Common Worship

*Services and Prayers
for the Church of England*

Church House Publishing

Published by	Church House Publishing
	Church House
	Great Smith Street
	London SW1P 3NZ

Copyright ©	*The Archbishops' Council 2000*

First published 2000

Cased black	0 7151 2000 X
Cased red	0 7151 2008 5
Cased blue	0 7151 2009 3
Cased burgundy	0 7151 2010 7
Bonded leather red	0 7151 2011 5
Bonded leather blue	0 7151 2012 3
Bonded leather burgundy	0 7151 2013 1
Calfskin black	0 7151 2014 X
Calfskin white	0 7151 2015 8
Calfskin tan	0 7151 2016 6

Texts for local use: the arrangements which apply to local editions of services cover reproduction on a non-commercial basis both for a single occasion and for repeated use. Details are available in the booklet *A Brief Guide to Liturgical Copyright* (see Copyright Information on page 817 for further information).

Printed and bound in the EU
for Cambridge University Press
on 55gsm Primapages Ivory

Typeset in 9 on 12 point Gill Sans
by John Morgan and Shirley Thompson/Omnific
Designed by Derek Birdsall RDI

Contents

¶ Authorization

Common Worship: Services and Prayers for the Church of England comprises

¶ services and prayers from *The Book of Common Prayer*;

¶ alternative services and other material authorized for use until further resolution of the General Synod;

¶ services which comply with the provisions of A Service of the Word;

¶ material commended by the House of Bishops; and

¶ material, the use of which falls within the discretion allowed to the minister under the provisions of Canon B 5.

For details, see page 815.

Canon B 3 provides that decisions as to which of the authorized services are to be used (other than occasional offices) shall be taken jointly by the incumbent and the parochial church council. In the case of occasional offices (other than Confirmation and Ordination), the decision is to be made by the minister conducting the service, subject to the right of any of the persons concerned to object beforehand to the form of service proposed.

¶ Preface

The publication of *Common Worship* is an occasion of great significance in the life of the Church of England, because the worship of God is central to the life of his Church.

The forms of worship authorized in the Church of England express our faith and help to create our identity. The Declaration of Assent is placed at the beginning of this volume to remind us of this. When ministers make the Declaration, they affirm their loyalty to the Church of England's inheritance of faith and accept their share in the responsibility to proclaim the faith 'afresh in each generation'.

Common Worship draws together the rich inheritance of the past and the very best of our contemporary forms of worship. In this volume we bring together the services of *The Book of Common Prayer* as they are used today and newer liturgies in both traditional and contemporary style. *The Book of Common Prayer* remains the permanently authorized provision for public worship in the Church of England, whereas the newer liturgies are authorized until further resolution of the General Synod. This combination of old and new provides for the diverse worshipping needs of our communities, within an ordered structure which affirms our essential unity and common life.

The services provided here are rich and varied. This reflects the multiplicity of contexts in which worship is offered today. They encourage an imaginative engagement in worship, opening the way for people in the varied circumstances of their lives to experience the love of God in Jesus Christ in the life and power of the Holy Spirit. In the worship of God the full meaning and beauty of our humanity is consummated and our lives are opened to the promise God makes for all creation – to transform and renew it in love and goodness.

The publication of these services is a challenge to us. It is a challenge to worship God better and to take the greatest care in preparing and celebrating worship. It is a challenge to draw the whole community of the people we serve into the worship of God. Central to our worship is the proclamation of the one, perfect self-offering of the Son to the Father. The Gospel of Jesus Christ is at the heart of *Common Worship*.

Those who make the Declaration of Assent are charged with bringing the grace and truth of Christ to this generation and making him known to those in their care. Worship not only strengthens Christians for witness and service, but is itself a forum in which Christ is made known. Worship is for the whole people of God, who are fellow pilgrims on a journey of faith, and those who attend services are all at different stages of that journey. Indeed, worship itself is a pilgrimage – a journey into the heart of the love of God. A number of the services themselves – particularly that of Holy Baptism – are celebrated in stages. In each case the journey through the liturgy has a clear structure with signposts for those less familiar with the way. It moves from the gathering of the community through the Liturgy of the Word to an opportunity of transformation, sacramental or non-sacramental, after which those present are sent out to put their faith into practice.

Common Worship is marked by diversity, not only in its content and in those who will use it, but also in the manner of its publication. It is not a single book. This volume contains all that is needed for worship on Sundays and on Principal Feasts and Holy Days; the *Common Worship* Initiation Services, Pastoral Services, Daily Office book and seasonal material are being published separately. Moreover, these volumes are not published solely in book form. *Common Worship* is not a series of books, but a collection of services and other liturgical material published on the World Wide Web and through other electronic media as well as in print.

Just as *Common Worship* is more than a book, so worship is more than what is said; it is also what is done and how it is done. *Common Worship* provides texts, contemporary as well as traditional, which are resonant and memorable, so that they will enter and remain in the Church of England's corporate memory – especially if they are sung. It is when the framework of worship is clear and familiar and the texts are known by heart that the poetry of praise and the passion of prayer can transcend the printed word. Then worship can take wing and become the living sacrifice of ourselves to the God whose majesty is beyond compare and whose truth is from everlasting.

¶ *The Declaration of Assent*

The Declaration of Assent is made by deacons, priests and bishops of the Church of England when they are ordained and on each occasion when they take up a new appointment (Canon C 15). Readers and Lay Workers make the declaration, without the words 'and administration of the sacraments', when they are admitted and when they are licensed (Canons E 5, E 6 and E 8).

Preface

The Church of England is part of the One, Holy, Catholic and Apostolic Church, worshipping the one true God, Father, Son and Holy Spirit. It professes the faith uniquely revealed in the Holy Scriptures and set forth in the catholic creeds, which faith the Church is called upon to proclaim afresh in each generation. Led by the Holy Spirit, it has borne witness to Christian truth in its historic formularies, the Thirty-nine Articles of Religion, *The Book of Common Prayer* and the Ordering of Bishops, Priests and Deacons. In the declaration you are about to make, will you affirm your loyalty to this inheritance of faith as your inspiration and guidance under God in bringing the grace and truth of Christ to this generation and making Him known to those in your care?

Declaration of Assent

I, *A B*, do so affirm, and accordingly declare my belief in the faith which is revealed in the Holy Scriptures and set forth in the catholic creeds and to which the historic formularies of the Church of England bear witness; and in public prayer and administration of the sacraments, I will use only the forms of service which are authorized or allowed by Canon.

The Calendar

For Rules to Order the Christian Year, see page 526.

In the printing of the Calendar, Principal Feasts and other Principal Holy Days are printed in **bold**; Festivals are printed in roman typeface; other Sundays and Lesser Festivals are printed in ordinary roman typeface, in black. Commemorations are printed in *italics*.

¶ *The Seasons*

Advent

The First Sunday of Advent
The Second Sunday of Advent
The Third Sunday of Advent
From 17 December (O Sapientia)
    begin the eight days of prayer before Christmas Day
The Fourth Sunday of Advent
Christmas Eve

Christmas

Christmas Day – *25 December*
The First Sunday of Christmas
The Second Sunday of Christmas

*The days after Christmas Day until the Epiphany traditionally form
a unity of days of special thanksgiving.*

Epiphany

The Epiphany – *6 January*
The Baptism of Christ – *The First Sunday of Epiphany*
The Second Sunday of Epiphany
The Third Sunday of Epiphany
The Fourth Sunday of Epiphany
The Presentation of Christ in the Temple (Candlemas)
    – *2 February*

Ordinary Time

This begins on the day following the Presentation

The Fifth Sunday before Lent
The Fourth Sunday before Lent
The Third Sunday before Lent
The Second Sunday before Lent
The Sunday next before Lent

Lent

Ash Wednesday
The First Sunday of Lent
The Second Sunday of Lent
The Third Sunday of Lent
The Fourth Sunday of Lent – *Mothering Sunday*
The Fifth Sunday of Lent *(Passiontide begins)*
Palm Sunday
Monday of Holy Week
Tuesday of Holy Week
Wednesday of Holy Week
Maundy Thursday
Good Friday
Easter Eve

Easter

Easter Day
Monday of Easter Week
Tuesday of Easter Week
Wednesday of Easter Week
Thursday of Easter Week
Friday of Easter Week
Saturday of Easter Week
The Second Sunday of Easter
The Third Sunday of Easter
The Fourth Sunday of Easter
The Fifth Sunday of Easter
The Sixth Sunday of Easter
Ascension Day
From Friday after Ascension Day
    begin the nine days of prayer before Pentecost
The Seventh Sunday of Easter – *Sunday after Ascension Day*
Pentecost (Whit Sunday)

Ordinary Time

This is resumed on the Monday following the Day of Pentecost

Trinity Sunday

The Thursday after Trinity Sunday may be observed as

The Day of Thanksgiving for the Institution of Holy Communion
    (Corpus Christi)

The First Sunday after Trinity

The Second Sunday after Trinity

The Third Sunday after Trinity

The Fourth Sunday after Trinity

The Fifth Sunday after Trinity

The Sixth Sunday after Trinity

The Seventh Sunday after Trinity

The Eighth Sunday after Trinity

The Ninth Sunday after Trinity

The Tenth Sunday after Trinity

The Eleventh Sunday after Trinity

The Twelfth Sunday after Trinity

The Thirteenth Sunday after Trinity

The Fourteenth Sunday after Trinity

The Fifteenth Sunday after Trinity

The Sixteenth Sunday after Trinity

The Seventeenth Sunday after Trinity

The Eighteenth Sunday after Trinity

The Nineteenth Sunday after Trinity

The Twentieth Sunday after Trinity

The Twenty-first Sunday after Trinity

The Last Sunday after Trinity

Dedication Festival – *The First Sunday in October or The Last Sunday
    after Trinity, if date unknown*

All Saints' Day – *1 November*

*The Sunday between 30 October and 5 November
    may be kept as All Saints' Sunday or as:*

The Fourth Sunday before Advent

The Third Sunday before Advent

The Second Sunday before Advent

Christ the King – *The Sunday next before Advent*

¶ Holy Days

For the key to the typography, see page 1.

January

1	The Naming and Circumcision of Jesus
2	Basil the Great and Gregory of Nazianzus, Bishops, Teachers of the Faith, 379 and 389
2	*Seraphim, Monk of Sarov, Spiritual Guide, 1833*
2	*Vedanayagam Samuel Azariah, Bishop in South India, Evangelist, 1945*
6	**The Epiphany**
10	*William Laud, Archbishop of Canterbury, 1645*
11	*Mary Slessor, Missionary in West Africa, 1915*
12	Aelred of Hexham, Abbot of Rievaulx, 1167
12	*Benedict Biscop, Abbot of Wearmouth, Scholar, 689*
13	Hilary, Bishop of Poitiers, Teacher of the Faith, 367
13	*Kentigern (Mungo), Missionary Bishop in Strathclyde and Cumbria, 603*
13	*George Fox, Founder of the Society of Friends (the Quakers), 1691*
17	Antony of Egypt, Hermit, Abbot, 356
17	*Charles Gore, Bishop, Founder of the Community of the Resurrection, 1932*
18–25	*Week of Prayer for Christian Unity*
19	Wulfstan, Bishop of Worcester, 1095
20	*Richard Rolle of Hampole, Spiritual Writer, 1349*
21	Agnes, Child Martyr at Rome, 304
22	*Vincent of Saragossa, Deacon, first Martyr of Spain, 304*
24	Francis de Sales, Bishop of Geneva, Teacher of the Faith, 1622
25	The Conversion of Paul
26	Timothy and Titus, Companions of Paul
28	Thomas Aquinas, Priest, Philosopher, Teacher of the Faith, 1274
30	Charles, King and Martyr, 1649
31	*John Bosco, Priest, Founder of the Salesian Teaching Order, 1888*

February

Alternative dates

Matthias may be celebrated on 24 February instead of 14 May.

March

1	David, Bishop of Menevia, Patron of Wales, c.601
2	Chad, Bishop of Lichfield, Missionary, 672
7	Perpetua, Felicity and their Companions, Martyrs at Carthage, 203
8	Edward King, Bishop of Lincoln, 1910
8	*Felix, Bishop, Apostle to the East Angles, 647*
8	*Geoffrey Studdert Kennedy, Priest, Poet, 1929*
17	Patrick, Bishop, Missionary, Patron of Ireland, c.460
18	*Cyril, Bishop of Jerusalem, Teacher of the Faith, 386*
19	Joseph of Nazareth
20	Cuthbert, Bishop of Lindisfarne, Missionary, 687
21	Thomas Cranmer, Archbishop of Canterbury, Reformation Martyr, 1556
24	*Walter Hilton of Thurgarton, Augustinian Canon, Mystic, 1396*
24	*Oscar Romero, Archbishop of San Salvador, Martyr, 1980*
25	**The Annunciation of Our Lord to the Blessed Virgin Mary**
26	*Harriet Monsell, Founder of the Community of St John the Baptist, 1883*
31	*John Donne, Priest, Poet, 1631*

Alternative dates

Chad may be celebrated with Cedd on 26 October
instead of 2 March.

Cuthbert may be celebrated on 4 September instead of 20 March.

April

May

1	Philip and James, Apostles
2	Athanasius, Bishop of Alexandria, Teacher of the Faith, 373
4	English Saints and Martyrs of the Reformation Era
8	Julian of Norwich, Spiritual Writer, c.1417
14	Matthias the Apostle
16	*Caroline Chisholm, Social Reformer, 1877*
19	Dunstan, Archbishop of Canterbury, Restorer of Monastic Life, 988
20	Alcuin of York, Deacon, Abbot of Tours, 804
21	*Helena, Protector of the Holy Places, 330*
24	John and Charles Wesley, Evangelists, Hymn Writers, 1791 and 1788
25	The Venerable Bede, Monk at Jarrow, Scholar, Historian, 735
25	*Aldhelm, Bishop of Sherborne, 709*
26	Augustine, first Archbishop of Canterbury, 605
26	*John Calvin, Reformer, 1564*
26	*Philip Neri, Founder of the Oratorians, Spiritual Guide, 1595*
28	*Lanfranc, Prior of Le Bec, Archbishop of Canterbury, Scholar, 1089*
30	Josephine Butler, Social Reformer, 1906
30	*Joan of Arc, Visionary, 1431*
30	*Apolo Kivebulaya, Priest, Evangelist in Central Africa, 1933*
31	The Visit of the Blessed Virgin Mary to Elizabeth

Alternative dates

Matthias may be celebrated on 24 February instead of 14 May.

The Visit of the Blessed Virgin Mary to Elizabeth may be celebrated on 2 July instead of 31 May.

June

1   Justin, Martyr at Rome, c.165

3   The Martyrs of Uganda, 1886 and 1978

4   Petroc, Abbot of Padstow, 6th century

5   **Boniface (Wynfrith) of Crediton, Bishop, Apostle of Germany, Martyr, 754**

6   Ini Kopuria, Founder of the Melanesian Brotherhood, 1945

8   **Thomas Ken, Bishop of Bath and Wells, Nonjuror, Hymn Writer, 1711**

9   **Columba, Abbot of Iona, Missionary, 597**

9   Ephrem of Syria, Deacon, Hymn Writer, Teacher of the Faith, 373

11   **Barnabas the Apostle**

14   Richard Baxter, Puritan Divine, 1691

15   Evelyn Underhill, Spiritual Writer, 1941 ·

16   **Richard, Bishop of Chichester, 1253**

16   Joseph Butler, Bishop of Durham, Philosopher, 1752

17   Samuel and Henrietta Barnett, Social Reformers, 1913 and 1936

18   Bernard Mizeki, Apostle of the MaShona, Martyr, 1896

19   Sundar Singh of India, Sadhu (holy man), Evangelist, Teacher of the Faith, 1929

22   **Alban, first Martyr of Britain, c.250**

23   **Etheldreda, Abbess of Ely, c.678**

24   **The Birth of John the Baptist**

27   Cyril, Bishop of Alexandria, Teacher of the Faith, 444

28   **Irenæus, Bishop of Lyons, Teacher of the Faith, c.200**

29   Peter and Paul, Apostles

Alternative dates

Peter the Apostle may be celebrated alone, without Paul, on 29 June.

July

1	*Henry, John, and Henry Venn the younger, Priests, Evangelical Divines, 1797, 1813 and 1873*
3	**Thomas the Apostle**
6	*Thomas More, Scholar, and John Fisher, Bishop of Rochester, Reformation Martyrs, 1535*
11	**Benedict of Nursia, Abbot of Monte Cassino, Father of Western Monasticism, c.550**
14	**John Keble, Priest, Tractarian, Poet, 1866**
15	**Swithun, Bishop of Winchester, c.862**
15	*Bonaventure, Friar, Bishop, Teacher of the Faith, 1274*
16	*Osmund, Bishop of Salisbury, 1099*
18	*Elizabeth Ferard, first Deaconess of the Church of England, Founder of the Community of St Andrew, 1883*
19	**Gregory, Bishop of Nyssa, and his sister Macrina, Deaconess, Teachers of the Faith, c.394 and c.379**
20	*Margaret of Antioch, Martyr, 4th century*
20	*Bartolomé de las Casas, Apostle to the Indies, 1566*
22	**Mary Magdalene**
23	*Bridget of Sweden, Abbess of Vadstena, 1373*
25	**James the Apostle**
26	**Anne and Joachim, Parents of the Blessed Virgin Mary**
27	*Brooke Foss Westcott, Bishop of Durham, Teacher of the Faith, 1901*
29	**Mary, Martha and Lazarus, Companions of Our Lord**
30	**William Wilberforce, Social Reformer, 1833**
31	*Ignatius of Loyola, Founder of the Society of Jesus, 1556*

Alternative dates

The Visit of the Blessed Virgin Mary to Elizabeth may be celebrated on 2 July instead of 31 May.

Thomas the Apostle may be celebrated on 21 December instead of 3 July.

Thomas Becket may be celebrated on 7 July instead of 29 December.

August

Alternative dates

The Blessed Virgin Mary may be celebrated on 8 September
instead of 15 August.

September

1	*Giles of Provence, Hermit, c.710*
2	*The Martyrs of Papua New Guinea, 1901 and 1942*
3	**Gregory the Great, Bishop of Rome, Teacher of the Faith, 604**
4	*Birinus, Bishop of Dorchester (Oxon), Apostle of Wessex, 650*
6	*Allen Gardiner, Missionary,* *Founder of the South American Mission Society, 1851*
8	**The Birth of the Blessed Virgin Mary**
9	*Charles Fuge Lowder, Priest, 1880*
13	**John Chrysostom, Bishop of Constantinople,** **Teacher of the Faith, 407**
14	**Holy Cross Day**
15	**Cyprian, Bishop of Carthage, Martyr, 258**
16	**Ninian, Bishop of Galloway, Apostle of the Picts, c.432**
16	*Edward Bouverie Pusey, Priest, Tractarian, 1882*
17	**Hildegard, Abbess of Bingen, Visionary, 1179**
19	*Theodore of Tarsus, Archbishop of Canterbury, 690*
20	**John Coleridge Patteson, First Bishop of Melanesia,** **and his Companions, Martyrs, 1871**
21	**Matthew, Apostle and Evangelist**
25	**Lancelot Andrewes, Bishop of Winchester, Spiritual Writer, 1626**
25	*Sergei of Radonezh, Russian Monastic Reformer, Teacher of the Faith, 1392*
26	*Wilson Carlile, Founder of the Church Army, 1942*
27	**Vincent de Paul, Founder of the Congregation of the Mission** **(Lazarists), 1660**
29	**Michael and All Angels**
30	*Jerome, Translator of the Scriptures, Teacher of the Faith, 420*

Alternative dates

Cuthbert may be celebrated on 4 September instead of 20 March.

October

Alternative dates

Chad may be celebrated with Cedd on 26 October
instead of 2 March.

November

December

1	*Charles de Foucauld, Hermit in the Sahara, 1916*
3	*Francis Xavier, Missionary, Apostle of the Indies, 1552*
4	*John of Damascus, Monk, Teacher of the Faith, c.749*
4	*Nicholas Ferrar, Deacon, Founder of the Little Gidding Community, 1637*
6	Nicholas, Bishop of Myra, c.326
7	Ambrose, Bishop of Milan, Teacher of the Faith, 397
8	The Conception of the Blessed Virgin Mary
13	Lucy, Martyr at Syracuse, 304
13	*Samuel Johnson, Moralist, 1784*
14	John of the Cross, Poet, Teacher of the Faith, 1591
17	*O Sapientia*
17	*Eglantine Jebb, Social Reformer, Founder of 'Save The Children', 1928*
24	Christmas Eve
25	**Christmas Day**
26	Stephen, Deacon, First Martyr
27	John, Apostle and Evangelist
28	The Holy Innocents
29	Thomas Becket, Archbishop of Canterbury, Martyr, 1170
31	*John Wyclif, Reformer, 1384*

Alternative dates

Thomas the Apostle may be celebrated on 21 December instead of 3 July.

Thomas Becket may be celebrated on 7 July instead of 29 December.

¶ The Date of Easter and Other Variable Dates

For the lectionary years, see page 538.

Year	Ash Wednesday	Easter Day	Ascension Day	Pentecost (Whit Sunday)	First Sunday of Advent
2001	28 February	15 April	24 May	3 June	2 December
2002	13 February	31 March	9 May	19 May	1 December
2003	5 March	20 April	29 May	8 June	30 November
2004	25 February	11 April	20 May	30 May	28 November
2005	9 February	27 March	5 May	15 May	27 November
2006	1 March	16 April	25 May	4 June	3 December
2007	21 February	8 April	17 May	27 May	2 December
2008	6 February	23 March	1 May	11 May	30 November
2009	25 February	12 April	21 May	31 May	29 November
2010	17 February	4 April	13 May	23 May	28 November
2011	9 March	24 April	2 June	12 June	27 November
2012	22 February	8 April	17 May	27 May	2 December
2013	13 February	31 March	9 May	19 May	1 December
2014	5 March	20 April	29 May	8 June	30 November
2015	18 February	5 April	14 May	24 May	29 November
2016	10 February	27 March	5 May	15 May	27 November
2017	1 March	16 April	25 May	4 June	3 December
2018	14 February	1 April	10 May	20 May	2 December
2019	6 March	21 April	30 May	9 June	1 December
2020	26 February	12 April	21 May	31 May	29 November
2021	17 February	4 April	13 May	23 May	28 November
2022	2 March	17 April	26 May	5 June	27 November
2023	22 February	9 April	18 May	28 May	3 December
2024	14 February	31 March	9 May	19 May	1 December
2025	5 March	20 April	29 May	8 June	30 November
2026	18 February	5 April	14 May	24 May	29 November
2027	10 February	28 March	6 May	16 May	28 November
2028	1 March	16 April	25 May	4 June	3 December
2029	14 February	1 April	10 May	20 May	2 December
2030	6 March	21 April	30 May	9 June	1 December

A Service of the Word,
Morning and Evening Prayer,
Night Prayer

Contents

A Service of the Word

¶ *Introduction*

A Service of the Word is unusual for an authorized Church of
England service. It consists almost entirely of notes and directions
and allows for considerable local variation and choice within
a common structure. It is important that those who prepare for
and take part in A Service of the Word should have a clear
understanding of the nature of worship and of how the component
parts of this service work together. Leading people in worship is
leading people into mystery, into the unknown and yet the familiar.
This spiritual activity is much more than getting the words or the
sections in the right order. The primary object in the careful
planning and leading of the service is the spiritual direction which
enables the whole congregation to come into the presence of God
to give him glory. Choices must be made responsibly by leaders
of this service or by groups planning worship with them, whether
the service is an occasional one, or a regular one which may use
a service card. The notes and the text of A Service of the Word
should be read together as they interpret one another.

The Liturgy of the Word

At the heart of the service is the Liturgy of the Word. This must not
be so lightly treated as to appear insignificant compared with other
parts of the service. The readings from Holy Scripture are central to
this part and, together with the season, may determine the theme of
the rest of the worship. At certain times of the year, as Note 5 says,
the readings come from an authorized lectionary, so that the whole
Church is together proclaiming the major events in the Christian
story. Telling that story and expounding it in the 'sermon' can be
done in many different and adventurous ways. Some are suggested
in Notes 5 and 7, but there are many others. The word 'sermon' is
used in the service, and explained in the note, precisely because it
would be too limiting to use words like 'address', 'talk', 'instruction',
or 'meditation'.

The items in the Liturgy of the Word may come in any order and more than once. So the sermon may be in parts and there may be more than one psalm or song, and of course hymns may be inserted as well. But on most occasions it will be appropriate for this part of the service to have a Creed or Affirmation of Faith as its climax.

Preparation

With the Liturgy of the Word becoming clear it will be easier to see how the Preparation for it, and the response to it in the Prayers, fit in. People need to know when the service has started (Note 1). What happens at the beginning can create the atmosphere for worship and set the tone and mood for what follows. The gathering of the congregation and the call to worship are to be marked by a liturgical greeting between minister and people. Leaders should have worked out exactly where this comes among the singing, Scripture sentence, introduction (perhaps to the theme) and opening prayer. All these should draw the members of the congregation together and focus their attention on almighty God.

This part of the service will usually include the Prayers of Penitence, though these may come later if, for instance, the theme of the Liturgy of the Word appropriately leads to penitence. Authorized Prayers of Penitence include all those confessions and absolutions in *The Book of Common Prayer* and in services in *Common Worship*, together with several other seasonal and thematic forms, mostly for occasional use, which are set out on pages 122–137. The climax of this part of the service is either the Collect or, if that is included in the Prayers, one of the items of praise, a hymn or the Gloria. The Collect does not have to be that of the day; it may be a thematic one based on the readings (in which case it should come immediately before the readings), or be used to sum up the Prayers.

Prayers

Part of the response to the Word is the Creed, but the response should be developed in the Prayers which follow. There are many different options for this part of the service. These range from a series of Collect-type prayers to congregational involvement in prayer groups, visual and processional prayers, with responsive forms and a number of people sharing the leading of intercessions in between. But, whatever the form, it is essential that the Prayers also include thanksgiving. A section of thanksgiving, which may include the spoken word, music and hymns, may be the proper climax to this part of the service.

Conclusion

Many different words have been used for the Conclusion, each of which has something to contribute to our understanding of how the service ends: dismissal, farewell, goodbye, departure, valediction, commission, blessing, ending, going out. What is essential, as with the way the service starts, is that it should have a clear liturgical ending: options are listed in Note 9.

Once the service is planned, leaders will want to check through to ensure that there is the right balance between the elements of word, prayer and praise, and between congregational activity and congregational passivity. Does the music come in the right places? Is there sufficient silence (Note 4)? This is something leaders can be afraid of, or fail to introduce properly. And is there a clear overall direction to the service: is it achieving the purpose of bringing the congregation together to give glory to God?

¶ A Service of the Word

Preparation

The minister welcomes the people with the **Greeting**.

Authorized Prayers of Penitence may be used here or in the **Prayers**.

The Venite, Kyries, Gloria, a hymn, song, or a set of responses may be used.

The **Collect** is said either here or in the **Prayers**.

The Liturgy of the Word

This includes
¶ **readings (or a reading) from Holy Scripture**
¶ a **psalm**, or, if occasion demands, a scriptural song
¶ a **sermon**
¶ an **authorized Creed**, or, if occasion demands,
   an **authorized Affirmation of Faith.**

Prayers

These include
¶ **intercessions and thanksgivings**
¶ **the Lord's Prayer**

Conclusion

The service concludes with a **blessing, dismissal** or other **liturgical ending**.

¶ A Service of the Word with a Celebration of Holy Communion

This rite requires careful preparation by the president and other participants, and is not normally to be used as the regular Sunday or weekday service.

Sections marked with an asterisk* must follow an authorized text.

Preparation

The people and the priest:

¶ greet each other in the Lord's name
¶ confess their sins and are assured of God's forgiveness*
¶ keep silence and pray a Collect*

The Liturgy of the Word

The people and the priest:

¶ proclaim and respond to the word of God

Prayers

The people and the priest:

¶ pray for the Church and the world

The Liturgy of the Sacrament

The people and the priest:

¶ exchange the Peace
¶ prepare the table
¶ pray the Eucharistic Prayer*
¶ break the bread
¶ receive Holy Communion

The Dismissal

The people and the priest:

¶ depart with God's blessing.

¶ Notes

In this form of service, the material is described as 'authorized' or 'suitable', which expressions shall have the following meanings:

¶ 'authorized' means approved by the General Synod in accordance with the provisions of Canon B 2.

¶ 'suitable' means a form used at the discretion of the minister conducting the form of service on any occasion, but such that the material so used shall be neither contrary to, nor indicative of any departure from, the doctrine of the Church of England in any essential matter.

This service is authorized as an alternative to Morning Prayer and Evening Prayer. It provides a structure for Sunday services, for daily prayer and for services of an occasional nature.

1 **Greeting**
The service should have a clear beginning. The liturgical greeting may follow some introductory singing, or a hymn or a sentence of Scripture, and may be followed by a brief introduction or an opening prayer.

2 **Prayers of Penitence**
Only authorized Prayers of Penitence should be used. They may be omitted except at the Principal Service on Sundays and Principal Holy Days. Authorized forms of Confession and Absolution may be found in *The Book of Common Prayer*, in the services in *Common Worship* and on pages 122–137. The minister may introduce the Confession with suitable words.

3 **Hymns, Canticles, Acclamations and the Peace**
Points are indicated for some of these, but if occasion requires they may occur elsewhere.

4 **Silence**
Periods of silence may be kept at different points of the service. It may be particularly appropriate at the beginning of the service, after the readings and the sermon, and during the prayers.

5   **Readings**
     There should preferably be at least two readings from the Bible,
     but it is recognized that if occasion demands there may be only
     one reading. It may be dramatized, sung or read responsively.
     The readings are taken from an authorized lectionary during the
     period from the Third Sunday of Advent to the Baptism of Christ,
     and from Palm Sunday to Trinity Sunday. When A Service of the
     Word is combined with Holy Communion on Sundays and Principal
     Holy Days, the readings of the day are normally used.

6   **Psalms**
     The service should normally include a psalm or psalms. These might
     be said or sung in the traditional way, but it is also possible to use a
     metrical version, a responsive form or a paraphrase such as can be
     found in many current hymn books. The psalm may occasionally be
     replaced by a song or canticle the words of which are taken directly
     from Scripture: a 'scriptural song'.

7   **Sermon**
     The term 'sermon' includes less formal exposition, the use of drama,
     interviews, discussion, audio-visuals and the insertion of hymns or
     other sections of the service between parts of the sermon. The
     sermon may come after one of the readings, or before or after the
     prayers, and may be omitted except on Sundays and Principal
     Holy Days.

8   **Sermon and Creed**
     The sermon, and a Creed or authorized Affirmation of Faith may be
     omitted except at the principal service on Sundays and Principal
     Holy Days.

9   **Ending**
     The service should have a clear ending. This takes one or more of
     the following forms: the Peace, the Grace or a suitable ascription
     or blessing. If a responsive conclusion is used, it comes last.

10   **A Service of the Word with a Celebration of Holy Communion**
     An order for this is provided (see page 25). The notes to the Order
     for the Celebration of Holy Communion (pages 158–159 and 330–335)
     apply equally to this service. In particular the Note on Ministries
     (pages 158–159) specifies that the president must be an episcopally
     ordained priest, but indicates that where necessary a deacon or lay
     person may preside over the Preparation and the Liturgy of the Word,
     including the Prayers. The order provided is not prescriptive.

Morning and Evening Prayer on Sunday

¶ *Introduction*

From earliest times, Christians gathered at regular hours during each day and night to respond to God's word with praise on behalf of all creation and with intercession for the salvation of the world. By the fourth century, if not earlier, morning and evening had emerged as the pre-eminent hours for the offering of this sacrifice of praise. They have remained so ever since, especially on Sundays when the Church commemorates both the first day of creation and the day of Christ's resurrection. These orders of service are examples of forms which comply with the provisions of A Service of the Word and are intended to help Christians of our own day take their part in this privilege and duty which belongs to all God's priestly people. They may be celebrated in a variety of different ways, for example, as:

¶   a simple form of prayer at the very beginning or end of the day;

¶   the Gathering and Liturgy of the Word for another service which is to follow immediately;

¶   the principal service of the day.

To meet diverse needs such as these, they are very flexible in arrangement. The central core, however, consists of the Liturgy of the Word interwoven with canticles to supply the response of praise, followed by intercessory prayer in one form or another. A variety of alternative endings is provided in the form of thanksgivings for different aspects of the Church's life. Whenever possible, the services should include some singing, especially of the Gospel canticle, which is the climax of the morning or evening praise for the work of God in Christ. If desired, metrical paraphrases may be substituted for any of the biblical canticles, and other hymns and songs may be added at appropriate points.

Provision for weekdays is published separately.

For Notes, see pages 57–58.

An Order for Morning Prayer on Sunday

Grace, mercy and peace
from God our Father
and the Lord Jesus Christ
be with you

All **and also with you.**

This is the day that the Lord has made.

All **Let us rejoice and be glad in it.**

(or)

O Lord, open our lips

All **and our mouth shall proclaim your praise.**

Give us the joy of your saving help

All **and sustain us with your life-giving Spirit.**

The minister may say

We have come together in the name of Christ
to offer our praise and thanksgiving,
to hear and receive God's holy word,
to pray for the needs of the world,
and to seek the forgiveness of our sins,
that by the power of the Holy Spirit
we may give ourselves to the service of God.

Prayers of Penitence are used when Morning Prayer is the principal
service and may be used on other occasions (see Note 3).

The following or another authorized confession and absolution is used

Jesus says, 'Repent, for the kingdom of heaven is close at hand.'
So let us turn away from our sin and turn to Christ,
confessing our sins in penitence and faith.

All **Lord God,**
we have sinned against you;
we have done evil in your sight.
We are sorry and repent.
Have mercy on us according to your love.
Wash away our wrongdoing and cleanse us from our sin.
Renew a right spirit within us
and restore us to the joy of your salvation;
through Jesus Christ our Lord. Amen.

May the Father of all mercies
cleanse *you* from *your* sins,
and restore *you* in his image
to the praise and glory of his name,
through Jesus Christ our Lord.

All **Amen.**

Blessed is the Lord,
All **for he has heard the voice of our prayer;**

therefore shall our hearts dance for joy
All **and in our song will we praise our God.**

*One or more of the following may conclude the Preparation
or they may be omitted.*

This prayer of thanksgiving may be said

Blessed are you, Lord our God,
creator and redeemer of all;
to you be glory and praise for ever.
From the waters of chaos you drew forth the world
and in your great love fashioned us in your image.
Now, through the deep waters of death,
you have brought your people to new birth
by raising your Son to life in triumph.
May Christ your light ever dawn in our hearts
as we offer you our sacrifice of thanks and praise.
Blessed be God, Father, Son and Holy Spirit:

All   **Blessed be God for ever.**

An opening canticle or a hymn may be said or sung.

This opening prayer may be said

The night has passed, and the day lies open before us;
let us pray with one heart and mind.

Silence is kept.

As we rejoice in the gift of this new day,
so may the light of your presence, O God,
set our hearts on fire with love for you;
now and for ever.

All   **Amen.**

The Word of God

Psalmody

The appointed psalmody is said or sung.

Each psalm or group of psalms may end with

Glory to the Father and to the Son
and to the Holy Spirit;
as it was in the beginning is now
and shall be for ever. Amen.

Old Testament Canticle

*If there are two Scripture readings, the first may be read here,
or both may be read after the Old Testament canticle.*

A suitable canticle is said or sung (see Note 5 on page 57).

Scripture Reading

*One or more readings appointed for the day are read.
The reading(s) may be followed by a time of silence.*

The reader may say

This is the word of the Lord.

All **Thanks be to God.**

*A suitable song or chant, or a responsory in this or another form,
may follow*

Awake, O sleeper, and arise from the dead.

All **And Christ shall give you light.**

You have died and your life is hid with Christ in God.

All **Awake, O sleeper, and arise from the dead.**

Set your minds on things that are above,
　　not on things that are on the earth.

All **And Christ shall give you light.**

When Christ our life appears you will appear with him in glory.

All **Awake, O sleeper, and arise from the dead,
　　and Christ shall give you light.**

Gospel Canticle

The Benedictus (The Song of Zechariah) is said or sung

1   Blessed be the Lord the God of Israel, ♦
     who has come to his people and set them free.

2   He has raised up for us a mighty Saviour, ♦
     born of the house of his servant David.

3   Through his holy prophets God promised of old ♦
     to save us from our enemies,
        from the hands of all that hate us,

4   To show mercy to our ancestors, ♦
     and to remember his holy covenant.

5   This was the oath God swore to our father Abraham: ♦
     to set us free from the hands of our enemies,

6   Free to worship him without fear, ♦
     holy and righteous in his sight
        all the days of our life.

7   And you, child, shall be called the prophet of the Most High, ♦
     for you will go before the Lord to prepare his way,

8   To give his people knowledge of salvation ♦
     by the forgiveness of all their sins.

9   In the tender compassion of our God ♦
     the dawn from on high shall break upon us,

10 To shine on those who dwell in darkness and the shadow of death, ♦
     and to guide our feet into the way of peace.   *Luke 1.68-79*

     Glory to the Father and to the Son
     and to the Holy Spirit;
     as it was in the beginning is now
     and shall be for ever. Amen.

A sermon is preached when Morning Prayer is the principal service (see Note 3).

Morning Prayer may conclude with one of the Thanksgivings (pages 46–56).

The Creed

When Morning Prayer is the principal service, the Apostles' Creed or an authorized Affirmation of Faith is said. It may be omitted on other occasions (see Note 3).

All　**I believe in God, the Father almighty,
creator of heaven and earth.**

**I believe in Jesus Christ, his only Son, our Lord,
who was conceived by the Holy Spirit,
born of the Virgin Mary,
suffered under Pontius Pilate,
was crucified, died, and was buried;
he descended to the dead.
On the third day he rose again;
he ascended into heaven,
he is seated at the right hand of the Father,
and he will come to judge the living and the dead.**

**I believe in the Holy Spirit,
the holy catholic Church,
the communion of saints,
the forgiveness of sins,
the resurrection of the body,
and the life everlasting.
Amen.**

Prayers

Intercessions are offered.

The Collect is said.

The Lord's Prayer is said

Gathering our prayers and praises into one,
as our Saviour has taught us, so we pray

All   **Our Father in heaven,**
hallowed be your name,
your kingdom come,
your will be done,
on earth as in heaven.
Give us today our daily bread.
Forgive us our sins
as we forgive those who sin against us.
Lead us not into temptation
but deliver us from evil.
For the kingdom, the power,
and the glory are yours
now and for ever.
Amen.

(or)

Gathering our prayers and praises into one,
let us pray with confidence as our Saviour has taught us

All   **Our Father, who art in heaven,**
hallowed be thy name;
thy kingdom come;
thy will be done;
on earth as it is in heaven.
Give us this day our daily bread.
And forgive us our trespasses,
as we forgive those who trespass against us.
And lead us not into temptation;
but deliver us from evil.
For thine is the kingdom,
the power, and the glory
for ever and ever.
Amen.

The Conclusion

The service ends with one of the following, or another blessing or ending.

The Blessing

The Lord bless us, and preserve us from all evil,
and keep us in eternal life.

All **Amen.**

[Let us bless the Lord.

All **Thanks be to God.**]

(or)

The Grace

All **The grace of our Lord Jesus Christ,
and the love of God,
and the fellowship of the Holy Spirit,
be with us all evermore.
Amen.**

(or)

The Peace

May the peace of God, which passes all understanding,
keep our hearts and minds in Christ Jesus.

All **Amen.**

The peace of the Lord be always with you

All **and also with you.**

These words may be added

Let us offer one another a sign of peace, God's seal on our prayers.

An Order for Evening Prayer on Sunday

Preparation

The light and peace of Jesus Christ be with you

All **and also with you.**

The glory of the Lord has risen upon us.

All **Let us rejoice and sing God's praise for ever.**

(or)

O God, make speed to save us.

All **O Lord, make haste to help us.**

Lead your people to freedom, O God.

All **And banish all darkness from our hearts and minds.**

The minister may say

We have come together in the name of Christ
to offer our praise and thanksgiving,
to hear and receive God's holy word,
to pray for the needs of the world,
and to seek the forgiveness of our sins,
that by the power of the Holy Spirit
we may give ourselves to the service of God.

Prayers of Penitence are used when Evening Prayer is the principal service and may be used on other occasions (see Note 3).

The following or another authorized confession and absolution is used

Jesus says, 'Repent, for the kingdom of heaven is close at hand.'
So let us turn away from our sin and turn to Christ,
confessing our sins in penitence and faith.

All **Most merciful God,
Father of our Lord Jesus Christ,
we confess that we have sinned
in thought, word and deed.
We have not loved you with our whole heart.
We have not loved our neighbours as ourselves.
In your mercy
forgive what we have been,
help us to amend what we are,
and direct what we shall be;
that we may do justly,
love mercy,
and walk humbly with you, our God.
Amen.**

May the God of love and power
forgive *you* and free *you* from *your* sins,
heal and strengthen *you* by his Spirit,
and raise *you* to new life in Christ our Lord.

All **Amen.**

One or more of the following may conclude the Preparation
or they may be omitted.

This prayer of thanksgiving may be said

Blessed are you, sovereign God,
our light and our salvation;
to you be glory and praise for ever.
You led your people to freedom
by a pillar of cloud by day and a pillar of fire by night.
May we who walk in the light of your presence
acclaim your Christ, rising victorious,
as he banishes all darkness from our hearts and minds.
Blessed be God, Father, Son and Holy Spirit:

All **Blessed be God for ever.**

An opening hymn may be sung.

Verses from Psalm 141 or from Psalm 104 may be said
(see pages 784–785).

This opening prayer may be said

The day is almost over, and the evening has come;
let us pray with one heart and mind.

Silence is kept.

As our evening prayer rises before you, O God,
so may your Spirit come down upon us
to set us free to sing your praise
for ever and ever.

All **Amen.**

The Word of God

The appointed psalmody is said or sung.

Each psalm or group of psalms may end with

Glory to the Father and to the Son
and to the Holy Spirit;
as it was in the beginning is now
and shall be for ever. Amen.

New Testament Canticle

If there are two Scripture readings, the first may be read here, or both may be read after the New Testament canticle.

A suitable canticle is said or sung (see Note 5 on page 57).

Scripture Reading

One or more readings appointed for the day are read.
The reading(s) may be followed by a time of silence.

The reader may say

This is the word of the Lord.

All **Thanks be to God.**

A suitable song or chant, or a responsory in this or another form, may follow

The Lord is my light and my salvation;
    the Lord is the strength of my life.

All **The Lord is my light and my salvation;**
    the Lord is the strength of my life.
The light shines in the darkness
    and the darkness has not overcome it.

All **The Lord is the strength of my life.**
Glory to the Father, and to the Son
    and to the Holy Spirit.

All **The Lord is my light and my salvation;**
    the Lord is the strength of my life.

The Magnificat (The Song of Mary) is said or sung

1 My soul proclaims the greatness of the Lord,
      my spirit rejoices in God my Saviour; ♦
   he has looked with favour on his lowly servant.

2 From this day all generations will call me blessed; ♦
   the Almighty has done great things for me
      and holy is his name.

3 He has mercy on those who fear him, ♦
   from generation to generation.

4 He has shown strength with his arm ♦
   and has scattered the proud in their conceit,

5 Casting down the mighty from their thrones ♦
   and lifting up the lowly.

6 He has filled the hungry with good things ♦
   and sent the rich away empty.

7 He has come to the aid of his servant Israel, ♦
   to remember his promise of mercy,

8 The promise made to our ancestors, ♦
   to Abraham and his children for ever.   *Luke 1.46-55*

   Glory to the Father and to the Son
   and to the Holy Spirit;
   as it was in the beginning is now
   and shall be for ever. Amen.

*A sermon is preached when Evening Prayer is the principal service
(see Note 3).*

*Evening Prayer may conclude with one of the Thanksgivings
(pages 46–56).*

The Creed

*When Evening Prayer is the principal service, the Apostles' Creed
or an authorized Affirmation of Faith is said. It may be omitted on other
occasions (see Note 3).*

All **I believe in God, the Father almighty,
creator of heaven and earth.**

**I believe in Jesus Christ, his only Son, our Lord,
who was conceived by the Holy Spirit,
born of the Virgin Mary,
suffered under Pontius Pilate,
was crucified, died, and was buried;
he descended to the dead.
On the third day he rose again;
he ascended into heaven,
he is seated at the right hand of the Father,
and he will come to judge the living and the dead.**

**I believe in the Holy Spirit,
the holy catholic Church,
the communion of saints,
the forgiveness of sins,
the resurrection of the body,
and the life everlasting.
Amen.**

Prayers

Intercessions are offered.

The Collect is said.

The Lord's Prayer is said

Gathering our prayers and praises into one,
as our Saviour has taught us, so we pray

All **Our Father in heaven,**
hallowed be your name,
your kingdom come,
your will be done,
on earth as in heaven.
Give us today our daily bread.
Forgive us our sins
as we forgive those who sin against us.
Lead us not into temptation
but deliver us from evil.
For the kingdom, the power,
and the glory are yours
now and for ever.
Amen.

(or)

Gathering our prayers and praises into one,
let us pray with confidence as our Saviour has taught us

All **Our Father, who art in heaven,**
hallowed be thy name;
thy kingdom come;
thy will be done;
on earth as it is in heaven.
Give us this day our daily bread.
And forgive us our trespasses,
as we forgive those who trespass against us.
And lead us not into temptation;
but deliver us from evil.
For thine is the kingdom,
the power, and the glory
for ever and ever.
Amen.

The Conclusion

The service ends with one of the following, or another blessing or ending.

The Blessing

The Lord bless us, and preserve us from all evil,
and keep us in eternal life.

All **Amen.**

[Let us bless the Lord.

All **Thanks be to God.**]

(or)

The Grace

All **The grace of our Lord Jesus Christ,
and the love of God,
and the fellowship of the Holy Spirit,
be with us all evermore.
Amen.**

(or)

The Peace

May the peace of God, which passes all understanding,
keep our hearts and minds in Christ Jesus.

All **Amen.**

The peace of the Lord be always with you

All **and also with you.**

These words may be added.

Let us offer one another a sign of peace, God's seal on our prayers.

Thanksgivings for Use at Morning and Evening Prayer on Sunday

¶ *Thanksgiving for the Word*

Your word is a lantern to our feet
All **and a light upon our path.**

This prayer of thanksgiving may be said

Blessed are you, Lord our God.
How sweet are your words to the taste,
sweeter than honey to the mouth.
How precious are your commands for our life,
more than the finest gold in our hands.
How marvellous is your will for the world,
unending is your love for the nations.
Our voices shall sing of your promises
and our lips declare your praise
for ever and ever.
All **Amen.**

After a suitable introduction, this or another authorized confession and absolution may be used

All **O King enthroned on high,**
filling the earth with your glory:
holy is your name,
Lord God almighty.
In our sinfulness we cry to you
to take our guilt away,
and to cleanse our lips to speak your word,
through Jesus Christ our Lord.
Amen.

May the God of all healing and forgiveness
draw *us* to himself,
and cleanse *us* from all *our* sins
that *we* may behold the glory of his Son,
the Word made flesh,
Jesus Christ our Lord.
All **Amen.**

Testimonies may be shared. The Apostles' Creed or an authorized Affirmation of Faith is said at a principal service and may be said on other occasions.

Intercessions are offered.

This or another Collect is said

Almighty God,
we thank you for the gift of your holy word.
May it be a lantern to our feet,
a light upon our paths,
and a strength to our lives.
Take us and use us
to love and serve all people
in the power of the Holy Spirit
and in the name of your Son,
Jesus Christ our Lord.

All **Amen.**

The Lord's Prayer is said.

The service ends either with the Peace or with the following proclamation to the world

The Word of life which was from the beginning
All **we proclaim to you.**
The darkness is passing away
and the true light is already shining;
All **the Word of life which was from the beginning.**
That which we heard, which we saw with our eyes,
and touched with our hands,
All **we proclaim to you.**
For our fellowship is with the Father,
and with his Son, Jesus Christ our Lord.
All **The Word of life, which was from the beginning, we proclaim to you.**

Let us bless the Lord.
All **Thanks be to God.**

¶ Thanksgiving for Holy Baptism

If possible, this Thanksgiving should be celebrated at the font.

I saw water flowing from the threshold of the temple.

All **Wherever the river flows**
everything will spring to life. Alleluia.

On the banks of the river grow trees bearing every kind of fruit.

All **Their leaves will not wither nor their fruit fail.**

Their fruit will serve for food,
their leaves for the healing of the nations.

All **For the river of the water of life**
flows from the throne of God and of the Lamb.

This prayer of thanksgiving is said and water may be poured into the font.

God in Christ gives us water welling up for eternal life.
With joy you will draw water from the wells of salvation.

All **Lord, give us this water and we shall thirst no more.**

Let us give thanks to the Lord our God.

All **It is right to give thanks and praise.**

Blessed are you, sovereign God of all,
to you be glory and praise for ever.
You are our light and our salvation.
From the deep waters of death
you have raised your Son to life in triumph.
Grant that all who have been born anew by water and the Spirit,
may daily be renewed in your image,
walk by the light of faith,
and serve you in newness of life;
through your anointed Son, Jesus Christ,
to whom with you and the Holy Spirit
we lift our voices of praise.
Blessed be God, Father, Son and Holy Spirit:

All **Blessed be God for ever.**

The Apostles' Creed or an authorized Affirmation of Faith is said.

Intercessions are offered. These should include prayer for those who are preparing for baptism and for those recently baptized.

This or another Collect is said

Almighty God,
in our baptism you have consecrated us
to be temples of your Holy Spirit.
May we, whom you have counted worthy,
nurture this gift of your indwelling Spirit with a lively faith
and worship you with upright lives;
through Jesus Christ our Lord.

All   **Amen.**

The water may be sprinkled over the people or they may be invited to use it to sign themselves with the cross.

The service ends either with the Peace or with the following blessing

May God, who in Christ gives us a spring of water
    welling up to eternal life,
perfect in you the image of his glory;
and may the blessing of God almighty,
the Father, the Son, and the Holy Spirit,
be among *you* and remain with *you* always.

All   **Amen.**

¶ Thanksgiving for the Healing Ministry of the Church

See Note 8 on page 58.

Bless the Lord, O my soul;

All **and forget not all his benefits.**

God forgives all our iniquities;

All **and heals all our diseases.**

God redeems our life from the pit;

All **and crowns us with love and mercy.**

James 5.13-16a or another suitable reading such as Mark 1.29-34 or Acts 3.1-10 follows.

This prayer of thanksgiving may be said

Blessed are you, sovereign God, gentle and merciful,
creator of heaven and earth.
Your word brought light out of darkness.
In Jesus Christ you proclaim good news to the poor,
liberty to captives, sight to the blind
and freedom for the oppressed.
Daily your Spirit renews the face of the earth,
bringing life and health, wholeness and peace.
In the renewal of our lives
you make known your heavenly glory.
Blessed be God, Father, Son and Holy Spirit:

All **Blessed be God for ever.**

The Apostles' Creed or an authorized Affirmation of Faith is said at a principal service and may be said on other occasions.

Intercessions for those in need and those who care for them may be offered in this or another form

Holy God, in whom we live and move and have our being,
we make our prayer to you, saying,
Lord, hear us.

All **Lord, graciously hear us.**

Grant to [*N and*] all who seek you
the assurance of your presence, your power and your peace.
Lord, hear us.

All **Lord, graciously hear us.**

Grant your healing grace to [*N and*] all who are sick
that they may be made whole in body, mind and spirit.
Lord, hear us.

All **Lord, graciously hear us.**

Grant to all who minister to the suffering
wisdom and skill, sympathy and patience.
Lord, hear us.

All **Lord, graciously hear us.**

Sustain and support the anxious and fearful
and lift up all who are brought low.
Lord, hear us.

All **Lord, graciously hear us.**

Hear us, Lord of life.

All **Heal us, and make us whole.**

This or another Collect is said

Almighty God,
whose Son revealed in signs and miracles
the wonder of your saving presence:
renew [*N, N, … and*] all your people
with your heavenly grace,
and in all our weakness
sustain us by your mighty power,
through Jesus Christ our Lord.

All **Amen.**

The Lord's Prayer is said.

The Ministry of Healing may take place here using these or other suitable prayers

Be with us, Spirit of God;

All **nothing can separate us from your love.**

Breathe on us, breath of God;

All **fill us with your saving power.**

Speak in us, wisdom of God;

All **bring strength, healing and peace.**

The Lord is here.

All **His Spirit is with us.**

Silence is kept.

If anointing is to be administered, a priest may use this prayer over the oil, if it has not previously been blessed

Lord, holy Father, giver of health and salvation,
as your apostles anointed those who were sick and healed them,
so continue the ministry of healing in your Church.
Sanctify this oil, that those who are anointed with it
may be freed from suffering and distress,
find inward peace, and know the joy of your salvation,
through your Son, our Saviour Jesus Christ.

All **Amen.**

The laying on of hands may be administered using these or other suitable words

In the name of God and trusting in his might alone,
receive Christ's healing touch to make you whole.

May Christ bring you wholeness of body, mind and spirit,
deliver you from every evil,
and give you his peace.

All **Amen.**

If anointing is administered by an authorized minister, these or other suitable words may be used

N, I anoint you in the name of God who gives you life.
Receive Christ's forgiveness, his healing and his love.

May the Father of our Lord Jesus Christ
grant you the riches of his grace,
his wholeness and his peace.

All **Amen.**

This prayer concludes the Ministry of Healing

The almighty Lord,
who is a strong tower for all who put their trust in him,
whom all things in heaven, on earth, and under the earth obey,
be now and evermore your defence.
May you believe and trust that the only name under heaven
given for health and salvation
is the name of our Lord Jesus Christ.

All **Amen.**

This responsory may be used

O magnify the Lord with me;
let us exalt his name together.

All **O magnify the Lord with me;**
let us exalt his name together.
I sought the Lord and he answered me;
he delivered me from all my fears.

All **O magnify the Lord with me.**
In my weakness I cried to the Lord;
he heard me and saved me from my troubles.

All **Let us exalt his name together.**
Glory to the Father, and to the Son
and to the Holy Spirit.

All **O magnify the Lord with me;**
let us exalt his name together.   *cf Psalm 34*

The service ends with the Grace or a blessing or the Peace

Peace to you from God our Father who hears our cry.
Peace from his Son Jesus Christ whose death brings healing.
Peace from the Holy Spirit who gives us life and strength.
The peace of the Lord be always with you

All **and also with you.**

¶ Thanksgiving for the Mission of the Church

A suitable Gospel reading may be introduced by this acclamation

We proclaim not ourselves, but Christ Jesus as Lord

All **and ourselves as your servants for Jesus' sake.**

For the God who said, Let light shine out of darkness,

All **has caused the light to shine within us:**

to give the light of the knowledge of the glory of God

All **in the face of Jesus Christ.**

Hear the Gospel of our Lord Jesus Christ according to *N.*

All **Glory to you, O Lord.**

After the Gospel reading

This is the Gospel of the Lord.

All **Praise to you, O Christ.**

This prayer of thanksgiving may be said

Blessed are you,
the God and Father of our Lord Jesus Christ,
for you have blessed us in Christ with every spiritual blessing.
You chose us in Christ before the foundation of the world
and destined us for adoption as your children.
In Christ we have the forgiveness of sins,
an inheritance in your kingdom, the seal of your Spirit,
and in him we live for the praise of your glory
for ever and ever.

All **Amen.**

The commissioning of those called and prepared to exercise particular ministries may take place here.

The Apostles' Creed or an authorized Affirmation of Faith and this affirmation of commitment are said at a principal service and may be said on other occasions.

Will you continue in the apostles' teaching and fellowship,
in the breaking of bread, and in the prayers?

All **With the help of God, I will.**

Will you persevere in resisting evil,
and, whenever you fall into sin, repent and return to the Lord?

All **With the help of God, I will.**

Will you proclaim by word and example
the good news of God in Christ?

All **With the help of God, I will.**

Will you seek and serve Christ in all people,
loving your neighbour as yourself?

All **With the help of God, I will.**

Will you acknowledge Christ's authority over human society,
by prayer for the world and its leaders,
by defending the weak, and by seeking peace and justice?

All **With the help of God, I will.**

May Christ dwell in your hearts through faith,
that you may be rooted and grounded in love
and bring forth the fruit of the Spirit.

All **Amen.**

Intercessions for those engaged in ministry and other prayers for the mission of the Church may be offered.

This Collect is said

Almighty God,
who called your Church to witness
that in Christ you were reconciling the world to yourself:
help us so to proclaim the good news of your love,
that all who hear it may be reconciled to you
through him who died for us and rose again
and reigns with you in the unity of the Holy Spirit,
one God, now and for ever.

All **Amen.**

The Lord's Prayer is said.

The service ends either with the Peace or with the following blessing

Let us bless the living God:
he was born of the Virgin Mary,

All **revealed in his glory,**
worshipped by angels,

All **proclaimed among the nations,**
believed in throughout the world,

All **exalted to the highest heavens.**

Blessed be God, our strength and our salvation,

All **now and for ever. Amen.**

Let us bless the Lord.

All **Thanks be to God.**

Notes to Orders for Morning and Evening Prayer on Sunday

In the services and the Notes square brackets indicate parts of the service which may be omitted.

1 **Hymns and Songs**
Hymns and songs may be sung at appropriate points in the service, and metrical paraphrases may be used in place of the biblical canticles.

2 **Sentences of Scripture**
Alternative sentences of Scripture appropriate to the day or the season may be substituted for those in these orders.

3 **Principal Services and Principal Holy Days**
An authorized confession and absolution, and the Apostles' Creed or another Creed or authorized Affirmation of Faith, and a sermon, must be included in Morning or Evening Prayer when it is the principal service on a Sunday or Principal Holy Day, but may be omitted at other times.

4 **Opening Canticle at Morning Prayer**
The following are suitable for use as the opening canticle at Morning Prayer:
Benedicite, A Song of Creation (pages 778–779), especially in
    Ordinary Time;
Jubilate, A Song of Joy (page 781), especially in festal seasons;
The Easter Anthems (page 782), especially during the Easter season;
Venite, A Song of Triumph (page 780), especially during Advent
    and Lent.

5 **Old and New Testament Canticles**
The following are suitable as Old Testament canticles at Morning Prayer and New Testament canticles at Evening Prayer, especially in the seasons indicated:

	Morning	**Evening**
Advent	A Song of the Wilderness (page 786)	A Song of the Spirit (page 792)
Christmas	A Song of the Messiah (page 787)	A Song of Redemption (page 793)
Epiphany	A Song of the New Jerusalem (page 788)	A Song of Praise (page 794)
Lent	A Song of Humility (page 789)	A Song of Christ the Servant (page 794)
Easter	The Song of Moses and Miriam (page 790)	A Song of Faith (page 795)
Pentecost	A Song of Ezekiel (page 791)	A Song of God's Children (page 796)
Ordinary Time	A Song of David (page 791)	A Song of the Lamb (page 796)

6   **Opening Hymn and Canticle at Evening Prayer**
Phos hilaron (A Song of the Light) is a suitable opening hymn
(see page 783). Verses from either Psalm 104 or Psalm 141 are
suitable opening canticles (see pages 784–785).

7   **Te Deum**
The canticle Te Deum, A Song of the Church (page 802),
may be used at Morning or Evening Prayer immediately before the
Conclusion.

8   **Thanksgivings**
In Morning or Evening Prayer, one of the Thanksgivings may follow
the sermon or, where a sermon is included in the Thanksgiving,
the Gospel canticle. The confession and absolution at the beginning
of Morning and Evening Prayer should be omitted where penitence
is included in the Thanksgiving for the Word. If the Thanksgiving
for the Healing Ministry of the Church is to include anointing,
the minister must be authorized for this ministry as required by
Canon B 37.

9   **Intercessions**
These should normally be broadly based, expressing a concern for
the whole of God's world and the ministry of the whole Church.
Nevertheless, where occasion demands, they may be focused on
more particular and local needs. Where another service follows
immediately, they may be brief.

10   **Morning and Evening Collects**
If it is desired to use the Morning and Evening Collects (page 101),
they should not be added after the Collect of the Day, but should
be used before the Blessing or other Ending.

11   **Commemoration of the Resurrection**
The Order for Morning Prayer may be arranged as a
commemoration of the resurrection (which is especially
appropriate during the Easter season) by the use of the following:

[*Opening Canticle*: Benedicite, A Song of Creation]
Psalmody: Psalm 118.14-29
[*First Reading*: Genesis 1.1-5; Exodus 14.21-31; 1 Corinthians 15.1-8;
   or Colossians 3.1-4]
Old Testament Canticle: The Song of Moses and Miriam
Gospel Reading: Matthew 28.1-10; Mark 16.1-8; Mark 16.9-20;
   Luke 24.1-9; John 20.1-10; John 20.11-18; *or* John 21.1-14
New Testament Canticle: The Easter Anthems

Morning and Evening Prayer
from *The Book of Common Prayer*
with permitted variations (see page 80)

¶ *Opening Sentences*

Seasonal Sentences

General

O worship the Lord in the beauty of holiness: let the whole earth stand in awe of him.   *Psalm 96.9*

God is Spirit: and they that worship him must worship him in spirit and in truth.   *John 4.24*

Advent

The night is far spent, and the day is at hand: let us therefore cast off the works of darkness, and let us put on the armour of light.
                                      Romans 13.12

Christmas

Behold, I bring you good tidings of great joy which shall be to all people: for unto you is born in the city of David, a Saviour, which is Christ the Lord.   *Luke 2.10,11*

Epiphany

From the rising of the sun even unto the going down of the same my name is great among the nations; and in every place incense is offered unto my name, and a pure offering: for my name is great among the nations, saith the Lord.   *Malachi 1.11*

Lent

The sacrifices of God are a broken spirit: a broken and a contrite heart, O God, thou wilt not despise.   *Psalm 51.17*

Passiontide

Is it nothing to you, all ye that pass by? Behold, and see if there be any sorrow like unto my sorrow.   *Lamentations 1.12*

Good Friday

God commendeth his love toward us, in that, while we were yet sinners, Christ died for us.   *Romans 5.8*

Easter Eve

Rest in the Lord and wait patiently for him; and he shall give thee thy heart's desire. *Psalm 37.7,4*

Easter

Blessed be the God and Father of our Lord Jesus Christ, who according to his great mercy hath begotten us again unto a living hope by the resurrection of Jesus Christ from the dead. *1 Peter 1.3*

Ascension Day

Seeing that we have a great high priest that is passed into the heavens, Jesus the Son of God, let us come boldly unto the throne of grace, that we may obtain mercy and find grace to help in time of need. *Hebrews 4.14,16*

Pentecost

The love of God hath been shed abroad in our hearts through the Holy Spirit which was given unto us. *Romans 5.5*

Trinity

God is love; and he that abideth in love abideth in God and God in him. *1 John 4.16*

Harvest

The earth is the Lord's, and the fullness thereof. *Psalm 24.1*

All Saints

Seeing we are compassed about with so great a cloud of witnesses, let us lay aside every weight, and the sin which doth so easily beset us, and let us run with patience the race that is set before us, looking unto Jesus, the author and perfecter of our faith.
Hebrews 12.1, 2

Saints' Days

The righteous shall be had in everlasting remembrance; the memory of the just is blessed. *Psalm 112.6; Proverbs 10.7*

Time of Trouble

God is our hope and strength: a very present help in trouble.
Psalm 46.1

Penitential Sentences

I will arise and go to my father, and will say unto him, Father, I have sinned against heaven, and before thee, and am no more worthy to be called thy son. *Luke 15.18, 19*

If we say that we have no sin, we deceive ourselves, and the truth is not in us: but if we confess our sins, he is faithful and just to forgive us our sins, and to cleanse us from all unrighteousness. *1 John 1.8, 9*

To the Lord our God belong mercies and forgivenesses, though we have rebelled against him: neither have we obeyed the voice of the Lord our God, to walk in his laws which he set before us.
Daniel 9.9, 10

Enter not into judgement with thy servant, O Lord; for in thy sight shall no man living be justified. *Psalm 143.2*

When the wicked man turneth away from his wickedness that he hath committed, and doeth that which is lawful and right, he shall save his soul alive. *Ezekiel 18.27*

I acknowledge my transgressions, and my sin is ever before me.
Psalm 51.3

Hide thy face from my sins, and blot out all mine iniquities.
Psalm 51.9

O Lord, correct me, but with judgement; not in thine anger, lest thou bring me to nothing. *Jeremiah 10.24; Psalm 6.1*

Repent ye; for the kingdom of heaven is at hand. *Matthew 3.2*

Rend your heart, and not your garments, and turn unto the Lord your God: for he is gracious and merciful, slow to anger, and of great kindness, and repenteth him of the evil. *Joel 2.13*

Morning Prayer from
The Book of Common Prayer

¶ *Introduction*

The minister may use a seasonal sentence before using one or more of the penitential sentences (see pages 59–61).

The minister introduces the service

Dearly beloved [brethren],
the Scripture moveth us in sundry places to acknowledge
    and confess our manifold sins and wickedness;

[and that we should not dissemble nor cloak them before
    the face of almighty God our heavenly Father;
but confess them with an humble, lowly, penitent and
    obedient heart;
to the end that we may obtain forgiveness of the same
    by his infinite goodness and mercy.
And although we ought at all times humbly to acknowledge
    our sins before God;
yet ought we most chiefly so to do,
when we assemble and meet together
to render thanks for the great benefits that we have
    received at his hands,
to set forth his most worthy praise,
to hear his most holy word,
and to ask those things which are requisite and necessary,
as well for the body as the soul.]

Wherefore I pray and beseech you,
as many as are here present,
to accompany me with a pure heart, and humble voice,
unto the throne of the heavenly grace, saying [after me]:

(or)

Beloved, we are come together in the presence of almighty God and of the whole company of heaven to offer unto him through our Lord Jesus Christ our worship and praise and thanksgiving; to make confession of our sins; to pray, as well for others as for ourselves, that we may know more truly the greatness of God's love and shew forth in our lives the fruits of his grace; and to ask on behalf of all men such things as their well-being doth require.

Wherefore let us kneel in silence, and remember God's presence with us now.

All **Almighty and most merciful Father,**
we have erred, and strayed from thy ways like lost sheep.
We have followed too much the devices and desires
      of our own hearts.
We have offended against thy holy laws.
We have left undone those things
      which we ought to have done;
and we have done those things
      which we ought not to have done;
and there is no health in us.
But thou, O Lord, have mercy upon us, miserable offenders.
Spare thou them, O God, which confess their faults.
Restore thou them that are penitent;
according to thy promises declared unto mankind
      in Christ Jesu our Lord.
And grant, O most merciful Father, for his sake,
that we may hereafter live a godly, righteous, and sober life,
to the glory of thy holy name.
Amen.

Almighty God, the Father of our Lord Jesus Christ,
who desireth not the death of a sinner,
but rather that he may turn from his wickedness and live;
and hath given power, and commandment, to his ministers
to declare and pronounce to his people, being penitent,
the absolution and remission of their sins:
he pardoneth and absolveth all them that truly repent
　　and unfeignedly believe his holy gospel.
Wherefore let us beseech him to grant us true repentance,
　　and his Holy Spirit,
that those things may please him which we do at this present;
and that the rest of our life hereafter may be pure and holy;
so that at the last we may come to his eternal joy;
through Jesus Christ our Lord.

All　**Amen.**

or other ministers may say

Grant, we beseech thee, merciful Lord,
to thy faithful people pardon and peace,
that they may be cleansed from all their sins,
and serve thee with a quiet mind;
through Jesus Christ our Lord.

All　**Amen.**

All　**Our Father, which art in heaven,**
hallowed be thy name;
thy kingdom come;
thy will be done,
in earth as it is in heaven.
Give us this day our daily bread.
And forgive us our trespasses,
as we forgive them that trespass against us.
And lead us not into temptation;
but deliver us from evil.
For thine is the kingdom,
the power and the glory,
for ever and ever.
Amen.

¶ *Morning Prayer*

The introduction to the service (pages 62–64) is used on Sundays, and may be used on any occasion.

These responses are used

O Lord, open thou our lips
All **and our mouth shall shew forth thy praise.**

O God, make speed to save us.
All **O Lord, make haste to help us.**

Glory be to the Father, and to the Son,
and to the Holy Ghost;
All **as it was in the beginning, is now, and ever shall be, world without end. Amen.**

Praise ye the Lord.
All **The Lord's name be praised.**

Venite, exultemus Domino

1   O come, let us sing unto the Lord :
let us heartily rejoice in the strength of our salvation.

2   Let us come before his presence with thanksgiving :
and shew ourselves glad in him with psalms.

3   For the Lord is a great God :
and a great King above all gods.

4   In his hand are all the corners of the earth :
and the strength of the hills is his also.

5   The sea is his, and he made it :
and his hands prepared the dry land.

6   O come, let us worship, and fall down :
and kneel before the Lord our Maker.

7   For he is the Lord our God :
and we are the people of his pasture, and the sheep of his hand.

[8   Today if ye will hear his voice, harden not your hearts :
as in the provocation,
     and as in the day of temptation in the wilderness;

9   When your fathers tempted me :
proved me, and saw my works.

10   Forty years long was I grieved with this generation, and said :
It is a people that do err in their hearts,
     for they have not known my ways.

11   Unto whom I sware in my wrath :
that they should not enter into my rest.]   *Psalm 95*

Glory be to the Father, and to the Son :
and to the Holy Ghost;
as it was in the beginning, is now, and ever shall be :
world without end. Amen.

Psalmody

At the end of each psalm these words are said or sung

Glory be to the Father, and to the Son :
and to the Holy Ghost;
as it was in the beginning, is now, and ever shall be :
world without end. Amen.

Old Testament Reading

Te Deum Laudamus

Either the Te Deum Laudamus (as follows) or Benedicite, omnia opera (page 807) is said or sung.

We praise thee, O God; we acknowledge thee to be the Lord.
All the earth doth worship thee, the Father everlasting.
To thee all angels cry aloud, the heavens and all the powers therein.
To thee cherubin and seraphin continually do cry,
Holy, Holy, Holy, Lord God of Sabaoth;
Heaven and earth are full of the majesty of thy glory.
The glorious company of the apostles praise thee.
The goodly fellowship of the prophets praise thee.
The noble army of martyrs praise thee.
The holy Church throughout all the world doth acknowledge thee:
the Father of an infinite majesty;
thine honourable, true and only Son;
also the Holy Ghost the Comforter.

Thou art the King of glory, O Christ.
Thou art the everlasting Son of the Father.
When thou tookest upon thee to deliver man,
    thou didst not abhor the Virgin's womb.
When thou hadst overcome the sharpness of death,
    thou didst open the kingdom of heaven to all believers.
Thou sittest at the right hand of God, in the glory of the Father.
We believe that thou shalt come to be our judge.
We therefore pray thee, help thy servants,
    whom thou hast redeemed with thy precious blood.
Make them to be numbered with thy saints in glory everlasting.

O Lord, save thy people and bless thine heritage.
Govern them and lift them up for ever.
Day by day we magnify thee;
and we worship thy name, ever world without end.
Vouchsafe, O Lord, to keep us this day without sin.
O Lord, have mercy upon us, have mercy upon us.
O Lord, let thy mercy lighten upon us, as our trust is in thee.
O Lord, in thee have I trusted; let me never be confounded.

New Testament Reading

Benedictus

Either the Benedictus (as follows) or Jubilate Deo (Psalm 100, page 810) is said or sung.

1   Blessed be the Lord God of Israel :
     for he hath visited, and redeemed his people;

2   And hath raised up a mighty salvation for us :
     in the house of his servant David;

3   As he spake by the mouth of his holy Prophets :
     which have been since the world began;

4   That we should be saved from our enemies :
     and from the hands of all that hate us;

5   To perform the mercy promised to our forefathers :
     and to remember his holy covenant;

6   To perform the oath which he sware to our forefather Abraham :
     that he would give us,

7   That we being delivered out of the hands of our enemies :
     might serve him without fear,

8   In holiness and righteousness before him :
     all the days of our life.

9   And thou, child, shalt be called the Prophet of the Highest :
     for thou shalt go before the face of the Lord to prepare his ways;

10   To give knowledge of salvation unto his people :
     for the remission of their sins;

11   Through the tender mercy of our God :
     whereby the day-spring from on high hath visited us;

12   To give light to them that sit in darkness,
          and in the shadow of death :
     and to guide our feet into the way of peace.   *Luke 1.68-79*

     Glory be to the Father, and to the Son :
     and to the Holy Ghost;
     as it was in the beginning, is now, and ever shall be :
     world without end. Amen.

All **I believe in God the Father almighty,**
maker of heaven and earth:
and in Jesus Christ his only Son our Lord,
who was conceived by the Holy Ghost,
born of the Virgin Mary,
suffered under Pontius Pilate,
was crucified, dead, and buried.
He descended into hell;
the third day he rose again from the dead;
he ascended into heaven,
and sitteth on the right hand of God the Father almighty;
from thence he shall come to judge the quick and the dead.
I believe in the Holy Ghost;
the holy catholic Church;
the communion of saints;
the forgiveness of sins;
the resurrection of the body,
and the life everlasting.
Amen.

The Lord be with you.

All **And with thy spirit.**

Let us pray.

Lord, have mercy upon us.

All **Christ, have mercy upon us.**
Lord, have mercy upon us.

All **Our Father, which art in heaven,**
hallowed be thy name;
thy kingdom come;
thy will be done,
in earth as it is in heaven.
Give us this day our daily bread.
And forgive us our trespasses,
as we forgive them that trespass against us.
And lead us not into temptation;
but deliver us from evil. Amen.

O Lord, shew thy mercy upon us.

All **And grant us thy salvation.**

O Lord, save the Queen.

All **And mercifully hear us when we call upon thee.**

Endue thy ministers with righteousness.

All **And make thy chosen people joyful.**

O Lord, save thy people.

All **And bless thine inheritance.**

Give peace in our time, O Lord.

All **Because there is none other that fighteth for us,**
but only thou, O God.

O God, make clean our hearts within us.

All **And take not thy Holy Spirit from us.**

Three Collects are said.

The Collect of the Day

The Collect for Peace

O God, who art the author of peace and lover of concord,
in knowledge of whom standeth our eternal life,
whose service is perfect freedom;
defend us thy humble servants in all assaults of our enemies;
that we, surely trusting in thy defence,
may not fear the power of any adversaries;
through the might of Jesus Christ our Lord.

All   **Amen.**

The Collect for Grace

O Lord, our heavenly Father,
almighty and everlasting God,
who hast safely brought us to the beginning of this day;
defend us in the same with thy mighty power;
and grant that this day we fall into no sin,
neither run into any kind of danger,
but that all our doings may be ordered by thy governance,
to do always that is righteous in thy sight;
through Jesus Christ our Lord.

All   **Amen.**

The order for the end of the service may include:

¶ *hymns or anthems*
¶ *a sermon*
¶ *further prayers (which may include prayers from pages 107–109)*

This prayer may be used to conclude the service

The grace of our Lord Jesus Christ,
and the love of God,
and the fellowship of the Holy Ghost,
be with us all evermore.

All   **Amen.**

Evening Prayer from
The Book of Common Prayer

¶ *Introduction*

The minister may use a seasonal sentence before using one or more of the penitential sentences (see pages 59–61).

The minister introduces the service

Dearly beloved [brethren],
the Scripture moveth us in sundry places to acknowledge
   and confess our manifold sins and wickedness;

[and that we should not dissemble nor cloak them before
   the face of almighty God our heavenly Father;
but confess them with an humble, lowly, penitent and
   obedient heart;
to the end that we may obtain forgiveness of the same
   by his infinite goodness and mercy.
And although we ought at all times humbly to acknowledge
   our sins before God;
yet ought we most chiefly so to do,
when we assemble and meet together
to render thanks for the great benefits that we have
   received at his hands,
to set forth his most worthy praise,
to hear his most holy word,
and to ask those things which are requisite and necessary,
as well for the body as the soul.]

Wherefore I pray and beseech you,
as many as are here present,
to accompany me with a pure heart, and humble voice,
unto the throne of the heavenly grace, saying [after me]:

(or)

Beloved, we are come together in the presence of almighty God and of the whole company of heaven to offer unto him through our Lord Jesus Christ our worship and praise and thanksgiving; to make confession of our sins; to pray, as well for others as for ourselves, that we may know more truly the greatness of God's love and shew forth in our lives the fruits of his grace; and to ask on behalf of all men such things as their well-being doth require.

Wherefore let us kneel in silence, and remember God's presence with us now.

All   **Almighty and most merciful Father,**
we have erred, and strayed from thy ways like lost sheep.
We have followed too much the devices and desires
of our own hearts.
We have offended against thy holy laws.
We have left undone those things
which we ought to have done;
and we have done those things
which we ought not to have done;
and there is no health in us.
But thou, O Lord, have mercy upon us, miserable offenders.
Spare thou them, O God, which confess their faults.
Restore thou them that are penitent;
according to thy promises declared unto mankind
in Christ Jesu our Lord.
And grant, O most merciful Father, for his sake,
that we may hereafter live a godly, righteous, and sober life,
to the glory of thy holy name.
Amen.

A priest says

Almighty God, the Father of our Lord Jesus Christ,
who desireth not the death of a sinner,
but rather that he may turn from his wickedness and live;
and hath given power, and commandment, to his ministers
to declare and pronounce to his people, being penitent,
the absolution and remission of their sins:
he pardoneth and absolveth all them that truly repent
    and unfeignedly believe his holy gospel.
Wherefore let us beseech him to grant us true repentance,
    and his Holy Spirit,
that those things may please him which we do at this present;
and that the rest of our life hereafter may be pure and holy;
so that at the last we may come to his eternal joy;
through Jesus Christ our Lord.

All **Amen.**

or other ministers may say

Grant, we beseech thee, merciful Lord,
to thy faithful people pardon and peace,
that they may be cleansed from all their sins,
and serve thee with a quiet mind;
through Jesus Christ our Lord.

All **Amen.**

All **Our Father, which art in heaven,**
       hallowed be thy name;
       thy kingdom come;
       thy will be done,
       in earth as it is in heaven.
       Give us this day our daily bread.
       And forgive us our trespasses,
       as we forgive them that trespass against us.
       And lead us not into temptation;
       but deliver us from evil.
       For thine is the kingdom,
       the power and the glory,
       for ever and ever.
       Amen.

¶ *Evening Prayer*

The introduction to the service (pages 72–74) is used on Sundays, and may be used on any occasion.

These responses are used

O Lord, open thou our lips

All **and our mouth shall shew forth thy praise.**

O God, make speed to save us.

All **O Lord, make haste to help us.**

Glory be to the Father, and to the Son,
and to the Holy Ghost;

All **as it was in the beginning, is now, and ever shall be,
world without end. Amen.**

Praise ye the Lord.

All **The Lord's name be praised.**

Psalmody

At the end of each psalm these words are said or sung

Glory be to the Father, and to the Son :
and to the Holy Ghost;
as it was in the beginning, is now, and ever shall be :
world without end. Amen.

Old Testament Reading

Magnificat

*Either the Magnificat (as follows) or Cantate Domino
(Psalm 98, page 812) is said or sung.*

1   My soul doth magnify the Lord :
    and my spirit hath rejoiced in God my Saviour.

2   For he hath regarded :
    the lowliness of his handmaiden.

3   For behold, from henceforth :
    all generations shall call me blessed.

4   For he that is mighty hath magnified me :
    and holy is his Name.

5   And his mercy is on them that fear him :
    throughout all generations.

6   He hath shewed strength with his arm :
    he hath scattered the proud in the imagination of their hearts.

7   He hath put down the mighty from their seat :
    and hath exalted the humble and meek.

8   He hath filled the hungry with good things :
    and the rich he hath sent empty away.

9   He remembering his mercy hath holpen his servant Israel :
    as he promised to our forefathers, Abraham and his seed for ever.

Luke 1.46-55

Glory be to the Father, and to the Son :
and to the Holy Ghost;
as it was in the beginning, is now, and ever shall be :
world without end. Amen.

New Testament Reading

Nunc dimittis

*Either the Nunc dimittis (as follows) or Deus misereatur
(Psalm 67, page 813) is said or sung.*

1 Lord, now lettest thou thy servant depart in peace :
   according to thy word.

2 For mine eyes have seen :
   thy salvation;

3 Which thou hast prepared :
   before the face of all people;

4 To be a light to lighten the Gentiles :
   and to be the glory of thy people Israel.   *Luke 2.29-32*

   Glory be to the Father, and to the Son :
   and to the Holy Ghost;
   as it was in the beginning, is now, and ever shall be :
   world without end. Amen.

The Apostles' Creed

All **I believe in God the Father almighty,
       maker of heaven and earth:
       and in Jesus Christ his only Son our Lord,
       who was conceived by the Holy Ghost,
       born of the Virgin Mary,
       suffered under Pontius Pilate,
       was crucified, dead, and buried.
       He descended into hell;
       the third day he rose again from the dead;
       he ascended into heaven,
       and sitteth on the right hand of God the Father almighty;
       from thence he shall come to judge the quick and the dead.
       I believe in the Holy Ghost;
       the holy catholic Church;
       the communion of saints;
       the forgiveness of sins;
       the resurrection of the body,
       and the life everlasting.
       Amen.**

The Lord be with you.

All **And with thy spirit.**

Let us pray.

Lord, have mercy upon us.

All **Christ, have mercy upon us.**
Lord, have mercy upon us.

All **Our Father, which art in heaven,**
hallowed be thy name;
thy kingdom come;
thy will be done,
in earth as it is in heaven.
Give us this day our daily bread.
And forgive us our trespasses,
as we forgive them that trespass against us.
And lead us not into temptation;
but deliver us from evil. Amen.

O Lord, shew thy mercy upon us.

All **And grant us thy salvation.**

O Lord, save the Queen.

All **And mercifully hear us when we call upon thee.**

Endue thy ministers with righteousness.

All **And make thy chosen people joyful.**

O Lord, save thy people.

All **And bless thine inheritance.**

Give peace in our time, O Lord.

All **Because there is none other that fighteth for us,**
but only thou, O God.

O God, make clean our hearts within us.

All **And take not thy Holy Spirit from us.**

Three Collects are said.

The Collect of the Day

The Collect for Peace

O God, from whom all holy desires, all good counsels,
  and all just works do proceed;
give unto thy servants that peace which the world cannot give;
that both, our hearts may be set to obey thy commandments,
and also that, by thee,
we being defended from the fear of our enemies
may pass our time in rest and quietness;
through the merits of Jesus Christ our Saviour.

All **Amen.**

The Collect for Aid against all Perils

Lighten our darkness, we beseech thee, O Lord;
and by thy great mercy defend us
  from all perils and dangers of this night;
for the love of thy only Son, our Saviour, Jesus Christ.

All **Amen.**

The order for the end of the service may include:

¶   *hymns or anthems*
¶   *a sermon*
¶   *further prayers (which may include prayers from pages 107–109)*

This prayer may be used to conclude the service

The grace of our Lord Jesus Christ,
and the love of God,
and the fellowship of the Holy Ghost,
be with us all evermore.

All **Amen.**

Schedule of Permitted Variations
to the *Book of Common Prayer* Orders for Morning and Evening Prayer where these occur in *Common Worship*

1   All or part of the material before 'O Lord, open thou our lips' may be omitted, at least on weekdays.

2   The minister may use a seasonal sentence before using one of the penitential sentences with which the service begins.

3   The minister may use an abbreviated form of the Bidding, 'Dearly beloved brethren …', or the form on pages 63 and 73 may be used.

4   When the officiating minister is not a priest, an authorized prayer for absolution in the 'us' form or else the Collect for Trinity 21 in *The Book of Common Prayer* is said by the minister in place of the prayer for absolution printed in *The Book of Common Prayer*.

5   The whole of the Gloria Patri, together with the words 'Praise ye the Lord' that follow, may be said or sung by the entire congregation, in which case the final response, 'The Lord's name be praised', may be omitted.

6   At Morning Prayer, verses 8 to 11 of the Venite may be omitted except in Lent. The Easter Anthems (page 805) may be used in place of the Venite throughout Eastertide.

7   Other prayers of intercession and thanksgiving may be used in addition to or in place of the five prayers printed at the end of the Order in *The Book of Common Prayer*.

8   Hymns may be sung at suitable points in the service, silence may be kept after the readings, a sermon may be preached and the service may end with a blessing.

An Order for Night Prayer
(Compline)

Note

The ancient office of Compline derives its name from a Latin word meaning 'completion' (*completorium*). It is above all a service of quietness and reflection before rest at the end of the day. It is most effective when the ending is indeed an ending, without additions, conversation or noise. If there is an address, or business to be done, it should come first. If the service is in church, those present depart in silence; if at home, they go quietly to bed.

For further Notes, see page 99.

Preparation

The Lord almighty grant us a quiet night and a perfect end.

All **Amen.**

Our help is in the name of the Lord

All **who made heaven and earth.**

A period of silence for reflection on the past day may follow.

The following or other suitable words of penitence may be used

All **Most merciful God,**
we confess to you,
before the whole company of heaven and one another,
that we have sinned in thought, word and deed
and in what we have failed to do.
Forgive us our sins,
heal us by your Spirit
and raise us to new life in Christ. Amen.

O God, make speed to save us.

All **O Lord, make haste to help us.**

All **Glory to the Father and to the Son**
and to the Holy Spirit;
as it was in the beginning is now
and shall be for ever. Amen.
Allelula.

The following or another suitable hymn may be sung

Before the ending of the day,
Creator of the world, we pray
That you, with steadfast love, would keep
Your watch around us while we sleep.

From evil dreams defend our sight,
From fears and terrors of the night;
Tread underfoot our deadly foe
That we no sinful thought may know.

O Father, that we ask be done
Through Jesus Christ, your only Son;
And Holy Spirit, by whose breath
Our souls are raised to life from death.

The Word of God

Psalmody

One or more of the following psalms may be used.

Psalm 4

1   Answer me when I call, O God of my righteousness; ♦
    you set me at liberty when I was in trouble;
        have mercy on me and hear my prayer.

2   How long will you nobles dishonour my glory; ♦
    how long will you love vain things and seek after falsehood?

3   But know that the Lord has shown me his marvellous kindness; ♦
    when I call upon the Lord, he will hear me.

4   Stand in awe, and sin not; ♦
    commune with your own heart upon your bed, and be still.

5   Offer the sacrifices of righteousness ♦
    and put your trust in the Lord.

6   There are many that say, 'Who will show us any good?' ♦
    Lord, lift up the light of your countenance upon us.

7   You have put gladness in my heart, ✦
     more than when their corn and wine and oil increase.

8   In peace I will lie down and sleep, ✦
     for it is you Lord, only, who make me dwell in safety.

Psalm 91

1   Whoever dwells in the shelter of the Most High ✦
     and abides under the shadow of the Almighty,

2   Shall say to the Lord, 'My refuge and my stronghold, ✦
     my God, in whom I put my trust.'

3   For he shall deliver you from the snare of the fowler ✦
     and from the deadly pestilence.

4   He shall cover you with his wings
         and you shall be safe under his feathers; ✦
     his faithfulness shall be your shield and buckler.

5   You shall not be afraid of any terror by night, ✦
     nor of the arrow that flies by day;

6   Of the pestilence that stalks in darkness, ✦
     nor of the sickness that destroys at noonday.

7   Though a thousand fall at your side
         and ten thousand at your right hand, ✦
     yet it shall not come near you.

8   Your eyes have only to behold ✦
     to see the reward of the wicked.

9   Because you have made the Lord your refuge ✦
     and the Most High your stronghold,

10   There shall no evil happen to you, ✦
     neither shall any plague come near your tent.

11   For he shall give his angels charge over you, ✦
     to keep you in all your ways.

12   They shall bear you in their hands, ✦
     lest you dash your foot against a stone.

13   You shall tread upon the lion and adder; ♦
the young lion and the serpent you shall trample underfoot.

14   Because they have set their love upon me,
       therefore will I deliver them; ♦
I will lift them up, because they know my name.

15   They will call upon me and I will answer them; ♦
I am with them in trouble,
       I will deliver them and bring them to honour.

16   With long life will I satisfy them ♦
and show them my salvation.

Psalm 134

1   Come, bless the Lord, all you servants of the Lord, ♦
you that by night stand in the house of the Lord.

2   Lift up your hands towards the sanctuary ♦
and bless the Lord.

3   The Lord who made heaven and earth ♦
give you blessing out of Zion.

At the end of the psalmody, the following is said or sung

Glory to the Father and to the Son
and to the Holy Spirit;
as it was in the beginning is now
and shall be for ever. Amen.

Scripture Reading

One of the following short lessons or another suitable passage is read

You, O Lord, are in the midst of us and we are called by your name; leave us not, O Lord our God.   *Jeremiah 14.9*

(or)

Be sober, be vigilant, because your adversary the devil is prowling round like a roaring lion, seeking for someone to devour. Resist him, strong in the faith.   *1 Peter 5.8, 9*

(or)

The servants of the Lamb shall see the face of God, whose name will be on their foreheads. There will be no more night: they will not need the light of a lamp or the light of the sun, for God will be their light, and they will reign for ever and ever.   *Revelation 22.4, 5*

The following responsory may be said

Into your hands, O Lord, I commend my spirit.

All **Into your hands, O Lord, I commend my spirit.**
For you have redeemed me, Lord God of truth.

All **I commend my spirit.**
Glory to the Father, and to the Son, and to the Holy Spirit.

All **Into your hands, O Lord, I commend my spirit.**

Or, in Easter

Into your hands, O Lord, I commend my spirit.
Alleluia, alleluia.

All **Into your hands, O Lord, I commend my spirit.**
Alleluia, alleluia.
For you have redeemed me, Lord God of truth.

All **Alleluia, alleluia.**
Glory to the Father, and to the Son, and to the Holy Spirit.

All **Into your hands, O Lord, I commend my spirit.**
Alleluia, alleluia.

Keep me as the apple of your eye.

All **Hide me under the shadow of your wings.**

Gospel Canticle

The Nunc dimittis (The Song of Simeon) is said or sung

All **Save us, O Lord, while waking,**
and guard us while sleeping,
that awake we may watch with Christ
and asleep may rest in peace.

1   Now, Lord, you let your servant go in peace: ♦
     your word has been fulfilled.

2   My own eyes have seen the salvation ♦
     which you have prepared in the sight of every people;

3   A light to reveal you to the nations ♦
     and the glory of your people Israel.   *Luke 2.29-32*

     Glory to the Father and to the Son
     and to the Holy Spirit;
     as it was in the beginning is now
     and shall be for ever. Amen.

All **Save us, O Lord, while waking,**
and guard us while sleeping,
that awake we may watch with Christ
and asleep may rest in peace.

Prayers

Intercessions and thanksgivings may be offered here.

The Collect

Silence may be kept.

Visit this place, O Lord, we pray,
and drive far from it the snares of the enemy;
may your holy angels dwell with us and guard us in peace,
and may your blessing be always upon us;
through Jesus Christ our Lord.

All **Amen.**

The Lord's Prayer may be said.

The Conclusion

In peace we will lie down and sleep;

All **for you alone, Lord, make us dwell in safety.**

Abide with us, Lord Jesus,

All **for the night is at hand and the day is now past.**

As the night watch looks for the morning,

All **so do we look for you, O Christ.**

[Come with the dawning of the day

All **and make yourself known in the breaking of the bread.**]

The Lord bless us and watch over us;
the Lord make his face shine upon us and be gracious to us;
the Lord look kindly on us and give us peace.

All **Amen.**

An Order for Night Prayer (Compline) in Traditional Language

Note

The ancient office of Compline derives its name from a Latin word meaning 'completion' (*completorium*). It is above all a service of quietness and reflection before rest at the end of the day. It is most effective when the ending is indeed an ending, without additions, conversation or noise. If there is an address, or business to be done, it should come first. If the service is in church, those present depart in silence; if at home, they go quietly to bed.

For further Notes, see page 99.

Preparation

The Lord almighty grant us a quiet night and a perfect end.

All **Amen.**

[Brethren,] be sober, be vigilant; because your adversary the devil, as a roaring lion, walketh about, seeking whom he may devour: whom resist, steadfast in the faith. *1 Peter 5.8, 9*

But thou, O Lord, have mercy upon us.

All **Thanks be to God.**

Our help is in the name of the Lord

All **who hath made heaven and earth.**

A period of silence for reflection on the past day may follow.

The following or other suitable words of penitence may be used

All **We confess to God almighty,
the Father, the Son and the Holy Ghost,
that we have sinned in thought, word and deed,
through our own grievous fault.
Wherefore we pray God to have mercy upon us.**

**Almighty God, have mercy upon us,
forgive us all our sins and deliver us from all evil,
confirm and strengthen us in all goodness,
and bring us to life everlasting;
through Jesus Christ our Lord.
Amen.**

A priest may say

May the almighty and merciful Lord
grant unto you pardon and remission of all your sins,
time for amendment of life,
and the grace and comfort of the Holy Spirit.

All **Amen.**

O God, make speed to save us.

All **O Lord, make haste to help us.**

Glory be to the Father, and to the Son,
and to the Holy Ghost;

All **as it was in the beginning, is now, and ever shall be,
world without end. Amen.**

Praise ye the Lord.

All **The Lord's name be praised.**

The following or another suitable hymn may be sung

Before the ending of the day,
Creator of the world we pray,
That with thy wonted favour thou
Wouldst be our guard and keeper now.

From all ill dreams defend our eyes,
From nightly fears and fantasies;
Tread underfoot our ghostly foe,
That no pollution we may know.

O Father, that we ask be done,
Through Jesus Christ, thine only Son;
Who, with the Holy Ghost and thee,
Doth live and reign eternally.

The Word of God

One or more of the following psalms may be used

Psalm 4

1   Hear me when I call, O God of my righteousness :
    thou hast set me at liberty when I was in trouble;
        have mercy upon me, and hearken unto my prayer.

2   O ye sons of men, how long will ye blaspheme mine honour :
    and have such pleasure in vanity, and seek after leasing?

3   Know this also, that the Lord hath chosen to himself
        the man that is godly :
    when I call upon the Lord, he will hear me.

4   Stand in awe, and sin not :
    commune with your own heart, and in your chamber, and be still.

5   Offer the sacrifice of righteousness :
    and put your trust in the Lord.

6   There be many that say :
    Who will shew us any good?

7   Lord, lift thou up :
    the light of thy countenance upon us.

8   Thou hast put gladness in my heart :
    since the time that their corn, and wine, and oil increased.

9   I will lay me down in peace, and take my rest :
    for it is thou, Lord, only, that makest me dwell in safety.

Psalm 31.1-6

1   In thee, O Lord, have I put my trust :
let me never be put to confusion, deliver me in thy righteousness.

2   Bow down thine ear to me :
make haste to deliver me.

3   And be thou my strong rock, and house of defence :
that thou mayest save me.

4   For thou art my strong rock, and my castle :
be thou also my guide, and lead me for thy name's sake.

5   Draw me out of the net, that they have laid privily for me :
for thou art my strength.

6   Into thy hands I commend my spirit :
for thou hast redeemed me, O Lord, thou God of truth.

Psalm 91

1   Whoso dwelleth under the defence of the Most High :
shall abide under the shadow of the Almighty.

2   I will say unto the Lord, Thou art my hope, and my stronghold :
my God, in him will I trust.

3   For he shall deliver thee from the snare of the hunter :
and from the noisome pestilence.

4   He shall defend thee under his wings,
        and thou shalt be safe under his feathers :
his faithfulness and truth shall be thy shield and buckler.

5   Thou shalt not be afraid for any terror by night :
nor for the arrow that flieth by day;

6   For the pestilence that walketh in darkness :
nor for the sickness that destroyeth in the noonday.

7   A thousand shall fall beside thee, and ten thousand at thy right hand :
but it shall not come nigh thee.

8   Yea, with thine eyes shalt thou behold :
and see the reward of the ungodly.

9   For thou, Lord, art my hope :
        thou hast set thine house of defence very high.

10   There shall no evil happen unto thee :
        neither shall any plague come nigh thy dwelling.

11   For he shall give his angels charge over thee :
        to keep thee in all thy ways.

12   They shall bear thee in their hands :
        that thou hurt not thy foot against a stone.

13   Thou shalt go upon the lion and adder :
        the young lion and the dragon shalt thou tread under thy feet.

14   Because he hath set his love upon me, therefore will I deliver him :
        I will set him up, because he hath known my name.

15   He shall call upon me, and I will hear him :
        yea, I am with him in trouble;
           I will deliver him, and bring him to honour.

16   With long life will I satisfy him :
        and shew him my salvation.

Psalm 134

1   Behold now, praise the Lord :
        all ye servants of the Lord;

2   Ye that by night stand in the house of the Lord :
        even in the courts of the house of our God.

3   Lift up your hands in the sanctuary :
        and praise the Lord.

4   The Lord that made heaven and earth :
        give thee blessing out of Sion.

At the end of the psalmody, the following is said or sung

Glory be to the Father, and to the Son :
and to the Holy Ghost;
as it was in the beginning, is now, and ever shall be :
world without end. Amen.

Scripture Reading

One of the following short lessons or another suitable passage is read

Thou, O Lord, art in the midst of us, and we are called by thy name; leave us not, O Lord our God. *Jeremiah 14.9*

(or)

Come unto me, all ye that labour and are heavy laden, and I will give you rest. Take my yoke upon you, and learn of me; for I am meek and lowly in heart: and ye shall find rest unto your souls. For my yoke is easy, and my burden is light. *Matthew 11.28-30*

(or)

Now the God of peace, that brought again from the dead our Lord Jesus, that great shepherd of the sheep, through the blood of the everlasting covenant, make you perfect in every good work to do his will, working in you that which is well-pleasing in his sight; through Jesus Christ, to whom be glory for ever and ever. Amen. *Hebrews 13.20,21*

All **Thanks be to God.**

The following responsory may be said

Into thy hands, O Lord, I commend my spirit.
All **Into thy hands, O Lord, I commend my spirit.**
For thou hast redeemed me, O Lord, thou God of truth.
All **I commend my spirit.**
Glory be to the Father, and to the Son, and to the Holy Ghost.
All **Into thy hands, O Lord, I commend my spirit.**

Or, in Easter

Into thy hands, O Lord, I commend my spirit.
  Alleluia, alleluia.
All **Into thy hands, O Lord, I commend my spirit.**
  Alleluia, alleluia.
For thou hast redeemed me, O Lord, thou God of truth.
All **Alleluia, alleluia.**
Glory be to the Father, and to the Son, and to the Holy Ghost.
All **Into thy hands, O Lord, I commend my spirit.**
  Alleluia, alleluia.

Keep me as the apple of an eye.

All **Hide me under the shadow of thy wings.**

Gospel Canticle

The Nunc dimittis (The Song of Simeon) is said or sung

All **Preserve us, O Lord, while waking,**
and guard us while sleeping,
that awake we may watch with Christ,
and asleep we may rest in peace.

1 Lord, now lettest thou thy servant depart in peace :
according to thy word.

2 For mine eyes have seen :
thy salvation;

3 Which thou hast prepared :
before the face of all people;

4 To be a light to lighten the Gentiles :
and to be the glory of thy people Israel. *Luke 2.29-32*

Glory be to the Father, and to the Son :
and to the Holy Ghost;
as it was in the beginning, is now, and ever shall be :
world without end. Amen.

All **Preserve us, O Lord, while waking,**
and guard us while sleeping,
that awake we may watch with Christ,
and asleep we may rest in peace.

Lord, have mercy upon us.

All **Christ, have mercy upon us.**

Lord, have mercy upon us.

All **Our Father, which art in heaven,**
hallowed be thy name;
thy kingdom come;
thy will be done,
in earth as it is in heaven.
Give us this day our daily bread.
And forgive us our trespasses,
as we forgive them that trespass against us.
And lead us not into temptation;
but deliver us from evil. Amen.

Blessed art thou, Lord God of our fathers:

All **to be praised and glorified above all for ever.**

Let us bless the Father, the Son, and the Holy Ghost:

All **let us praise him and magnify him for ever.**

Blessed art thou, O Lord, in the firmament of heaven:

All **to be praised and glorified above all for ever.**

The almighty and most merciful Lord guard us
and give us his blessing.

All **Amen.**

[Wilt thou not turn again and quicken us;

All **that thy people may rejoice in thee?**

O Lord, shew thy mercy upon us;

All **and grant us thy salvation.**

Vouchsafe, O Lord, to keep us this night without sin;

All **O Lord, have mercy upon us, have mercy upon us.**

O Lord, hear our prayer;

All **and let our cry come unto thee.]**

Let us pray.

One or more of the following Collects is said

Visit, we beseech thee, O Lord, this place,
and drive from it all the snares of the enemy;
let thy holy angels dwell herein to preserve us in peace;
and may thy blessing be upon us evermore;
through Jesus Christ our Lord.

All   **Amen.**

Lighten our darkness, we beseech thee, O Lord;
and by thy great mercy defend us
     from all perils and dangers of this night;
for the love of thy only Son, our Saviour, Jesus Christ.

All   **Amen.**

O Lord Jesus Christ, son of the living God,
who at this evening hour didst rest in the sepulchre,
and didst thereby sanctify the grave
to be a bed of hope to thy people:
make us so to abound in sorrow for our sins,
which were the cause of thy passion,
that when our bodies lie in the dust,
our souls may live with thee;
who livest and reignest with the Father and the Holy Ghost,
one God, world without end.

All   **Amen.**

Look down, O Lord, from thy heavenly throne,
illuminate the darkness of this night with thy celestial brightness,
and from the sons of light banish the deeds of darkness;
through Jesus Christ our Lord.

All   **Amen.**

Be present, O merciful God,
and protect us through the silent hours of this night,
so that we who are wearied
by the changes and chances of this fleeting world,
may repose upon thy eternal changelessness;
through Jesus Christ our Lord.

All   **Amen.**

The Conclusion

We will lay us down in peace and take our rest.

All **For it is thou, Lord, only that makest us dwell in safety.**

Abide with us, O Lord,

All **for it is toward evening and the day is far spent.**

As the watchmen look for the morning,

All **so do we look for thee, O Christ.**

[Come with the dawning of the day

All **and make thyself known in the breaking of bread.]**

The Lord be with you

All **and with thy spirit.**

Let us bless the Lord.

All **Thanks be to God.**

The almighty and merciful Lord,
the Father, the Son and the Holy Ghost,
bless us and preserve us.

All **Amen.**

Notes to Night Prayer (Compline)

1 **Psalms**
   If it is desired to use an unchanging pattern of psalmody for Night
   Prayer, the psalms printed in the text are used. However, verses
   from other psalms may be used instead, particularly if Night Prayer
   is said daily – Saturday: as set; Sunday: Psalm 104; Monday: Psalm 86;
   Tuesday: Psalm 143; Wednesday: Psalm 31; Thursday: Psalm 16;
   Friday: Psalm 139.

2 **Thanksgiving**
   Night Prayer may begin with the Prayer of Thanksgiving from
   Evening Prayer (page 40).

3 **Gospel Reading**
   On suitable occasions, particularly Saturday night and before other
   festivals, the Gospel for the following day may be read before the
   Office.

4 **Preparation**
   When the confession is being used, it may be replaced by another
   act of penitence. However, all that precedes 'O God, make speed
   to save us' may be omitted; this is particularly appropriate if Holy
   Communion has been celebrated in the evening.

5 **Alleluia**
   The Alleluias included in the Easter form of the Responsory are for
   use from Easter Day until the Day of Pentecost, not at other times.
   The Alleluia following the opening versicles and responses is always
   used, except in Lent.

6 **Blessing**
   The response in square brackets [ ] is normally used only if Holy
   Communion is to be celebrated the following morning.

7 **Seasons**
   The hymn, the Scripture reading, the refrain to the Gospel Canticle,
   the Collect and the blessing may change seasonally and on Festivals.

Prayers for Various Occasions

A Morning Collect

Almighty and everlasting God,
we thank you that you have brought us safely
to the beginning of this day.
Keep us from falling into sin
or running into danger,
order us in all our doings
and guide us to do always
what is righteous in your sight;
through Jesus Christ our Lord.

All **Amen.**

An Evening Collect

Lighten our darkness,
Lord, we pray,
and in your great mercy
defend us from all perils and dangers of this night,
for the love of your only Son,
our Saviour Jesus Christ.

All **Amen.**

A Prayer for the Sovereign

Almighty God, the fountain of all goodness,
bless our Sovereign Lady, *Queen Elizabeth,*
and all who are in authority under her;
that they may order all things
in wisdom and equity, righteousness and peace,
to the honour of your name,
and the good of your Church and people;
through Jesus Christ our Lord.

All **Amen.**

A Prayer for the Royal Family

Almighty God, the fountain of all goodness,
bless, we pray, *Elizabeth the Queen Mother,*
Philip Duke of Edinburgh, Charles Prince of Wales,
and all the Royal Family.
Endue them with your Holy Spirit;
enrich them with your heavenly grace;
prosper them with all happiness;
and bring them to your everlasting kingdom;
through Jesus Christ our Lord.

All   **Amen.**

A Prayer for Those who Govern

Eternal God,
fount and source of all authority and wisdom,
hear our prayer for those who govern.
Give to *Elizabeth our Queen* grace
as the symbol of loyalty and unity
for all our different peoples;
give to the parliaments in these islands,
and especially to our own Government,
wisdom and skill, imagination and energy;
give to the members of the European institutions
vision, understanding and integrity,
that all may live in peace and happiness, truth and prosperity;
through Jesus Christ our Lord.

All   **Amen.**

A Prayer for Bishops and other Pastors

Almighty and everlasting God,
the only worker of great marvels,
send down upon our bishops and other pastors
and all congregations committed to their care
the spirit of your saving grace;
and that they may truly please you,
pour upon them the continual dew of your blessing.
Grant this, O Lord,
for the honour of our advocate and mediator, Jesus Christ.

All   **Amen.**

A Prayer of Dedication

All **Almighty God,**
we thank you for the gift of your holy word.
May it be a lantern to our feet,
a light to our paths,
and a strength to our lives.
Take us and use us
to love and serve
in the power of the Holy Spirit
and in the name of your Son,
Jesus Christ our Lord.
Amen.

Additional Collects

Where a Collect ends 'through Jesus Christ...', the following longer Trinitarian ending may be added

who is alive and reigns with you,
in the unity of the Holy Spirit,
one God, now and for ever.

This longer ending is to be preferred at Holy Communion.

The Collect for the Fifth Sunday after Trinity (pages 410 and 482) may be used as a Collect for the ministry of all Christian people.

The Collect for the Thirteenth Sunday after Trinity (pages 416 and 488) may be used as a Collect for mission and evangelism.

Further Collects for special occasions are published in the President's edition of Common Worship.

For the Guidance of the Holy Spirit

God, who from of old
taught the hearts of your faithful people
by sending to them the light of your Holy Spirit:
grant us by the same Spirit
to have a right judgement in all things
and evermore to rejoice in his holy comfort;
through the merits of Christ Jesus our Saviour.

For the Guidance of the Holy Spirit
at a Synod or Parochial Church Council meeting

Almighty God,
you have given your Holy Spirit to the Church
to lead us into all truth:
bless with the Spirit's grace and presence
    the members of this *synod/PCC/etc.*;
keep *us/them* steadfast in faith and united in love,
that *we/they* may manifest your glory
and prepare the way of your kingdom;
through Jesus Christ your Son our Lord.

For Those who Work on Land or Sea
(Rogation)

Almighty God,
whose will it is that the earth and the sea
    should bear fruit in due season:
bless the labours of those who work on land and sea,
grant us a good harvest
and the grace always to rejoice in your fatherly care;
through Jesus Christ your Son our Lord.

For Those Engaged in Commerce and Industry
(Rogation)

Almighty God and Father,
you have so ordered our life
    that we are dependent on one another:
prosper those engaged in commerce and industry
and direct their minds and hands
that they may rightly use your gifts in the service of others;
through Jesus Christ your Son our Lord.

For the Unity of the Church (1)

Heavenly Father,
you have called us in the Body of your Son Jesus Christ
to continue his work of reconciliation
and reveal you to the world:
forgive us the sins which tear us apart;
give us the courage to overcome our fears
and to seek that unity which is your gift and your will;
through Jesus Christ your Son our Lord.

For the Unity of the Church (2)

Lord Jesus Christ,
who said to your apostles,
'Peace I leave with you, my peace I give to you':
look not on our sins but on the faith of your Church
and grant it the peace and unity of your kingdom;
where you are alive and reign with the Father
in the unity of the Holy Spirit,
one God, now and for ever.

For the Peace of the World

Almighty God,
from whom all thoughts of truth and peace proceed:
kindle, we pray, in the hearts of all, the true love of peace
and guide with your pure and peaceable wisdom
those who take counsel for the nations of the earth
that in tranquillity your kingdom may go forward,
till the earth is filled with the knowledge of your love;
through Jesus Christ your Son our Lord.

For Social Justice and Responsibility

Eternal God,
in whose perfect realm
no sword is drawn but the sword of righteousness,
and no strength known but the strength of love:
so guide and inspire the work of those who seek your kingdom
that all your people may find their security
in that love which casts out fear
and in the fellowship revealed to us
in Jesus Christ our Saviour.

For Vocations

Almighty God,
you have entrusted to your Church
a share in the ministry of your Son our great high priest:
inspire by your Holy Spirit the hearts of many
to offer themselves for the ministry of your Church,
that strengthened by his power,
they may work for the increase of your kingdom
and set forward the eternal praise of your name;
through Jesus Christ your Son our Lord.

A Text of the Lord's Prayer

This text may be used on suitable occasions

As we look for the coming of the kingdom, so we pray

All   **Our Father in heaven,
hallowed be your name,
your kingdom come,
your will be done,
on earth as in heaven.
Give us today our daily bread.
Forgive us our sins
as we forgive those who sin against us.
Save us from the time of trial
and deliver us from evil.
For the kingdom, the power,
and the glory are yours
now and for ever.
Amen.**

Prayers from *The Book of Common Prayer*

A Prayer for the Queen's Majesty

O Lord our heavenly Father,
high and mighty, King of kings, Lord of lords, the only Ruler of princes,
who dost from thy throne behold all the dwellers upon earth;
most heartily we beseech thee with thy favour
    to behold our most gracious Sovereign Lady, *Queen Elizabeth*;
and so replenish her with the grace of thy Holy Spirit,
that she may alway incline to thy will, and walk in thy way:
endue her plenteously with heavenly gifts;
grant her in health and wealth long to live;
strengthen her that she may vanquish and overcome all her enemies;
and finally, after this life, she may attain everlasting joy and felicity;
through Jesus Christ our Lord.

All **Amen.**

A Collect for the Queen

Almighty and everlasting God,
we are taught by thy holy Word,
    that the hearts of kings are in thy rule and governance,
and that thou dost dispose and turn them
    as it seemeth best to thy godly wisdom:
we humbly beseech thee so to dispose and govern the heart of
    Elizabeth thy Servant, our *Queen* and Governor,
that, in all her thoughts, words, and works,
she may ever seek thy honour and glory,
and study to preserve thy people committed to her charge,
    in wealth, peace, and godliness:
grant this, O merciful Father, for thy dear Son's sake,
    Jesus Christ our Lord.

All **Amen.**

A Prayer for the Royal Family

Almighty God, the fountain of all goodness,
we humbly beseech thee to bless *Elizabeth the Queen Mother*,
Philip Duke of Edinburgh, Charles Prince of Wales,
and all the Royal Family.
Endue them with thy Holy Spirit;
enrich them with thy heavenly grace;
prosper them with all happiness;
and bring them to thine everlasting kingdom;
through Jesus Christ our Lord.

All   **Amen.**

A Prayer for the Clergy and People

Almighty and everlasting God,
who alone workest great marvels,
send down upon our bishops and curates,
and all congregations committed to their charge,
the healthful spirit of thy grace;
and that they may truly please thee,
pour upon them the continual dew of thy blessing.
Grant this, O Lord,
for the honour of our advocate and mediator, Jesus Christ.

All   **Amen.**

A Prayer of St Chrysostom

Almighty God,
who hast given us grace at this time
with one accord to make our common supplications unto thee;
and dost promise
that when two or three are gathered together in thy Name
thou wilt grant their requests:
fulfil now, O Lord, the desires and petitions of thy servants,
as may be most expedient for them;
granting us in this world knowledge of thy truth,
and in the world to come life everlasting.

All   **Amen.**

A General Thanksgiving

Almighty God, Father of all mercies,
we thine unworthy servants
    do give thee most humble and hearty thanks
for all thy goodness and loving-kindness to us and to all men;
* [*particularly to those who desire now to offer up their praises
and thanksgivings for thy late mercies vouchsafed unto them.*]
We bless thee for our creation, preservation,
    and all the blessings of this life;
but above all for thine inestimable love
in the redemption of the world by our Lord Jesus Christ,
for the means of grace, and for the hope of glory.
And we beseech thee, give us that due sense of all thy mercies,
that our hearts may be unfeignedly thankful,
and that we shew forth thy praise, not only with our lips,
    but in our lives;
by giving up ourselves to thy service,
and by walking before thee in holiness and righteousness
    all our days;
through Jesus Christ our Lord,
to whom with thee and the Holy Ghost
be all honour and glory, world without end.

All **Amen.**

  * *This to be said when any that have been prayed for
desire to return praise.*

¶ Endings and Blessings

1

The grace of our Lord Jesus Christ, and the love of God, and the fellowship of the Holy Spirit be with us all evermore.

All **Amen.**   *cf 2 Corinthians 13.13*

2

Now to him who is able to do immeasurably more than all we can ask or conceive, by the power which is at work among us, to him be glory in the Church and in Christ Jesus throughout all ages.

All **Amen.**

3

The Lord be with you

All **and also with you.**

Let us bless the Lord.

All **Thanks be to God.**

4

The Lord bless *you* and watch over *you*,
the Lord make his face shine upon *you*
and be gracious to *you*,
the Lord look kindly on *you*
and give *you* peace;
and the blessing of God almighty,
the Father, the Son, and the Holy Spirit,
be among *you* and remain with *you* always.

All **Amen.**

5

The love of the Lord Jesus
draw *you* to himself,
the power of the Lord Jesus
strengthen *you* in his service,
the joy of the Lord Jesus fill *your* hearts;
and the blessing of God almighty,
the Father, the Son, and the Holy Spirit,
be among *you* and remain with *you* always.

All **Amen.**

The Litany

Sections I and VII must always be used, but a selection of appropriate suffrages may be made from Sections II, III, IV, V and VI.

I

Let us pray.

God the Father,

All **have mercy upon us.**

God the Son,

All **have mercy upon us.**

God the Holy Spirit,

All **have mercy upon us.**

Holy, blessed and glorious Trinity,

All **have mercy upon us.**

II

From all evil and mischief;
from pride, vanity and hypocrisy;
from envy, hatred and malice;
and from all evil intent,

All **good Lord, deliver us.**

From sloth, worldliness and love of money;
from hardness of heart
and contempt for your word and your laws,

All **good Lord, deliver us.**

From sins of body and mind;
from the deceits of the world, the flesh and the devil,

All **good Lord, deliver us.**

From famine and disaster;
from violence, murder and dying unprepared,

All **good Lord, deliver us.**

In all times of sorrow;
in all times of joy;
in the hour of death,
and at the day of judgement,

All **good Lord, deliver us.**

III

By the mystery of your holy incarnation;
by your birth, childhood and obedience;
by your baptism, fasting and temptation,

All **good Lord, deliver us.**

By your ministry in word and work;
by your mighty acts of power;
and by your preaching of the kingdom,

All **good Lord, deliver us.**

By your agony and trial;
by your cross and passion;
and by your precious death and burial,

All **good Lord, deliver us.**

By your mighty resurrection;
by your glorious ascension;
and by your sending of the Holy Spirit,

All **good Lord, deliver us.**

IV

Hear our prayers, O Lord our God.

All **Hear us, good Lord.**

Govern and direct your holy Church;
fill it with love and truth;
and grant it that unity which is your will.

All **Hear us, good Lord.**

Give us boldness to preach the gospel in all the world,
and to make disciples of all the nations.

All **Hear us, good Lord.**

Enlighten *N* our Bishop and all who minister
with knowledge and understanding,
that by their teaching and their lives they may proclaim your word.

All **Hear us, good Lord.**

Give your people grace to hear and receive your word,
and to bring forth the fruit of the Spirit.

All **Hear us, good Lord.**

Bring into the way of truth all who have erred
and are deceived.

All **Hear us, good Lord.**

Strengthen those who stand;
comfort and help the faint-hearted;
raise up the fallen;
and finally beat down Satan under our feet.

All **Hear us, good Lord.**

V

Guide the leaders of the nations
into the ways of peace and justice.

All **Hear us, good Lord.**

Guard and strengthen your servant *Elizabeth our Queen*,
that she may put her trust in you,
and seek your honour and glory.

All **Hear us, good Lord.**

Endue the High Court of Parliament
and all the Ministers of the Crown
with wisdom and understanding.

All **Hear us, good Lord.**

Bless those who administer the law,
that they may uphold justice, honesty and truth.

All **Hear us, good Lord.**

Give us the will to use the resources of the earth to your glory,
and for the good of all creation.

All **Hear us, good Lord.**

Bless and keep all your people.

All **Hear us, good Lord.**

Bring your joy into all families;
strengthen and deliver those in childbirth,
watch over children and guide the young,
bring reconciliation to those in discord
and peace to those in stress.

All **Hear us, good Lord.**

VI

Help and comfort the lonely, the bereaved and the oppressed.

All **Lord, have mercy.**

Keep in safety those who travel, and all who are in danger.

All **Lord, have mercy.**

Heal the sick in body and mind,
and provide for the homeless, the hungry and the destitute.

All **Lord, have mercy.**

Show your pity on prisoners and refugees,
and all who are in trouble.

All **Lord, have mercy.**

Forgive our enemies, persecutors and slanderers,
and turn their hearts.

All **Lord, have mercy.**

Hear us as we remember
 those who have died in the peace of Christ,
both those who have confessed the faith
and those whose faith is known to you alone,
and grant us with them a share in your eternal kingdom.

All **Lord, have mercy.**

VII

Give us true repentance;
forgive us our sins of negligence and ignorance
and our deliberate sins;
and grant us the grace of your Holy Spirit
to amend our lives according to your holy word.

All **Holy God,**
holy and strong,
holy and immortal,
have mercy upon us.

*When the Litany is said instead of the Prayers at Morning or
Evening Prayer, the Collect of the Day, the Lord's Prayer and the
Grace are added here.*

The Litany from
The Book of Common Prayer

O God the Father of heaven:
have mercy upon us miserable sinners.

All   **O God the Father of heaven:
have mercy upon us miserable sinners.**

O God the Son, Redeemer of the world:
have mercy upon us miserable sinners.

All   **O God the Son, Redeemer of the world:
have mercy upon us miserable sinners.**

O God the Holy Ghost, proceeding from the Father and the Son:
have mercy upon us miserable sinners.

All   **O God the Holy Ghost,
      proceeding from the Father and the Son:
have mercy upon us miserable sinners.**

O holy, blessed, and glorious Trinity, three Persons and one God:
have mercy upon us miserable sinners.

All   **O holy, blessed, and glorious Trinity,
      three Persons and one God:
have mercy upon us miserable sinners.**

Remember not, Lord, our offences,
      nor the offences of our forefathers;
neither take thou vengeance of our sins:
spare us, good Lord, spare thy people,
      whom thou hast redeemed with thy most precious blood,
and be not angry with us for ever.

All   **Spare us, good Lord.**

From all evil and mischief;
from sin, from the crafts and assaults of the devil;
from thy wrath, and from everlasting damnation,

All **good Lord, deliver us.**

From all blindness of heart;
from pride, vain-glory, and hypocrisy;
from envy, hatred, and malice, and all uncharitableness,

All **good Lord, deliver us.**

From fornication, and all other deadly sin;
and from all the deceits of the world, the flesh, and the devil,

All **good Lord, deliver us.**

From lightning and tempest;
from plague, pestilence, and famine;
from battle and murder, and from sudden death,

All **good Lord, deliver us.**

From all sedition, privy conspiracy, and rebellion;
from all false doctrine, heresy, and schism;
from hardness of heart,
    and contempt of thy Word and Commandment,

All **good Lord, deliver us.**

By the mystery of thy holy Incarnation;
by thy holy Nativity and Circumcision;
by thy Baptism, Fasting, and Temptation,

All **good Lord, deliver us.**

By thine Agony and bloody Sweat;
by thy Cross and Passion;
by thy precious Death and Burial;
by thy glorious Resurrection and Ascension;
and by the coming of the Holy Ghost,

All **good Lord, deliver us.**

In all time of our tribulation; in all time of our wealth;
in the hour of death, and in the day of judgement,

All **good Lord, deliver us.**

We sinners do beseech thee to hear us, O Lord God;
and that it may please thee to rule and govern
    thy holy Church universal in the right way,

All **we beseech thee to hear us, good Lord.**

That it may please thee to keep and strengthen
    in the true worshipping of thee,
in righteousness and holiness of life,
thy Servant *Elizabeth*, our most gracious *Queen* and Governor,

All **we beseech thee to hear us, good Lord.**

That it may please thee to rule her heart in thy faith, fear, and love,
and that she may evermore have affiance in thee,
and ever seek thy honour and glory,

All **we beseech thee to hear us, good Lord.**

That it may please thee to be her defender and keeper,
giving her the victory over all her enemies,

All **we beseech thee to hear us, good Lord.**

That it may please thee to bless and preserve
    Elizabeth the Queen Mother,
    Philip Duke of Edinburgh, Charles Prince of Wales,
    and all the Royal Family,

All **we beseech thee to hear us, good Lord.**

That it may please thee to illuminate
    all Bishops, Priests, and Deacons,
with true knowledge and understanding of thy Word;
and that both by their preaching and living
    they may set it forth and shew it accordingly,

All **we beseech thee to hear us, good Lord.**

That it may please thee to endue the Lords of the Council,
    and all the Nobility,†
with grace, wisdom, and understanding,

All **we beseech thee to hear us, good Lord.**

That it may please thee to bless and keep the Magistrates,
giving them grace to execute justice, and to maintain truth,

All **we beseech thee to hear us, good Lord.**

That it may please thee to bless and keep all thy people,

All **we beseech thee to hear us, good Lord.**

† or the High Court of Parliament and all the Ministers of the Crown

That it may please thee to give to all nations
    unity, peace, and concord,

All   **we beseech thee to hear us, good Lord.**

That it may please thee to give us an heart to love and dread thee,
and diligently to live after thy commandments,

All   **we beseech thee to hear us, good Lord.**

That it may please thee to give to all thy people increase of grace,
to hear meekly thy Word, and to receive it with pure affection,
and to bring forth the fruits of the Spirit,

All   **we beseech thee to hear us, good Lord.**

That it may please thee to bring into the way of truth
    all such as have erred, and are deceived,

All   **we beseech thee to hear us, good Lord.**

That it may please thee to strengthen such as do stand;
and to comfort and help the weak-hearted;
and to raise up them that fall;
and finally to beat down Satan under our feet,

All   **we beseech thee to hear us, good Lord.**

That it may please thee to succour, help, and comfort
all that are in danger, necessity, and tribulation,

All   **we beseech thee to hear us, good Lord.**

That it may please thee to preserve all that travel
    by land or by water, †
all women labouring of child, all sick persons, and young children;
and to shew thy pity upon all prisoners and captives,

All   **we beseech thee to hear us, good Lord.**

That it may please thee to defend, and provide for,
    the fatherless children, and widows,
and all that are desolate and oppressed,

All   **we beseech thee to hear us, good Lord.**

That it may please thee to have mercy upon all men,

All   **we beseech thee to hear us, good Lord.**

† *or* by land or air or water

That it may please thee to forgive our enemies,
   persecutors, and slanderers,
and to turn their hearts,

All   **we beseech thee to hear us, good Lord.**

That it may please thee to give and preserve to our use
   the kindly fruits of the earth,
so as in due time we may enjoy them,

All   **we beseech thee to hear us, good Lord.**

That it may please thee to give us true repentance;
to forgive us all our sins, negligences, and ignorances;
and to endue us with the grace of thy Holy Spirit,
to amend our lives according to thy holy Word,

All   **we beseech thee to hear us, good Lord.**

Son of God: we beseech thee to hear us.

All   **Son of God: we beseech thee to hear us.**

O Lamb of God: that takest away the sins of the world,

All   **grant us thy peace.**

O Lamb of God: that takest away the sins of the world,

All   **have mercy upon us.**

O Christ, hear us.

All   **O Christ, hear us.**

Lord, have mercy upon us.

All   **Lord, have mercy upon us.**

Christ, have mercy upon us.

All   **Christ, have mercy upon us.**

Lord, have mercy upon us.

All   **Lord, have mercy upon us.**

All **Our Father, which art in heaven,
hallowed be thy name;
thy kingdom come;
thy will be done,
in earth as it is in heaven.
Give us this day our daily bread.
And forgive us our trespasses,
as we forgive them that trespass against us.
And lead us not into temptation;
but deliver us from evil.
Amen.**

O Lord, deal not with us after our sins.

All **Neither reward us after our iniquities.**

Let us pray.

O God, merciful Father,
that despisest not the sighing of a contrite heart,
nor the desire of such as be sorrowful:
mercifully assist our prayers that we make before thee
 in all our troubles and adversities, whensoever they oppress us;
and graciously hear us, that those evils,
which the craft and subtilty of the devil or man worketh against us,
be brought to nought,
and by the providence of thy goodness they may be dispersed;
that we thy servants, being hurt by no persecutions,
may evermore give thanks unto thee in thy holy Church;
through Jesus Christ our Lord.

All **O Lord, arise, help us, and deliver us for thy Name's sake.**

O God, we have heard with our ears,
and our fathers have declared unto us,
the noble works that thou didst in their days,
and in the old time before them.

All **O Lord, arise, help us, and deliver us for thine honour.**

Glory be to the Father, and to the Son
and to the Holy Ghost;

All **as it was in the beginning, is now, and ever shall be
world without end. Amen.**

From our enemies defend us, O Christ.

All **Graciously look upon our afflictions.**

Pitifully behold the sorrows of our hearts.

All **Mercifully forgive the sins of thy people.**

Favourably with mercy hear our prayers.

All **O Son of David, have mercy upon us.**

Both now and ever vouchsafe to hear us, O Christ.

All **Graciously hear us, O Christ;**
graciously hear us, O Lord Christ.

O Lord, let thy mercy be shewed upon us;

All **as we do put our trust in thee.**

Let us pray.

We humbly beseech thee, O Father,
mercifully to look upon our infirmities;
and for the glory of thy Name
turn from us all those evils that we most righteously have deserved;
and grant that in all our troubles
we may put our whole trust and confidence in thy mercy,
and evermore serve thee in holiness and pureness of living,
to thy honour and glory;
through our only Mediator and Advocate,
Jesus Christ our Lord.

All **Amen.**

Almighty God,
who hast given us grace at this time
with one accord to make our common supplications unto thee;
and dost promise
that when two or three are gathered together in thy Name
thou wilt grant their requests:
fulfil now, O Lord, the desires and petitions of thy servants,
as may be most expedient for them;
granting us in this world knowledge of thy truth,
and in the world to come life everlasting.

All **Amen.**

The grace of our Lord Jesus Christ,
and the love of God,
and the fellowship of the Holy Ghost,
be with us all evermore.   *2 Corinthians 13.13*

All **Amen.**

Authorized Forms of Confession and Absolution

The forms of confession in the Order of Holy Communion and Morning and Evening Prayer in The Book of Common Prayer *may be used on any occasion. These or one of the forms in the services in* Common Worship *should normally be used.*

It may sometimes be helpful to vary the form on particular occasions, in which case one of the confessions and absolutions which follow should be used. If possible, an absolution should be chosen which reflects the style, in language and length, of the confession. 'Us' and 'our' are said by those who are not ordained priest: words in italics indicate the points where changes may be necessary.

¶ Confessions

Incarnation, Christmas

Christ the light of the world has come to dispel the darkness of our hearts. In his light let us examine ourselves and confess our sins.

Silence is kept.

Lord of grace and truth,
we confess our unworthiness
to stand in your presence as your children.
We have sinned:

All **forgive and heal us.**

The Virgin Mary accepted your call
to be the mother of Jesus.
Forgive our disobedience to your will.
We have sinned:

All **forgive and heal us.**

Your Son our Saviour
was born in poverty in a manger.
Forgive our greed and rejection of your ways.
We have sinned:

All **forgive and heal us.**

The shepherds left their flocks
to go to Bethlehem.
Forgive our self-interest and lack of vision.
We have sinned:

All **forgive and heal us.**

The wise men followed the star
to find Jesus the King.
Forgive our reluctance to seek you.
We have sinned:

All **forgive and heal us.**

Lent, Penitence

Let us admit to God the sin which always confronts us.

All **Lord God,**
we have sinned against you;
we have done evil in your sight.
We are sorry and repent.
Have mercy on us according to your love.
Wash away our wrongdoing and cleanse us from our sin.
Renew a right spirit within us
and restore us to the joy of your salvation,
through Jesus Christ our Lord.   *cf Psalm 51*
Amen.

Cross, Failure in Discipleship

Lord Jesus Christ,
we confess we have failed you as did your first disciples.
We ask for your mercy and your help.

Our selfishness betrays you:
Lord, forgive us.

All **Christ have mercy.**

We fail to share the pain of your suffering:
Lord, forgive us.

All **Christ have mercy.**

We run away from those who abuse you:
Lord, forgive us.

All **Christ have mercy.**

We are afraid of being known to belong to you:
Lord, forgive us.

All **Christ have mercy.**

Resurrection, Heaven, Glory,
Transfiguration, Death, Funerals

Jesus Christ, risen Master and triumphant Lord,
we come to you in sorrow for our sins,
and confess to you our weakness and unbelief.

We have lived by our own strength,
and not by the power of your resurrection.
In your mercy, forgive us.

All **Lord, hear us and help us.**

We have lived by the light of our own eyes,
as faithless and not believing.
In your mercy, forgive us.

All **Lord, hear us and help us.**

We have lived for this world alone,
and doubted our home in heaven.
In your mercy, forgive us.

All **Lord, hear us and help us.**

Trinity, Mission

All **O King enthroned on high,**
filling the earth with your glory:
holy is your name,
Lord God almighty.
In our sinfulness we cry to you
to take our guilt away,
and to cleanse our lips to speak your word,
through Jesus Christ our Lord.
Amen.

We confess our sin, and the sins of our society,
in the misuse of God's creation.

God our Father, we are sorry
for the times when we have used your gifts carelessly,
and acted ungratefully.
Hear our prayer, and in your mercy:

All **forgive us and help us.**

We enjoy the fruits of the harvest,
but sometimes forget that you have given them to us.
Father, in your mercy:

All **forgive us and help us.**

We belong to a people who are full and satisfied,
but ignore the cry of the hungry.
Father, in your mercy:

All **forgive us and help us.**

We are thoughtless,
and do not care enough for the world you have made.
Father, in your mercy:

All **forgive us and help us.**

We store up goods for ourselves alone,
as if there were no God and no heaven.
Father, in your mercy:

All **forgive us and help us.**

Lord God, our maker and our redeemer,
this is your world and we are your people:
come among us and save us.

We have wilfully misused your gifts of creation;
Lord, be merciful:

All **forgive us our sin.**

We have seen the ill-treatment of others
and have not gone to their aid;
Lord, be merciful:

All **forgive us our sin.**

We have condoned evil and dishonesty
and failed to strive for justice;
Lord, be merciful:

All **forgive us our sin.**

We have heard the good news of Christ,
but have failed to share it with others;
Lord, be merciful:

All **forgive us our sin.**

We have not loved you with all our heart,
nor our neighbours as ourselves;
Lord, be merciful:

All **forgive us our sin.**

Reconciliation

Let us return to the Lord our God and say to him:

All **Father,**
we have sinned against heaven and against you.
We are not worthy to be called your children.
We turn to you again.
Have mercy on us,
bring us back to yourself
as those who once were dead
but now have life through Christ our Lord.   *cf Luke 15*
Amen.

Come, let us return to the Lord and say:

All **Lord our God,**
in our sin we have avoided your call.
Our love for you is like a morning cloud,
like the dew that goes away early.
Have mercy on us;
deliver us from judgement;
bind up our wounds and revive us;
in Jesus Christ our Lord.   *cf Hosea 6*
Amen.

General

God our Father,
we come to you in sorrow for our sins.

For turning away from you,
and ignoring your will for our lives;
Father, forgive us:

All **save us and help us.**

For behaving just as we wish,
without thinking of you;
Father, forgive us:

All **save us and help us.**

For failing you by what we do,
and think and say;
Father, forgive us:

All **save us and help us.**

For letting ourselves be drawn away from you
by temptations in the world about us;
Father, forgive us:

All **save us and help us.**

For living as if we were ashamed
to belong to your Son;
Father, forgive us:

All **save us and help us.**

All **God our Father,**
long-suffering, full of grace and truth,
you create us from nothing and give us life.
You give your faithful people new life in the water of baptism.
You do not turn your face from us,
nor cast us aside.
We confess that we have sinned
against you and our neighbour.
We have wounded your love and marred your image in us.
Restore us for the sake of your Son,
and bring us to heavenly joy,
in Jesus Christ our Lord.
Amen.

All **Almighty and most merciful Father,**
we have wandered and strayed from your ways
like lost sheep.
We have followed too much the devices and desires
of our own hearts.
We have offended against your holy laws.
We have left undone those things
that we ought to have done;
and we have done those things
that we ought not to have done;
and there is no health in us.
But you, O Lord, have mercy upon us sinners.
Spare those who confess their faults.
Restore those who are penitent,
according to your promises declared to mankind
in Christ Jesus our Lord.
And grant, O most merciful Father, for his sake,
that we may live a disciplined, righteous and godly life,
to the glory of your holy name.
Amen.

All **Almighty God,**
Father of our Lord Jesus Christ,
maker of all things, judge of all people,
we acknowledge and confess
the grievous sins and wickedness
which we have so often committed
by thought, word and deed
against your divine majesty,
provoking most justly your anger
and indignation against us.
We earnestly repent,
and are deeply sorry for these our wrongdoings;
the memory of them weighs us down,
the burden of them is too great for us to bear.
Have mercy upon us,
have mercy upon us, most merciful Father,
for your Son our Lord Jesus Christ's sake,
forgive us all that is past;
and grant that from this time onwards
we may always serve and please you
in newness of life,
to the honour and glory of your name,
through Jesus Christ our Lord.
Amen.

Man born of woman has but a short time to live.†
We have our fill of sorrow.
We blossom like a flower and wither away.
We slip away like a shadow and do not stay.

All **Holy God,**
holy and strong,
holy and immortal,
have mercy upon us.

In the midst of life we are in death;
where can we turn for help?
Only to you, Lord,
who are justly angered by our sins.

All **Holy God,**
holy and strong,
holy and immortal,
have mercy upon us.

Shut not your ears to our prayers,
but spare us, O Lord.

All **Holy God,**
holy and strong,
holy and immortal,
have mercy upon us.

You know the secrets of our hearts;
forgive us our sins.

All **Holy God,**
holy and strong,
holy and immortal,
have mercy upon us.

Eternal and merciful judge,
both in life and when we come to die,
let us not fall away from you.

All **Holy God,**
holy and mighty,
holy and merciful Saviour,
do not abandon us to the bitterness of eternal death.

† *or* Those born of women have but a short time to live.

General

All   **Almighty God,**
long-suffering and of great goodness:
I confess to you,
I confess with my whole heart
my neglect and forgetfulness of your commandments,
my wrong doing, thinking, and speaking;
the hurts I have done to others,
and the good I have left undone.
O God, forgive me, for I have sinned against you;
and raise me to newness of life;
through Jesus Christ our Lord.
Amen.

General

All   **My God, for love of you**
I desire to hate and forsake all sins
by which I have ever displeased you;
and I resolve by the help of your grace
to commit them no more;
and to avoid all opportunities of sin.
Help me to do this,
through Jesus Christ our Lord.
Amen.

¶ Kyrie Confessions

Short sentences may be inserted between the petitions of the Kyrie, suitable for particular seasons or themes. The insertion of such sentences may replace any form of confession, provided that the sentences are of a penitential character and are followed by an authorized form of absolution. Some examples follow (see also pages 277–278).

Spirit

You raise the dead to life in the Spirit:
Lord, have mercy.

All **Lord, have mercy.**

You bring pardon and peace to the broken in heart:
Christ, have mercy.

All **Christ, have mercy.**

You make one by your Spirit the torn and divided:
Lord, have mercy.

All **Lord, have mercy.**

Word

May your loving mercy come to me, O Lord,
and your salvation according to your word:
Lord, have mercy.

All **Lord, have mercy.**

Your word is a lantern to my feet and a light to my path:
Christ, have mercy.

All **Christ, have mercy.**

O let your mercy come to me that I may live,
for your law is my delight:
Lord, have mercy.

All **Lord, have mercy.**

God be gracious to us and bless us,
and make your face shine upon us:
Lord, have mercy.

All **Lord, have mercy.**

May your ways be known on the earth,
your saving power among the nations:
Christ, have mercy.

All **Christ, have mercy.**

You, Lord, have made known your salvation,
and reveal your justice in the sight of the nations:
Lord, have mercy.

All **Lord, have mercy.**

City

Lord Jesus, you wept over the sins of your city.
On our city: Lord, have mercy.

All **Lord, have mercy.**

Lord Jesus, you heal the wounds of sin and division,
      jealousy and bitterness.
On us: Christ, have mercy.

All **Christ, have mercy.**

Lord Jesus, you bring pardon and peace to the sinner.
Grant us peace: Lord, have mercy.

All **Lord, have mercy.**

¶ Absolutions

May the God of all healing and forgiveness
draw *us* to himself,
and cleanse *us* from all *our* sins
that *we* may behold the glory of his Son,
the Word made flesh,
Jesus Christ our Lord.

All **Amen.**

May almighty God,
who sent his Son into the world to save sinners,
bring *you* his pardon and peace, now and for ever.

All **Amen.**

May the Father of all mercies
cleanse *us* from *our* sins,
and restore *us* in his image
to the praise and glory of his name,
through Jesus Christ our Lord.

All **Amen.**

May the God of love and power
forgive *you* and free *you* from *your* sins,
heal and strengthen *you* by his Spirit,
and raise *you* to new life in Christ our Lord.

All **Amen.**

May the Father forgive *us*
by the death of his Son
and strengthen *us*
to live in the power of the Spirit
all *our* days.

All **Amen.**

The Lord enrich *you* with his grace,
and nourish *you* with his blessing;
the Lord defend *you* in trouble and keep *you* from all evil;
the Lord accept *your* prayers,
and absolve *you* from *your* offences,
for the sake of Jesus Christ, our Saviour.

All **Amen.**

May God who loved the world so much
that he sent his Son to be our Saviour
forgive *us our* sins
and make *us* holy to serve him in the world,
through Jesus Christ our Lord.

All **Amen.**

May God our Father forgive *us our* sins,
and bring *us* to the fellowship of his table
with his saints for ever.

All **Amen.**

May the God of love
bring *us* back to himself,
forgive *us our* sins,
and assure *us* of his eternal love
in Jesus Christ our Lord.

All **Amen.**

The almighty and merciful Lord
grant *you* pardon and forgiveness of all *your* sins,
time for amendment of life,
and the grace and strength of the Holy Spirit.

All **Amen.**

Almighty God,
who in Jesus Christ has given us
a kingdom that cannot be destroyed,
forgive *us our* sins,
open *our* eyes to God's truth,
strengthen *us* to do God's will
and give *us* the joy of his kingdom,
through Jesus Christ our Lord.

All **Amen.**

May almighty God have mercy on *us*,
forgive *us our* sins,
and bring *us* to everlasting life,
through Jesus Christ our Lord.

All **Amen.**

God, the Father of mercies,
has reconciled the world to himself
through the death and resurrection of his Son, Jesus Christ,
not counting our trespasses against us,
but sending his Holy Spirit
to shed abroad his love among us.
By the ministry of reconciliation
entrusted by Christ to his Church,
receive his pardon and peace
to stand before him in his strength alone,
this day and evermore.

All **Amen.**

Creeds and Authorized Affirmations of Faith

¶ Creeds

At a celebration of Holy Communion, the Apostles' Creed or the Athanasian Creed in an authorized form may be used in place of the Nicene Creed, or an authorized Affirmation of Faith may be used. Suitable words of introduction or conclusion (such as 'Let us declare our faith in God, Father, Son and Holy Spirit') to the Creed or Affirmation of Faith may be used.

The Nicene Creed

The text of the Nicene Creed is printed in the Orders for the Celebration of Holy Communion on pages 173, 213, 234, and 253.

The Nicene Creed may be used responsively as follows

We believe in one God,
the Father, the Almighty,

All **maker of heaven and earth,
of all that is,
seen and unseen.**

We believe in one Lord, Jesus Christ,
the only Son of God,
eternally begotten of the Father,

All **God from God, Light from Light,
true God from true God,**
begotten, not made,
of one Being with the Father.

All **Through him all things were made.**
For us and for our salvation he came down from heaven,
was incarnate from the Holy Spirit and the Virgin Mary,
and was made man.

All **For our sake he was crucified under Pontius Pilate;
he suffered death and was buried.**
On the third day he rose again
in accordance with the Scriptures;

All **he ascended into heaven
and is seated at the right hand of the Father.
He will come again in glory to judge the living and the dead,
and his kingdom will have no end.**

We believe in the Holy Spirit,

All **the Lord, the giver of life,**
who proceeds from the Father and the Son.

All **With the Father and the Son he is worshipped and glorified.**
He has spoken through the prophets.

All **We believe in one holy, catholic and apostolic Church.**
We acknowledge one baptism for the forgiveness of sins.

All **We look for the resurrection of the dead,
and the life of the world to come. Amen.**

An Alternative Text of the Nicene Creed

This text of the Nicene Creed, which omits the phrase 'and the Son'
in the third paragraph, may be used on suitable ecumenical occasions

All **We believe in one God,**
the Father, the Almighty,
maker of heaven and earth,
of all that is,
seen and unseen.

We believe in one Lord, Jesus Christ,
the only Son of God,
eternally begotten of the Father,
God from God, Light from Light,
true God from true God,
begotten, not made,
of one Being with the Father;
through him all things were made.
For us and for our salvation he came down from heaven,
was incarnate of the Holy Spirit and the Virgin Mary
and was made man.
For our sake he was crucified under Pontius Pilate;
he suffered death and was buried.
On the third day he rose again
in accordance with the Scriptures;
he ascended into heaven
and is seated at the right hand of the Father.
He will come again in glory to judge the living and the dead,
and his kingdom will have no end.

We believe in the Holy Spirit,
the Lord, the giver of life,
who proceeds from the Father,
who with the Father and the Son is worshipped and glorified,
who has spoken through the prophets.
We believe in one holy catholic and apostolic Church.
We acknowledge one baptism for the forgiveness of sins.
We look for the resurrection of the dead,
and the life of the world to come.
Amen.

The Apostles' Creed

The origin of the Apostles' Creed is the profession of faith made at baptism. This association may have implications for the occasion when it is used at Holy Communion.

All   **I believe in God, the Father almighty,**
creator of heaven and earth.

I believe in Jesus Christ, his only Son, our Lord,
who was conceived by the Holy Spirit,
born of the Virgin Mary,
suffered under Pontius Pilate,
was crucified, died, and was buried;
he descended to the dead.
On the third day he rose again;
he ascended into heaven,
he is seated at the right hand of the Father,
and he will come to judge the living and the dead.

I believe in the Holy Spirit,
the holy catholic Church,
the communion of saints,
the forgiveness of sins,
the resurrection of the body,
and the life everlasting.
Amen.

(or)

All   **I believe in God the Father almighty,**
maker of heaven and earth:

And in Jesus Christ his only Son our Lord,
who was conceived by the Holy Ghost,
born of the Virgin Mary,
suffered under Pontius Pilate,
was crucified, dead and buried.
He descended into hell;
the third day he rose again from the dead;
he ascended into heaven,
and sitteth on the right hand of God the Father almighty;
from thence he shall come to judge the quick and the dead.

I believe in the Holy Ghost;
the holy catholic Church;
the communion of saints;
the forgiveness of sins;
the resurrection of the body,
and the life everlasting.
Amen.

Do you believe and trust in God the Father?

All **I believe in God, the Father almighty,
creator of heaven and earth.**

Do you believe and trust in his Son Jesus Christ?

All **I believe in Jesus Christ, his only Son, our Lord,
who was conceived by the Holy Spirit,
born of the Virgin Mary,
suffered under Pontius Pilate,
was crucified, died, and was buried;
he descended to the dead.
On the third day he rose again;
he ascended into heaven,
he is seated at the right hand of the Father,
and he will come to judge the living and the dead.**

Do you believe and trust in the Holy Spirit?

All **I believe in the Holy Spirit,
the holy catholic Church,
the communion of saints,
the forgiveness of sins,
the resurrection of the body,
and the life everlasting.
Amen.**

The Athanasian Creed

The authorized form of the Athanasian Creed is that contained in
The Book of Common Prayer.

¶ *Authorized Affirmations of Faith*

In addition to the Nicene Creed, the Apostles' Creed and the Athanasian Creed, the following forms of the Creeds and these Affirmations of Faith are also authorized.

I

Do you believe and trust in God the Father,
source of all being and life,
the one for whom we exist?

All **We believe and trust in him.**

Do you believe and trust in God the Son,
who took our human nature,
died for us and rose again?

All **We believe and trust in him.**

Do you believe and trust in God the Holy Spirit,
who gives life to the people of God
and makes Christ known in the world?

All **We believe and trust in him.**

This is the faith of the Church.

All **This is our faith.**
We believe and trust in one God,
Father, Son and Holy Spirit.
Amen.

2

We proclaim the Church's faith in Jesus Christ.

All **We believe and declare that our Lord Jesus Christ,
the Son of God, is both divine and human.**

God, of the being of the Father,
the only Son from before time began;
human from the being of his mother, born in the world;

All **fully God and fully human;
human in both mind and body.**

As God he is equal to the Father,
as human he is less than the Father.

All **Although he is both divine and human
he is not two beings but one Christ.**

One, not by turning God into flesh,
but by taking humanity into God;

All **truly one, not by mixing humanity with Godhead,
but by being one person.**

For as mind and body form one human being
so the one Christ is both divine and human.

All **The Word became flesh and lived among us;
we have seen his glory,
the glory of the only Son from the Father,
full of grace and truth.**   *from the Athanasian Creed*

3

All   We believe in God the Father,
God almighty, by whose plan
earth and heaven sprang to being,
all created things began.
We believe in Christ the Saviour,
Son of God in human frame,
virgin-born, the child of Mary
upon whom the Spirit came.

Christ, who on the cross forsaken,
like a lamb to slaughter led,
suffered under Pontius Pilate,
he descended to the dead.
We believe in Jesus risen,
heaven's king to rule and reign,
to the Father's side ascended
till as judge he comes again.

We believe in God the Spirit;
in one Church, below, above:
saints of God in one communion,
one in holiness and love.
So by faith, our sins forgiven,
Christ our Saviour, Lord and friend,
we shall rise with him in glory
to the life that knows no end.

(May be sung to any 87 87 or 87 87D tune.)

4

Let us affirm our faith in Jesus Christ the Son of God.

All   **Though he was divine,**
he did not cling to equality with God,
but made himself nothing.
Taking the form of a slave,
he was born in human likeness.
He humbled himself
and was obedient to death,
even the death of the cross.
Therefore God has raised him on high,
and given him the name above every name:
that at the name of Jesus
every knee should bow,
and every voice proclaim that Jesus Christ is Lord,
to the glory of God the Father.   *cf Philippians 2.6-11*
Amen.

5

Let us declare our faith
in the resurrection of our Lord Jesus Christ.

All   **Christ died for our sins**
in accordance with the Scriptures;
he was buried;
he was raised to life on the third day
in accordance with the Scriptures;
afterwards he appeared to his followers,
and to all the apostles:
this we have received,
and this we believe.   *cf 1 Corinthians 15.3-7*
Amen.

6

We say together in faith

All **Holy, holy, holy**
is the Lord God almighty,
who was, and is, and is to come.

We believe in God the Father,
who created all things:

All **for by his will they were created**
and have their being.

We believe in God the Son,
who was slain:

All **for with his blood,**
he purchased us for God,
from every tribe and language,
from every people and nation.

We believe in God the Holy Spirit:

All **the Spirit and the Bride say, 'Come!'**
Even so come, Lord Jesus!   *cf Revelation 4.8, 11; 5.9; 22.17, 20*
Amen.

7

Let us declare our faith in God.

All **We believe in God the Father,**
from whom every family
in heaven and on earth is named.

We believe in God the Son,
who lives in our hearts through faith,
and fills us with his love.

We believe in God the Holy Spirit,
who strengthens us
with power from on high.

We believe in one God;
Father, Son and Holy Spirit.   *cf Ephesians 3*
Amen.

¶ A Form for the Corporate Renewal of Baptismal Vows

when celebrated within a service other than Baptism or Confirmation

Notes

1　This form should be used only when there has been due notice and proper preparation. It is recommended that it is used no more than once or twice in any one year. Suitable opportunities include Easter, Pentecost, the Baptism of Christ in Epiphany, and the inauguration of a new ministry.

2　This form is a corporate affirmation for use within a service. When it is used it replaces the Creed or other Affirmation of Faith.

3　Where it is customary for the assembly to be sprinkled with water from the font or to sign themselves with water from the font, this may take place immediately after the Profession of Faith or during a hymn, canticle or song at the conclusion of this form.

A Corporate Renewal of Baptismal Vows

The president may use words of introduction to this part of the service.

A large candle may be lit. The president may address the congregation as follows

In baptism, God calls us out of darkness into his marvellous light.
To follow Christ means dying to sin and rising to new life with him.
Therefore I ask:

Do you reject the devil and all rebellion against God?

All **I reject them.**

Do you renounce the deceit and corruption of evil?

All **I renounce them.**

Do you repent of the sins that separate us from God and neighbour?

All **I repent of them.**

Do you turn to Christ as Saviour?

All **I turn to Christ.**

Do you submit to Christ as Lord?

All **I submit to Christ.**

Do you come to Christ, the way, the truth and the life?

All **I come to Christ.**

The president may say

May almighty God who has given you the desire to follow Christ
give you the strength to continue in the way.

The Profession of Faith

The president addresses the congregation

Brothers and sisters, I ask you to profess the faith of the Church.

Do you believe and trust in God the Father?

All **I believe in God, the Father almighty,**
creator of heaven and earth.

Do you believe and trust in his Son Jesus Christ?

All   **I believe in Jesus Christ, his only Son, our Lord,**
who was conceived by the Holy Spirit,
born of the Virgin Mary,
suffered under Pontius Pilate,
was crucified, died, and was buried;
he descended to the dead.
On the third day he rose again;
he ascended into heaven,
he is seated at the right hand of the Father,
and he will come to judge the living and the dead.

Do you believe and trust in the Holy Spirit?

All   **I believe in the Holy Spirit,**
the holy catholic Church,
the communion of saints,
the forgiveness of sins,
the resurrection of the body,
and the life everlasting.
Amen.

The president says

Almighty God,
we thank you for our fellowship in the household of faith
with all who have been baptized into your name.
Keep us faithful to our baptism,
and so make us ready for that day
when the whole creation shall be made perfect in your Son,
our Saviour Jesus Christ.

All   **Amen.**

The president may use the Affirmation of Commitment (page 152).

The president concludes the Renewal of Vows saying

May Christ dwell in your hearts through faith,
that you may be rooted and grounded in love
and bring forth the fruit of the Spirit.

All   **Amen.**

¶ *Affirmation of Commitment*

This Affirmation of Commitment may be used after an authorized Creed or Affirmation of Faith

Will you continue in the apostles' teaching and fellowship,
in the breaking of bread, and in the prayers?

All **With the help of God, I will.**

Will you persevere in resisting evil and,
whenever you fall into sin, repent and return to the Lord?

All **With the help of God, I will.**

Will you proclaim by word and example
the good news of God in Christ?

All **With the help of God, I will.**

Will you seek and serve Christ in all people,
loving your neighbour as yourself?

All **With the help of God, I will.**

Will you acknowledge Christ's authority over human society,
by prayer for the world and its leaders,
by defending the weak, and by seeking peace and justice?

All **With the help of God, I will.**

The Order for the Celebration of
Holy Communion
also called
The Eucharist
and
The Lord's Supper

Contents

¶ General Notes

¶ Preparation

Careful devotional preparation before the service is recommended for every communicant. A Form of Preparation for public or private use is provided (page 161).

¶ Ministries

Holy Communion is celebrated by the whole people of God gathered for worship. The ministry of the members of the congregation is expressed through their active participation together in the words and actions of the service, but also by some of them reading the Scripture passages, leading the prayers of intercession, and, if authorized, assisting with the distribution of communion.

In some traditions the ministry of the deacon at Holy Communion has included some of the following elements: the bringing in of the Book of the Gospels, the invitation to confession, the reading of the Gospel, the preaching of the sermon when licensed to do so, a part in the prayers of intercession, the preparation of the table and the gifts, a part in the distribution, the ablutions and the dismissal.

The deacon's liturgical ministry provides an appropriate model for the ministry of an assisting priest, a Reader, or another episcopally authorized minister in a leadership ministry that complements that of the president.

The unity of the liturgy is served by the ministry of the president, who in presiding over the whole service holds word and sacrament together and draws the congregation into a worshipping community.

The president at Holy Communion (who, in accordance with the provisions of Canon B 12 'Of the Ministry of the Holy Communion', must have been episcopally ordained priest) expresses this ministry by saying the opening Greeting, the Absolution, the Collect, the Peace and the Blessing. The president must say the Eucharistic Prayer, break the consecrated bread and receive the sacrament on every occasion. When appropriate, the president may, after greeting the people, delegate the leadership of all or parts of the Gathering and the Liturgy of the Word to a deacon, Reader or other authorized lay person.

In the absence of a priest for the first part of the service, a deacon, Reader or other authorized lay person may lead the entire Gathering and Liturgy of the Word.

When the bishop is present, he normally presides over the whole service.

As provided in Canon B 18 the sermon shall be preached by a duly authorized minister, deaconess, Reader or lay worker or, at the invitation of the minister having the cure of souls and with the permission of the bishop, another person.

¶   **Communicant members of other Churches**

Baptized persons who are communicant members of other Churches which subscribe to the doctrine of the Holy Trinity and are in good standing in their own Church shall be admitted to Communion in accordance with Canon B 15A.

For further Notes, see pages 330–335.

A Form of Preparation

This form may be used in any of three ways.

It may be used by individuals as part of their preparation for Holy Communion.

It may be used corporately on suitable occasions within Holy Communion where it replaces the sections entitled 'Prayer of Preparation' and 'Prayers of Penitence'.

It may be used as a separate service of preparation. When used in this way, there should be added at the beginning a greeting and at the end the Peace and the Lord's Prayer. Hymns, psalms and other suitable liturgical material may also be included.

Come, Holy Ghost *(Veni creator Spiritus)*

All   **Come, Holy Ghost, our souls inspire,**
And lighten with celestial fire;
Thou the anointing Spirit art,
Who dost thy sevenfold gifts impart.

Thy blessed unction from above
Is comfort, life and fire of love;
Enable with perpetual light
The dullness of our blinded sight.

Anoint and cheer our soiled face
With the abundance of thy grace;
Keep far our foes, give peace at home;
Where thou art guide no ill can come.

Teach us to know the Father, Son,
And thee, of Both, to be but One;
That through the ages all along
This may be our endless song:

Praise to thy eternal merit,
Father, Son and Holy Spirit.
Amen.

Exhortation

As we gather at the Lord's table we must recall the promises and
warnings given to us in the Scriptures and so examine ourselves and
repent of our sins. We should give thanks to God for his redemption
of the world through his Son Jesus Christ and, as we remember
Christ's death for us and receive the pledge of his love, resolve
to serve him in holiness and righteousness all the days of our life.

The Commandments

Hear the commandments which God has given to his people,
and examine your hearts.

I am the Lord your God: you shall have no other gods but me.

All **Amen. Lord, have mercy.**

You shall not make for yourself any idol.

All **Amen. Lord, have mercy.**

You shall not dishonour the name of the Lord your God.

All **Amen. Lord, have mercy.**

Remember the Sabbath and keep it holy.

All **Amen. Lord, have mercy.**

Honour your father and your mother.

All **Amen. Lord, have mercy.**

You shall not commit murder.

All **Amen. Lord, have mercy.**

You shall not commit adultery.

All **Amen. Lord, have mercy.**

You shall not steal.

All **Amen. Lord, have mercy.**

You shall not bear false witness against your neighbour.

All **Amen. Lord, have mercy.**

You shall not covet anything which belongs to your neighbour.

All **Amen. Lord, have mercy upon us
and write all these your laws in our hearts.**

*Or one of the forms of the Commandments in the Supplementary Texts
(pages 269–271) may be used.*

Or, in place of the Commandments, one of these texts may be used.

Summary of the Law

Our Lord Jesus Christ said:
The first commandment is this:
'Hear, O Israel, the Lord our God is the only Lord.
You shall love the Lord your God with all your heart,
with all your soul, with all your mind,
and with all your strength.'

The second is this: 'Love your neighbour as yourself.'
There is no other commandment greater than these.
On these two commandments hang all the law and the prophets.

All **Amen. Lord, have mercy**.

(or)

The Comfortable Words

Hear the words of comfort our Saviour Christ says
to all who truly turn to him:

Come to me, all who labour and are heavy laden,
and I will give you rest.   *Matthew 11.28*

God so loved the world that he gave his only-begotten Son,
that whoever believes in him should not perish
but have eternal life.   *John 3.16*

Hear what Saint Paul says:
This saying is true, and worthy of full acceptance,
that Christ Jesus came into the world to save sinners. *1 Timothy 1.15*

Hear what Saint John says:
If anyone sins, we have an advocate with the Father,
Jesus Christ the righteous;
and he is the propitiation for our sins.   *1 John 2.1, 2*

(or)

The Beatitudes

Let us hear our Lord's blessing on those who follow him.

Blessed are the poor in spirit,
for theirs is the kingdom of heaven.

Blessed are those who mourn,
for they shall be comforted.

Blessed are the meek,
for they shall inherit the earth.

Blessed are those who hunger and thirst after righteousness,
for they shall be satisfied.

Blessed are the merciful,
for they shall obtain mercy.

Blessed are the pure in heart,
for they shall see God.

Blessed are the peacemakers,
for they shall be called children of God.

Blessed are those who suffer persecution for righteousness' sake,
for theirs is the kingdom of heaven.

Silence for Reflection

Confession

All **Father eternal, giver of light and grace,**
we have sinned against you and against our neighbour,
in what we have thought,
in what we have said and done,
through ignorance, through weakness,
through our own deliberate fault.
We have wounded your love
and marred your image in us.
We are sorry and ashamed
and repent of all our sins.
For the sake of your Son Jesus Christ,
who died for us,
forgive us all that is past
and lead us out from darkness
to walk as children of light.
Amen.

Or another authorized confession may be used.

Absolution

Almighty God, our heavenly Father,
who in his great mercy
has promised forgiveness of sins
to all those who with heartfelt repentance and true faith
    turn to him:
have mercy on *you*;
pardon and deliver *you* from all *your* sins;
confirm and strengthen *you* in all goodness;
and bring *you* to everlasting life;
through Jesus Christ our Lord.

All **Amen.**

Order One

The people and the priest

¶ greet each other in the Lord's name

¶ confess their sins and are assured of God's forgiveness

¶ keep silence and pray a Collect

¶ proclaim and respond to the word of God

¶ pray for the Church and the world

¶ exchange the Peace

¶ prepare the table

¶ pray the Eucharistic Prayer

¶ break the bread

¶ receive communion

¶ depart with God's blessing

For Notes, see pages 158–159 and 330–334.

Order One

¶ *The Gathering*

At the entry of the ministers a hymn may be sung.

The president may say

In the name of the Father,
and of the Son,
and of the Holy Spirit.

All **Amen.**

The Greeting

The president greets the people

The Lord be with you

All **and also with you.**

(or)

Grace, mercy and peace
from God our Father
and the Lord Jesus Christ
be with you

All **and also with you.**

From Easter Day to Pentecost this acclamation follows

Alleluia. Christ is risen.

All **He is risen indeed. Alleluia.**

Words of welcome or introduction may be said.

Prayer of Preparation

This prayer may be said

All   **Almighty God,**
to whom all hearts are open,
all desires known,
and from whom no secrets are hidden:
cleanse the thoughts of our hearts
by the inspiration of your Holy Spirit,
that we may perfectly love you,
and worthily magnify your holy name;
through Christ our Lord.
Amen.

Prayers of Penitence

The Commandments, the Beatitudes, the Comfortable Words
(pages 269–273) or the following Summary of the Law may be used

Our Lord Jesus Christ said:
The first commandment is this:
'Hear, O Israel, the Lord our God is the only Lord.
You shall love the Lord your God with all your heart,
with all your soul, with all your mind,
and with all your strength.'

The second is this: 'Love your neighbour as yourself.'
There is no other commandment greater than these.
On these two commandments hang all the law and the prophets.

All   **Amen. Lord, have mercy.**

A minister uses a seasonal invitation to confession or these or other
suitable words

God so loved the world
that he gave his only Son Jesus Christ
to save us from our sins,
to be our advocate in heaven,
and to bring us to eternal life.

Let us confess our sins in penitence and faith,
firmly resolved to keep God's commandments
and to live in love and peace with all.

All **Almighty God, our heavenly Father,**
we have sinned against you
and against our neighbour
in thought and word and deed,
through negligence, through weakness,
through our own deliberate fault.
We are truly sorry
and repent of all our sins.
For the sake of your Son Jesus Christ,
who died for us,
forgive us all that is past
and grant that we may serve you in newness of life
to the glory of your name.
Amen.

(or)

All **Most merciful God,**
Father of our Lord Jesus Christ,
we confess that we have sinned
in thought, word and deed.
We have not loved you with our whole heart.
We have not loved our neighbours as ourselves.
In your mercy
forgive what we have been,
help us to amend what we are,
and direct what we shall be;
that we may do justly,
love mercy,
and walk humbly with you, our God.
Amen.

Or, with suitable penitential sentences, the Kyrie eleison may be used

Lord, have mercy.

All **Lord, have mercy.**

Christ, have mercy.

All **Christ, have mercy.**

Lord, have mercy.

All **Lord, have mercy.**

If another confession has already been used, the Kyrie eleison may be used without interpolation here or after the absolution.

The president says

Almighty God,
who forgives all who truly repent,
have mercy upon *you*,
pardon and deliver *you* from all *your* sins,
confirm and strengthen *you* in all goodness,
and keep *you* in life eternal;
through Jesus Christ our Lord.

All **Amen.**

Gloria in Excelsis

The Gloria in excelsis may be used

All **Glory to God in the highest,**
     and peace to his people on earth.

     Lord God, heavenly King,
     almighty God and Father,
     we worship you, we give you thanks,
     we praise you for your glory.

     Lord Jesus Christ, only Son of the Father,
     Lord God, Lamb of God,
     you take away the sin of the world:
     have mercy on us;
     you are seated at the right hand of the Father:
     receive our prayer.

     For you alone are the Holy One,
     you alone are the Lord,
     you alone are the Most High, Jesus Christ,
     with the Holy Spirit,
     in the glory of God the Father.
     Amen.

The Collect

*The president introduces a period of silent prayer with the words
'Let us pray' or a more specific bidding.*

The Collect is said, and all respond

All **Amen.**

¶ *The Liturgy of the Word*

Readings

Either one or two readings from Scripture precede the Gospel reading.

At the end of each the reader may say

This is the word of the Lord.

All **Thanks be to God.**

The psalm or canticle follows the first reading; other hymns and songs may be used between the readings.

Gospel Reading

An acclamation may herald the Gospel reading.

When the Gospel is announced the reader says

Hear the Gospel of our Lord Jesus Christ according to N.

All **Glory to you, O Lord.**

At the end

This is the Gospel of the Lord.

All **Praise to you, O Christ.**

Sermon

The Creed

*On Sundays and Principal Holy Days an authorized translation of
the Nicene Creed is used, or on occasion the Apostles' Creed or
an authorized Affirmation of Faith may be used (see pages 138–148).*

All   **We believe in one God,
the Father, the Almighty,
maker of heaven and earth,
of all that is,
seen and unseen.**

**We believe in one Lord, Jesus Christ,
the only Son of God,
eternally begotten of the Father,
God from God, Light from Light,
true God from true God,
begotten, not made,
of one Being with the Father;
through him all things were made.
For us and for our salvation he came down from heaven,
was incarnate from the Holy Spirit and the Virgin Mary
and was made man.
For our sake he was crucified under Pontius Pilate;
he suffered death and was buried.
On the third day he rose again
in accordance with the Scriptures;
he ascended into heaven
and is seated at the right hand of the Father.
He will come again in glory to judge the living and the dead,
and his kingdom will have no end.**

**We believe in the Holy Spirit,
the Lord, the giver of life,
who proceeds from the Father and the Son,
who with the Father and the Son is worshipped and glorified,
who has spoken through the prophets.
We believe in one holy catholic and apostolic Church.
We acknowledge one baptism for the forgiveness of sins.
We look for the resurrection of the dead,
and the life of the world to come.
Amen.**

Prayers of Intercession

One of the forms on pages 281–289 or other suitable words may be used.

The prayers usually include these concerns and may follow this sequence:

¶   *The Church of Christ*

¶   *Creation, human society, the Sovereign and those in authority*

¶   *The local community*

¶   *Those who suffer*

¶   *The communion of saints*

These responses may be used

Lord, in your mercy
All   **hear our prayer.**

(or)

Lord, hear us.
All   **Lord, graciously hear us.**

And at the end

Merciful Father,
All   **accept these prayers**
for the sake of your Son,
our Saviour Jesus Christ.
Amen.

¶ The Liturgy of the Sacrament

The Peace

The president may introduce the Peace with a suitable sentence, and then says

The peace of the Lord be always with you

All **and also with you.**

These words may be added
Let us offer one another a sign of peace.

All may exchange a sign of peace.

Preparation of the Table
Taking of the Bread and Wine

A hymn may be sung.

The gifts of the people may be gathered and presented.

The table is prepared and bread and wine are placed upon it.

One or more of the prayers at the preparation of the table may be said.

The president takes the bread and wine.

The Eucharistic Prayer

An authorized Eucharistic Prayer is used (pages 184–205).

The president says

The Lord be with you	*(or)*	The Lord is here.
All **and also with you.**		**His Spirit is with us.**

Lift up your hearts.
All **We lift them to the Lord.**

Let us give thanks to the Lord our God.
All **It is right to give thanks and praise.**

The president praises God for his mighty acts and all respond

All **Holy, holy, holy Lord,**
God of power and might,
heaven and earth are full of your glory.
Hosanna in the highest.
[Blessed is he who comes in the name of the Lord.
Hosanna in the highest.]

The president recalls the Last Supper,
and one of these four acclamations may be used

[Great is the mystery of faith:]
All **Christ has died:**
Christ is risen:
Christ will come again.

[Praise to you, Lord Jesus:]
Dying you destroyed
our death,
rising you restored our life:
Lord Jesus, come in glory.

[Christ is the bread of life:]
All **When we eat this bread**
and drink this cup,
we proclaim your death,
Lord Jesus,
until you come in glory.

[Jesus Christ is Lord:]
Lord, by your cross and
resurrection
you have set us free.
You are the Saviour of the
world.

The Prayer continues and leads into the doxology,
to which all respond boldly

All **Amen.**

Prayer A
page 184

This response may be used

All **To you be glory and praise for ever.**

and the Prayer ends

All **Blessing and honour and glory and power
be yours for ever and ever.
Amen.**

Prayer D
page 194

These words are used

This is his/our story.
All **This is our song:
Hosanna in the highest.**

and the Prayer ends

All **Blessing and honour and glory and power
be yours for ever and ever.
Amen.**

Prayer F
page 198

These responses may be used

All **Amen. Lord, we believe.**

All **Amen. Come, Lord Jesus.**

All **Amen. Come, Holy Spirit.**

Prayer G
page 201

Prayer G ends

All **Blessing and honour and glory and power
be yours for ever and ever.
Amen.**

Prayer H
page 204

For Prayer H, see page 204.

The Lord's Prayer

As our Saviour taught us, so we pray

All **Our Father in heaven,**
hallowed be your name,
your kingdom come,
your will be done,
on earth as in heaven.
Give us today our daily bread.
Forgive us our sins
as we forgive those who sin against us.
Lead us not into temptation
but deliver us from evil.
For the kingdom, the power,
and the glory are yours
now and for ever.
Amen.

(or)

Let us pray with confidence as our Saviour has taught us

All **Our Father, who art in heaven,**
hallowed be thy name;
thy kingdom come;
thy will be done;
on earth as it is in heaven.
Give us this day our daily bread.
And forgive us our trespasses,
as we forgive those who trespass against us.
And lead us not into temptation;
but deliver us from evil.
For thine is the kingdom,
the power and the glory,
for ever and ever.
Amen.

Breaking of the Bread

The president breaks the consecrated bread.

We break this bread
to share in the body of Christ.

All **Though we are many, we are one body,
because we all share in one bread.**

(or)

Every time we eat this bread
and drink this cup,

All **we proclaim the Lord's death
until he comes.**

The Agnus Dei may be used as the bread is broken

All **Lamb of God,
you take away the sin of the world,
have mercy on us.**

**Lamb of God,
you take away the sin of the world,
have mercy on us.**

**Lamb of God,
you take away the sin of the world,
grant us peace.**

(or)

All **Jesus, Lamb of God,
have mercy on us.**

**Jesus, bearer of our sins,
have mercy on us.**

**Jesus, redeemer of the world,
grant us peace.**

Giving of Communion

The president says one of these invitations to communion

Draw near with faith.
Receive the body of our Lord Jesus Christ
which he gave for you,
and his blood which he shed for you.
Eat and drink
in remembrance that he died for you,
and feed on him in your hearts
by faith with thanksgiving.

(or)

Jesus is the Lamb of God
who takes away the sin of the world.
Blessed are those who are called to his supper.

All **Lord, I am not worthy to receive you,
but only say the word, and I shall be healed.**

(or)

God's holy gifts
for God's holy people.

All **Jesus Christ is holy,
Jesus Christ is Lord,
to the glory of God the Father.**

or, from Easter Day to Pentecost

Alleluia. Christ our passover is sacrificed for us.

All **Therefore let us keep the feast. Alleluia.**

One of these prayers may be said before the distribution

All   **We do not presume
to come to this your table, merciful Lord,
trusting in our own righteousness,
but in your manifold and great mercies.
We are not worthy
so much as to gather up the crumbs under your table.
But you are the same Lord
whose nature is always to have mercy.
Grant us therefore, gracious Lord,
so to eat the flesh of your dear Son Jesus Christ
and to drink his blood,
that our sinful bodies may be made clean by his body
and our souls washed through his most precious blood,
and that we may evermore dwell in him, and he in us.
Amen.**

(or)

All   **Most merciful Lord,
your love compels us to come in.
Our hands were unclean,
our hearts were unprepared;
we were not fit
even to eat the crumbs from under your table.
But you, Lord, are the God of our salvation,
and share your bread with sinners.
So cleanse and feed us
with the precious body and blood of your Son,
that he may live in us and we in him;
and that we, with the whole company of Christ,
may sit and eat in your kingdom.
Amen.**

The president and people receive communion.

Authorized words of distribution are used and the communicant replies

Amen.

During the distribution hymns and anthems may be sung.

If either or both of the consecrated elements are likely to prove insufficient, the president returns to the holy table and adds more, saying the words on page 296.

Any consecrated bread and wine which is not required for purposes of communion is consumed at the end of the distribution or after the service.

Prayer after Communion

Silence is kept.

The Post Communion or another suitable prayer is said.

All may say one of these prayers

All   **Almighty God,**
we thank you for feeding us
with the body and blood of your Son Jesus Christ.
Through him we offer you our souls and bodies
to be a living sacrifice.
Send us out
in the power of your Spirit
to live and work
to your praise and glory.
Amen.

(or)

All   **Father of all,**
we give you thanks and praise,
that when we were still far off
you met us in your Son and brought us home.
Dying and living, he declared your love,
gave us grace, and opened the gate of glory.
May we who share Christ's body live his risen life;
we who drink his cup bring life to others;
we whom the Spirit lights give light to the world.
Keep us firm in the hope you have set before us,
so we and all your children shall be free,
and the whole earth live to praise your name;
through Christ our Lord.
Amen.

¶ The Dismissal

A hymn may be sung.

The president may use the seasonal blessing, or another suitable blessing

(or)

The peace of God,
which passes all understanding,
keep your hearts and minds
in the knowledge and love of God,
and of his Son Jesus Christ our Lord;
and the blessing of God almighty,
the Father, the Son, and the Holy Spirit,
be among you and remain with you always.

All **Amen.**

A minister says

Go in peace to love and serve the Lord.

All **In the name of Christ. Amen.**

(or)

Go in the peace of Christ.

All **Thanks be to God.**

or, from Easter Day to Pentecost

Go in the peace of Christ. Alleluia, alleluia.

All **Thanks be to God. Alleluia, alleluia.**

The ministers and people depart.

¶ *Eucharistic Prayers for use in Order One*

Proper Prefaces are to be found on pages 294 and 300–329.

Prayer A

*If an extended Preface (pages 294 and 300–329) is used,
it replaces all words between the opening dialogue and the Sanctus.*

The Lord be with you   *(or)*   The Lord is here.
All   **and also with you.**   **His Spirit is with us.**

Lift up your hearts.
All   **We lift them to the Lord.**

Let us give thanks to the Lord our God.
All   **It is right to give thanks and praise.**

It is indeed right,
it is our duty and our joy,
at all times and in all places
to give you thanks and praise,
holy Father, heavenly King,
almighty and eternal God,
through Jesus Christ your Son our Lord.

The following may be omitted if a short Proper Preface is used

For he is your living Word;
through him you have created all things from the beginning,
and formed us in your own image.

[*All*]   **To you be glory and praise for ever.**]

Through him you have freed us from the slavery of sin,
giving him to be born of a woman and to die upon the cross;
you raised him from the dead
and exalted him to your right hand on high.

[*All*]   **To you be glory and praise for ever.**]

Through him you have sent upon us
your holy and life-giving Spirit,
and made us a people for your own possession.

[*All*]   **To you be glory and praise for ever.**]

Therefore with angels and archangels,
and with all the company of heaven,
we proclaim your great and glorious name,
for ever praising you and *saying:*

All **Holy, holy, holy Lord,**
God of power and might,
heaven and earth are full of your glory.
Hosanna in the highest.
[Blessed is he who comes in the name of the Lord.
Hosanna in the highest.]

Accept our praises, heavenly Father,
through your Son our Saviour Jesus Christ,
and as we follow his example and obey his command,
grant that by the power of your Holy Spirit
these gifts of bread and wine
may be to us his body and his blood;

who, in the same night that he was betrayed,
took bread and gave you thanks;
he broke it and gave it to his disciples, saying:
Take, eat; this is my body which is given for you;
do this in remembrance of me.

[*All* **To you be glory and praise for ever.**]

In the same way, after supper
he took the cup and gave you thanks;
he gave it to them, saying:
Drink this, all of you;
this is my blood of the new covenant,
which is shed for you and for many for the forgiveness of sins.
Do this, as often as you drink it,
in remembrance of me.

[*All* **To you be glory and praise for ever.**]

Therefore, heavenly Father,
we remember his offering of himself
made once for all upon the cross;
we proclaim his mighty resurrection and glorious ascension;
we look for the coming of your kingdom,
and with this bread and this cup
we make the memorial of Christ your Son our Lord.

One of these four acclamations is used

[Great is the mystery of faith:]

All **Christ has died:**
Christ is risen:
Christ will come again.

(or)

[Praise to you, Lord Jesus:]

All **Dying you destroyed our death,**
rising you restored our life:
Lord Jesus, come in glory.

(or)

[Christ is the bread of life:]

All **When we eat this bread and drink this cup,**
we proclaim your death, Lord Jesus,
until you come in glory.

(or)

[Jesus Christ is Lord:]

All **Lord, by your cross and resurrection**
you have set us free.
You are the Saviour of the world.

Accept through him, our great high priest,
this our sacrifice of thanks and praise,
and as we eat and drink these holy gifts
in the presence of your divine majesty,
renew us by your Spirit,
inspire us with your love
and unite us in the body of your Son,
Jesus Christ our Lord.

[*All*   **To you be glory and praise for ever.**]

Through him, and with him, and in him,
in the unity of the Holy Spirit,
with all who stand before you in earth and heaven,
we worship you, Father almighty,
in songs of everlasting praise:

All   **Blessing and honour and glory and power
be yours for ever and ever.
Amen.**

The service continues with the Lord's Prayer on page 178.

Prayer B

If an extended Preface (pages 294 and 300–329) is used, it replaces all words between the opening dialogue and the Sanctus.

The Lord be with you   *(or)*   The Lord is here.
All **and also with you.**   **His Spirit is with us.**

Lift up your hearts.
All **We lift them to the Lord.**

Let us give thanks to the Lord our God.
All **It is right to give thanks and praise.**

Father, we give you thanks and praise
through your beloved Son Jesus Christ, your living Word,
through whom you have created all things;
who was sent by you in your great goodness to be our Saviour.

By the power of the Holy Spirit he took flesh;
as your Son, born of the blessed Virgin,
he lived on earth and went about among us;
he opened wide his arms for us on the cross;
he put an end to death by dying for us;
and revealed the resurrection by rising to new life;
so he fulfilled your will and won for you a holy people.

Short Proper Preface, when appropriate

Therefore with angels and archangels,
and with all the company of heaven,
we proclaim your great and glorious name,
for ever praising you and *saying*:

All **Holy, holy, holy Lord,**
God of power and might,
heaven and earth are full of your glory.
Hosanna in the highest.
[Blessed is he who comes in the name of the Lord.
Hosanna in the highest.]

Lord, you are holy indeed, the source of all holiness;
grant that by the power of your Holy Spirit,
and according to your holy will,
these gifts of bread and wine
may be to us the body and blood of our Lord Jesus Christ;

who, in the same night that he was betrayed,
took bread and gave you thanks;
he broke it and gave it to his disciples, saying:
Take, eat; this is my body which is given for you;
do this in remembrance of me.

In the same way, after supper
he took the cup and gave you thanks;
he gave it to them, saying:
Drink this, all of you;
this is my blood of the new covenant,
which is shed for you and for many for the forgiveness of sins.
Do this, as often as you drink it,
in remembrance of me.

One of these four acclamations is used

[Great is the mystery of faith:]

All **Christ has died:**
Christ is risen:
Christ will come again.

(or)

[Praise to you, Lord Jesus:]

All **Dying you destroyed our death,**
rising you restored our life:
Lord Jesus, come in glory.

(or)

[Christ is the bread of life:]

All **When we eat this bread and drink this cup,**
we proclaim your death, Lord Jesus,
until you come in glory.

(or)

[Jesus Christ is Lord:]

All **Lord, by your cross and resurrection**
you have set us free.
You are the Saviour of the world.

And so, Father, calling to mind his death on the cross,
his perfect sacrifice made once for the sins of the whole world;
rejoicing in his mighty resurrection and glorious ascension,
and looking for his coming in glory,
we celebrate this memorial of our redemption.
As we offer you this our sacrifice of praise and thanksgiving,
we bring before you this bread and this cup
and we thank you for counting us worthy
to stand in your presence and serve you.

Send the Holy Spirit on your people
and gather into one in your kingdom
all who share this one bread and one cup,
so that we, in the company of [N and] all the saints,
may praise and glorify you for ever,
through Jesus Christ our Lord;

by whom, and with whom, and in whom,
in the unity of the Holy Spirit,
all honour and glory be yours, almighty Father,
for ever and ever.

All   **Amen.**

The service continues with the Lord's Prayer on page 178.

Prayer C

The Lord be with you   *(or)*   The Lord is here.
All **and also with you.**   **His Spirit is with us.**

Lift up your hearts.
All **We lift them to the Lord.**

Let us give thanks to the Lord our God.
All **It is right to give thanks and praise.**

It is indeed right,
it is our duty and our joy,
at all times and in all places
to give you thanks and praise,
holy Father, heavenly King,
almighty and eternal God,
through Jesus Christ our Lord.

Short Proper Preface, when appropriate

[or, when there is no Proper Preface

For he is our great high priest,
who has loosed us from our sins
and has made us to be a royal priesthood to you,
our God and Father.]

Therefore with angels and archangels,
and with all the company of heaven,
we proclaim your great and glorious name,
for ever praising you and *saying*:

All **Holy, holy, holy Lord,**
God of power and might,
heaven and earth are full of your glory.
Hosanna in the highest.
[Blessed is he who comes in the name of the Lord.
Hosanna in the highest.]

All glory be to you, our heavenly Father,
who, in your tender mercy,
gave your only Son our Saviour Jesus Christ
to suffer death upon the cross for our redemption;
who made there by his one oblation of himself once offered
a full, perfect and sufficient sacrifice, oblation and satisfaction
    for the sins of the whole world;
he instituted, and in his holy gospel commanded us to continue,
a perpetual memory of his precious death until he comes again.

Hear us, merciful Father, we humbly pray,
and grant that, by the power of your Holy Spirit,
we receiving these gifts of your creation, this bread and this wine,
according to your Son our Saviour Jesus Christ's holy institution,
in remembrance of his death and passion,
may be partakers of his most blessed body and blood;

who, in the same night that he was betrayed,
took bread and gave you thanks;
he broke it and gave it to his disciples, saying:
Take, eat; this is my body which is given for you;
do this in remembrance of me.

In the same way, after supper
he took the cup and gave you thanks;
he gave it to them, saying:
Drink this, all of you;
this is my blood of the new covenant,
which is shed for you and for many for the forgiveness of sins.
Do this, as often as you drink it,
in remembrance of me.

One of these four acclamations is used

[Great is the mystery of faith:]

All **Christ has died:**
Christ is risen:
Christ will come again.

[Praise to you, Lord Jesus:]

Dying you destroyed
    our death,
rising you restored our life:
Lord Jesus, come in glory.

[Christ is the bread of life:]

All **When we eat this bread**
    and drink this cup,
we proclaim your death,
    Lord Jesus,
until you come in glory.

[Jesus Christ is Lord:]

Lord, by your cross and
    resurrection
you have set us free.
You are the Saviour of the
    world.

Therefore, Lord and heavenly Father,
in remembrance of the precious death and passion,
the mighty resurrection and glorious ascension
of your dear Son Jesus Christ,
we offer you through him this our sacrifice of praise
    and thanksgiving.

Grant that by his merits and death,
and through faith in his blood,
we and all your Church may receive forgiveness of our sins
and all other benefits of his passion.
Although we are unworthy, through our manifold sins,
to offer you any sacrifice,
yet we pray that you will accept this
the duty and service that we owe.
Do not weigh our merits, but pardon our offences,
and fill us all who share in this holy communion
with your grace and heavenly blessing;

through Jesus Christ our Lord,
by whom, and with whom, and in whom,
in the unity of the Holy Spirit,
all honour and glory be yours, almighty Father,
for ever and ever.

All **Amen.**

The service continues with the Lord's Prayer on page 178.

Prayer D

| | The Lord be with you | *(or)* | The Lord is here. |
All **and also with you.** **His Spirit is with us.**

Lift up your hearts.
All **We lift them to the Lord.**

Let us give thanks to the Lord our God.
All **It is right to give thanks and praise.**

Almighty God, good Father to us all,
your face is turned towards your world.
In love you gave us Jesus your Son
to rescue us from sin and death.
Your Word goes out to call us home
to the city where angels sing your praise.
We join with them in heaven's song:

All **Holy, holy, holy Lord,**
God of power and might,
heaven and earth are full of your glory.
Hosanna in the highest.
[Blessed is he who comes in the name of the Lord.
Hosanna in the highest.]

Father of all, we give you thanks
for every gift that comes from heaven.

To the darkness Jesus came as your light.
With signs of faith and words of hope
he touched untouchables with love and washed the guilty clean.

This is his story.
All **This is our song:**
Hosanna in the highest.

The crowds came out to see your Son,
yet at the end they turned on him.
On the night he was betrayed
he came to table with his friends
to celebrate the freedom of your people.

This is his story.
All **This is our song:**
Hosanna in the highest.

Jesus blessed you, Father, for the food;
he took bread, gave thanks, broke it and said:
This is my body, given for you all.
Jesus then gave thanks for the wine;
he took the cup, gave it and said:
This is my blood, shed for you all
    for the forgiveness of sins.
Do this in remembrance of me.

This is our story.

All **This is our song:**
Hosanna in the highest.

Therefore, Father, with this bread and this cup
we celebrate the cross
on which he died to set us free.
Defying death he rose again
and is alive with you to plead for us and all the world.

This is our story.

All **This is our song:**
Hosanna in the highest.

Send your Spirit on us now
that by these gifts we may feed on Christ
    with opened eyes and hearts on fire.

May we and all who share this food
offer ourselves to live for you
and be welcomed at your feast in heaven
    where all creation worships you,
Father, Son and Holy Spirit:

All **Blessing and honour and glory and power**
be yours for ever and ever.
Amen.

The service continues with the Lord's Prayer on page 178.

Prayer E

The Lord be with you   *(or)*   The Lord is here.
All   **and also with you.**   **His Spirit is with us.**

Lift up your hearts.
All   **We lift them to the Lord.**

Let us give thanks to the Lord our God.
All   **It is right to give thanks and praise.**

*Here follows an extended Preface (pages 294 and 300–329)
or the following*

Father, you made the world and love your creation.
You gave your Son Jesus Christ to be our Saviour.
His dying and rising have set us free from sin and death.
And so we gladly thank you,
with saints and angels praising you, and *saying*:

All   **Holy, holy, holy Lord,**
God of power and might,
heaven and earth are full of your glory.
Hosanna in the highest.
[Blessed is he who comes in the name of the Lord.
Hosanna in the highest.]

We praise and bless you, loving Father,
through Jesus Christ, our Lord;
and as we obey his command,
send your Holy Spirit,
that broken bread and wine outpoured
may be for us the body and blood of your dear Son.

On the night before he died he had supper with his friends
and, taking bread, he praised you.
He broke the bread, gave it to them and said:
Take, eat; this is my body which is given for you;
do this in remembrance of me.

When supper was ended he took the cup of wine.
Again he praised you, gave it to them and said:
Drink this, all of you;
this is my blood of the new covenant,
which is shed for you and for many for the forgiveness of sins.
Do this, as often as you drink it, in remembrance of me.

So, Father, we remember all that Jesus did,
in him we plead with confidence his sacrifice
    made once for all upon the cross.

Bringing before you the bread of life and cup of salvation,
we proclaim his death and resurrection
until he comes in glory.

One of these four acclamations is used

[Great is the mystery of faith:]

All **Christ has died:**
Christ is risen:
Christ will come again.

[Praise to you, Lord Jesus:]

Dying you destroyed
    our death,
rising you restored our life:
Lord Jesus, come in glory.

[Christ is the bread of life:]

All **When we eat this bread**
    and drink this cup,
we proclaim your death,
    Lord Jesus,
until you come in glory.

[Jesus Christ is Lord:]

Lord, by your cross and
    resurrection
you have set us free.
You are the Saviour of the
    world.

Lord of all life,
help us to work together for that day
when your kingdom comes
and justice and mercy will be seen in all the earth.

Look with favour on your people,
gather us in your loving arms
and bring us with [N and] all the saints
to feast at your table in heaven.

Through Christ, and with Christ, and in Christ,
in the unity of the Holy Spirit,
all honour and glory are yours, O loving Father,
for ever and ever.

All **Amen.**

The service continues with the Lord's Prayer on page 178.

Prayer F

The Lord be with you   *(or)*   The Lord is here.
All and also with you.   **His Spirit is with us.**

Lift up your hearts.
All We lift them to the Lord.

Let us give thanks to the Lord our God.
All It is right to give thanks and praise.

You are worthy of our thanks and praise,
Lord God of truth,
for by the breath of your mouth
you have spoken your word,
and all things have come into being.

You fashioned us in your image
and placed us in the garden of your delight.
Though we chose the path of rebellion
you would not abandon your own.

Again and again you drew us into your covenant of grace.
You gave your people the law and taught us by your prophets
to look for your reign of justice, mercy and peace.

As we watch for the signs of your kingdom on earth,
we echo the song of the angels in heaven,
evermore praising you and *saying*:

**All Holy, holy, holy Lord,
God of power and might,
heaven and earth are full of your glory.
Hosanna in the highest.
[Blessed is he who comes in the name of the Lord.
Hosanna in the highest.]**

Lord God, you are the most holy one,
enthroned in splendour and light,
yet in the coming of your Son Jesus Christ
you reveal the power of your love
made perfect in our human weakness.

[All Amen. Lord, we believe.]

Embracing our humanity,
Jesus showed us the way of salvation;
loving us to the end,
he gave himself to death for us;
dying for his own,
he set us free from the bonds of sin,
that we might rise and reign with him in glory.

[*All*   **Amen. Lord, we believe.**]

On the night he gave up himself for us all
he took bread and gave you thanks;
he broke it and gave it to his disciples, saying:
Take, eat; this is my body which is given for you;
do this in remembrance of me.

[*All*   **Amen. Lord, we believe.**]

In the same way, after supper
he took the cup and gave you thanks;
he gave it to them, saying:
Drink this, all of you; this is my blood of the new covenant
which is shed for you and for many for the forgiveness of sins.
Do this, as often as you drink it, in remembrance of me.

[*All*   **Amen. Lord, we believe.**]

Therefore we proclaim the death that he suffered on the cross,
we celebrate his resurrection, his bursting from the tomb,
we rejoice that he reigns at your right hand on high
and we long for his coming in glory.

[*All*   **Amen. Come, Lord Jesus.**]

As we recall the one, perfect sacrifice of our redemption,
Father, by your Holy Spirit let these gifts of your creation
be to us the body and blood of our Lord Jesus Christ;
form us into the likeness of Christ
and make us a perfect offering in your sight.

[*All*   **Amen. Come, Holy Spirit.**]

Look with favour on your people
and in your mercy hear the cry of our hearts.
Bless the earth,
heal the sick,
let the oppressed go free
and fill your Church with power from on high.

[*All* **Amen. Come, Holy Spirit.**]

Gather your people from the ends of the earth
to feast with [*N and*] all your saints
at the table in your kingdom,
where the new creation is brought to perfection
in Jesus Christ our Lord;

by whom, and with whom, and in whom,
in the unity of the Holy Spirit,
all honour and glory be yours, almighty Father,
for ever and ever.

All **Amen.**

The service continues with the Lord's Prayer on page 178.

Prayer G

The Lord be with you   *(or)*   The Lord is here.

All **and also with you.**   **His Spirit is with us.**

Lift up your hearts.

All **We lift them to the Lord.**

Let us give thanks to the Lord our God.

All **It is right to give thanks and praise.**

Blessed are you, Lord God,
our light and our salvation;
to you be glory and praise for ever.

From the beginning you have created all things
and all your works echo the silent music of your praise.
In the fullness of time you made us in your image,
the crown of all creation.

You give us breath and speech, that with angels and archangels
and all the powers of heaven
we may find a voice to sing your praise:

All **Holy, holy, holy Lord,**
God of power and might,
heaven and earth are full of your glory.
Hosanna in the highest.
[Blessed is he who comes in the name of the Lord.
Hosanna in the highest.]

How wonderful the work of your hands, O Lord.
As a mother tenderly gathers her children,
you embraced a people as your own.
When they turned away and rebelled
your love remained steadfast.

From them you raised up Jesus our Saviour, born of Mary,
to be the living bread,
in whom all our hungers are satisfied.

He offered his life for sinners,
and with a love stronger than death
he opened wide his arms on the cross.

On the night before he died,
he came to supper with his friends
and, taking bread, he gave you thanks.
He broke it and gave it to them, saying:
Take, eat; this is my body which is given for you;
do this in remembrance of me.

At the end of supper, taking the cup of wine,
he gave you thanks, and said:
Drink this, all of you; this is my blood of the new covenant,
which is shed for you and for many for the forgiveness of sins.
Do this, as often as you drink it, in remembrance of me.

One of these four acclamations is used

[Great is the mystery of faith:]

All **Christ has died:**
Christ is risen:
Christ will come again.

(or)

[Praise to you, Lord Jesus:]

All **Dying you destroyed our death,**
rising you restored our life:
Lord Jesus, come in glory.

(or)

[Christ is the bread of life:]

All **When we eat this bread and drink this cup**
we proclaim your death, Lord Jesus,
until you come in glory.

(or)

[Jesus Christ is Lord:]

All **Lord, by your cross and resurrection**
you have set us free.
You are the Saviour of the world.

Father, we plead with confidence
his sacrifice made once for all upon the cross;
we remember his dying and rising in glory,
and we rejoice that he intercedes for us at your right hand.

Pour out your Holy Spirit as we bring before you
these gifts of your creation;
may they be for us the body and blood of your dear Son.

As we eat and drink these holy things in your presence,
form us in the likeness of Christ,
and build us into a living temple to your glory.

[Remember, Lord, your Church in every land.
Reveal her unity, guard her faith,
and preserve her in peace ...]

Bring us at the last with [N and] all the saints
to the vision of that eternal splendour
for which you have created us;
through Jesus Christ, our Lord,
by whom, with whom, and in whom,
with all who stand before you in earth and heaven,
we worship you, Father almighty, in songs of everlasting praise:

All **Blessing and honour and glory and power
be yours for ever and ever.
Amen.**

The service continues with the Lord's Prayer on page 178.

Prayer H

The Lord be with you   *(or)*   The Lord is here.

All   **and also with you.**   **His Spirit is with us.**

Lift up your hearts.

All   **We lift them to the Lord.**

Let us give thanks to the Lord our God.

All   **It is right to give thanks and praise.**

It is right to praise you, Father, Lord of all creation;
in your love you made us for yourself.

When we turned away
you did not reject us,
but came to meet us in your Son.

All   **You embraced us as your children**
      and welcomed us to sit and eat with you.

In Christ you shared our life
that we might live in him and he in us.

All   **He opened his arms of love upon the cross**
      and made for all the perfect sacrifice for sin.

On the night he was betrayed,
at supper with his friends
he took bread, and gave you thanks;
he broke it and gave it to them, saying:
Take, eat; this is my body which is given for you;
do this in remembrance of me.

All   **Father, we do this in remembrance of him:**
      his body is the bread of life.

At the end of supper, taking the cup of wine,
he gave you thanks, and said:
Drink this, all of you; this is my blood of the new covenant,
which is shed for you for the forgiveness of sins;
do this in remembrance of me.

All   **Father, we do this in remembrance of him:**
      his blood is shed for all.

As we proclaim his death and celebrate his rising in glory,
send your Holy Spirit that this bread and this wine
may be to us the body and blood of your dear Son.

All **As we eat and drink these holy gifts
make us one in Christ, our risen Lord.**

With your whole Church throughout the world
we offer you this sacrifice of praise
and lift our voice to join the eternal song of heaven:

All **Holy, holy, holy Lord,
God of power and might,
Heaven and earth are full of your glory.
Hosanna in the highest.**

The service continues with the Lord's Prayer on page 178.

Order One *in Traditional Language*

¶ *The Gathering*

At the entry of the ministers a hymn may be sung.

The president may say

In the name of the Father,
and of the Son,
and of the Holy Spirit.

All **Amen.**

The Greeting

The president greets the people

The Lord be with you
All **and with thy spirit.**

(or)

Grace, mercy and peace
from God our Father
and the Lord Jesus Christ
be with you
All **and with thy spirit.**

From Easter Day to Pentecost this acclamation follows

Alleluia. Christ is risen.
All **He is risen indeed. Alleluia.**

Words of welcome or introduction may be said.

Prayer of Preparation

This prayer may be said

All   **Almighty God,**
unto whom all hearts be open,
all desires known,
and from whom no secrets are hid:
cleanse the thoughts of our hearts
by the inspiration of thy Holy Spirit,
that we may perfectly love thee,
and worthily magnify thy holy name;
through Christ our Lord.
Amen.

Prayers of Penitence

The Commandments, the Beatitudes, the Comfortable Words
(pages 269–273) or the following Summary of the Law may be used

Our Lord Jesus Christ said:
Hear, O Israel, the Lord our God is one Lord;
and thou shalt love the Lord thy God with all thy heart,
and with all thy soul, and with all thy mind,
and with all thy strength.
This is the first commandment.

And the second is like, namely this:
Thou shalt love thy neighbour as thyself.
There is none other commandment greater than these.
On these two commandments hang all the law and the prophets.

All   **Lord, have mercy upon us, and write all these thy laws**
in our hearts, we beseech thee.

A minister uses a seasonal invitation to confession or these or other suitable words

God so loved the world
that he gave his only Son Jesus Christ
to save us from our sins,
to be our advocate in heaven,
and to bring us to eternal life.

Let us confess our sins in penitence and faith,
firmly resolved to keep God's commandments
and to live in love and peace with all.

All **Almighty God, our heavenly Father,
we have sinned against thee
and against our neighbour,
in thought and word and deed,
through negligence, through weakness,
through our own deliberate fault.
We are heartily sorry
and repent of all our sins.
For the sake of thy Son Jesus Christ,
who died for us,
forgive us all that is past,
and grant that we may serve thee in newness of life
to the glory of thy name.
Amen.**

(or)

All **Most merciful God,
Father of our Lord Jesus Christ,
we confess that we have sinned
in thought, word and deed.
We have not loved thee with our whole heart.
We have not loved our neighbours as ourselves.
In thy mercy
forgive what we have been,
help us to amend what we are,
and direct what we shall be;
that we may do justly,
love mercy,
and walk humbly with thee, our God.
Amen.**

Or, with suitable penitential sentences, the Kyrie eleison may be used

Lord, have mercy.

All **Lord, have mercy.**

Christ, have mercy.

All **Christ, have mercy.**

Lord, have mercy.

All **Lord, have mercy.**

If another confession has already been used, the Kyrie eleison may be used without interpolation here or after the absolution.

The president says

Almighty God,
who forgives all who truly repent,
have mercy upon *you*,
pardon and deliver *you* from all *your* sins,
confirm and strengthen *you* in all goodness,
and keep *you* in life eternal;
through Jesus Christ our Lord.

All **Amen.**

Gloria in Excelsis

The Gloria in excelsis may be used

All **Glory be to God on high,**
and in earth peace, good will towards men.

We praise thee, we bless thee,
we worship thee, we glorify thee,
we give thanks to thee for thy great glory,
O Lord God, heavenly King,
God the Father almighty.

O Lord, the only-begotten Son, Jesus Christ:
O Lord God, Lamb of God, Son of the Father,
that takest away the sins of the world,
have mercy upon us.
Thou that takest away the sins of the world,
receive our prayer.
Thou that sittest at the right hand of God the Father,
have mercy upon us.

For thou only art holy;
thou only art the Lord;
thou only, O Christ,
with the Holy Ghost,
art the Most High,
in the glory of God the Father.
Amen.

The Collect

The president introduces a period of silent prayer with the words
'Let us pray' or a more specific bidding.

The Collect is said, and all respond

All **Amen.**

¶ *The Liturgy of the Word*

Readings

Either one or two readings from Scripture precede the Gospel reading.

At the end of each the reader may say

This is the word of the Lord.

All **Thanks be to God.**

The psalm or canticle follows the first reading; other hymns and songs may be used between the readings.

Gospel Reading

An acclamation may herald the Gospel reading.

When the Gospel is announced, the reader says

Hear the Gospel of our Lord Jesus Christ according to N.

All **Glory be to thee, O Lord.**

At the end

This is the Gospel of the Lord.

All **Praise be to thee, O Christ.**

Sermon

The Creed

On Sundays and Principal Holy Days an authorized translation
of the Nicene Creed is used, or on occasion the Apostles' Creed
or an authorized Affirmation of Faith may be used (see pages 138–148).

All I believe in one God the Father almighty,
maker of heaven and earth,
and of all things
visible and invisible:

And in one Lord Jesus Christ,
the only-begotten Son of God,
begotten of his Father before all worlds,
God of God, Light of Light,
very God of very God,
begotten, not made,
being of one substance with the Father,
by whom all things were made;
who for us men and for our salvation
came down from heaven,
and was incarnate by the Holy Ghost of the Virgin Mary,
and was made man,
and was crucified also for us under Pontius Pilate.
He suffered and was buried,
and the third day he rose again
according to the Scriptures,
and ascended into heaven,
and sitteth on the right hand of the Father.
And he shall come again with glory
to judge both the quick and the dead:
whose kingdom shall have no end.

And I believe in the Holy Ghost,
the Lord, the giver of life,
who proceedeth from the Father and the Son,
who with the Father and the Son together
is worshipped and glorified,
who spake by the prophets.
And I believe one holy catholic and apostolic Church.
I acknowledge one baptism for the remission of sins.
And I look for the resurrection of the dead,
and the life of the world to come.

Prayers of Intercession

*One of the forms on pages 281–289 or other suitable words may
be used.*

*The prayers usually include these concerns and may follow this
sequence:*

¶   *The Church of Christ*

¶   *Creation, human society, the Sovereign and those in authority*

¶   *The local community*

¶   *Those who suffer*

¶   *The communion of saints*

These responses may be used

Lord, in thy mercy
All   **hear our prayer.**

(or)

Lord, hear us.
All   **Lord, graciously hear us.**

And at the end

Merciful Father,
All   **accept these prayers
for the sake of thy Son,
our Saviour Jesus Christ.
Amen.**

¶ *The Liturgy of the Sacrament*

The Peace

The president may introduce the Peace with a suitable sentence, and then says

The peace of the Lord be always with you

All   **and with thy spirit.**

These words may be added
Let us offer one another a sign of peace.

All may exchange a sign of peace.

Preparation of the Table
Taking of the Bread and Wine

A hymn may be sung.

The gifts of the people may be gathered and presented.

The table is prepared and bread and wine are placed upon it.

One or more of the prayers at the preparation of the table may be said.

The president takes the bread and wine.

The Eucharistic Prayer

One of the following Eucharistic Prayers is used:
Prayer A below, or Prayer C on page 219.

Prayer A

The Lord be with you   *(or)*   The Lord is here.
All **and with thy spirit.**   **His Spirit is with us.**

Lift up your hearts.
All **We lift them up unto the Lord.**

Let us give thanks unto the Lord our God.
All **It is meet and right so to do.**

It is very meet, right and our bounden duty,
that we should at all times and in all places give thanks unto thee,
O Lord, holy Father,
almighty, everlasting God,
through Jesus Christ thine only Son our Lord.

The following may be omitted if a short Proper Preface is used

For he is thy living Word;
through him thou hast created all things from the beginning,
and fashioned us in thine own image.

Through him thou didst redeem us from the slavery of sin,
giving him to be born of a woman,
to die upon the cross,
and to rise again for us.

Through him thou hast made us a people for thine own possession,
exalting him to thy right hand on high,
and sending forth through him thy holy and life-giving Spirit.

Short Proper Preface, when appropriate

Therefore with angels and archangels,
and with all the company of heaven,
we laud and magnify thy glorious name,
evermore praising thee and *saying*:

All **Holy, holy, holy, Lord God of hosts,
heaven and earth are full of thy glory.
Glory be to thee, O Lord most high.
[Blessed is he that cometh in the name of the Lord.
Hosanna in the highest.]**

Accept our praises, heavenly Father,
through thy Son our Saviour Jesus Christ,
and as we follow his example and obey his command,
grant that by the power of thy Holy Spirit
these gifts of bread and wine
may be unto us his body and his blood;

who, in the same night that he was betrayed, took bread;
and when he had given thanks to thee,
he broke it and gave it to his disciples, saying:
Take, eat; this is my body which is given for you;
do this in remembrance of me.

Likewise after supper he took the cup;
and when he had given thanks to thee, he gave it to them, saying:
Drink ye all of this;
for this is my blood of the new covenant,
which is shed for you and for many for the forgiveness of sins.
Do this, as oft as ye shall drink it,
in remembrance of me.

Wherefore, O Lord and heavenly Father,
we remember his offering of himself
made once for all upon the cross;
we proclaim his mighty resurrection and glorious ascension;
we look for the coming of his kingdom
and with this bread and this cup
we make the memorial of Christ thy Son our Lord.

One of the following may be used

[Great is the mystery of faith:]

All **Christ has died:**
Christ is risen:
Christ will come again.

(or)

[Jesus Christ is Lord:]

All **O Saviour of the world,**
who by thy cross and precious blood hast redeemed us,
save us, and help us, we humbly beseech thee, O Lord.

Accept through him, our great high priest,
this our sacrifice of thanks and praise,
and as we eat and drink these holy gifts
in the presence of thy divine majesty,
renew us by thy Holy Spirit,
inspire us with thy love,
and unite us in the body of thy Son,
Jesus Christ our Lord,

by whom, and with whom, and in whom,
in the unity of the Holy Spirit,
all honour and glory be unto thee,
O Father almighty,
world without end.

All **Amen.**

The service continues with the Lord's Prayer on page 222.

Prayer C

The Lord be with you   *(or)*   The Lord is here.
All **and with thy spirit.**   **His Spirit is with us.**

Lift up your hearts.
All **We lift them up unto the Lord.**

Let us give thanks unto the Lord our God.
All **It is meet and right so to do.**

It is very meet, right and our bounden duty,
that we should at all times and in all places give thanks unto thee,
O Lord, holy Father,
almighty, everlasting God,
through Jesus Christ thine only Son our Lord.

Short Proper Preface, when appropriate

[or, when there is no Proper Preface

For he is the great high priest,
who has loosed us from our sins
and has made us to be a royal priesthood unto thee,
our God and Father.]

Therefore with angels and archangels,
and with all the company of heaven,
we laud and magnify thy glorious name,
evermore praising thee and *saying*:

All **Holy, holy, holy, Lord God of hosts,**
heaven and earth are full of thy glory.
Glory be to thee, O Lord most high.
[Blessed is he that cometh in the name of the Lord.
Hosanna in the highest.]

All glory be to thee,
almighty God, our heavenly Father,
who, of thy tender mercy,
didst give thine only Son Jesus Christ
to suffer death upon the cross for our redemption;
who made there,
by his one oblation of himself once offered,
a full, perfect and sufficient sacrifice, oblation and satisfaction
     for the sins of the whole world;
and did institute,
and in his holy gospel command us to continue,
a perpetual memory of that his precious death,
until his coming again.

Hear us, O merciful Father, we most humbly beseech thee,
and grant that, by the power of thy Holy Spirit,
we receiving these thy creatures of bread and wine,
according to thy Son our Saviour Jesus Christ's holy institution,
in remembrance of his death and passion,
may be partakers of his most blessed body and blood;

who, in the same night that he was betrayed, took bread;
and when he had given thanks to thee,
he broke it and gave it to his disciples, saying:
Take, eat; this is my body which is given for you;
do this in remembrance of me.

Likewise after supper he took the cup;
and when he had given thanks to thee, he gave it to them, saying:
Drink ye all of this;
for this is my blood of the new covenant,
which is shed for you and for many for the forgiveness of sins.
Do this, as oft as ye shall drink it,
in remembrance of me.

One of the following may be used

[Great is the mystery of faith:]

All **Christ has died:**
Christ is risen:
Christ will come again.

(or)

[Jesus Christ is Lord:]

All **O Saviour of the world,**
who by thy cross and precious blood hast redeemed us,
save us, and help us, we humbly beseech thee, O Lord.

Wherefore, O Lord and heavenly Father,
we thy humble servants,
having in remembrance
the precious death and passion of thy dear Son,
his mighty resurrection and glorious ascension,
entirely desire thy fatherly goodness
mercifully to accept this our sacrifice of praise
    and thanksgiving;
most humbly beseeching thee to grant that
by the merits and death of thy Son Jesus Christ,
and through faith in his blood,
we and all thy whole Church may obtain remission
    of our sins,
and all other benefits of his passion.
And although we be unworthy, through our manifold sins,
to offer unto thee any sacrifice,
yet we beseech thee
to accept this our bounden duty and service,
not weighing our merits, but pardoning our offences;
and to grant that all we, who are partakers of this holy communion,
may be fulfilled with thy grace and heavenly benediction;

through Jesus Christ our Lord,
by whom, and with whom, and in whom,
in the unity of the Holy Spirit,
all honour and glory be unto thee,
O Father almighty,
world without end.

All **Amen.**

The service continues with the Lord's Prayer on page 222.

The Lord's Prayer

Let us pray with confidence as our Saviour has taught us

All   **Our Father, who art in heaven,**
hallowed be thy name;
thy kingdom come;
thy will be done;
on earth as it is in heaven.
Give us this day our daily bread.
And forgive us our trespasses,
as we forgive those who trespass against us.
And lead us not into temptation;
but deliver us from evil.
For thine is the kingdom,
the power and the glory,
for ever and ever.
Amen.

(or)

As our Saviour taught us, so we pray

All   **Our Father in heaven,**
hallowed be your name,
your kingdom come,
your will be done,
on earth as in heaven.
Give us today our daily bread.
Forgive us our sins
as we forgive those who sin against us.
Lead us not into temptation
but deliver us from evil.
For the kingdom, the power,
and the glory are yours
now and for ever.
Amen.

Breaking of the Bread

The president breaks the consecrated bread.

We break this bread
to share in the body of Christ.

All **Though we are many, we are one body,
because we all share in one bread.**

(or)

Every time we eat this bread
and drink this cup,

All **we proclaim the Lord's death
until he comes.**

The Agnus Dei may be used as the bread is broken

All **O Lamb of God,
that takest away the sins of the world,
have mercy upon us.**

**O Lamb of God,
that takest away the sins of the world,
have mercy upon us.**

**O Lamb of God,
that takest away the sins of the world,
grant us thy peace.**

Giving of Communion

The president says one of these invitations to communion

Draw near with faith.
Receive the body of our Lord Jesus Christ
which he gave for you,
and his blood which he shed for you.
Eat and drink
in remembrance that he died for you,
and feed on him in your hearts
by faith with thanksgiving.

(or)

Jesus is the Lamb of God
who takes away the sin of the world.
Blessed are those who are called to his supper.

All   **Lord, I am not worthy that thou shouldest
     come under my roof,
but speak the word only and my soul shall be healed.**

(or)

God's holy gifts
for God's holy people.

All   **Jesus Christ is holy,
Jesus Christ is Lord,
to the glory of God the Father.**

or, from Easter Day to Pentecost

Alleluia. Christ our passover is sacrificed for us.

All   **Therefore let us keep the feast. Alleluia.**

This prayer may be said before the distribution

All **We do not presume**
to come to this thy table, O merciful Lord,
trusting in our own righteousness,
but in thy manifold and great mercies.
We are not worthy
so much as to gather up the crumbs under thy table.
But thou art the same Lord
whose nature is always to have mercy.
Grant us therefore, gracious Lord,
so to eat the flesh of thy dear Son Jesus Christ
and to drink his blood,
that our sinful bodies may be made clean by his body
and our souls washed through his most precious blood,
and that we may evermore dwell in him, and he in us.
Amen.

The president and people receive communion.

Authorized words of distribution are used and the communicant replies

Amen.

During the distribution hymns and anthems may be sung.

If either or both of the consecrated elements are likely to prove insufficient, the president returns to the holy table and adds more, saying the words on page 296.

Any consecrated bread and wine which is not required for purposes of communion is consumed at the end of the distribution or after the service.

Prayer after Communion

Silence is kept.

The Post Communion, or this or another suitable prayer is said

Almighty and ever-living God, we most heartily thank thee, for
that thou dost vouchsafe to feed us, who have duly received these
holy mysteries, with the spiritual food of the most precious body
and blood of thy Son our Saviour Jesus Christ; and dost assure us
thereby of thy favour and goodness towards us; and that we are very
members incorporate in the mystical body of thy Son, which is the
blessed company of all faithful people, and are also heirs through
hope of thy everlasting kingdom, by the merits of the most precious
death and passion of thy dear Son. And we most humbly beseech
thee, O heavenly Father, so to assist us with thy grace, that we
may continue in that holy fellowship, and do all such good works as
thou hast prepared for us to walk in; through Jesus Christ our Lord,
to whom, with thee and the Holy Spirit, be all honour and glory,
world without end.

All　**Amen.**

All may say this prayer

All　**Almighty God,**
we thank thee for feeding us
with the body and blood of thy Son Jesus Christ.
Through him we offer thee our souls and bodies
to be a living sacrifice.
Send us out
in the power of thy Spirit
to live and work
to thy praise and glory.
Amen.

¶ The Dismissal

A hymn may be sung.

The president may use the seasonal blessing, or another suitable blessing

(or)

The peace of God,
which passes all understanding,
keep your hearts and minds
in the knowledge and love of God,
and of his Son Jesus Christ our Lord;
and the blessing of God almighty,
the Father, the Son, and the Holy Spirit,
be among you and remain with you always.

All **Amen.**

A minister says

Go in peace to love and serve the Lord.

All **In the name of Christ. Amen.**

(or)

Go in the peace of Christ.

All **Thanks be to God.**

or, from Easter Day to Pentecost

Go in the peace of Christ. Alleluia, alleluia.

All **Thanks be to God. Alleluia, alleluia.**

The ministers and people depart.

Order Two   *Structure*

The people and the priest

¶   prepare for worship

¶   hear and respond to the commandments of God

¶   keep silence and pray a Collect

¶   proclaim and respond to the word of God

¶   prepare the table

¶   pray for the Church and the world

¶   confess their sins and are assured of God's forgiveness

¶   praise God for his goodness

¶   pray the Consecration Prayer

¶   receive communion

¶   respond with thanksgiving

¶   depart with God's blessing

For Notes, see pages 158–159, 330–334 and 335.

Order Two

A hymn may be sung.

The Lord's Prayer

Our Father, which art in heaven,
hallowed be thy name;
thy kingdom come;
thy will be done,
in earth as it is in heaven.
Give us this day our daily bread.
And forgive us our trespasses,
as we forgive them that trespass against us.
And lead us not into temptation;
but deliver us from evil. Amen.

Prayer of Preparation

Almighty God,
unto whom all hearts be open,
all desires known,
and from whom no secrets are hid:
cleanse the thoughts of our hearts
by the inspiration of thy Holy Spirit,
that we may perfectly love thee,
and worthily magnify thy holy name;
through Christ our Lord.

All　**Amen.**

The Commandments

*The priest reads the Ten Commandments and the people make
the response. Or, except on the first Sundays of Advent and Lent,
the Summary of the Law or Kyrie eleison may be used.*

God spake these words and said:
I am the Lord thy God; thou shalt have none other gods but me.

All **Lord, have mercy upon us,**
and incline our hearts to keep this law.

Thou shalt not make to thyself any graven image,
nor the likeness of any thing that is in heaven above,
or in the earth beneath, or in the water under the earth.
Thou shalt not bow down to them, nor worship them:
for I the Lord thy God am a jealous God,
and visit the sins of the fathers upon the children
    unto the third and fourth generation of them that hate me,
and shew mercy unto thousands in them that love me
    and keep my commandments.

All **Lord, have mercy upon us,**
and incline our hearts to keep this law.

Thou shalt not take the name of the Lord thy God in vain:
for the Lord will not hold him guiltless that taketh his name in vain.

All **Lord, have mercy upon us,**
and incline our hearts to keep this law.

Remember that thou keep holy the Sabbath day.
Six days shalt thou labour, and do all that thou hast to do;
but the seventh day is the Sabbath of the Lord thy God.
In it thou shalt do no manner of work,
thou, and thy son, and thy daughter,
thy manservant, and thy maidservant,
thy cattle, and the stranger that is within thy gates.
For in six days the Lord made heaven and earth,
the sea, and all that in them is,
and rested the seventh day:
wherefore the Lord blessed the seventh day, and hallowed it.

All **Lord, have mercy upon us,**
and incline our hearts to keep this law.

Honour thy father and thy mother;
that thy days may be long in the land
   which the Lord thy God giveth thee.

All   **Lord, have mercy upon us,**
and incline our hearts to keep this law.

Thou shalt do no murder.

All   **Lord, have mercy upon us,**
and incline our hearts to keep this law.

Thou shalt not commit adultery.

All   **Lord, have mercy upon us,**
and incline our hearts to keep this law.

Thou shalt not steal.

All   **Lord, have mercy upon us,**
and incline our hearts to keep this law.

Thou shalt not bear false witness against thy neighbour.

All   **Lord, have mercy upon us,**
and incline our hearts to keep this law.

Thou shalt not covet thy neighbour's house,
thou shalt not covet thy neighbour's wife, nor his servant,
nor his maid, nor his ox, nor his ass, nor anything that is his.

All   **Lord, have mercy upon us,**
and write all these thy laws in our hearts, we beseech thee.

Or this Summary of the Law may be said

Our Lord Jesus Christ said:
Hear, O Israel, the Lord our God is one Lord;
and thou shalt love the Lord thy God with all thy heart,
and with all thy soul, and with all thy mind,
and with all thy strength.
This is the first commandment.

And the second is like, namely this:
Thou shalt love thy neighbour as thyself.
There is none other commandment greater than these.
On these two commandments hang all the law
   and the prophets.

All   **Lord, have mercy upon us,**
and write all these thy laws in our hearts,
we beseech thee.

Or the Kyrie eleison may be sung or said

Lord, have mercy.
All **Lord, have mercy.**
Lord, have mercy.

All **Christ, have mercy.**
Christ, have mercy.
All **Christ, have mercy.**

Lord, have mercy.
All **Lord, have mercy.**
Lord, have mercy.

(or)

Kyrie, eleison.
All **Kyrie, eleison**.
Kyrie, eleison.

All **Christe, eleison.**
Christe, eleison.
All **Christe, eleison.**

Kyrie, eleison.
All **Kyrie, eleison**.
Kyrie, eleison.

The Collect for the Sovereign may be said

Almighty God, whose kingdom is everlasting, and power infinite:
have mercy upon the whole Church; and so rule the heart of
thy chosen servant *Elizabeth, our Queen* and Governor, that she
(knowing whose minister she is) may above all things seek thy
honour and glory: and that we and all her subjects (duly considering
whose authority she hath) may faithfully serve, honour and humbly
obey her, in thee, and for thee, according to thy blessed word and
ordinance; through Jesus Christ our Lord, who with thee and the
Holy Ghost liveth and reigneth, ever one God, world without end.
All **Amen.**

The Collect

The priest may say

The Lord be with you

All **and with thy spirit.**
Let us pray.

The priest says the Collect of the Day.

Epistle

A Lesson from the Old Testament may be read and a Psalm may be used.

The reader says

The Lesson is written in the ... chapter of ... beginning at the ... verse.

At the end

Here endeth the Lesson.

The reader says

The Epistle is written in the ... chapter of ... beginning at the ... verse.

At the end

Here endeth the Epistle.

A hymn may be sung.

Gospel

The reader says

The holy Gospel is written in the ... chapter of the Gospel according to Saint ..., beginning at the ... verse.

All may respond

All **Glory be to thee, O Lord.**

At the end the reader may say

This is the Gospel of the Lord.

All may respond

All **Praise be to thee, O Christ.**

The Creed

*The Creed is used on every Sunday and Holy Day
and may be used on other days also.*

All I believe in one God the Father almighty,
maker of heaven and earth,
and of all things
visible and invisible:

And in one Lord Jesus Christ,
the only-begotten Son of God,
begotten of his Father before all worlds,
God of God, Light of Light,
very God of very God,
begotten, not made,
being of one substance with the Father,
by whom all things were made;
who for us men and for our salvation
came down from heaven,
and was incarnate by the Holy Ghost of the Virgin Mary,
and was made man,
and was crucified also for us under Pontius Pilate.
He suffered and was buried,
and the third day he rose again
according to the Scriptures,
and ascended into heaven,
and sitteth on the right hand of the Father.
And he shall come again with glory
to judge both the quick and the dead:
whose kingdom shall have no end.

And I believe in the Holy Ghost,
the Lord and giver of life,
who proceedeth from the Father and the Son,
who with the Father and the Son together
is worshipped and glorified,
who spake by the prophets.
And I believe one catholic and apostolic Church.
I acknowledge one baptism for the remission of sins.
And I look for the resurrection of the dead,
and the life of the world to come.
Amen.

Banns of marriage may be published and notices given.

Sermon

Offertory

One of the following or another sentence of Scripture is used

Let your light so shine before men, that they may see your good works, and glorify your Father which is in heaven.   *Matthew 5.16*

Lay not up for yourselves treasure upon the earth, where the rust and moth doth corrupt, and where thieves break through and steal: but lay up for yourselves treasures in heaven; where neither rust nor moth doth corrupt, and where thieves do not break through and steal.   *Matthew 6.19*

All things come of thee, and of thine own do we give thee.
1 Chronicles 29.14

Whoso hath this world's good, and seeth his brother have need, and shutteth up his compassion from him, how dwelleth the love of God in him?   *1 John 3.17*

A hymn may be sung.

The gifts of the people may be gathered and presented.

The priest places the bread and wine upon the table.

Intercession

Brief biddings may be given.

Let us pray for the whole state of Christ's Church militant here in earth.

Almighty and ever-living God, who by thy holy apostle hast taught us to make prayers and supplications, and to give thanks, for all men: we humbly beseech thee most mercifully [to accept our alms and oblations, and] to receive these our prayers, which we offer unto thy divine majesty; beseeching thee to inspire continually the universal Church with the spirit of truth, unity, and concord: and grant, that all they that do confess thy holy name may agree in the truth of thy holy word, and live in unity and godly love.

We beseech thee also to save and defend all Christian kings, princes and governors; and specially thy servant *Elizabeth our Queen*, that under her we may be godly and quietly governed: and grant unto her whole Council, and to all that are put in authority under her, that they may truly and impartially minister justice, to the punishment of wickedness and vice, and to the maintenance of thy true religion and virtue.

Give grace, O heavenly Father, to all bishops, priests and deacons, that they may both by their life and doctrine set forth thy true and lively word, and rightly and duly administer thy holy sacraments: and to all thy people give thy heavenly grace; and specially to this congregation here present; that, with meek heart and due reverence, they may hear and receive thy holy word; truly serving thee in holiness and righteousness all the days of their life.

And we most humbly beseech thee of thy goodness, O Lord, to comfort and succour all them, who in this transitory life are in trouble, sorrow, need, sickness, or any other adversity.

And we also bless thy holy name for all thy servants departed this life in thy faith and fear; beseeching thee to give us grace so to follow their good examples, that with them we may be partakers of thy heavenly kingdom.

Grant this, O Father, for Jesus Christ's sake, our only mediator and advocate.

All **Amen.**

The priest may read the Exhortation (page 245) or one of the other Exhortations in The Book of Common Prayer.

Invitation to Confession

Ye that do truly and earnestly repent you of your sins, and are in love and charity with your neighbours, and intend to lead a new life, following the commandments of God, and walking from henceforth in his holy ways: draw near with faith, and take this holy sacrament to your comfort; and make your humble confession to almighty God, meekly kneeling upon your knees.

Confession

All **Almighty God,**
Father of our Lord Jesus Christ,
maker of all things, judge of all men:
we acknowledge and bewail
    our manifold sins and wickedness,
which we, from time to time,
    most grievously have committed,
by thought, word and deed,
against thy divine majesty,
provoking most justly thy wrath and indignation against us.
We do earnestly repent,
and are heartily sorry for these our misdoings;
the remembrance of them is grievous unto us;
the burden of them is intolerable.
Have mercy upon us,
have mercy upon us, most merciful Father;
for thy Son our Lord Jesus Christ's sake,
forgive us all that is past;
and grant that we may ever hereafter
serve and please thee in newness of life,
to the honour and glory of thy name;
through Jesus Christ our Lord.
Amen.

Absolution

The priest says

Almighty God, our heavenly Father,
who of his great mercy
hath promised forgiveness of sins
to all them that with hearty repentance and true faith
    turn unto him:
have mercy upon *you*;
pardon and deliver *you* from all *your* sins;
confirm and strengthen *you* in all goodness;
and bring *you* to everlasting life;
through Jesus Christ our Lord.

All   **Amen.**

The Comfortable Words

Hear what comfortable words our Saviour Christ saith
unto all that truly turn to him:

Come unto me, all that travail and are heavy laden,
and I will refresh you.   *Matthew 11.28*

So God loved the world, that he gave his only-begotten Son,
to the end that all that believe in him should not perish,
but have everlasting life.   *John 3.16*

Hear also what Saint Paul saith:
This is a true saying, and worthy of all men to be received,
that Christ Jesus came into the world to save sinners. *1 Timothy 1.15*

Hear also what Saint John saith:
If any man sin, we have an advocate with the Father,
Jesus Christ the righteous;
and he is the propitiation for our sins.   *1 John 2.1,2*

Preface

The priest and the people praise God for his goodness.

> The Lord be with you
>
> All **and with thy spirit.**

Lift up your hearts.

All **We lift them up unto the Lord.**

Let us give thanks unto our Lord God.

All **It is meet and right so to do.**

The priest says

It is very meet, right and our bounden duty,
that we should at all times, and in all places, give thanks unto thee,
O Lord, holy Father,
almighty, everlasting God.

A Proper Preface may follow (see Note 28).

Therefore with angels and archangels,
and with all the company of heaven,
we laud and magnify thy glorious name,
evermore praising thee, and *saying*:

All **Holy, holy, holy, Lord God of hosts,
heaven and earth are full of thy glory.
Glory be to thee, O Lord most high.
[Amen.]**

> *These words may also be used*
>
> All **Blessed is he that cometh in the name of the Lord.
> Hosanna in the highest.**

Prayer of Humble Access

We do not presume
to come to this thy table, O merciful Lord,
trusting in our own righteousness,
but in thy manifold and great mercies.
We are not worthy
so much as to gather up the crumbs under thy table.
But thou art the same Lord,
whose property is always to have mercy:
grant us therefore, gracious Lord,
so to eat the flesh of thy dear Son Jesus Christ,
and to drink his blood,
that our sinful bodies may be made clean by his body,
and our souls washed through his most precious blood,
and that we may evermore dwell in him, and he in us.

All **Amen.**

The Prayer of Consecration

The priest, standing at the table, says the Prayer of Consecration

Almighty God, our heavenly Father, who of thy tender mercy didst give thine only Son Jesus Christ to suffer death upon the cross for our redemption; who made there (by his one oblation of himself once offered) a full, perfect and sufficient sacrifice, oblation and satisfaction for the sins of the whole world; and did institute, and in his holy gospel command us to continue, a perpetual memory of that his precious death, until his coming again:

Hear us, O merciful Father, we most humbly beseech thee;
and grant that we receiving these thy creatures of bread and wine, according to thy Son our Saviour Jesus Christ's holy institution, in remembrance of his death and passion, may be partakers of his most blessed body and blood:

who, in the same night that he was betrayed, took bread;

Here the priest is to take the paten.

and, when he had given thanks, he brake it,

Here the priest shall break the bread.

and gave it to his disciples, saying, Take, eat;

Here the priest is to lay a hand on all the bread.

this is my body which is given for you:
do this in remembrance of me.
Likewise after supper he took the cup;

Here the priest is to take the cup.

and, when he had given thanks, he gave it to them, saying,
Drink ye all of this;

Here the priest is to lay a hand on every vessel
in which there is wine to be consecrated.

for this is my blood of the new testament,
which is shed for you and for many for the remission of sins:
do this, as oft as ye shall drink it, in remembrance of me.

All **Amen.**

The following may be used

All **O Lamb of God**
that takest away the sins of the world,
have mercy upon us.

O Lamb of God
that takest away the sins of the world,
have mercy upon us.

O Lamb of God
that takest away the sins of the world,
grant us thy peace.

Giving of Communion

The priest and people receive communion. To each is said

The body of our Lord Jesus Christ, which was given for thee,
preserve thy body and soul unto everlasting life.
Take and eat this in remembrance that Christ died for thee,
and feed on him in thy heart by faith with thanksgiving.

The blood of our Lord Jesus Christ, which was shed for thee,
preserve thy body and soul unto everlasting life.
Drink this in remembrance that Christ's blood was shed for thee,
    and be thankful.

*Or, when occasion requires, these words may be said once to each row
of communicants, or to a convenient number within each row.*

*If either or both of the consecrated elements are likely to prove
insufficient, the priest returns to the holy table and adds more,
saying the words on page 296.*

*What remains of the consecrated bread and wine which is not required
for purposes of communion is consumed now or at the end of the service.*

The Lord's Prayer

The priest may say

As our Saviour Christ hath commanded and taught us,
we are bold to say

All **Our Father, which art in heaven,
hallowed be thy name;
thy kingdom come;
thy will be done,
in earth as it is in heaven.
Give us this day our daily bread.
And forgive us our trespasses,
as we forgive them that trespass against us.
And lead us not into temptation;
but deliver us from evil.
For thine is the kingdom,
the power and the glory,
for ever and ever.
Amen.**

Prayer after Communion

The priest says either the Prayer of Oblation or the Prayer of Thanksgiving.

Prayer of Oblation

O Lord and heavenly Father, we thy humble servants entirely desire
thy fatherly goodness mercifully to accept this our sacrifice of praise
and thanksgiving; most humbly beseeching thee to grant, that by
the merits and death of thy Son Jesus Christ, and through faith in
his blood, we and all thy whole Church may obtain remission of our
sins, and all other benefits of his passion. And here we offer and
present unto thee, O Lord, ourselves, our souls and bodies, to be
a reasonable, holy and lively sacrifice unto thee; humbly beseeching
thee, that all we, who are partakers of this holy communion, may
be fulfilled with thy grace and heavenly benediction. And although
we be unworthy, through our manifold sins, to offer unto thee any
sacrifice, yet we beseech thee to accept this our bounden duty
and service; not weighing our merits, but pardoning our offences,
through Jesus Christ our Lord; by whom, and with whom, in the
unity of the Holy Ghost, all honour and glory be unto thee,
O Father almighty, world without end.

All   **Amen.**

Prayer of Thanksgiving

Almighty and ever-living God, we most heartily thank thee, for that
thou dost vouchsafe to feed us, who have duly received these holy
mysteries, with the spiritual food of the most precious body and
blood of thy Son our Saviour Jesus Christ; and dost assure us
thereby of thy favour and goodness towards us; and that we are
very members incorporate in the mystical body of thy Son, which
is the blessed company of all faithful people; and are also heirs
through hope of thy everlasting kingdom, by the merits of the most
precious death and passion of thy dear Son. And we most humbly
beseech thee, O heavenly Father, so to assist us with thy grace, that
we may continue in that holy fellowship, and do all such good works
as thou hast prepared for us to walk in; through Jesus Christ our
Lord, to whom, with thee and the Holy Ghost, be all honour and
glory, world without end.

All   **Amen.**

Gloria in Excelsis

All   **Glory be to God on high,**
and in earth peace, good will towards men.

We praise thee, we bless thee,
we worship thee, we glorify thee,
we give thanks to thee for thy great glory,
O Lord God, heavenly King,
God the Father almighty.

O Lord, the only-begotten Son Jesu Christ;
O Lord God, Lamb of God, Son of the Father,
that takest away the sins of the world,
have mercy upon us.
Thou that takest away the sins of the world,
have mercy upon us.
Thou that takest away the sins of the world,
receive our prayer.
Thou that sittest at the right hand of God the Father,
have mercy upon us.

For thou only art holy;
thou only art the Lord;
thou only, O Christ,
with the Holy Ghost,
art most high
in the glory of God the Father.
Amen.

The Blessing

The priest says

The peace of God, which passeth all understanding, keep your
hearts and minds in the knowledge and love of God, and of his
Son Jesus Christ our Lord: and the blessing of God almighty,
the Father, the Son, and the Holy Ghost, be amongst you and
remain with you always.

All   **Amen.**

A hymn may be sung.

Third Exhortation from
The Book of Common Prayer

Dearly beloved in the Lord, ye that mind to come to the holy Communion of the Body and Blood of our Saviour Christ, must consider how Saint Paul exhorteth all persons diligently to try and examine themselves, before they presume to eat of that Bread, and drink of that Cup. For as the benefit is great, if with a true penitent heart and lively faith we receive that holy Sacrament; (for then we spiritually eat the flesh of Christ and drink his blood; then we dwell in Christ, and Christ in us; we are one with Christ, and Christ with us;) so is the danger great, if we receive the same unworthily. For then we are guilty of the Body and Blood of Christ our Saviour; we eat and drink our own damnation, not considering the Lord's Body; we kindle God's wrath against us; we provoke him to plague us with divers diseases, and sundry kinds of death. Judge therefore yourselves, brethren, that ye be not judged of the Lord; repent you truly for your sins past; have a lively and steadfast faith in Christ our Saviour; amend your lives, and be in perfect charity with all men; so shall ye be meet partakers of those holy mysteries. And above all things ye must give most humble and hearty thanks to God, the Father, the Son and the Holy Ghost, for the redemption of the world by the death and passion of our Saviour Christ, both God and man; who did humble himself, even to the death upon the Cross, for us miserable sinners, who lay in darkness and the shadow of death; that he might make us the children of God, and exalt us to everlasting life. And to the end that we should always remember the exceeding great love of our Master and only Saviour Jesus Christ, thus dying for us, and the innumerable benefits which by his precious blood-shedding he hath obtained to us; he hath instituted and ordained holy mysteries, as pledges of his love, and for a continual remembrance of his death, to our great and endless comfort. To him, therefore, with the Father and the Holy Ghost, let us give (as we are most bounden) continual thanks; submitting ourselves wholly to his holy will and pleasure, and studying to serve him in true holiness and righteousness all the days of our life.

All **Amen.**

Proper Prefaces from
The Book of Common Prayer

For additional Prefaces, see Note 28 and texts on pages 300–329.

Christmas

Because thou didst give Jesus Christ thine only Son to be born
as at this time for us; who, by the operation of the Holy Ghost,
was made very man of the substance of the Virgin Mary his mother;
and that without spot of sin, to make us clean from all sin.
Therefore with angels …

Easter

But chiefly are we bound to praise thee for the glorious resurrection
of thy Son Jesus Christ our Lord: for he is the very paschal lamb,
which was offered for us, and hath taken away the sin of the world;
who by his death hath destroyed death, and by his rising to life again
hath restored to us everlasting life.
Therefore with angels …

Ascension

Through thy most dearly beloved Son Jesus Christ our Lord;
who after his most glorious resurrection manifestly appeared to all
his apostles, and in their sight ascended up into heaven to prepare
a place for us; that where he is, thither we might also ascend, and
reign with him in glory.
Therefore with angels …

Pentecost (Whitsun)

Through Jesus Christ our Lord; according to whose most true
promise, the Holy Ghost came down as at this time from heaven
with a sudden great sound, as it might have been a mighty wind,
in the likeness of fiery tongues, lighting upon the apostles, to teach
them, and to lead them to all truth; giving them both the gift of
divers languages, and also boldness with fervent zeal constantly to
preach the gospel unto all nations; whereby we have been brought
out of darkness and error into the clear light and true knowledge
of thee, and of thy Son Jesus Christ.
Therefore with angels ...

Trinity Sunday

Who art one God, one Lord; not one only Person, but three Persons
in one Substance. For that which we believe of the glory of the
Father, the same we believe of the Son, and of the Holy Ghost,
without any difference or inequality.
Therefore with angels ...

*When this Preface is used, the words 'holy Father' must be omitted in the
preceding paragraph.*

Order Two *in Contemporary Language*

A hymn may be sung.

The Lord's Prayer may be said.

Prayer of Preparation

Almighty God,
to whom all hearts are open,
all desires known,
and from whom no secrets are hidden:
cleanse the thoughts of our hearts
by the inspiration of your Holy Spirit,
that we may perfectly love you,
and worthily magnify your holy name;
through Christ our Lord.

All **Amen.**

The Commandments

*The president reads the Ten Commandments and the people make the
response. Or, except on the first Sundays of Advent and Lent, the Summary
of the Law (page 268) or Kyrie eleison may be used. At the discretion of
the minister, responses may be used only after the fourth and tenth
Commandments, or only after the tenth Commandment.*

God spoke these words and said: I am the Lord your God
[who brought you out of the land of Egypt, out of the house of slavery]
you shall have no other gods but me.

All **Lord, have mercy upon us,
and incline our hearts to keep this law.**

You shall not make for yourself any idol,
whether in the form of anything that is in heaven above,
or that is on the earth beneath, or that is in the water under the earth.
You shall not bow down to them or worship them.
[For I the Lord your God am a jealous God,
punishing children for the iniquity of parents
to the third and the fourth generation of those who reject me,
but showing steadfast love to a thousand generations of those
    who love me
and keep my commandments.]

All **Lord, have mercy upon us,
and incline our hearts to keep this law.**

You shall not take the name of the Lord your God in vain
[for the Lord will not hold him guiltless who takes his name in vain].

All **Lord, have mercy upon us,
and incline our hearts to keep this law.**

Remember the Sabbath day, and keep it holy.
For six days you shall labour and do all your work.
But the seventh day is a Sabbath to the Lord your God.
[You shall not do any work –
you, your son or your daughter,
your slaves, your livestock,
or the foreigner who lives among you.
For in six days the Lord made heaven and earth,
the sea, and all that is in them,
but rested the seventh day;
therefore the Lord blessed the seventh day and consecrated it.]

All **Lord, have mercy upon us,
and incline our hearts to keep this law.**

Honour your father and your mother
[so that your days may be long in the land
that the Lord your God is giving you].

All **Lord, have mercy upon us,
and incline our hearts to keep this law.**

You shall not murder.

All **Lord, have mercy upon us,
and incline our hearts to keep this law.**

You shall not commit adultery.

All **Lord, have mercy upon us,
and incline our hearts to keep this law.**

You shall not steal.

All **Lord, have mercy upon us,
and incline our hearts to keep this law.**

You shall not bear false witness [against your neighbour].

All **Lord, have mercy upon us,
and incline our hearts to keep this law.**

You shall not covet [your neighbour's house;
you shall not covet your neighbour's wife, or slaves, or ox, or donkey,
or anything that belongs to your neighbour].

All **Lord, have mercy upon us,
and write all these your laws in our hearts.**

The Collect for the Sovereign may be said

Almighty God,
the fountain of all goodness,
bless our Sovereign *Lady, Queen Elizabeth,*
and all who are in authority under her;
that they may order all things
    in wisdom and equity, righteousness and peace,
to the honour and glory of your name
and the good of your Church and people;
through Jesus Christ your Son our Lord,
who is alive and reigns with you,
in the unity of the Holy Spirit,
one God, now and for ever.

All **Amen.**

The Collect

The president introduces a period of silent prayer with the words 'Let us pray' or a more specific bidding.

The Collect is said, and all respond

All **Amen.**

Readings

Either one or two readings from Scripture precede the Gospel reading.

At the end of each the reader may say

This is the word of the Lord.
All **Thanks be to God.**

The psalm or canticle follows the first reading, and other hymns and songs may be used between the readings.

Gospel Reading

An acclamation may herald the Gospel reading.

When the Gospel is announced the reader says

Hear the Gospel of our Lord Jesus Christ according to N.
All **Glory to you, O Lord.**

At the end the reader may say

This is the Gospel of the Lord.
All **Praise to you, O Christ.**

The Creed

On Sundays and Principal Holy Days an authorized translation of the Nicene Creed is used, or on occasion the Apostles' Creed or an authorized Affirmation of Faith may be used (see pages 138–148).

All   **We believe in one God,**
the Father, the Almighty,
maker of heaven and earth,
of all that is,
seen and unseen.

We believe in one Lord, Jesus Christ,
the only Son of God,
eternally begotten of the Father,
God from God, Light from Light,
true God from true God,
begotten, not made,
of one Being with the Father;
through him all things were made.
For us and for our salvation he came down from heaven,
was incarnate from the Holy Spirit and the Virgin Mary
and was made man.
For our sake he was crucified under Pontius Pilate;
he suffered death and was buried.
On the third day he rose again
in accordance with the Scriptures;
he ascended into heaven
and is seated at the right hand of the Father.
He will come again in glory to judge the living and the dead,
and his kingdom will have no end.

We believe in the Holy Spirit,
the Lord, the giver of life,
who proceeds from the Father and the Son,
who with the Father and the Son is worshipped and glorified,
who has spoken through the prophets.
We believe in one holy catholic and apostolic Church.
We acknowledge one baptism for the forgiveness of sins.
We look for the resurrection of the dead,
and the life of the world to come.
Amen.

Sermon

Offertory

One of the following or another sentence of Scripture is used.

Let your light shine before others, so that they may see your good works, and give glory to your Father in heaven.   *Matthew 5.16*

Do not store up for yourselves treasures on earth; where moth and rust consume, and where thieves break in and steal: but store up for yourselves treasures in heaven, where neither rust nor moth consume, and where thieves do not break in and steal.

Matthew 6.19

All things come from you, and of your own have we given you.

1 Chronicles 29.14

How does God's love abide in anyone who has the world's goods and sees a brother or sister in need and yet refuses help?

1 John 3.17

A hymn may be sung.

The gifts of the people may be gathered and presented.

The president places the bread and wine on the table.

Prayers of Intercession

One of the forms on pages 281–289 or other suitable words may be used.

The prayers usually include these concerns and may follow this sequence:

¶   *The Church of Christ*

¶   *Creation, human society, the Sovereign and those in authority*

¶   *The local community*

¶   *Those who suffer*

¶   *The communion of saints*

These responses may be used

Lord, in your mercy
All   **hear our prayer.**

(or)

Lord, hear us.
All   **Lord, graciously hear us.**

And at the end

Merciful Father,
All   **accept these prayers**
for the sake of your Son,
our Saviour Jesus Christ.
Amen.

Prayers of Penitence

A minister reads this shorter exhortation

Brothers and sisters in Christ,
as we gather at the Lord's table
we must recall the promises and warnings
    given to us in the Scriptures.
Let us therefore examine ourselves and repent of our sins.
Let us give thanks to God
    for his redemption of the world through his Son Jesus Christ,
and as we remember Christ's death for us,
and receive this pledge of his love,
let us resolve to serve him in holiness and righteousness
all the days of our life.

Invitation to Confession

A minister uses a seasonal invitation to confession or these
or other suitable words

You then, who truly and earnestly repent of your sins,
and are in love and charity with your neighbours,
and intend to lead a new life,
following the commandments of God,
and walking from this day forward in his holy ways:
draw near with faith,
and take this holy sacrament to your comfort;
and make your humble confession to almighty God.

Confession

Either of these forms, or form 2 on page 276 may be used.

All   **Almighty God,**
Father of our Lord Jesus Christ,
maker of all things, judge of all people,
we acknowledge and lament our many sins
and the wickedness we have committed time after time,
by thought, word and deed against your divine majesty.
We have provoked your righteous anger
and your indignation against us.
We earnestly repent,
and are deeply sorry for these our wrongdoings;
the memory of them weighs us down,
the burden of them is too great for us to bear.
Have mercy upon us,
have mercy upon us, most merciful Father.
For your Son our Lord Jesus Christ's sake,
forgive us all that is past;
and grant that from this time forward
we may always serve and please you in newness of life,
to the honour and glory of your name;
through Jesus Christ our Lord.
Amen.

(or)

All   **Father eternal, giver of light and grace,**
we have sinned against you and against our neighbour,
in what we have thought,
in what we have said and done,
through ignorance, through weakness,
through our own deliberate fault.
We have wounded your love,
and marred your image in us.
We are sorry and ashamed,
and repent of all our sins.
For the sake of your Son Jesus Christ,
who died for us,
forgive us all that is past;
and lead us out from darkness
to walk as children of light
Amen.

Absolution

The president says

Almighty God, our heavenly Father,
who in his great mercy
has promised forgiveness of sins
to all those who with heartfelt repentance and true faith
    turn to him:
have mercy on *you*,
pardon and deliver *you* from all *your* sins,
confirm and strengthen *you* in all goodness,
and bring *you* to everlasting life,
through Jesus Christ our Lord.

All **Amen.**

The Comfortable Words

Hear the words of comfort our Saviour Christ says
to all who truly turn to him:

Come to me, all who labour and are heavy laden,
and I will give you rest. *Matthew 11.28*

God so loved the world that he gave his only-begotten Son,
that whoever believes in him should not perish
but have eternal life. *John 3.16*

Hear what Saint Paul says:
This saying is true and worthy of full acceptance,
that Christ Jesus came into the world to save sinners. *1 Timothy 1.15*

Hear what Saint John says:
If anyone sins, we have an advocate with the Father,
Jesus Christ the righteous;
and he is the propitiation for our sins. *1 John 2.1,2*

Preface

The president and the people praise God for his goodness.

Lift up your hearts.

All **We lift them to the Lord.**

Let us give thanks to the Lord our God.

All **It is right to give thanks and praise.**

It is indeed right,
it is our duty and our joy,
at all times and in all places
to give you thanks and praise,
holy Father, heavenly King,
almighty and eternal God.

A Proper Preface may follow (see Note 28).

Therefore with angels and archangels,
and with all the company of heaven,
we proclaim your great and glorious name,
for ever praising you, and *saying*:

All **Holy, holy, holy Lord,**
God of power and might,
heaven and earth are full of your glory.
Hosanna in the highest.

Prayer of Humble Access

One of these prayers is said

We do not presume
to come to this your table, merciful Lord,
trusting in our own righteousness,
but in your manifold and great mercies.
We are not worthy
so much as to gather up the crumbs under your table.
But you are the same Lord
whose nature is always to have mercy.
Grant us therefore, gracious Lord,
so to eat the flesh of your dear Son Jesus Christ
and to drink his blood,
that our sinful bodies may be made clean by his body,
and our souls washed through his most precious blood,
and that we may evermore dwell in him, and he in us.

All **Amen.**

(or)

Most merciful Lord,
your love compels us to come in.
Our hands were unclean,
our hearts were unprepared;
we were not fit
even to eat the crumbs from under your table.
But you, Lord, are the God of our salvation,
and share your bread with sinners.
So cleanse and feed us
with the precious body and blood of your Son,
that he may live in us and we in him;
and that we, with the whole company of Christ,
may sit and eat in your kingdom.

All **Amen**.

The Prayer of Consecration

The president, standing at the table, says the Prayer of Consecration

Almighty God, our heavenly Father,
who, in your tender mercy,
gave your only Son our Saviour Jesus Christ
to suffer death upon the cross for our redemption;
who made there by his one oblation of himself once offered
a full, perfect and sufficient sacrifice, oblation and satisfaction
    for the sins of the whole world;
he instituted, and in his holy gospel commanded us to continue,
a perpetual memory of his precious death until he comes again.

Hear us, merciful Father, we humbly pray,
and grant that we receiving these gifts of your creation,
    this bread and this wine,
according to your Son our Saviour Jesus Christ's holy institution,
in remembrance of his death and passion,
may be partakers of his most blessed body and blood;

who, in the same night that he was betrayed,
took bread and gave you thanks;

      Here the president takes the paten.

he broke it and gave it to his disciples, saying:

      Here the president breaks the bread.

Take, eat, this is my body which is given for you;

      Here the president lays a hand on all the bread.

do this in remembrance of me.
In the same way, after supper, he took the cup;

      Here the president takes the cup.

and when he had given thanks, he gave it to them, saying:
Drink this, all of you, this is my blood of the new covenant,
which is shed for you and for many
for the forgiveness of sins.

      Here the president is to lay a hand on every vessel
         in which there is wine to be consecrated.

Do this, as often as you drink it,
in remembrance of me.

All   **Amen.**

Giving of Communion

The president and people receive communion.

To each is said

The body of our Lord Jesus Christ,
which was given for you,
preserve your body and soul to everlasting life.
Take and eat this in remembrance that Christ died for you,
and feed on him in your heart by faith with thanksgiving.

The blood of our Lord Jesus Christ,
which was shed for you,
preserve your body and soul to everlasting life.
Drink this in remembrance that Christ's blood was shed for you,
    and be thankful.

*Or, when occasion requires, these words may be said once to each row
of communicants, or to a convenient number within each row.*

*If either or both of the consecrated elements are likely to prove
insufficient, the president returns to the holy table and adds more,
saying the words on page 296.*

*What remains of the consecrated bread and wine which is not required
for purposes of communion is consumed now or at the end of the service.*

The Lord's Prayer

The Lord's Prayer is said

As our Saviour taught us, so we pray

All **Our Father in heaven,**
hallowed be your name,
your kingdom come,
your will be done,
on earth as in heaven.
Give us today our daily bread.
Forgive us our sins
as we forgive those who sin against us.
Lead us not into temptation
but deliver us from evil.
For the kingdom, the power,
and the glory are yours
now and for ever.
Amen.

(or)

Let us pray with confidence as our Saviour has taught us

All **Our Father, who art in heaven,**
hallowed be thy name;
thy kingdom come;
thy will be done;
on earth as it is in heaven.
Give us this day our daily bread.
And forgive us our trespasses,
as we forgive those who trespass against us.
And lead us not into temptation;
but deliver us from evil.
For thine is the kingdom,
the power and the glory,
for ever and ever.
Amen.

Prayer after Communion

The president says one of the following prayers or the prayer on page 298.

Lord and heavenly Father,
we offer you through your dear Son Jesus Christ
    this our sacrifice of praise and thanksgiving.
Grant that by his merits and death,
and through faith in his blood,
we and all your Church may receive forgiveness of our sins
and all other benefits of his passion.

And here we offer and present to you, O Lord,
    ourselves, our souls and our bodies,
to be a reasonable, holy and living sacrifice;
fill us all who share in this holy communion
with your grace and heavenly blessing.

Although we are unworthy, through our manifold sins,
to offer you any sacrifice,
yet we pray that you will accept this
the duty and service that we owe.
Do not weigh our merits, but pardon our offences,
through Jesus Christ our Lord,
by whom, and with whom, and in whom,
in the unity of the Holy Spirit,
all honour and glory be yours, almighty Father,
for ever and ever.

All   **Amen.**

(or)

Father of all,
we give you thanks and praise,
that when we were still far off
you met us in your Son and brought us home.
Dying and living, he declared your love,
gave us grace, and opened the gate of glory.
May we who share Christ's body live his risen life;
we who drink his cup bring life to others;
we whom the Spirit lights give light to the world.
Keep us firm in the hope you have set before us,
so we and all your children shall be free,
and the whole earth live to praise your name;
through Christ our Lord.

All   **Amen.**

Gloria in Excelsis

All   **Glory to God in the highest,
and peace to his people on earth.**

**Lord God, heavenly King,
almighty God and Father,
we worship you, we give you thanks,
we praise you for your glory.**

**Lord Jesus Christ, only Son of the Father,
Lord God, Lamb of God,
you take away the sin of the world:
have mercy on us;
you are seated at the right hand of the Father:
receive our prayer.**

**For you alone are the Holy One,
you alone are the Lord,
you alone are the Most High, Jesus Christ,
with the Holy Spirit,
in the glory of God the Father.
Amen.**

Or another song of praise may be used.

The Blessing

The president may use a seasonal blessing or another suitable blessing, or

The peace of God,
which passes all understanding,
keep your hearts and minds
in the knowledge and love of God,
and of his Son Jesus Christ our Lord;
and the blessing of God almighty,
the Father, the Son, and the Holy Spirit,
be among you, and remain with you always.

All   **Amen.**

A hymn may be sung.

Supplementary Texts

¶ *Penitential Material*

Summary of the Law

This may be used with or without the congregational response.

Our Lord Jesus Christ said:
The first commandment is this:
'Hear, O Israel, the Lord our God is the only Lord.
You shall love the Lord your God with all your heart,
with all your soul, with all your mind,
and with all your strength.'

The second is this: 'Love your neighbour as yourself.'
There is no other commandment greater than these.
On these two commandments hang all the law and the prophets.

All **Amen. Lord, have mercy.**

(or)

Our Lord Jesus Christ said:
Hear, O Israel, the Lord our God is one Lord;
and thou shalt love the Lord thy God with all thy heart,
and with all thy soul, and with all thy mind,
and with all thy strength.
This is the first commandment.

And the second is like, namely this:
Thou shalt love thy neighbour as thyself.
There is none other commandment greater than these.
On these two commandments hang all the law and the prophets.

All **Lord, have mercy upon us,**
and write all these thy laws in our hearts, we beseech thee.

The Commandments

I

Hear these commandments which God has given to his people
and examine your hearts.

God spake these words and said:
I am the Lord thy God; thou shalt have none other gods but me.

All **Lord, have mercy upon us,**
and incline our hearts to keep this law.

Thou shalt not make to thyself any graven image,
nor the likeness of any thing that is in heaven above,
or in the earth beneath, or in the water under the earth.
Thou shalt not bow down to them, nor worship them.
[For I the Lord thy God am a jealous God,
and visit the sins of the fathers upon the children
    unto the third and fourth generation of them that hate me,
and shew mercy unto thousands in them that love me
    and keep my commandments.]

All **Lord, have mercy upon us,**
and incline our hearts to keep this law.

Thou shalt not take the name of the Lord thy God in vain
[for the Lord will not hold him guiltless that taketh his name in vain].

All **Lord, have mercy upon us,**
and incline our hearts to keep this law.

Remember that thou keep holy the Sabbath day.
Six days shalt thou labour, and do all that thou hast to do;
but the seventh day is the Sabbath of the Lord thy God.
[In it thou shalt do no manner of work,
thou, and thy son, and thy daughter,
thy manservant, and thy maidservant,
thy cattle, and the stranger that is within thy gates.
For in six days the Lord made heaven and earth,
the sea, and all that in them is,
and rested the seventh day:
wherefore the Lord blessed the seventh day, and hallowed it.]

All **Lord, have mercy upon us,**
and incline our hearts to keep this law.

Honour thy father and thy mother
[that thy days may be long in the land
which the Lord thy God giveth thee].

All   **Lord, have mercy upon us,
and incline our hearts to keep this law.**

Thou shalt do no murder.

All   **Lord, have mercy upon us,
and incline our hearts to keep this law.**

Thou shalt not commit adultery.

All   **Lord, have mercy upon us,
and incline our hearts to keep this law.**

Thou shalt not steal.

All   **Lord, have mercy upon us,
and incline our hearts to keep this law.**

Thou shalt not bear false witness [against thy neighbour].

All   **Lord, have mercy upon us,
and incline our hearts to keep this law.**

Thou shalt not covet [thy neighbour's house,
thou shalt not covet thy neighbour's wife, nor his servant,
nor his maid, nor his ox, nor his ass, nor anything that is his].

All   **Lord, have mercy upon us,
and write all these thy laws in our hearts, we beseech thee.**

2

Hear these commandments which God has given to his people,
and examine your hearts.

I am the Lord your God: you shall have no other gods but me.
You shall love the Lord your God with all your heart,
with all your soul, with all your mind, and with all your strength.

All   **Amen. Lord, have mercy.**

You shall not make for yourself any idol.
God is spirit, and those who worship him must worship in spirit
and in truth.

All   **Amen. Lord, have mercy.**

You shall not dishonour the name of the Lord your God.
You shall worship him with awe and reverence.

All **Amen. Lord, have mercy.**

Remember the Sabbath and keep it holy.
Christ is risen from the dead: set your minds on things that are
above, not on things that are on the earth.

All **Amen. Lord, have mercy.**

Honour your father and mother.
Live as servants of God; let us work for the good of all,
especially members of the household of faith.

All **Amen. Lord, have mercy.**

You shall not commit murder.
Live peaceably with all; overcome evil with good.

All **Amen. Lord, have mercy.**

You shall not commit adultery.
Know that your body is a temple of the Holy Spirit.

All **Amen. Lord, have mercy.**

You shall not steal.
Be honest in all that you do, and care for those in need.

All **Amen. Lord, have mercy.**

You shall not be a false witness.
Let everyone speak the truth.

All **Amen. Lord, have mercy.**

You shall not covet anything which belongs to your neighbour.
Remember the words of the Lord Jesus:
'It is more blessed to give than to receive.'
Love your neighbour as yourself, for love is the fulfilling of the law.

All **Amen. Lord, have mercy.**

The Beatitudes

Silence is kept between each Beatitude.

Let us hear our Lord's blessing on those who follow him.

Blessed are the poor in spirit,
for theirs is the kingdom of heaven.

Blessed are those who mourn,
for they shall be comforted.

Blessed are the meek,
for they shall inherit the earth.

Blessed are those who hunger and thirst after righteousness,
for they shall be satisfied.

Blessed are the merciful,
for they shall obtain mercy.

Blessed are the pure in heart,
for they shall see God.

Blessed are the peacemakers,
for they shall be called children of God.

Blessed are those who suffer persecution for righteousness' sake,
for theirs is the kingdom of heaven.

Let us confess our many failures to keep this way of truth and life.

The confession follows without further invitation.

The Comfortable Words

One or more of these sentences may be used

Hear the words of comfort our Saviour Christ says
to all who truly turn to him:

Come to me, all who labour and are heavy laden,
and I will give you rest. *Matthew 11.28*

God so loved the world that he gave his only-begotten Son,
that whoever believes in him should not perish
but have eternal life. *John 3.16*

Hear what Saint Paul says:
This saying is true, and worthy of full acceptance,
that Christ Jesus came into the world to save sinners. *1 Timothy 1.15*

Hear what Saint John says:
If anyone sins, we have an advocate with the Father,
Jesus Christ the righteous;
and he is the propitiation for our sins. *1 John 2.1,2*

[Let us confess our sins in penitence and faith.]

(or)

Hear what comfortable words our Saviour Christ saith
unto all that truly turn to him:

Come unto me, all that travail and are heavy laden,
and I will refresh you. *Matthew 11.28*

So God loved the world, that he gave his only-begotten Son,
to the end that all that believe in him should not perish,
but have everlasting life. *John 3.16*

Hear what Saint Paul saith:
This is a true saying, and worthy of all men to be received,
that Christ Jesus came into the world to save sinners. *1 Timothy 1.15*

Hear what Saint John saith:
If any man sin, we have an advocate with the Father,
Jesus Christ the righteous;
and he is the propitiation for our sins. *1 John 2.1,2*

[Let us confess our sins in penitence and faith.]

Exhortation

Brothers and sisters in Christ,
as we gather at the Lord's table
we must recall the promises and warnings
    given to us in the Scriptures.
Let us therefore examine ourselves and repent of our sins.
Let us give thanks to God
    for his redemption of the world through his Son Jesus Christ,
and as we remember Christ's death for us,
and receive this pledge of his love,
let us resolve to serve him in holiness and righteousness
all the days of our life.

Invitations to Confession

The provision made for seasons and Principal Holy Days
(see pages 300–329) may be used at other times when appropriate.

1

My brothers and sisters,
as we prepare to celebrate the presence of Christ
in word and sacrament,
let us call to mind and confess our sins.

2

Jesus said:
Before you offer your gift,
go and be reconciled.
As brothers and sisters in God's family,
we come together to ask our Father for forgiveness.

3

Ye that do truly and earnestly repent you of your sins,
and are in love and charity with your neighbours,
and intend to lead a new life,
following the commandments of God,
and walking from henceforth in his holy ways:
draw near with faith,
and take this holy sacrament to your comfort;
and make your humble confession to almighty God.

4

This invitation may be used after the Commandments,
the Comfortable Words or the Exhortation, or may be introduced
by a penitential sentence of Scripture

You then, who truly and earnestly repent of your sins,
and are in love and charity with your neighbours,
and intend to lead a new life,
following the commandments of God
and walking from henceforth in his holy ways:
draw near with faith,
and take this holy sacrament to your comfort;
and make your humble confession to almighty God.

The confession follows without further invitation.

Confessions

For other authorized confessions, see pages 123–134.

1

All **Father eternal, giver of light and grace,**
we have sinned against you and against our neighbour,
in what we have thought,
in what we have said and done,
through ignorance, through weakness,
through our own deliberate fault.
We have wounded your love,
and marred your image in us.
We are sorry and ashamed,
and repent of all our sins.
For the sake of your Son Jesus Christ,
who died for us,
forgive us all that is past;
and lead us out from darkness
to walk as children of light.
Amen.

2

All **Almighty God, our heavenly Father,**
we have sinned against you,
through our own fault,
in thought, and word, and deed,
and in what we have left undone.
We are heartily sorry,
and repent of all our sins.
For your Son our Lord Jesus Christ's sake,
forgive us all that is past;
and grant that we may serve you in newness of life
to the glory of your name.
Amen.

3

All　**Almighty God,**
Father of our Lord Jesus Christ,
maker of all things, judge of all men:
we acknowledge and bewail
　　our manifold sins and wickedness,
which we, from time to time,
　　most grievously have committed,
by thought, word and deed,
against thy divine majesty,
provoking most justly thy wrath and indignation against us.
We do earnestly repent,
and are heartily sorry for these our misdoings;
the remembrance of them is grievous unto us;
the burden of them is intolerable.
Have mercy upon us,
have mercy upon us, most merciful Father;
for thy Son our Lord Jesus Christ's sake,
forgive us all that is past;
and grant that we may ever hereafter
serve and please thee in newness of life,
to the honour and glory of thy name;
through Jesus Christ our Lord.
Amen.

4

Wash me thoroughly from my wickedness
and cleanse me from my sin.
Lord, have mercy.

All　**Lord, have mercy.**

Make me a clean heart, O God,
and renew a right spirit within me.
Christ, have mercy.

All　**Christ, have mercy.**

Cast me not away from your presence
and take not your holy spirit from me.
Lord, have mercy.

All　**Lord, have mercy.**

5

In the wilderness we find your grace;
you love us with an everlasting love.
Lord, have mercy.

All **Lord, have mercy.**

There is none but you to uphold our cause;
our sin cries out and our guilt is great.
Christ, have mercy.

All **Christ, have mercy.**

Heal us, O Lord, and we shall be healed;
restore us and we shall know your joy.
Lord, have mercy.

All **Lord, have mercy.**

6

Remember, Lord, your compassion and love,
for they are everlasting.
Lord, have mercy.

All **Lord, have mercy.**

Remember not the sins of my youth or my transgressions,
but think on me in your goodness, O Lord,
    according to your steadfast love.
Christ, have mercy.

All **Christ, have mercy.**

O keep my soul and deliver me;
let me not be put to shame, for I have put my trust in you.
Lord, have mercy.

All **Lord, have mercy.**

Absolutions

For other authorized absolutions, see pages 135–137.

1
Almighty God, our heavenly Father,
who of his great mercy
hath promised forgiveness of sins
to all them that with hearty repentance and true faith
    turn unto him:
have mercy upon *you*;
pardon and deliver *you* from all *your* sins;
confirm and strengthen *you* in all goodness;
and bring *you* to everlasting life;
through Jesus Christ our Lord.

All **Amen.**

2
May almighty God have mercy on *you*,
forgive *you your* sins,
and bring *you* to everlasting life.

All **Amen.**

¶ Gospel Acclamations for Ordinary Time

1

Alleluia, alleluia.
Speak, Lord, for your servant is listening.
You have the words of eternal life.   *1 Samuel 3.9; John 6.68*

All   **Alleluia.**

2

Alleluia, alleluia.
I am the light of the world, says the Lord.
Whoever follows me will never walk in darkness
but will have the light of life.   *cf John 8.12*

All   **Alleluia.**

3

Alleluia, alleluia.
My sheep hear my voice, says the Lord.
I know them, and they follow me.   *cf John 10.27*

All   **Alleluia.**

4

Alleluia, alleluia.
I am the way, the truth, and the life, says the Lord.
No one comes to the Father except through me.   *cf John 14.6*

All   **Alleluia.**

5

Alleluia, alleluia.
We do not live by bread alone,
but by every word that comes from the mouth of God.

All   **Alleluia.**   *cf Matthew 4.4*

6

Alleluia, alleluia.
Welcome with meekness the implanted word
that has the power to save your souls.   *James 1.21*

All   **Alleluia.**

7

Alleluia, alleluia.
The word of the Lord endures for ever.
The word of the Lord is the good news announced to you.

All   **Alleluia.**   *cf 1 Peter 1.25*

¶ Forms of Intercession

I

This form may be used either with the insertion of specific subjects between the paragraphs or as a continuous whole, with or without brief biddings addressed to the people before the prayer begins.

Not all paragraphs need to be used on every occasion.

Individual names may be added at the places indicated.

The responses indicated in the service order may be used at appropriate points in the text.

At the end of this form of intercession, silence may be kept and a Collect or other ending may be said (see page 288).

In the power of the Spirit and in union with Christ,
let us pray to the Father.

Almighty God, our heavenly Father,
you promised through your Son Jesus Christ
to hear us when we pray in faith.

Strengthen *N* our bishop and all your Church in the service of Christ,
that those who confess your name may be united in your truth,
live together in your love, and reveal your glory in the world.

Bless and guide *Elizabeth our Queen*; give wisdom to all in authority;
and direct this and every nation in the ways of justice and of peace;
that we may honour one another, and seek the common good.

Give grace to us, our families and friends, and to all our neighbours,
that we may serve Christ in one another, and love as he loves us.

Comfort and heal all those who suffer in body, mind, or spirit …;
give them courage and hope in their troubles;
and bring them the joy of your salvation.

Hear us as we remember those who have died in the faith of Christ …;
according to your promises,
grant us with them a share in your eternal kingdom.

Rejoicing in the fellowship of [*N and of*] all your saints,
we commend ourselves and the whole creation to your unfailing love.

Silence may be kept and a Collect or other ending may be said.

2

This form may be used either with the insertion of specific subjects at the points indicated or as a continuous whole, with or without brief biddings addressed to the people before the prayer begins.

The responses indicated in the service order may be used at appropriate points in the text.

In the power of the Spirit and in union with Christ,
let us pray to the Father.

O God, the creator and preserver of all,
we pray for people in every kind of need;
make your ways known on earth,
your saving health among all nations ...

We pray for the good estate of the catholic Church;
guide and govern us by your good Spirit,
that all who profess and call themselves Christians
may be led into the way of truth,
and hold the faith in unity of spirit,
in the bond of peace and in righteousness of life ...

We commend to your fatherly goodness
all those who are any ways afflicted or distressed,
in mind, body or estate;
comfort and relieve them in their need,
give them patience in their sufferings,
and bring good out of all their afflictions ...

We remember those who have gone before us
in the peace of Christ,
and we give you praise for all your faithful ones,
with whom we rejoice in the communion of saints ...

All this we ask for Jesus Christ's sake.

All **Amen.**

3

*This form is used as a continuous whole without interpolation
except, if desired, the inclusion of responses printed in the service order.
However, biddings may be addressed to the people before the prayer
begins. Not all paragraphs need be used on every occasion.*

In the power of the Spirit and in union with Christ, let us pray to
the Father.

Almighty and ever-living God, who by thy holy apostle hast taught
us to make prayers and supplications, and to give thanks, for all
men: we humbly beseech thee most mercifully to receive these our
prayers, which we offer unto thy divine majesty; beseeching thee
to inspire continually the universal Church with the spirit of truth,
unity and concord; and grant that all they that do confess thy holy
name may agree in the truth of thy holy word, and live in unity and
godly love.

We beseech thee also to lead all nations in the way of righteousness
and peace; and so to direct all kings and rulers, that under them
thy people may be godly and quietly governed. And grant unto thy
servant *Elizabeth our Queen*, and to all that are put in authority
under her, that they may truly and impartially administer justice,
to the punishment of wickedness and vice, and to the maintenance
of thy true religion and virtue.

Give grace, O heavenly Father, to all bishops, priests and deacons,
especially to thy servant *N* our bishop, that they may both by their
life and doctrine set forth thy true and lively word, and rightly and
duly administer thy holy sacraments.

Guide and prosper, we pray thee, those who are labouring for the
spread of thy gospel among the nations, and enlighten with thy Spirit
all places of education and learning; that the whole world may be
filled with the knowledge of thy truth.

And to all thy people give thy heavenly grace; and specially to this
congregation here present, that, with meek heart and due
reverence, they may hear and receive thy holy word, truly serving
thee in holiness and righteousness all the days of their life.

And we most humbly beseech thee of thy goodness, O Lord,
to comfort and succour all them who in this transitory life are
in trouble, sorrow, need, sickness, or any other adversity.

And we commend to thy gracious keeping, O Lord, all thy servants departed this life in thy faith and fear, beseeching thee, according to thy promises, to grant them refreshment, light and peace.

And here we give thee most high praise and hearty thanks for all thy saints, who have been the chosen vessels of thy grace, and lights of the world in their several generations; and we pray that, rejoicing in their fellowship and following their good examples, we may be partakers with them of thy heavenly kingdom.

Grant this, O Father, for Jesus Christ's sake, our only mediator and advocate.

All **Amen.**

4

At the end of this form of intercession, silence may be kept and a Collect or other ending may be said (see page 288).

In the power of the Spirit and in union with Christ,
let us pray to the Father.

Hear our prayers, O Lord our God.

All **Hear us, good Lord.**

Govern and direct your holy Church; fill it with love and truth;
and grant it that unity which is your will.

All **Hear us, good Lord.**

Give us boldness to preach the gospel in all the world,
and to make disciples of all the nations.

All **Hear us, good Lord.**

Enlighten *N* our bishop and all your ministers with knowledge
and understanding, that by their teaching and their lives
they may proclaim your word.

All **Hear us, good Lord.**

Give your people grace to hear and receive your word,
and to bring forth the fruit of the Spirit.

All **Hear us, good Lord.**

Bring into the way of truth all who have erred and are deceived.

All **Hear us, good Lord.**

Strengthen those who stand, comfort and help the faint-hearted;
raise up the fallen; and finally beat down Satan under our feet.

All **Hear us, good Lord.**

Guide the leaders of the nations into the ways of peace and justice.

All **Hear us, good Lord.**

Guard and strengthen your servant *Elizabeth our Queen,*
that she may put her trust in you, and seek your honour and glory.

All **Hear us, good Lord.**

Endue the High Court of Parliament and all the ministers of
the Crown with wisdom and understanding.

All **Hear us, good Lord.**

Bless those who administer the law, that they may uphold
justice, honesty and truth.

All **Hear us, good Lord.**

Give us the will to use the fruits of the earth to your glory,
and for the good of all creation.

All **Hear us, good Lord.**

Bless and keep all your people.

All **Hear us, good Lord.**

Help and comfort the lonely, the bereaved and the oppressed.

All **Lord, have mercy.**

Keep in safety those who travel, and all who are in danger.

All **Lord, have mercy.**

Heal the sick in body and mind, and provide for the homeless,
the hungry, and the destitute.

All **Lord, have mercy.**

Show your pity on prisoners and refugees, and all who are in trouble.

All **Lord, have mercy.**

Forgive our enemies, persecutors and slanderers, and turn
their hearts.

All **Lord, have mercy.**

Hear us as we remember those who have died in the peace
of Christ, both those who have confessed the faith and those
whose faith is known to you alone, and grant us with them
a share in your eternal kingdom.

All **Lord, have mercy.**

Silence may be kept and a Collect or other ending may be said.

5

At the end of this form of intercession, silence may be kept and a Collect or other ending may be said (see page 288).

In the power of the Spirit and in union with Christ,
let us pray to the Father.

For the peace of the whole world,
for the welfare of the Holy Church of God,
and for the unity of all,
let us pray to the Lord.

All **Lord, have mercy.**

For *N* our bishop,
for the leaders of our sister Churches,
and for all clergy and people,
let us pray to the Lord.

All **Lord, have mercy.**

For *Elizabeth our Queen*,
for the leaders of the nations,
and for all in authority,
let us pray to the Lord.

All **Lord, have mercy.**

For this community,
for every city, town and village,
and for all the people who live within them,
let us pray to the Lord.

All **Lord, have mercy.**

For good weather,
and for abundant harvests for all to share,
let us pray to the Lord.

All **Lord, have mercy.**

For those who travel by land, air, or water,
for the sick and the suffering,
[*for* ... ,]
for prisoners and captives,
and for their safety, health and salvation,
let us pray to the Lord.

All **Lord, have mercy.**

For our deliverance from all affliction, strife and need,
and for the absolution of our sins and offences,
let us pray to the Lord.

All **Lord, have mercy.**

Remembering [... *and*]
all who have gone before us in faith,
and in communion with [... *and*] all the saints,
we commit ourselves, one another,
and our whole life to Christ our God;

All **to you, O Lord.**

Silence may be kept and a Collect or other ending may be said.

¶ *Collects and Other Endings for Intercession*

For use by the president or those leading intercessions.

1

Heavenly Father,
you have promised through your Son Jesus Christ,
that when we meet in his name,
and pray according to his mind,
he will be among us and hear our prayer:
in your love and mercy fulfil our desires,
and give us your greatest gift,
which is to know you, the only true God,
and your Son Jesus Christ our Lord.

All **Amen.**

2

Be with us, Lord, in all our prayers,
and direct our way toward the attainment of salvation,
that among the changes and chances of this mortal life,
we may always be defended by your gracious help;
through Jesus Christ our Lord.

All **Amen.**

3

Almighty God, the fountain of all wisdom,
you know our needs before we ask,
and our ignorance in asking:
have compassion on our weakness,
and give us those things
which for our unworthiness we dare not,
and for our blindness we cannot ask,
for the sake of your Son Jesus Christ our Lord.

All **Amen.**

4

Almighty God,
you have promised to hear the prayers
of those who ask in your Son's name;
we pray that what we have asked faithfully
we may obtain effectually;
through Jesus Christ our Lord.

All **Amen.**

5

Almighty God,
by your Holy Spirit you have made us one
with your saints in heaven and on earth:
grant that in our earthly pilgrimage
we may ever be supported by this fellowship of love and prayer,
and know ourselves surrounded by their witness
    to your power and mercy;
through Jesus Christ our Lord.

All   **Amen.**

6

Bring us all to your heavenly city,
to the joyful gathering of thousands of angels,
to the assembly of your firstborn,
to the spirits of the saints made perfect,
to Jesus the mediator of the new covenant
and to the sprinkled blood that promises peace.
Merciful Father

All   **accept these prayers**
for the sake of your Son,
our Saviour Jesus Christ.
Amen.

7

Hasten, Lord, the day when people will come
from east and west,
from north and south,
and sit at table in your kingdom
and we shall see your Son in his glory.
Merciful Father ...

8

Almighty God,
who hast given us grace at this time with one accord
to make our common supplications unto thee;
and dost promise
that when two or three are gathered together in thy name
thou wilt grant their requests:
fulfil now, O Lord, the desires and petitions of thy servants,
as may be most expedient for them;
granting us in this world knowledge of thy truth,
and in the world to come life everlasting.

All   **Amen.**

¶ Introductions to the Peace

1

Christ is our peace.
He has reconciled us to God
in one body by the cross.
We meet in his name and share his peace.

2

We are the body of Christ.
In the one Spirit we were all baptized into one body.
Let us then pursue all that makes for peace
and builds up our common life.

3

May the God of peace make you perfect and holy,
that you may be kept safe and blameless
in spirit, soul and body,
for the coming of our Lord Jesus Christ.

4

Blessed are the peacemakers:
they shall be called children of God.
We meet in the name of Christ and share his peace.

5

God is love
and those who live in love live in God
and God lives in them.

6

'Where two or three are gathered together in my name,'
says the Lord, 'there am I in the midst of them.'

7

We are all one in Christ Jesus.
We belong to him through faith,
heirs of the promise of the Spirit of peace.

The provision made for seasons and Principal Holy Days
(see pages 300–329) may be used at other times when appropriate.

¶ Prayers at the Preparation of the Table

1

Yours, Lord, is the greatness, the power,
the glory, the splendour, and the majesty;
for everything in heaven and on earth is yours.

All **All things come from you,
and of your own do we give you.**

2

Generous God,
creator, redeemer, sustainer,
at your table we present this money,
symbol of the work you have given us to do;
use it, use us,
in the service of your world
to the glory of your name.

All **Amen.**

3

God of life, saviour of the poor,
receive with this money
gratitude for your goodness,
penitence for our pride
and dedication to your service
in Jesus Christ our Lord.

All **Amen.**

4

Blessed are you, Lord God of all creation:
through your goodness we have this bread to set before you,
which earth has given and human hands have made.
It will become for us the bread of life.

All **Blessed be God for ever.**

Blessed are you, Lord God of all creation:
through your goodness we have this wine to set before you,
fruit of the vine and work of human hands.
It will become for us the cup of salvation.

All **Blessed be God for ever.**

5

Be present, be present,
Lord Jesus Christ,
our risen high priest;
make yourself known in the breaking of bread.

All **Amen.**

6

As the grain once scattered in the fields
and the grapes once dispersed on the hillside
are now reunited on this table in bread and wine,
so, Lord, may your whole Church soon be gathered together
from the corners of the earth
into your kingdom.

All **Amen.**

7

Wise and gracious God,
you spread a table before us;
nourish your people with the word of life
and the bread of heaven.

All **Amen.**

8

*In this prayer, the texts for single voice need not be spoken by
the president. It will sometimes be appropriate to ask children to
speak them.*

With this bread that we bring

All **we shall remember Jesus.**

With this wine that we bring

All **we shall remember Jesus.**

Bread for his body,
wine for his blood,
gifts from God to his table we bring.

All **We shall remember Jesus.**

9

Blessed be God,
by whose grace creation is renewed,
by whose love heaven is opened,
by whose mercy we offer our sacrifice of praise.

All   **Blessed be God for ever.**

10

Blessed be God,
who feeds the hungry,
who raises the poor,
who fills our praise.

All   **Blessed be God for ever.**

11

Look upon us in mercy not in judgement;
draw us from hatred to love;
make the frailty of our praise
a dwelling place for your glory.

All   **Amen.**

12

Pour upon the poverty of our love,
and the weakness of our praise,
the transforming fire of your presence.

All   **Amen.**

¶ *Prefaces for the Sundays before Lent and after Trinity*

Short Prefaces
And now we give you thanks
because you are the source of light and life;
you made us in your image
and called us to new life in him.

(or)

And now we give you thanks
because on the first day of the week
he overcame death and the grave
and opened to us the way of everlasting life.

(or)

And now we give you thanks
because by water and the Holy Spirit
you have made us in him a new people to show forth your glory.

Extended Preface
It is truly right and just, our duty and our salvation,
always and everywhere to give you thanks,
holy Father, almighty and eternal God.
From sunrise to sunset this day is holy,
for Christ has risen from the tomb
and scattered the darkness of death
with light that will not fade.
This day the risen Lord walks with your gathered people,
unfolds for us your word,
and makes himself known in the breaking of the bread.
And though the night will overtake this day
you summon us to live in endless light,
the never-ceasing sabbath of the Lord.
And so, with choirs of angels
and with all the heavenly host,
we proclaim your glory
and join their unending song of praise:

¶ Words at the Giving of Communion

1

The body of our Lord Jesus Christ,
which was given for you,
preserve your body and soul unto everlasting life.
Take and eat this in remembrance that Christ died for you,
and feed on him in your heart by faith with thanksgiving.

The blood of our Lord Jesus Christ,
which was shed for you,
preserve your body and soul unto everlasting life.
Drink this in remembrance that Christ's blood was shed for you,
and be thankful.

2

The body of Christ.
The blood of Christ.

3

The body of Christ keep you in eternal life.
The blood of Christ keep you in eternal life.

4

The body of Christ, broken for you.
The blood of Christ, shed for you.

5

The bread of heaven in Christ Jesus.
The cup of life in Christ Jesus.

¶ *Supplementary Consecration*

If either or both of the consecrated elements are likely to prove insufficient, the president returns to the holy table and adds more, saying these words

Father, having given thanks over the bread and the cup
according to the institution of your Son Jesus Christ,
who said,
'Take, eat; this is my body'
[*and/or* 'Drink this; this is my blood'],
we pray that by the power of your Holy Spirit
this *bread/wine* also
may be to us his *body/blood,*
to be received in remembrance of him.

or (traditional language)

Father, having given thanks over the bread and the cup
according to the institution of thy Son Jesus Christ,
who said,
'Take, eat; this is my body'
[*and/or* 'Drink ye all of this; this is my blood'],
we pray that by the power of thy Holy Spirit
this *bread/wine* also
may be unto us his *body/blood,*
to be received in remembrance of him.

¶ *Prayers after Communion*

1

All **We thank you, Lord,**
that you have fed us in this sacrament,
united us with Christ,
and given us a foretaste of the heavenly banquet
prepared for all peoples.
Amen.

2

All **Faithful God,**
in baptism you have adopted us as your children,
made us members of the body of Christ
and chosen us as inheritors of your kingdom:
we thank you that in this Eucharist
you renew your promises within us,
empower us by your Spirit to witness and to serve,
and send us out as disciples of your Son,
Jesus Christ our Lord.
Amen.

3

All **You have opened to us the Scriptures, O Christ,**
and you have made yourself known
in the breaking of the bread.
Abide with us, we pray,
that, blessed by your royal presence,
we may walk with you
all the days of our life,
and at its end behold you
in the glory of the eternal Trinity,
one God for ever and ever.
Amen.

4

Almighty and ever-living God,
we thank you that you graciously feed us,
who have duly received these holy mysteries,
with the spiritual food of the body and blood
    of our Saviour Jesus Christ.
By this you assure us of your favour and goodness towards us:
we are incorporated into the mystical body of your Son,
    the blessed company of all faithful people;
we are heirs, through hope, of your everlasting kingdom,
by the merits of Christ's precious death and passion.
Assist us with your grace, heavenly Father,
that we may continue in that holy fellowship,
and walk in goodness the way you have prepared for us;
through Jesus Christ our Lord,
to whom, with you and the Holy Spirit,
be all honour and glory, now and for ever.

All   **Amen.**

¶ Blessings

1

God the Father,
by whose glory Christ was raised from the dead,
strengthen you to walk with him in his risen life;
and the blessing …

2

Christ the good shepherd,
who laid down his life for the sheep,
draw you and all who hear his voice,
to be one flock within one fold;
and the blessing …

3

The God of all grace,
who called you to his eternal glory in Christ Jesus,
establish, strengthen and settle you in the faith;
and the blessing …

4

Christ, who has nourished us with himself the living bread,
make you one in praise and love,
and raise you up at the last day;
and the blessing …

5

May the Father from whom every family
in earth and heaven receives its name
strengthen you with his Spirit in your inner being,
so that Christ may dwell in your hearts by faith;
and the blessing …

6

The God of hope fill you with all joy and peace in believing;
and the blessing …

7

May God, who in Christ gives us a spring of water welling up to
    eternal life,
perfect in you the image of his glory; and the blessing …

The provision made for seasons and Principal Holy Days
(see pages 300–329) may be used at other times when appropriate.

Seasonal Provisions

From the First Sunday of Advent until Christmas Eve

Invitation to Confession
When the Lord comes,
he will bring to light the things now hidden in darkness,
and will disclose the purposes of the heart.
Therefore in the light of Christ let us confess our sins.

1 Corinthians 4.5

Gospel Acclamation
Alleluia, alleluia.
Prepare the way of the Lord, make his paths straight,
and all flesh shall see the salvation of God.   *cf Isaiah 40.3-5*

All **Alleluia.**

Introduction to the Peace
In the tender mercy of our God,
the dayspring from on high shall break upon us,
to give light to those who dwell in darkness
        and in the shadow of death
and to guide our feet into the way of peace.   *Luke 1.78,79*

Eucharistic Prefaces

Short Preface (contemporary language)
And now we give you thanks
because you sent him to redeem us from sin and death
        and to make us inheritors of everlasting life;
that when he shall come again in power and great triumph
        to judge the world,
we may with joy behold his appearing,
and in confidence may stand before him.

Short Preface (traditional language)
And now we give thee thanks
because thou didst send him to redeem us from sin and death
        and to make us inheritors of everlasting life;

that when he shall come again in power and great triumph
    to judge the world,
we may with joy behold his appearing,
    and in confidence may stand before him.

Extended Preface for use with Eucharistic Prayers A, B and E
(from the First Sunday of Advent until 16 December)
It is indeed right and good to give you thanks and praise,
almighty God and everlasting Father,
through Jesus Christ your Son.
For when he humbled himself to come among us in human flesh,
he fulfilled the plan you formed before the foundation of the world
to open for us the way of salvation.
Confident that your promise will be fulfilled,
we now watch for the day
when Christ our Lord will come again in glory.
And so we join our voices with angels and archangels
and with all the company of heaven
to proclaim your glory,
for ever praising you and *saying:*

(from 17 December until Christmas Eve)
It is indeed right and good to give you thanks and praise,
almighty God and everlasting Father,
through Jesus Christ your Son.
He is the one foretold by all the prophets,
whom the Virgin Mother bore with love beyond all telling.
John the Baptist was his herald
and made him known when at last he came.
In his love Christ fills us with joy
as we prepare to celebrate his birth,
so that when he comes again he may find us watching in prayer,
our hearts filled with wonder and praise.
And so, with angels and archangels,
and with all the company of heaven,
we proclaim your glory,
and join in their unending hymn of praise:

Blessing
Christ the Sun of Righteousness shine upon you,
scatter the darkness from before your path,
and make you ready to meet him when he comes in glory;
and the blessing …

From Christmas Day
until the Eve of the Epiphany

Invitation to Confession
Hear the words of the angel to Joseph:
'You shall call his name Jesus,
for he will save his people from their sins.'
Therefore let us seek the forgiveness of God
through Jesus the Saviour of the world.   *cf Matthew 1.21*

Gospel Acclamation
Alleluia, alleluia.
The Word became flesh and dwelt among us,
and we have seen his glory.   *John 1.14*

All **Alleluia.**

Introduction to the Peace
Unto us a child is born, unto us a son is given,
and his name shall be called the Prince of Peace.   *Isaiah 9.6*

Eucharistic Prefaces

Short Preface (contemporary language)
And now we give you thanks
because, by the power of the Holy Spirit,
he took our nature upon him
and was born of the Virgin Mary his mother,
that being himself without sin,
he might make us clean from all sin.

Short Preface (traditional language)
And now we give thee thanks
because, by the power of the Holy Spirit,
he took our nature upon him
and was born of the Virgin Mary his mother,
that being himself without sin,
he might make us clean from all sin.

Extended Preface for use with Eucharistic Prayers A, B and E
All glory and honour be yours always and everywhere,
mighty creator, ever-living God.
We give you thanks and praise for your Son,
our Saviour Jesus Christ,
who for love of our fallen race humbled himself,
was born of the Virgin Mary by the power of your Spirit,
and lived as one of us.
In this mystery of the Word made flesh
you have caused his light to shine in our hearts,
to give knowledge of your glory in the face of Jesus Christ.
In him we see our God made visible
and so are caught up in the love of the God we cannot see.
Therefore with all the angels of heaven
we lift our voices to proclaim the glory of your name
and sing our joyful hymn of praise:

Blessing
Christ, who by his incarnation gathered into one
    things earthly and heavenly,
fill you with peace and goodwill
and make you partakers of the divine nature;
and the blessing ...

From the Epiphany
until the Eve of the Presentation

Invitation to Confession
The grace of God has dawned upon the world
    through our Saviour Jesus Christ,
      who sacrificed himself for us to purify a people as his own.
Let us confess our sins.   *cf Titus 2.11-14*

Gospel Acclamation
Alleluia, alleluia.
Christ was revealed in flesh, proclaimed among the nations
and believed in throughout the world.   *cf 1 Timothy 3.16*

All   **Alleluia.**

Introduction to the Peace
Our Saviour Christ is the Prince of Peace.
Of the increase of his government and of peace
there shall be no end.   *cf Isaiah 9.6,7*

Eucharistic Prefaces

Short Preface (contemporary language)
And now we give you thanks
because, in the incarnation of the Word,
a new light has dawned upon the world,
that all the nations may be brought out of darkness
to see the radiance of your glory.

Short Preface (traditional language)
And now we give thee thanks
because, in the incarnation of the Word,
a new light has dawned upon the world,
that all the nations may be brought out of darkness
to see the radiance of thy glory.

Extended Preface for use with Eucharistic Prayers A, B and E
All honour and praise be yours always and everywhere,
mighty creator, ever-living God,
through Jesus Christ your only Son our Lord:
for at this time we celebrate your glory
made present in our midst.
In the coming of the Magi
the King of all the world was revealed to the nations.
In the waters of baptism
Jesus was revealed as the Christ,
the Saviour sent to redeem us.
In the water made wine
the new creation was revealed at the wedding feast.
Poverty was turned to riches, sorrow into joy.
Therefore with all the angels of heaven
we lift our voices to proclaim the glory of your name
and sing our joyful hymn of praise:

Blessing
Christ the Son of God perfect in you the image of his glory
and gladden your hearts with the good news of his kingdom;
and the blessing ...

The Presentation of Christ in the Temple

Invitation to Confession
Hear the words of our Saviour Jesus Christ:
'I am the light of the world.
Whoever follows me shall never walk in darkness
but shall have the light of life.'
Let us therefore bring our sins into his light
and confess them in penitence and faith.   *cf John 8.12*

Gospel Acclamation
Alleluia, alleluia.
This child is the light to enlighten the nations,
and the glory of your people Israel.   *cf Luke 2.32*

All **Alleluia.**

Introduction to the Peace
In the tender mercy of our God
the dayspring from on high has broken upon us,
to give light to those who dwell in darkness
     and in the shadow of death
and to guide our feet into the way of peace.   *cf Luke 1.78,79*

Eucharistic Prefaces

Short Preface (contemporary language)
And now we give you thanks
because, by appearing in the temple,
he comes near to us in judgement;
the Word made flesh searches the hearts of all your people
and brings to light the brightness of your splendour.

Short Preface (traditional language)
And now we give thee thanks
because, by appearing in the temple,
he comes near to us in judgement;
the Word made flesh searches the hearts of all thy people
and brings to light the brightness of thy splendour.

Extended Preface for use with Eucharistic Prayers A, B and E
It is indeed right and good,
always and everywhere to give you thanks and praise
through Jesus Christ, who is one with you from all eternity.
For on this day he appeared in the temple
in substance of our flesh
to come near to us in judgement.
He searches the hearts of all your people
and brings to light the image of your splendour.
Your servant Simeon acclaimed him as the light to lighten the nations
while Anna spoke of him to all who looked for your redemption.
Destined for the falling and rising of many,
he was lifted high upon the cross
and a sword of sorrow pierced his mother's heart
when by his sacrifice he made our peace with you.
And now we rejoice and glorify your name
that we, too, have seen your salvation
and join with angels and archangels
in their unending hymn of praise:

Blessing
Christ the Son of God, born of Mary,
fill you with his grace to trust his promises and obey his will;
and the blessing ...

From Ash Wednesday
until the Saturday after
the Fourth Sunday of Lent

Invitation to Confession
The sacrifice of God is a broken spirit;
a broken and contrite heart God will not despise.
Let us come to the Lord, who is full of compassion,
and acknowledge our transgressions in penitence and faith.

cf Psalm 51.17

Gospel Acclamation
Praise to you, O Christ, King of eternal glory.
The Lord is a great God, O that today you would listen to his voice.
Harden not your hearts. *cf Psalm 95.3,7,8*

All **Praise to you, O Christ, King of eternal glory.**

Introduction to the Peace
Since we are justified by faith,
we have peace with God through our Lord Jesus Christ,
who has given us access to his grace. *Romans 5.1,2*

Eucharistic Prefaces

Short Preface (contemporary language)
And now we give you thanks
because you give us the spirit of discipline,
that we may triumph over evil and grow in grace,
as we prepare to celebrate the paschal mystery
    with mind and heart renewed.

Short Preface (traditional language)
And now we give thee thanks
because thou dost give us the spirit of discipline,
that we may triumph over evil and grow in grace,
as we prepare to celebrate the paschal mystery
    with mind and heart renewed.

Extended Preface for use with Eucharistic Prayers A, B and E
It is indeed right and good
to give you thanks and praise,
almighty God and everlasting Father,
through Jesus Christ your Son.
For in these forty days
you lead us into the desert of repentance
that through a pilgrimage of prayer and discipline
we may grow in grace
and learn to be your people once again.
Through fasting, prayer and acts of service
you bring us back to your generous heart.
Through study of your holy word
you open our eyes to your presence in the world
and free our hands to welcome others
into the radiant splendour of your love.
As we prepare to celebrate the Easter feast
with joyful hearts and minds
we bless you for your mercy
and join with saints and angels
for ever praising you and *saying*:

Blessing
Christ give you grace to grow in holiness,
to deny yourselves, take up your cross, and follow him;
and the blessing ...

The Annunciation of Our Lord

Invitation to Confession

The grace of God has dawned upon the world
    through our Saviour Jesus Christ,
    who sacrificed himself for us to purify a people as his own.
Let us confess our sins. *cf Titus 2.11-14*

Gospel Acclamation

Praise to you, O Christ, King of eternal glory.
The Word became flesh and lived among us,
and we have seen his glory. *John 1.14*

All   **Praise to you, O Christ, King of eternal glory.**

*(Note: If the Annunciation falls in Easter, use the text provided
for Christmas.)*

Introduction to the Peace

In the tender mercy of our God,
the dayspring from on high shall break upon us,
to give light to those who dwell in darkness
    and in the shadow of death
and to guide our feet into the way of peace. *Luke 1.78,79*
(In Easter, add Alleluia.*)*

Eucharistic Prefaces

Short Preface (contemporary language)

And now we give you thanks
because, by the power of the Holy Spirit,
he took our nature upon him
and was born of the Virgin Mary his mother,
that being himself without sin,
he might make us clean from all sin.

Short Preface (traditional language)

And now we give thee thanks
because, by the power of the Holy Spirit,
he took our nature upon him
and was born of the Virgin Mary his mother,
that being himself without sin,
he might make us clean from all sin.

Extended Preface for use with Eucharistic Prayers A, B and E
It is indeed right and good,
our duty and our salvation,
always and everywhere to give you thanks,
holy Father, almighty and eternal God,
through Jesus Christ your Son our Lord.
We give you thanks and praise
that the Virgin Mary heard with faith the message of the angel,
and by the power of your Holy Spirit
conceived and bore the Word made flesh.
From the warmth of her womb
to the stillness of the grave
he shared our life in human form.
In him new light has dawned upon the world
and you have become one with us
that we might become one with you
in your glorious kingdom.
Therefore earth unites with heaven
to sing a new song of praise;
we too join with angels and archangels
as they proclaim your glory without end:

Blessing
Christ the Son of God, born of Mary,
fill you with his grace to trust his promises and obey his will;
and the blessing ...

From the Fifth Sunday of Lent until the Wednesday of Holy Week

Invitation to Confession

God shows his love for us
    in that, while we were still sinners, Christ died for us.
Let us then show our love for him
by confessing our sins in penitence and faith.   *Romans 5.8*

Gospel Acclamation

Praise to you, O Christ, King of eternal glory.
Christ humbled himself and became obedient unto death,
even death on a cross.
Therefore God has highly exalted him
and given him the name that is above every name.   *Philippians 2.8,9*

All **Praise to you, O Christ, King of eternal glory.**

Introduction to the Peace

Once we were far off,
but now in union with Christ Jesus we have been brought near
    through the shedding of Christ's blood,
for he is our peace.   *Ephesians 2.13*

Eucharistic Prefaces

Short Preface (contemporary language)

And now we give you thanks
because, for our salvation,
he was obedient even to death on the cross.
The tree of shame was made the tree of glory;
and where life was lost, there life has been restored.

Short Preface (traditional language)

And now we give thee thanks
because, for our salvation,
he was obedient even to death on the cross.
The tree of shame was made the tree of glory;
and where life was lost, there life has been restored.

Extended Preface for use with Eucharistic Prayers A, B and E
It is indeed right and just,
our duty and our salvation,
always and everywhere to give you thanks,
holy Father, almighty and eternal God,
through Jesus Christ our Lord.
For as the time of his passion and resurrection draws near
the whole world is called to acknowledge his hidden majesty.
The power of the life-giving cross
reveals the judgement that has come upon the world
and the triumph of Christ crucified.
He is the victim who dies no more,
the Lamb once slain, who lives for ever,
our advocate in heaven to plead our cause,
exalting us there to join with angels and archangels,
for ever praising you and *saying*:

Blessing
Christ crucified draw you to himself,
to find in him a sure ground for faith,
a firm support for hope,
and the assurance of sins forgiven;
and the blessing ...

Maundy Thursday

Invitation to Confession
Our Lord Jesus Christ says:
'If you love me, keep my commandments.'
'Unless I wash you, you have no part in me.'
Let us confess to almighty God our sins against his love,
and ask him to cleanse us.   *cf John 14.15; 13.8*

Gospel Acclamation
Praise to you, O Christ, King of eternal glory.
I give you a new commandment, says the Lord:
Love one another as I have loved you.   *cf John 13.34*

All **Praise to you, O Christ, King of eternal glory.**

Introduction to the Peace
Jesus says: 'Peace I leave with you; my peace I give to you.
Do not let your hearts be troubled, neither let them be afraid.'
                                                  cf John 14.27

Eucharistic Prefaces

Short Preface (contemporary language)
And now we give you thanks
because, having loved his own who were in the world,
he loved them to the end;
and on the night before he suffered,
sitting at table with his disciples,
he instituted these holy mysteries,
that we, redeemed by his death
    and restored to life by his resurrection,
might be partakers of his divine nature.

Short Preface (traditional language)
And now we give thee thanks
because, having loved his own who were in the world,
he loved them to the end;
and on the night before he suffered,
sitting at table with his disciples,
he instituted these holy mysteries,
that we, redeemed by his death
    and restored to life by his resurrection,
might be partakers of his divine nature.

Extended Preface for use with Eucharistic Prayers A, B and E
It is indeed right to give you thanks,
Father most holy, through Jesus Christ our Lord.
For on this night he girded himself with a towel
and, taking the form of a servant,
washed the feet of his disciples.
He gave us a new commandment
that we should love one another as he has loved us.
Knowing that his hour had come,
in his great love he gave this supper to his disciples
to be a memorial of his passion,
that we might proclaim his death until he comes again,
and feast with him in his kingdom.
Therefore earth unites with heaven
to sing a new song of praise;
we too join with angels and archangels
as they proclaim your glory without end:

There is no blessing at the end of the Maundy Thursday liturgy.

From Easter Day
until the Eve of the Ascension

Invitation to Confession
Christ our passover lamb has been sacrificed for us.
Let us therefore rejoice by putting away all malice and evil
and confessing our sins with a sincere and true heart.

1 Corinthians 5.7,8

Gospel Acclamation
Alleluia, alleluia.
I am the first and the last, says the Lord, and the living one;
I was dead, and behold I am alive for evermore.

All **Alleluia.** *cf Revelation 1.17,18*

Introduction to the Peace
The risen Christ came and stood among his disciples
    and said, 'Peace be with you.'
Then were they glad when they saw the Lord. Alleluia.

John 20.19,20

Eucharistic Prefaces

Short Preface (contemporary language)
But chiefly are we bound to praise you
because you raised him gloriously from the dead.
For he is the true paschal lamb who was offered for us,
and has taken away the sin of the world.
By his death he has destroyed death,
and by his rising to life again he has restored to us everlasting life.

Short Preface (traditional language)
But chiefly are we bound to praise thee
because thou didst raise him gloriously from the dead.
For he is the true paschal lamb who was offered for us,
and has taken away the sin of the world.
By his death he has destroyed death,
and by his rising to life again he has restored to us everlasting life.

Extended Preface for use with Eucharistic Prayers A, B and E
It is indeed right, our duty and our joy,
always and everywhere to give you thanks,
almighty and eternal Father,
and in these days of Easter
to celebrate with joyful hearts
the memory of your wonderful works.
For by the mystery of his passion
Jesus Christ, your risen Son,
has conquered the powers of death and hell
and restored in men and women the image of your glory.
He has placed them once more in paradise
and opened to them the gate of life eternal.
And so, in the joy of this Passover,
earth and heaven resound with gladness,
while angels and archangels and the powers of all creation
sing for ever the hymn of your glory:

Blessing
The God of peace,
who brought again from the dead our Lord Jesus,
that great shepherd of the sheep,
through the blood of the eternal covenant,
make you perfect in every good work to do his will,
working in you that which is well-pleasing in his sight;
and the blessing ...

Ascension Day

Invitation to Confession
Seeing we have a great high priest who has passed into the heavens,
    Jesus the Son of God,
let us draw near with a true heart, in full assurance of faith,
and make our confession to our heavenly Father.

Hebrews 4.14; 10.22

Gospel Acclamation
Alleluia, alleluia.
Go and make disciples of all nations, says the Lord.
Remember, I am with you always, to the end of the age.

All **Alleluia.**   *cf Matthew 28.19,20*

Introduction to the Peace
Jesus says: 'Peace I leave with you; my peace I give to you.
If you love me, rejoice because I am going to the Father.' Alleluia.

John 14.27,28

Eucharistic Prefaces

Short Preface (contemporary language)
And now we give you thanks
because, after his most glorious resurrection,
he appeared to his disciples,
and in their sight ascended into heaven to prepare a place for us;
that where he is, thither we might also ascend,
and reign with him in glory.

Short Preface (traditional language)
And now we give thee thanks
because, after his most glorious resurrection,
he appeared to his disciples,
and in their sight ascended into heaven to prepare a place for us;
that where he is, thither we might also ascend,
and reign with him in glory.

Extended Preface for use with Eucharistic Prayers A, B and E
It is indeed right and good,
our duty and our joy,
always and everywhere to give you thanks,
holy Father, almighty and eternal God,
through Jesus Christ the King of glory.
Born of a woman,
he came to the rescue of our human race.
Dying for us,
he trampled death and conquered sin.
By the glory of his resurrection
he opened the way to life eternal
and by his ascension,
gave us the sure hope
that where he is we may also be.
Therefore the universe resounds with Easter joy
and with choirs of angels we sing for ever to your praise:

Blessing
Christ our ascended King pour upon you the abundance of his gifts
    and bring you to reign with him in glory;
and the blessing ...

From the day after Ascension Day
until the Day of Pentecost

Invitation to Confession
What God has prepared for those who love him,
he has revealed to us through the Spirit;
for the Spirit searches everything.
Therefore, let us in penitence open our hearts to the Lord,
who has prepared good things for those who love him.

1 Corinthians 2.9,10

Gospel Acclamation
Alleluia, alleluia.
Come, Holy Spirit, fill the hearts of your faithful people
and kindle in them the fire of your love.

All **Alleluia.**

Introduction to the Peace
God has made us one in Christ.
He has set his seal upon us and, as a pledge of what is to come,
has given the Spirit to dwell in our hearts. Alleluia.

cf 2 Corinthians 1.22

Eucharistic Prefaces

Short Preface (contemporary language)
And now we give you thanks
that, after he had ascended far above all heavens,
and was seated at the right hand of your majesty,
he sent forth upon the universal Church your holy and
    life-giving Spirit;
that through his glorious power the joy of the everlasting gospel
    might go forth into all the world.

Short Preface (traditional language)
And now we give thee thanks
that, after he had ascended far above all heavens,
and was seated at the right hand of thy majesty,
he sent forth upon the universal Church thy holy and
    life-giving Spirit;
that through his glorious power the joy of the everlasting gospel
    might go forth into all the world.

*Extended Preface for use with Eucharistic Prayers A, B and E on days
between Ascension Day and Pentecost*

It is indeed right, our duty and our joy,
always and everywhere to give you thanks,
holy Father, almighty and eternal God,
through Jesus Christ our Lord.
For he is our great high priest
who has entered once for all
into the heavenly sanctuary,
evermore to pour upon your Church
the grace and comfort of your Holy Spirit.
He is the one who has gone before us,
who calls us to be united in prayer
as were his disciples in the upper room
while they awaited his promised gift,
the life-giving Spirit of Pentecost.
Therefore all creation yearns with eager longing
as angels and archangels sing the endless hymn of praise:

(on the Day of Pentecost only)
It is indeed right, it is our duty and our joy,
always and everywhere to give you thanks,
holy Father, almighty and everlasting God,
through Jesus Christ, your only Son our Lord.
This day we give you thanks
because in fulfilment of your promise
you pour out your Spirit upon us,
filling us with your gifts, leading us into all truth,
and uniting peoples of many tongues in the confession of one faith.
Your Spirit gives us grace to call you Father,
to proclaim your gospel to all nations
and to serve you as a royal priesthood.
Therefore we join our voices with angels and archangels,
and with all those in whom the Spirit dwells,
to proclaim the glory of your name,
for ever praising you and *saying*:

Blessing
The Spirit of truth lead you into all truth,
give you grace to confess that Jesus Christ is Lord,
and strengthen you to proclaim the word and works of God;
and the blessing …

Trinity Sunday

Invitation to Confession
God the Father forgives us in Christ and heals us by the Holy Spirit.
Let us therefore put away all anger and bitterness,
    all slander and malice,
and confess our sins to God our redeemer.   *cf Ephesians 4.30,32*

Gospel Acclamation
Alleluia, alleluia.
Glory to the Father, and to the Son, and to the Holy Spirit,
one God, who was, and who is, and who is to come,
the Almighty.   *cf Revelation 1.8*

All   **Alleluia.**

Introduction to the Peace
Peace to you from God our heavenly Father.
Peace from his Son Jesus Christ who is our peace.
Peace from the Holy Spirit, the life-giver.
The peace of the triune God be always with you.

Eucharistic Prefaces

Short Preface (contemporary language)
And now we give you thanks
because you have revealed the glory of your eternal fellowship
    of love with your Son and with the Holy Spirit,
three persons equal in majesty, undivided in splendour,
yet one God,
ever to be worshipped and adored.

Short Preface (traditional language)
And now we give thee thanks
because thou hast revealed the glory of thine eternal fellowship
    of love with thy Son and with the Holy Spirit,
three persons equal in majesty, undivided in splendour,
yet one God,
ever to be worshipped and adored.

Extended Preface for use with Eucharistic Prayers A, B and E
It is indeed right, our duty and our joy,
always and everywhere to give you thanks,
holy Father, almighty and eternal God.
For with your only-begotten Son and the Holy Spirit
you are one God, one Lord.
All that you reveal of your glory,
the same we believe of the Son
and of the Holy Spirit, without any difference or inequality.
We, your holy Church, acclaim you,
Father of majesty unbounded,
your true and only Son, worthy of all worship,
and the Holy Spirit, advocate and guide.
Three Persons we adore,
one in being and equal in majesty.
And so with angels and archangels,
with cherubim and seraphim,
we sing for ever of your glory:

Blessing
God the Holy Trinity make you strong in faith and love,
defend you on every side, and guide you in truth and peace;
and the blessing ...

All Saints' Day

Invitation to Confession
Since we are surrounded by a great cloud of witnesses,
let us also lay aside every weight and the sin that clings so closely,
looking to Jesus in penitence and faith.   *Hebrews 12.1*

Gospel Acclamation
Alleluia, alleluia.
You are a chosen race, a royal priesthood,
a holy nation, God's own people,
called out of darkness into his marvellous light.   *1 Peter 2.9*

All **Alleluia.**

Introduction to the Peace
We are fellow-citizens with the saints and of the household of God,
through Christ our Lord, who came and preached peace
    to those who were far off and those who were near.
                         Ephesians 2.19,17

Eucharistic Prefaces

Short Preface (contemporary language)
And now we give you thanks
for the glorious pledge of the hope of our calling
    which you have given us in your saints;
that, following their example and strengthened by their fellowship,
we may run with perseverance the race that is set before us,
and with them receive the unfading crown of glory.

Short Preface (traditional language)
And now we give thee thanks
for the glorious pledge of the hope of our calling
    which thou hast given us in thy saints;
that, following their example and strengthened by their fellowship,
we may run with perseverance the race that is set before us,
and with them receive the unfading crown of glory.

Extended Preface for use with Eucharistic Prayers A, B and E
It is indeed right, our duty and our joy,
always and everywhere to give you thanks,
holy Father, almighty and eternal God,
through Jesus Christ our Lord.
And now we give you thanks, most gracious God,
surrounded by a great cloud of witnesses
and glorified in the assembly of your saints.
The glorious company of apostles praise you.
The noble fellowship of prophets praise you.
The white-robed army of martyrs praise you.
We, your holy Church, acclaim you.
In communion with angels and archangels,
and with all who served you on earth
and worship you now in heaven,
we raise our voice to proclaim your glory,
for ever praising you and *saying*:

Blessing
God, who has prepared for us a city with eternal foundations,
give you grace to share the inheritance of the saints in glory;
and the blessing ...

From the day after All Saints' Day
until the day before
the First Sunday of Advent

Invitation to Confession
Jesus says, 'Repent, for the kingdom of heaven is close at hand.'
So let us turn away from sin and turn to Christ,
confessing our sins in penitence and faith.   *cf Matthew 3.2*

Gospel Acclamation
Alleluia, alleluia.
Blessed is the king who comes in the name of the Lord.
Peace in heaven and glory in the highest heaven.   *Luke 19.38*

All   **Alleluia.**

Introduction to the Peace
To crown all things there must be love,
to bind all together and complete the whole.
Let the peace of Christ rule in our hearts.   *Colossians 3.14,15*

Eucharistic Prefaces

Short Preface (contemporary language)
And now we give you thanks
that he is the King of glory,
who overcomes the sting of death
and opens the kingdom of heaven to all believers.
He is seated at your right hand in glory
and we believe that he will come to be our judge.

Short Preface (traditional language)
And now we give thee thanks
that he is the King of glory,
who overcomes the sting of death
and opens the kingdom of heaven to all believers.
He is seated at thy right hand in glory
and we believe that he will come to be our judge.

Extended Preface for use with Eucharistic Prayers A, B and E
It is indeed right, our duty and our joy
that we should always sing of your glory,
holy Father, almighty and eternal God,
through Jesus Christ your Son our Lord.
For you are the hope of the nations,
the builder of the city that is to come.
Your love made visible in Jesus Christ
brings home the lost,
restores the sinner
and gives dignity to the despised.
In his face your light shines out,
flooding lives with goodness and truth,
gathering into one in your kingdom
a divided and broken humanity.
Therefore with all who can give voice in your creation
we glorify your name,
for ever praising you and *saying*:

(on the Feast of Christ the King only)
It is indeed right, our duty and our joy,
always and everywhere to give you thanks,
holy Father, almighty and eternal God.
For with the oil of gladness
you have anointed Christ the Lord, your only Son,
to be our great high priest and king of all creation.
As priest, he offered himself once for all upon the altar of the cross
and redeemed the human race by this perfect sacrifice of peace.
As king he claims dominion over all your creatures,
that he may bring before your infinite majesty
a kingdom of truth and life,
a kingdom of holiness and grace,
a kingdom of justice, love and peace.
And so with angels and archangels
and all the heavenly host,
we proclaim your glory
and join in their unending hymn of praise:

Blessing
Christ our King make you faithful and strong to do his will,
that you may reign with him in glory;
and the blessing …

On Saints' Days

Invitation to Confession
The saints were faithful unto death
and now dwell in the heavenly kingdom for ever.
As we celebrate their joy,
let us bring to the Lord our sins and weaknesses,
and ask for his mercy.

Gospel Acclamation
Alleluia, alleluia.
I have called you friends, says the Lord,
for all that I have heard from my Father
I have made known to you.   *cf John 15.15*

All **Alleluia.**

or, in Lent
Praise to you, O Christ, King of eternal glory.
I have called you friends, says the Lord,
for all that I have heard from my Father
I have made known to you.   *cf John 15.15*

All **Praise to you, O Christ, King of eternal glory.**

Introduction to the Peace
May the God of peace sanctify you:
may he so strengthen your hearts in holiness
that you may be blameless before him
at the coming of our Lord Jesus with his saints.
                                   1 Thessalonians 5.23; 3.13

Eucharistic Prefaces

Short Preface (contemporary language)
And now we give you thanks
that your glory is revealed in [*N and*] all the saints.
In their lives you have given us an example of faithfulness to Christ.
In their holiness we find encouragement and hope.
In our communion with them we share the unity of your kingdom.

Short Preface (traditional language)
And now we give thee thanks
that thy glory is revealed in [*N and*] all the saints.
In their lives thou hast given us an example of faithfulness to Christ.
In their holiness we find encouragement and hope.
In our communion with them we share the unity of thy kingdom.

Extended Preface for use with Eucharistic Prayers A, B and E
It is indeed right, our duty and our joy,
always and everywhere to give you thanks,
holy Father, almighty and eternal God,
through Jesus Christ your Son our Lord.
We rejoice in the glorious splendour of your majesty
for you have given us a share with *N*
in the inheritance of the saints in light.
In the darkness of this passing age
they proclaim the glory of your kingdom.
Chosen as lights in the world,
they surround our steps as we journey on
towards the city of eternal light
where they sing the everlasting song of triumph.
In communion with angels and archangels
and all who have served you on earth
and worship you now in heaven,
we raise our voices to proclaim your glory,
for ever praising you and *saying*:

Blessing
God give you grace to follow his saints
in faith and hope and love;
and the blessing ...

Notes

Notes 1 to 23 apply to Order One. They should be followed in Order Two insofar as they are applicable. Notes 24 to 29 apply to Order Two only.

The use of a lighter typeface for some texts reflects a decision of the General Synod to give more weight to one choice within a range of options.

1 **Posture**
   Local custom may be followed and developed in relation to posture. The people should stand for the reading of the Gospel, for the Creed, for the Peace and for the Dismissal. Any changes in posture during the Eucharistic Prayer should not detract from the essential unity of that prayer. It is appropriate that, on occasions, the congregation should kneel for prayers of penitence.

2 **Traditional Texts**
   In addition to the places where they are printed in the service, traditional versions of texts may be used.

3 **Hymns, Psalms, Canticles, the Collection and Presentation of the Offerings of the People, and the Preparation of the Table**
   Points are indicated for these, but they may occur elsewhere.

4 **Sentences**
   Sentences of Scripture appropriate to the season and the place in the service may be used as part of the president's greeting, in the Invitation to Confession, at the Peace, before the gifts of the people are collected and after the distribution of communion (from Easter Day to Pentecost 'Alleluia' is appropriately added to such sentences).

5 **Acclamations**
   Acclamations, which may include congregational response (such as 'The Lord is here: his Spirit is with us' and 'Christ is risen: he is risen indeed') may be used at appropriate points in the service (with 'Alleluia' except in Lent). Seasonal acclamations for use before the Gospel are provided on pages 280 and 300–329.

6   Entry
At the entry of the ministers, a Bible or Book of the Gospels may be carried into the assembly.

7   Greetings
In addition to the points where greetings are provided, at other suitable points (e.g. before the Gospel and before the blessing or dismissal), the greeting 'The Lord be with you' with its response 'and also with you' or 'and with thy spirit' may be used.

8   Silence
Silence is particularly appropriate within the Prayers of Penitence and of Intercession, before the Collect, in response to the reading of the Scriptures, after the Eucharistic Prayer and after the distribution.

9   Notices
Banns of marriage and other notices may be published before the Gathering (if possible by a minister other than the president), before the Prayers of Intercession or before the Dismissal.

10   The Prayers of Penitence
This section may be transposed to a later point in the service as a response to the Liturgy of the Word. In the special seasonal rites for certain days it is particularly appropriate at the later point.

On certain occasions, for a special service, this section may precede the opening hymn and greeting. A Form of Preparation is provided on page 161.

The Invitation to Confession may take the form of the Summary of the Law, the Commandments, the Beatitudes, the Comfortable Words or the Exhortation.

When the Kyrie eleison is used as a confession, short penitential sentences are inserted between the petitions, suitable for seasons or themes. This form of confession should not be the norm on Sundays.

Authorized alternative forms of confession and absolution may be used in place of those in the main text.

11   The Gloria in Excelsis
This canticle may be omitted during Advent and Lent, and on weekdays which are not Principal Holy Days or Festivals.
See also Note 3.

12 The Readings

The readings at Holy Communion are governed by authorized lectionary provision and are not a matter for local decision except where that provision permits.

Whenever possible, all three readings are used at Holy Communion on Sundays. When only two are read, the minister should ensure that, in any year, a balance is maintained between readings from the Old and New Testaments in the choice of the first reading. The psalm provided relates to the first reading in the lectionary. Where possible it should be used after that reading.

When announcing the Gospel, if it is desired to give book, chapter and verse or page number, the reader may do this informally before saying 'Hear the Gospel of our Lord Jesus Christ according to *N.*'

13 The Sermon

The sermon is an integral part of the Liturgy of the Word. A sermon should normally be preached at all celebrations on Sundays and Principal Holy Days.

The sermon may on occasion include less formal exposition of Scripture, the use of drama, interviews, discussion and audio-visual aids.

14 The Creed

The Creed may be preceded by the president saying 'Let us declare our faith in God, Father, Son and Holy Spirit'.

15 The Prayers of Intercession

Intercession frequently arises out of thanksgiving; nevertheless these prayers are primarily prayers of intercession. They are normally broadly based, expressing a concern for the whole of God's world and the ministry of the whole Church.

Several forms of intercession are provided; other suitable forms may be used. They need not always conform to the sequence indicated

Prayer for the nation is properly focused in prayer for the sovereign by name, and prayer for the Church in prayer for the bishop of the diocese by name.

The Supplementary Texts provide a number of Collects and other endings to conclude intercession. In some circumstances it may be appropriate for the president to say both the opening invitation and these concluding words.

16 The Peace

The Peace follows naturally from the Prayers of Intercession and begins the Liturgy of the Sacrament. But this section may be transposed to be the opening greeting or may be used later in the service, as part of either the breaking of bread or the Dismissal. Introductions can be found in the Supplementary Texts.

17 The Taking

In Holy Communion the Church, following the example of the Lord, takes, gives thanks, breaks and gives. The bread and wine must be taken into the president's hands and replaced upon the table either after the table has been prepared or during the Eucharistic Prayer.

18 The Eucharistic Prefaces and Optional Acclamations

Short Prefaces may be inserted in Eucharistic Prayers A, B and C in Order One and in both prayers in Order One in Traditional Language. Texts of these are to be found on pages 300–329.

When the short Prefaces given on pages 300–329 are used with Order Two and Order Two in Contemporary Language the phrase 'through Jesus Christ our Lord' must be inserted.

Extended Prefaces may be used with Eucharistic Prayers A, B and E for Order One (pages 294 and 300–329). When an extended Preface is used it replaces the entire text between the opening dialogue and the text of the Sanctus. It will be noted that in Prayer E the short text provided on page 196 must be used if no extended Preface is used.

There are optional acclamations suggested for use in Prayers A and F. Those provided for Prayer F echo the style of those in the Liturgy of St Basil and might, especially when sung, be led by a deacon or minister other than the president, then repeated by the whole congregation. Other acclamations may be used.

19 The Lord's Prayer

On any occasion when the text of an alternative service authorized under the provisions of Canon B 2 provides for the Lord's Prayer to be said or sung, it may be used in the form included in *The Book of Common Prayer* or in either of the two other forms included in services in *Common Worship*. The text included in Prayers for Various Occasions (page 106) may be used on suitable occasions.

20 Breaking of the Bread

Sufficient bread for the whole congregation to share may be broken by the president, if necessary assisted by other ministers, at this point in the service. The Agnus Dei may accompany this action.

The words provided at the breaking of the bread must be used on Sundays and Principal Holy Days. On other days the bread may be broken in silence or during the Agnus Dei.

21 Non-communicants

At the distribution, any of those distributing the sacrament, ordained or lay, may pray for any non-communicants who come forward in these or other suitable words: 'May God be with you' or 'May God bless you'.

22 Prayers after Communion

One or two prayers may be used after communion. If two are used, the first is normally a presidential text, the second a congregational text. If only one is used, either a presidential or congregational text is chosen. The presidential text is normally the authorized Post Communion of the day. The congregational text is normally one of those printed in the main text or one of those in the supplementary texts.

23 A Service without Communion

When there is no communion, the minister leads the service as far as the Prayers of Intercession or the Peace, and then adds the Lord's Prayer, the General Thanksgiving, and/or other prayers, ending with the Grace.

The following notes apply to Order Two only

Frequently used additions to the text of The Book of Common Prayer *are included in Order Two but are indented from the left hand margin.*

24 **Posture**
It is appropriate for the people to kneel for the opening prayer and Commandments, the Prayers of Intercession, the confession, absolution and Comfortable Words, the Prayer of Consecration and prayers after the distribution.

25 **Supplementary Material**
Supplementary Texts may be used with Order Two when they are compatible with that Order. The third form of intercession in the Supplementary Texts (page 283) may be used in place of the form printed.

26 **The Sermon**
At the discretion of the priest, the sermon may precede the Creed.

27 **Alternative Order**
Where customary, the Prayer of Humble Access may precede 'Lift up your hearts'; 'Amen' may be omitted at the end of the Prayer of Consecration, and the Prayer of Oblation follow immediately; the Lord's Prayer may follow the Prayer of Oblation; the versicle 'The peace of the Lord be always with you' with the response 'And with thy spirit' may follow the Lord's Prayer and precede the Agnus Dei. In Order Two, but not in Order Two in Contemporary Language, the breaking of the bread may be deferred until the Agnus Dei.

28 **Proper Prefaces**
The short Proper Prefaces in the Seasonal Provisions (pages 300–329) may be used with Order Two. In such case the priest inserts the words 'through Jesus Christ our Lord' after 'almighty, everlasting God'. The texts of the Proper Prefaces from *The Book of Common Prayer* for use with Order Two are given on pages 246–247.

29 **The Gloria in Excelsis**
If the Gloria in excelsis is not to be used on every occasion, it is appropriately omitted on Sundays in Advent and Lent and on all weekdays that are not Principal Holy Days or Festivals.

Thanksgiving for the Gift of a Child

Notes

1   This service is provided for a number of different occasions:

¶   the private celebration of a birth or adoption, at home
    or in church with only family and close friends present;

¶   the public celebration of the birth or adoption of a number
    of children, perhaps in church on a Sunday afternoon;

¶   the public celebration of the birth or adoption of a number
    of children as part of a main Sunday act of worship.

It is designed to meet the needs of:

¶   parents who see this as a preliminary to baptism;

¶   parents who do not wish their children to be baptized
    immediately;

¶   others, who do not ask for baptism, but who recognize that
    something has happened for which they wish to give thanks
    to God.

2   In preparing for the service, the minister should consult the
    Notes and Supplementary Texts to the service of Thanksgiving
    for the Gift of a Child in *Common Worship: Pastoral Services*.
    The Supplementary Texts include liturgical greetings, a list of
    suitable readings and additional prayers.

¶ Pastoral Introduction

This may be read by those present before the service begins.

The birth or adoption of a child is a cause for celebration. Many people are overcome by a sense of awe at the creation of new life and want to express their thanks to God. This service provides an opportunity for parents and families to give thanks for the birth or adoption of a child and to pray for family life. It may be a private celebration at home or in hospital, or it may be a public celebration in church, sometimes with a number of children.

This service is not the same as Baptism (sometimes called Christening), which is the sacrament of initiation into membership of the Church, the Body of Christ. If you are interested in exploring the Christian faith, or finding out more about preparation for Baptism, ask the minister taking this service.

Structure

¶ Introduction

¶ Reading(s) and Sermon

¶ Thanksgiving and Blessing

¶ Giving of the Gospel

¶ Prayers

¶ Ending

Thanksgiving for the Gift of a Child

Introduction

*The minister welcomes the people using a liturgical greeting
or other suitable words (see Note 2).*

A hymn or song may be sung.

The service may be introduced in these or similar words

We are here today to give thanks for *these children*, with *their* family
and friends, and to support *their* parents in their responsibilities with
prayer and love. God became one of us in Jesus, and understands all
that surrounds the arrival and upbringing of children. It is God's
purpose that children should know love within the stability of their
home, grow in faith, and come at last to the eternal city where his
love reigns supreme.

The following may be used

The works of the Lord are great:

All **his mercy endures for ever.**

Mary gave birth to a child and called him Jesus:

All **he will save his people from their sins.**

He will be called the Prince of Peace:

All **his kingdom will last for ever.**

The minister says

Loving God,
you hold all things in life
and call us into your kingdom of peace;
help us to walk the path of your truth
and fill our lives with gratitude and faith,
through Jesus Christ our Lord.

All **Amen.**

Reading(s) and Sermon

A suitable passage from the Bible is read (see Note 2).

A sermon may be preached.

A hymn may be sung.

Thanksgiving and Blessing

Where parents wish to recognize the role of supporting friends it may be appropriate for them to stand with the parents at the thanksgiving. One of them may present the children to the minister, and informal words may be said.

The minister says

Do you receive *these children* as a gift from God?
We do.

Do you wish to give thanks to God and seek his blessing?
We do.

The minister says

God our creator,
we thank you for the wonder of new life
and for the mystery of human love.
We thank you for all whose support and skill
surround and sustain the beginning of life.
We thank you that we are known to you by name
and loved by you from all eternity.
We thank you for Jesus Christ,
who has opened to us the way of love.
We praise you, Father, Son, and Holy Spirit.

All **Blessed be God for ever.**

The minister may say for each child

What name have you given this child?

A parent or supporting friend replies
His/her name is N.

The minister may take the child.
The minister says

As Jesus took children in his arms and blessed them,
so now we ask God's blessing on *N*.

Heavenly Father, we praise you for *his/her* birth;
surround *him/her* with your blessing
that *he/she* may know your love,
be protected from evil,
and know your goodness all *his/her* days.

When all the children have been prayed for

All   **May they learn to love all that is true,**
      grow in wisdom and strength
      and, in due time, come through faith and baptism
      to the fullness of your grace;
      through Jesus Christ, our Lord. Amen.

The minister prays for the parents

May God the Father of all bless *these parents*
and give *them* grace to love and care for *their children*.
May God give *them* wisdom, patience and faith,
help *them* to provide for the *children's* needs
and, by *their* example,
reveal the love and truth that are in Jesus Christ.

All   **Amen.**

Giving of the Gospel

A copy of a Gospel is presented, with these words

Receive this book.
It is the good news of God's love.
Take it as your guide.

The minister may address the supporting friends and say

Will you do all that you can to help and support *N* and *N*
in the bringing up of *N*?
With the help of God, we will.

The minister may address the wider family and friends and say

Will you do all that you can to help and support *this family*?
With the help of God, we will.

Prayers

This prayer may be said by the parents or by the whole congregation

God our creator,
we thank you for the gift of *these children*,
entrusted to our care.
May we be patient and understanding,
ready to guide and to forgive,
so that through our love
***they* may come to know your love;**
through Jesus Christ our Lord.
Amen.

The minister may say additional prayers (see Note 2),
ending with the Lord's Prayer.

Jesus taught us to call God our Father,
and so in faith and trust we say

All   **Our Father in heaven,**
hallowed be your name,
your kingdom come,
your will be done,
on earth as in heaven.
Give us today our daily bread.
Forgive us our sins
as we forgive those who sin against us.
Lead us not into temptation
but deliver us from evil.
For the kingdom, the power,
and the glory are yours
now and for ever.
Amen.

(or)

Jesus taught us to call God our Father,
and so we have the courage to say

All   **Our Father, who art in heaven,**
hallowed be thy name;
thy kingdom come;
thy will be done;
on earth as it is in heaven.
Give us this day our daily bread.
And forgive us our trespasses,
as we forgive those who trespass against us.
And lead us not into temptation;
but deliver us from evil.
For thine is the kingdom,
the power and the glory,
for ever and ever.
Amen.

Ending

The minister says one of these or another suitable blessing

The love of the Lord Jesus
draw *you* to himself,
the power of the Lord Jesus
strengthen *you* in his service,
the joy of the Lord Jesus fill *your* hearts;
and the blessing of God almighty,
the Father, the Son, and the Holy Spirit,
be among *you* and remain with *you* always.

All   **Amen.**

(or)

The Lord bless *you* and watch over *you*,
the Lord make his face shine upon *you*
and be gracious to *you*,
the Lord look kindly on *you* and give *you* peace;
and the blessing of God almighty,
the Father, the Son, and the Holy Spirit,
be among *you* and remain with *you* always.

All   **Amen.**

Holy Baptism

Notes

1   In preparing for the service, the minister should consult the
    full Notes and Supplementary Texts to the service of Holy Baptism
    in *Common Worship: Initiation Services* and the President's edition
    of *Common Worship*. The Supplementary Texts include the
    Thanksgiving Prayer for a Child and seasonal texts for the
    Introduction, Collect, Peace, Prayers of Intercession, Prayer after
    Communion and Blessing.

2   When the Renewal of Baptismal Vows takes place within a service
    of Holy Baptism and/or Confirmation, the responses of the people
    follow the responses of the candidates, for example:

    Do you reject ...?

Candidates   **I reject** ...

All   **I reject** ...

¶ Pastoral Introduction

This may be read by those present before the service begins.

Baptism marks the beginning of a journey with God which continues for the rest of our lives, the first step in response to God's love. For all involved, particularly the candidates but also parents, godparents and sponsors, it is a joyful moment when we rejoice in what God has done for us in Christ, making serious promises and declaring the faith. The wider community of the local church and friends welcome the new Christian, promising support and prayer for the future. Hearing and doing these things provides an opportunity to remember our own baptism and reflect on the progress made on that journey, which is now to be shared with this new member of the Church.

The service paints many vivid pictures of what happens on the Christian way. There is the sign of the cross, the badge of faith in the Christian journey, which reminds us of Christ's death for us. Our 'drowning' in the water of baptism, where we believe we die to sin and are raised to new life, unites us to Christ's dying and rising, a picture that can be brought home vividly by the way the baptism is administered. Water is also a sign of new life, as we are born again by water and the Spirit, as Jesus was at his baptism. And as a sign of that new life, there may be a lighted candle, a picture of the light of Christ conquering the darkness of evil. Everyone who is baptized walks in that light for the rest of their lives.

As you pray for the candidates, picture them with yourself and the whole Church throughout the ages, journeying into the fullness of God's love.

Jesus said, 'I came that they may have life, and have it abundantly.'

John 10.10

Holy Baptism within a Celebration of Holy Communion

Structure

¶ **Preparation**

The Greeting
 Thanksgiving Prayer for a Child
Introduction *
 † *Presentation of the Candidates*
The Collect *

¶ **The Liturgy of the Word**

Readings and Psalm
Gospel Reading
Sermon

¶ **The Liturgy of Baptism**

† Presentation of the Candidates
The Decision
Signing with the Cross
Prayer over the Water *
Profession of Faith *
Baptism
Commission
† Prayers of Intercession *
The Welcome and Peace *
 † *Prayers of Intercession* *

¶ **The Liturgy of the Eucharist**

Preparation of the Table
Taking of the Bread and Wine
The Eucharistic Prayer
The Lord's Prayer
Breaking of the Bread
Giving of Communion
Prayer after Communion *

¶ **The Sending Out**

The Blessing *
Giving of a Lighted Candle
The Dismissal

† indicates alternative position allowed and shown indented in italics

* indicates alternative texts are provided

Holy Baptism apart from a Celebration of Holy Communion

Structure

¶ **Preparation**

The Greeting
    Thanksgiving Prayer for a Child
Introduction *
    † Presentation of the Candidates
The Collect *

¶ **The Liturgy of the Word**

Readings and Psalm
Gospel Reading
Sermon

¶ **The Liturgy of Baptism**

† Presentation of the Candidates
The Decision
Signing with the Cross
Prayer over the Water *
Profession of Faith *
Baptism
Commission
    † Prayers of Intercession *
The Welcome and Peace *
† Prayers of Intercession *
The Lord's Prayer

¶ **The Sending Out**

The Blessing *
Giving of a Lighted Candle
The Dismissal

† indicates alternative position allowed and shown indented in italics

* indicates alternative texts are provided

Holy Baptism

¶ *Preparation*

At the entry of the ministers a hymn may be sung.

The Greeting

The president says

The grace of our Lord Jesus Christ,
the love of God
and the fellowship of the Holy Spirit
be with you all

All **and also with you.**

Words of welcome or introduction may be said.

*The president may use the prayer of thanksgiving
(see Note 1, page 344).*

Introduction

The president may use these or other words

Our Lord Jesus Christ has told us
that to enter the kingdom of heaven
we must be born again of water and the Spirit,
and has given us baptism as the sign and seal of this new birth.
Here we are washed by the Holy Spirit and made clean.
Here we are clothed with Christ,
dying to sin that we may live his risen life.
As children of God, we have a new dignity
and God calls us to fullness of life.

The Gloria in excelsis may be used.

The Collect

The president introduces a period of silent prayer with the words 'Let us pray' or a more specific bidding.

Either the Collect of the Day, or this Collect is said

Heavenly Father,
by the power of your Holy Spirit
you give to your faithful people new life in the water of baptism.
Guide and strengthen us by the same Spirit,
that we who are born again may serve you in faith and love,
and grow into the full stature of your Son, Jesus Christ,
who is alive and reigns with you in the unity of the Holy Spirit
now and for ever.

All **Amen.**

¶ *The Liturgy of the Word*

Readings

The readings of the day are normally used on Sundays and Principal Festivals.

Either one or two readings from Scripture may precede the Gospel reading.

At the end of each the reader may say

This is the word of the Lord.

All **Thanks be to God.**

The psalm or canticle follows the first reading; other hymns and songs may be used between the readings.

Gospel Reading

An acclamation may herald the Gospel reading.

When the Gospel is announced the reader says

Hear the Gospel of our Lord Jesus Christ according to N.

All **Glory to you, O Lord.**

At the end

This is the Gospel of the Lord.

All **Praise to you, O Christ.**

Sermon

¶ *The Liturgy of Baptism*

Presentation of the Candidates

The candidates may be presented to the congregation. Where appropriate, they may be presented by their godparents or sponsors.

The president asks those candidates for baptism who are able to answer for themselves

Do you wish to be baptized?
I do.

Testimony by the candidate(s) may follow.

The president addresses the whole congregation

Faith is the gift of God to his people.
In baptism the Lord is adding to our number
    those whom he is calling.
People of God, will you welcome *these children/candidates*
    and uphold *them* in *their* new life in Christ?

All   **With the help of God, we will.**

At the baptism of children, the president then says to the parents and godparents

Parents and godparents, the Church receives *these children* with joy.
Today we are trusting God for *their* growth in faith.
Will you pray for *them*,
draw *them* by your example into the community of faith
and walk with *them* in the way of Christ?
With the help of God, we will.

In baptism *these children* begin their journey in faith.
You speak for *them* today.
Will you care for *them*,
and help *them* to take *their* place
within the life and worship of Christ's Church?
With the help of God, we will.

The Decision

A large candle may be lit. The president addresses the candidates directly, or through their parents, godparents and sponsors

In baptism, God calls us out of darkness into his marvellous light.
To follow Christ means dying to sin and rising to new life with him.
Therefore I ask:

Do you reject the devil and all rebellion against God?
I reject them.

Do you renounce the deceit and corruption of evil?
I renounce them.

Do you repent of the sins that separate us from God and neighbour?
I repent of them.

Do you turn to Christ as Saviour?
I turn to Christ.

Do you submit to Christ as Lord?
I submit to Christ.

Do you come to Christ, the way, the truth and the life?
I come to Christ.

Where there are strong pastoral reasons, the alternative form of the Decision (page 372) may be used.

Signing with the Cross

The president or another minister makes the sign of the cross on the forehead of each candidate, saying

Christ claims you for his own.
Receive the sign of his cross.

The president may invite parents, godparents and sponsors to sign the candidates with the cross. When all the candidates have been signed, the president says

Do not be ashamed to confess the faith of Christ crucified.

All **Fight valiantly as a disciple of Christ**
against sin, the world and the devil,
and remain faithful to Christ to the end of your life.

May almighty God deliver you from the powers of darkness,
restore in you the image of his glory,
and lead you in the light and obedience of Christ.

All **Amen.**

Prayer over the Water

The ministers and candidates gather at the baptismal font.
A canticle, psalm, hymn or litany may be used (see page 370).

The president stands before the water of baptism and says
(optional seasonal and responsive forms are provided on
pages 364–369)

Praise God who made heaven and earth,

All **who keeps his promise for ever.**

Let us give thanks to the Lord our God.

All **It is right to give thanks and praise.**

We thank you, almighty God, for the gift of water
to sustain, refresh and cleanse all life.
Over water the Holy Spirit moved in the beginning of creation.
Through water you led the children of Israel
from slavery in Egypt to freedom in the Promised Land.
In water your Son Jesus received the baptism of John
and was anointed by the Holy Spirit as the Messiah, the Christ,
to lead us from the death of sin to newness of life.

We thank you, Father, for the water of baptism.
In it we are buried with Christ in his death.
By it we share in his resurrection.
Through it we are reborn by the Holy Spirit.
Therefore, in joyful obedience to your Son,
we baptize into his fellowship those who come to him in faith.

Now sanctify this water that, by the power of your Holy Spirit,
they may be cleansed from sin and born again.
Renewed in your image, may they walk by the light of faith
and continue for ever in the risen life of Jesus Christ our Lord;
to whom with you and the Holy Spirit
be all honour and glory, now and for ever.

All **Amen.**

Profession of Faith

The president addresses the congregation

Brothers and sisters, I ask you to profess
together with *these candidates*
the faith of the Church.

Do you believe and trust in God the Father?

All   **I believe in God, the Father almighty,
creator of heaven and earth.**

Do you believe and trust in his Son Jesus Christ?

All   **I believe in Jesus Christ, his only Son, our Lord,
who was conceived by the Holy Spirit,
born of the Virgin Mary,
suffered under Pontius Pilate,
was crucified, died, and was buried;
he descended to the dead.
On the third day he rose again;
he ascended into heaven,
he is seated at the right hand of the Father,
and he will come to judge the living and the dead.**

Do you believe and trust in the Holy Spirit?

All   **I believe in the Holy Spirit,
the holy catholic Church,
the communion of saints,
the forgiveness of sins,
the resurrection of the body,
and the life everlasting.
Amen.**

*Where there are strong pastoral reasons the alternative Profession
of Faith (page 373) may be used.*

If the candidate(s) can answer for themselves, the president may say to each one

N, is this your faith?

Each candidate answers in their own words, or

This is my faith.

The president or another minister dips each candidate in water, or pours water on them, saying

N, I baptize you
in the name of the Father,
and of the Son,
and of the Holy Spirit.

All **Amen.**

If the newly baptized are clothed with a white robe, a hymn or song may be used, and then a minister may say

You have been clothed with Christ.
As many as are baptized into Christ have put on Christ.

If those who have been baptized were not signed with the cross immediately after the Decision, the president signs each one now.

The president says

May God, who has received you by baptism into his Church,
pour upon you the riches of his grace,
that within the company of Christ's pilgrim people
you may daily be renewed by his anointing Spirit,
and come to the inheritance of the saints in glory.

All **Amen.**

The president and those who have been baptized may return from the font.

Commission

Either *Where the newly baptized are unable to answer for themselves,
a minister addresses the congregation, parents and godparents,
using these or similar words*

We have brought *these children* to baptism knowing that Jesus died
and rose again for *them* and trusting in the promise that God hears
and answers prayer. We have prayed that in Jesus Christ *they* will
know the forgiveness of *their* sins and the new life of the Spirit.

As *they* grow up, *they* will need the help and encouragement of the
Christian community, so that *they* may learn to know God in public
worship and private prayer, follow Jesus Christ in the life of faith,
serve *their* neighbour after the example of Christ, and in due course
come to confirmation.

As part of the Church of Christ, we all have a duty to support *them*
by prayer, example and teaching. As *their* parents and godparents,
you have the prime responsibility for guiding and helping *them* in
their early years. This is a demanding task for which you will need
the help and grace of God. Therefore let us now pray for grace in
guiding *these children* in the way of faith.

One or more of the following prayers may be used

Faithful and loving God,
bless those who care for *these children*
and grant them your gifts of love, wisdom and faith.
Pour upon them your healing and reconciling love,
and protect their home from all evil.
Fill them with the light of your presence
and establish them in the joy of your kingdom,
through Jesus Christ our Lord.

All   **Amen.**

God of grace and life,
in your love you have given us
a place among your people;
keep us faithful to our baptism,
and prepare us for that glorious day
when the whole creation will be made perfect
in your Son our Saviour Jesus Christ.

All   **Amen.**

These words may be added

N and N,
today God has touched you with his love
and given you a place among his people.
God promises to be with you
in joy and in sorrow,
to be your guide in life,
and to bring you safely to heaven.
In baptism God invites you on a life-long journey.
Together with all God's people
you must explore the way of Jesus
and grow in friendship with God,
in love for his people,
and in serving others.
With us you will listen to the word of God
and receive the gifts of God.

or *To the newly baptized who are able to answer for themselves,
a minister may say*

Those who are baptized are called to worship and serve God.

Will you continue in the apostles' teaching and fellowship,
in the breaking of bread, and in the prayers?
With the help of God, I will.

Will you persevere in resisting evil,
and, whenever you fall into sin, repent and return to the Lord?
With the help of God, I will.

Will you proclaim by word and example
the good news of God in Christ?
With the help of God, I will.

Will you seek and serve Christ in all people,
loving your neighbour as yourself?
With the help of God, I will.

Will you acknowledge Christ's authority over human society,
by prayer for the world and its leaders,
by defending the weak, and by seeking peace and justice?
With the help of God, I will.

May Christ dwell in your heart(s) through faith,
that you may be rooted and grounded in love
and bring forth the fruit of the Spirit.
Amen.

Prayers of Intercession

Either here or after the Welcome and Peace, intercessions may be led by the president or others. These or other suitable words may be used. The intercession may conclude with a Collect.

As a royal priesthood, let us pray to the Father
through Christ who ever lives to intercede for us.

Reveal your kingdom among the nations;
may peace abound and justice flourish.
Especially for …
Your name be hallowed.

All **Your kingdom come.**

Send down upon us the gift of the Spirit
and renew your Church with power from on high.
Especially for …
Your name be hallowed.

All **Your kingdom come.**

Deliver the oppressed, strengthen the weak,
heal and restore your creation.
Especially for …
Your name be hallowed.

All **Your kingdom come.**

Rejoicing in the fellowship of the Church on earth,
we join our prayers with all the saints in glory.
Your name be hallowed.

All **Your kingdom come.**

The Welcome and Peace

There is one Lord, one faith, one baptism:
N and N, by one Spirit we are all baptized into one body.

All   **We welcome you into the fellowship of faith;**
we are children of the same heavenly Father;
we welcome you.

The congregation may greet the newly baptized.

The president introduces the Peace in these or other suitable words

We are all one in Christ Jesus.
We belong to him through faith,
heirs of the promise of the Spirit of peace.

The peace of the Lord be always with you
All   **and also with you.**

A minister may say
Let us offer one another a sign of peace.

All may exchange a sign of peace.

If the Liturgy of the Eucharist does not follow immediately, the service continues with suitable prayers, ending with the Lord's Prayer and the Sending Out (page 363).

¶ *The Liturgy of the Eucharist*

The Order for Celebration of Holy Communion continues with

Preparation of the Table

Taking of the Bread and Wine

The Eucharistic Prayer

This short Proper Preface may be used

And now we give you thanks
because by water and the Holy Spirit
you have made us a holy people in Jesus Christ our Lord;
you raise us to new life in him
and renew in us the image of your glory.

The Lord's Prayer

Breaking of the Bread

Giving of Communion

Prayer after Communion

The authorized Post Communion of the Day,
or a seasonal form, or the following is used

Eternal God, our beginning and our end,
preserve in your people the new life of baptism;
as Christ receives us on earth,
so may he guide us through the trials of this world
and enfold us in the joy of heaven,
where you live and reign,
one God for ever and ever.

All **Amen.**

¶ *The Sending Out*

The Blessing

The president may use a seasonal blessing, or another suitable blessing, or

The God of all grace,
who called you to his eternal glory in Christ Jesus,
establish, strengthen and settle you in the faith;
and the blessing of God almighty,
the Father, the Son, and the Holy Spirit,
be upon you and remain with you always.

All **Amen.**

Giving of a Lighted Candle

The president or another person may give each of the newly baptized a lighted candle. These may be lit from the candle used at the Decision.

When all the newly baptized have received a candle, the president says

God has delivered us from the dominion of darkness
and has given us a place with the saints in light.

You have received the light of Christ;
walk in this light all the days of your life.

All **Shine as a light in the world**
to the glory of God the Father.

The Dismissal

Go in the light and peace of Christ.

All **Thanks be to God.**

From Easter Day to Pentecost Alleluia, alleluia *may be added to both the versicle and the response.*

Supplementary Texts

¶ *Responsive Form of the Prayer over the Water*

*The refrain **Lord of life, renew your creation** may be said
or sung by all.*
*The first phrase **Lord of life** (italicized) may be said or sung
by a deacon or other minister.*

Praise God who made heaven and earth,

All **who keeps his promise for ever.**

Let us give thanks to the Lord our God.

All **It is right to give thanks and praise.**

We thank you, almighty God, for the gift of water
to sustain, refresh and cleanse all life.
Over water the Holy Spirit moved in the beginning of creation.
Through water you led the children of Israel
from slavery in Egypt to freedom in the Promised Land.
In water your Son Jesus received the baptism of John
and was anointed by the Holy Spirit as the Messiah, the Christ,
to lead us from the death of sin to newness of life.
Lord of life,

All **renew your creation.**

We thank you, Father, for the water of baptism.
In it we are buried with Christ in his death.
By it we share in his resurrection.
Through it we are reborn by the Holy Spirit.
Therefore, in joyful obedience to your Son,
we baptize into his fellowship those who come to him in faith.
Lord of life,

All **renew your creation.**

Now sanctify this water that, by the power of your Holy Spirit,
they may be cleansed from sin and born again.
Renewed in your image, may they walk by the light of faith
and continue for ever in the risen life of Jesus Christ our Lord;
to whom with you and the Holy Spirit
be all honour and glory, now and for ever. Amen.
Lord of life,

All **renew your creation.**

¶ *Seasonal Prayers over the Water*

*The headings (Epiphany/Baptism of Christ/Trinity, Easter/Pentecost and
All Saints) indicate the seasonal emphases of the material. However,
these texts may be used on any occasion to meet pastoral circumstances.*

Epiphany/Baptism of Christ/Trinity

Praise God who made heaven and earth,

All **who keeps his promise for ever.**

Let us give thanks to the Lord our God.

All **It is right to give thanks and praise.**

Father, we give you thanks and praise
for your gift of water in creation;
for your Spirit, sweeping over the waters,
bringing light and life;
for your Son Jesus Christ our Lord,
baptized in the river Jordan.

We bless you for your new creation,
brought to birth by water and the Spirit,
and for your grace bestowed upon us your children,
washing away our sins.

May your holy and life-giving Spirit
move upon these waters.
Restore through them the beauty of your creation,
and bring those who are baptized
to new birth in the family of your Church.

Drown sin in the waters of judgement,
anoint your children with power from on high,
and make them one with Christ
in the freedom of your kingdom.
For all might, majesty, dominion and power are yours,
now and for ever.

All **Alleluia. Amen.**

Praise God who made heaven and earth,
All **who keeps his promise for ever.**

Let us give thanks to the Lord our God.
All **It is right to give thanks and praise.**

Father, for your gift of water in creation,
All **we give you thanks and praise.**

For your Spirit, sweeping over the waters,
bringing light and life,
All **we give you thanks and praise.**

For your Son Jesus Christ our Lord,
baptized in the river Jordan,
All **we give you thanks and praise.**

For your new creation,
brought to birth by water and the Spirit,
All **we give you thanks and praise.**

For your grace bestowed upon us your children,
washing away our sins,
All **we give you thanks and praise.**

Father, accept our sacrifice of praise;
may your holy and life-giving Spirit
move upon these waters.
All **Lord, receive our prayer.**

Restore through them the beauty of your creation,
and bring those who are baptized
to new birth in the family of your Church.
All **Lord, receive our prayer.**

Drown sin in the waters of judgement,
anoint your children with power from on high,
and make them one with Christ
in the freedom of your kingdom.
All **Lord, receive our prayer.**

For all might, majesty, dominion and power are yours,
now and for ever.
All **Alleluia. Amen.**

Easter/Pentecost

The bracketed refrain **Saving God, give us life** *is optional.*
If it is used, it may be said or sung by all.
The first phrase **Saving God** *(italicized) may be said or sung*
by a deacon or other minister.

Praise God who made heaven and earth,

All **who keeps his promise for ever.**

Let us give thanks to the Lord our God.

All **It is right to give thanks and praise.**

Almighty God, whose Son Jesus Christ
was baptized in the river Jordan,
we thank you for the gift of water
to cleanse us and revive us.
[*Saving God,*

All **give us life.]**

We thank you that through the waters of the Red Sea
you led your people out of slavery
to freedom in the Promised Land.
[*Saving God,*

All **give us life.]**

We thank you that through the deep waters of death
     you brought your Son,
and raised him to life in triumph.
[*Saving God,*

All **give us life.]**

Bless this water, that your servants who are washed in it
may be made one with Christ in his death and in his resurrection,
to be cleansed and delivered from all sin.
[*Saving God,*

All **give us life.]**

Send your Holy Spirit upon them,
bring them to new birth in the household of faith
and raise them with Christ to full and eternal life;
for all might, majesty, authority and power are yours,
now and for ever. Amen.
[*Saving God,*

All **give us life.]**

All Saints

The bracketed refrain **Hope of the saints, make known your glory**
is optional. If it is used, it may be said or sung.
The first phrase **Hope of the saints** *(italicized) may be said or sung by*
a deacon or other minister.

Praise God who made heaven and earth,

All **who keeps his promise for ever.**

Let us give thanks to the Lord our God.

All **It is right to give thanks and praise.**

Lord of the heavens,
we bless your name for all your servants
who have been a sign of your grace through the ages.
[Hope of the saints,

All **make known your glory.]**

You delivered Noah from the waters of destruction;
you divided the waters of the sea,
and by the hand of Moses
you led your people from slavery
into the Promised Land.
[Hope of the saints,

All **make known your glory.]**

You made a new covenant in the blood of your Son,
that all who confess his name
may, by the Holy Spirit,
enter the covenant of grace,
receive a pledge of the kingdom of heaven,
and share in the divine nature.
[Hope of the saints,

All **make known your glory.]**

Fill these waters, we pray, with the power of that same Spirit,
that all who enter them may be reborn
and rise from the grave
to new life in Christ.
[*Hope of the saints,*
All **make known your glory.]**

As the apostles and prophets, the confessors and martyrs,
faithfully served you in their generation,
may we be built into an eternal dwelling for you,
through Jesus Christ our Lord,
to whom with you and the Holy Spirit
be honour and glory, now and for ever. Amen.
[*Hope of the saints,*
All **make known your glory.]**

¶ A Litany of the Resurrection

which may be used in Procession to the Baptismal Font

O give thanks to the Lord, for he is gracious:

All **and his mercy endures for ever.**

He has loved us from all eternity:

All **for his mercy endures for ever.**

And remembered us when we were in trouble:

All **for his mercy endures for ever.**

For us and for our salvation he came down from heaven:

All **for his mercy endures for ever.**

He became incarnate of the Holy Spirit and the Virgin Mary
and was made man:

All **for his mercy endures for ever.**

By his cross and passion he has redeemed the world:

All **for his mercy endures for ever.**

And has washed us from our sins in his own blood:

All **for his mercy endures for ever.**

On the third day he rose again:

All **for his mercy endures for ever.**

And has given us the victory:

All **for his mercy endures for ever.**

He ascended into heaven:

All **for his mercy endures for ever.**

And opened wide for us the everlasting doors:

All **for his mercy endures for ever.**

He is seated at the right hand of the Father:

All **for his mercy endures for ever.**

And ever lives to make intercession for us:

All **for his mercy endures for ever.**

All **Glory to the Father and to the Son
and to the Holy Spirit;
as it was in the beginning is now
and shall be for ever.
Amen.**

For the gift of his Spirit:

All **blessed be Christ.**

For the catholic Church:

All **blessed be Christ.**

For the means of grace:

All **blessed be Christ.**

For the hope of glory:

All **blessed be Christ.**

For the triumphs of his gospel:

All **blessed be Christ.**

For the lives of his saints:

All **blessed be Christ.**

In joy and in sorrow:

All **blessed be Christ.**

In life and in death:

All **blessed be Christ.**

Now and to the end of the ages:

All **blessed be Christ.**

*This litany may be used in two parts, reserving the clauses following
the Gloria for a return procession from the place of baptism.*

¶ *An Alternative Form of the Decision*

Where there are strong pastoral reasons, the following may be used in place of the Decision in the service of Holy Baptism.

The president addresses the candidates directly, or through their parents, godparents and sponsors

Therefore I ask:

Do you turn to Christ?
I turn to Christ.

Do you repent of your sins?
I repent of my sins.

Do you renounce evil?
I renounce evil.

¶ *An Alternative Profession of Faith*

Where there are strong pastoral reasons, the following may be used in place of the Profession of Faith in the service of Holy Baptism.

The president says

Let us affirm,
together with these who are being baptized,
our common faith in Jesus Christ.

Do you believe and trust in God the Father,
source of all being and life,
the one for whom we exist?

All   **I believe and trust in him.**

Do you believe and trust in God the Son,
who took our human nature,
died for us and rose again?

All   **I believe and trust in him.**

Do you believe and trust in God the Holy Spirit,
who gives life to the people of God
and makes Christ known in the world?

All   **I believe and trust in him.**

This is the faith of the Church.

All   **This is our faith.**
We believe and trust in one God,
Father, Son and Holy Spirit.

Collects and Post Communions for Sundays, Principal Holy Days and Festivals

Notes

1 Collects and Post Communions for Lesser Festivals and Special Occasions, with Commons of the Saints, are published in the President's edition of *Common Worship*.

2 Normally on any occasion only one Collect is used.

3 The Collect for each Sunday is used on the following weekdays, except where other provision is made.

4 At Evening Prayer on Saturdays other than Easter Eve, Christmas Eve or Principal Feasts or Festivals, the Collect appointed for the ensuing Sunday shall be used. When Evening Prayer on the day before a Festival makes use of the lessons relating to that Festival, the Collect of that Festival shall be used.

5 Where a Collect ends 'Through Jesus Christ … now and for ever', the minister may use the shorter ending, 'Through Jesus Christ our Lord', to which the people respond 'Amen', and omit the longer Trinitarian ending. The longer ending is to be preferred at Holy Communion.

For Rules, see page 525.

Contents

For Collects and Post Communions in Traditional Language, see page 448.

The First Sunday of Advent *Purple*

Collect

Almighty God,
give us grace to cast away the works of darkness
and to put on the armour of light,
now in the time of this mortal life,
in which your Son Jesus Christ came to us in great humility;
that on the last day,
when he shall come again in his glorious majesty
    to judge the living and the dead,
we may rise to the life immortal;
through him who is alive and reigns with you,
in the unity of the Holy Spirit,
one God, now and for ever.

*This Collect may be used as the Post Communion on any day from
the Second Sunday of Advent until Christmas Eve instead of the
Post Communion provided.*

Post Communion

O Lord our God,
make us watchful and keep us faithful
as we await the coming of your Son our Lord;
that, when he shall appear,
he may not find us sleeping in sin
but active in his service
and joyful in his praise;
through Jesus Christ our Lord.

The Second Sunday of Advent

Collect

O Lord, raise up, we pray, your power
and come among us,
and with great might succour us;
that whereas, through our sins and wickedness
we are grievously hindered
in running the race that is set before us,
your bountiful grace and mercy
may speedily help and deliver us;
through Jesus Christ your Son our Lord,
to whom with you and the Holy Spirit,
be honour and glory, now and for ever.

Post Communion

Father in heaven,
who sent your Son to redeem the world
and will send him again to be our judge:
give us grace so to imitate him
    in the humility and purity of his first coming
that, when he comes again,
we may be ready to greet him
with joyful love and firm faith;
through Jesus Christ our Lord.

The Third Sunday of Advent

Collect

O Lord Jesus Christ,
who at your first coming sent your messenger
to prepare your way before you:
grant that the ministers and stewards of your mysteries
may likewise so prepare and make ready your way
by turning the hearts of the disobedient to the wisdom of the just,
that at your second coming to judge the world
we may be found an acceptable people in your sight;
for you are alive and reign with the Father
in the unity of the Holy Spirit,
one God, now and for ever.

Post Communion

We give you thanks, O Lord, for these heavenly gifts;
kindle in us the fire of your Spirit
that when your Christ comes again
we may shine as lights before his face;
who is alive and reigns now and for ever.

The Fourth Sunday of Advent

This provision is not used on weekdays after 23 December.

Collect

God our redeemer,
who prepared the Blessed Virgin Mary
to be the mother of your Son:
grant that, as she looked for his coming as our saviour,
so we may be ready to greet him
when he comes again as our judge;
who is alive and reigns with you,
in the unity of the Holy Spirit,
one God, now and for ever.

Post Communion

Heavenly Father,
who chose the Blessed Virgin Mary
to be the mother of the promised saviour:
fill us your servants with your grace,
that in all things we may embrace your holy will
and with her rejoice in your salvation;
through Jesus Christ our Lord.

24 December   **Christmas Eve**   *Purple*

Collect

Almighty God,
you make us glad with the yearly remembrance
    of the birth of your Son Jesus Christ:
grant that, as we joyfully receive him as our redeemer,
so we may with sure confidence behold him
when he shall come to be our judge;
who is alive and reigns with you,
in the unity of the Holy Spirit,
one God, now and for ever.

Post Communion

Eternal God, for whom we wait,
you have fed us with the bread of eternal life:
keep us ever watchful,
that we may be ready to stand before the Son of man,
Jesus Christ our Lord.

¶ Christmas

25 December **Christmas Night** *Gold or*
Principal Feast *White*

Collect

Eternal God,
who made this most holy night
to shine with the brightness of your one true light:
bring us, who have known the revelation of that light on earth,
to see the radiance of your heavenly glory;
through Jesus Christ your Son our Lord,
who is alive and reigns with you,
in the unity of the Holy Spirit,
one God, now and for ever.

Post Communion

God our Father,
in this night you have made known to us again
the coming of our Lord Jesus Christ:
confirm our faith and fix our eyes on him
until the day dawns
and Christ the Morning Star rises in our hearts.
To him be glory both now and for ever.

Christmas Day

Principal Feast

Collect

Almighty God,
you have given us your only-begotten Son
to take our nature upon him
and as at this time to be born of a pure virgin:
grant that we, who have been born again
and made your children by adoption and grace,
may daily be renewed by your Holy Spirit;
through Jesus Christ your Son our Lord,
who is alive and reigns with you,
in the unity of the Holy Spirit,
one God, now and for ever.

Post Communion

God our Father,
whose Word has come among us
in the Holy Child of Bethlehem:
may the light of faith illumine our hearts
    and shine in our words and deeds;
through him who is Christ the Lord.

The First Sunday of Christmas

White

This provision is not used on weekdays after 5 January.

Collect

Almighty God,
who wonderfully created us in your own image
and yet more wonderfully restored us
through your Son Jesus Christ:
grant that, as he came to share in our humanity,
so we may share the life of his divinity;
who is alive and reigns with you,
in the unity of the Holy Spirit,
one God, now and for ever.

Post Communion

Heavenly Father,
whose blessed Son shared at Nazareth the life of an earthly home:
help your Church to live as one family,
united in love and obedience,
and bring us all at last to our home in heaven;
through Jesus Christ our Lord.

The Second Sunday of Christmas White

This provision is not used on weekdays after 5 January.

Collect

Almighty God,
in the birth of your Son
you have poured on us the new light of your incarnate Word,
and shown us the fullness of your love:
help us to walk in his light and dwell in his love
that we may know the fullness of his joy;
who is alive and reigns with you,
in the unity of the Holy Spirit,
one God, now and for ever.

Post Communion

All praise to you,
almighty God and heavenly king,
who sent your Son into the world
to take our nature upon him
and to be born of a pure virgin:
grant that, as we are born again in him,
so he may continually dwell in us
and reign on earth as he reigns in heaven,
now and for ever.

¶ *Epiphany*

The Epiphany
Principal Feast

Gold or White

Collect

O God,
who by the leading of a star
manifested your only Son to the peoples of the earth:
mercifully grant that we,
who know you now by faith,
may at last behold your glory face to face;
through Jesus Christ your Son our Lord,
who is alive and reigns with you,
in the unity of the Holy Spirit,
one God, now and for ever.

Post Communion

Lord God,
the bright splendour whom the nations seek:
may we who with the wise men have been drawn by your light
discern the glory of your presence in your Son,
the Word made flesh, Jesus Christ our Lord.

The Baptism of Christ
The First Sunday of Epiphany

Gold or White

Collect

Eternal Father,
who at the baptism of Jesus
revealed him to be your Son,
anointing him with the Holy Spirit:
grant to us, who are born again by water and the Spirit,
that we may be faithful to our calling as your adopted children;
through Jesus Christ your Son our Lord,
who is alive and reigns with you,
in the unity of the Holy Spirit,
one God, now and for ever.

Post Communion

Lord of all time and eternity,
you opened the heavens and revealed yourself as Father
in the baptism of Jesus your beloved Son:
by the power of your Spirit
complete the heavenly work of our rebirth
through the waters of the new creation;
through Jesus Christ our Lord.

The Second Sunday of Epiphany   *White*

Collect

Almighty God,
in Christ you make all things new:
transform the poverty of our nature by the riches of your grace,
and in the renewal of our lives
make known your heavenly glory;
through Jesus Christ your Son our Lord,
who is alive and reigns with you,
in the unity of the Holy Spirit,
one God, now and for ever.

Post Communion

God of glory,
you nourish us with your Word
who is the bread of life:
fill us with your Holy Spirit
that through us the light of your glory
may shine in all the world.
We ask this in the name of Jesus Christ our Lord.

The Third Sunday of Epiphany *White*

Collect

Almighty God,
whose Son revealed in signs and miracles
the wonder of your saving presence:
renew your people with your heavenly grace,
and in all our weakness
sustain us by your mighty power;
through Jesus Christ your Son our Lord,
who is alive and reigns with you,
in the unity of the Holy Spirit,
one God, now and for ever.

Post Communion

Almighty Father,
whose Son our Saviour Jesus Christ is the light of the world:
may your people,
illumined by your word and sacraments,
shine with the radiance of his glory,
that he may be known, worshipped, and obeyed
    to the ends of the earth;
for he is alive and reigns, now and for ever.

The Fourth Sunday of Epiphany *White*

Collect

God our creator,
who in the beginning
commanded the light to shine out of darkness:
we pray that the light of the glorious gospel of Christ
may dispel the darkness of ignorance and unbelief,
shine into the hearts of all your people,
and reveal the knowledge of your glory
    in the face of Jesus Christ your Son our Lord,
who is alive and reigns with you,
in the unity of the Holy Spirit,
one God, now and for ever.

Post Communion

Generous Lord,
in word and eucharist we have proclaimed the mystery of your love:
help us so to live out our days
that we may be signs of your wonders in the world;
through Jesus Christ our Saviour.

The Presentation of Christ in the Temple

Candlemas

Principal Feast

Gold or White

Collect

Almighty and ever-living God,
clothed in majesty,
whose beloved Son was this day presented in the Temple,
in substance of our flesh:
grant that we may be presented to you
with pure and clean hearts,
by your Son Jesus Christ our Lord,
who is alive and reigns with you,
in the unity of the Holy Spirit,
one God, now and for ever.

Post Communion

Lord, you fulfilled the hope of Simeon and Anna,
who lived to welcome the Messiah:
may we, who have received these gifts beyond words,
prepare to meet Christ Jesus when he comes
    to bring us to eternal life;
for he is alive and reigns, now and for ever.

The Fifth Sunday before Lent *Green*

This provision is always used from the day after the Presentation of Christ in the Temple until the first of the Sundays before Lent.

Collect

Almighty God,
by whose grace alone we are accepted
    and called to your service:
strengthen us by your Holy Spirit
and make us worthy of our calling;
through Jesus Christ your Son our Lord,
who is alive and reigns with you,
in the unity of the Holy Spirit,
one God, now and for ever.

Post Communion

God of truth,
we have seen with our eyes
    and touched with our hands the bread of life:
strengthen our faith
that we may grow in love for you and for each other;
through Jesus Christ our Lord.

Collect

O God,
you know us to be set
in the midst of so many and great dangers,
that by reason of the frailty of our nature
we cannot always stand upright:
grant to us such strength and protection
as may support us in all dangers
and carry us through all temptations;
through Jesus Christ your Son our Lord,
who is alive and reigns with you,
in the unity of the Holy Spirit,
one God, now and for ever.

Post Communion

Go before us, Lord, in all we do
with your most gracious favour,
and guide us with your continual help,
that in all our works
begun, continued and ended in you,
we may glorify your holy name,
and finally by your mercy receive everlasting life;
through Jesus Christ our Lord.

The Third Sunday before Lent

Collect

Almighty God,
who alone can bring order
to the unruly wills and passions of sinful humanity:
give your people grace
so to love what you command
and to desire what you promise,
that, among the many changes of this world,
our hearts may surely there be fixed
where true joys are to be found;
through Jesus Christ your Son our Lord,
who is alive and reigns with you,
in the unity of the Holy Spirit,
one God, now and for ever.

Post Communion

Merciful Father,
who gave Jesus Christ to be for us the bread of life,
that those who come to him should never hunger:
draw us to the Lord in faith and love,
that we may eat and drink with him
at his table in the kingdom,
where he is alive and reigns, now and for ever.

Collect

Almighty God,
you have created the heavens and the earth
and made us in your own image:
teach us to discern your hand in all your works
and your likeness in all your children;
through Jesus Christ your Son our Lord,
who with you and the Holy Spirit reigns supreme over all things,
now and for ever.

Post Communion

God our creator,
by your gift
the tree of life was set at the heart of the earthly paradise,
and the bread of life at the heart of your Church:
may we who have been nourished at your table on earth
be transformed by the glory of the Saviour's cross
and enjoy the delights of eternity;
through Jesus Christ our Lord.

The Sunday next before Lent

This provision is not used on or after Ash Wednesday.

Collect

Almighty Father,
whose Son was revealed in majesty
before he suffered death upon the cross:
give us grace to perceive his glory,
that we may be strengthened to suffer with him
and be changed into his likeness, from glory to glory;
who is alive and reigns with you,
in the unity of the Holy Spirit,
one God, now and for ever.

Post Communion

Holy God,
we see your glory in the face of Jesus Christ:
may we who are partakers at his table
reflect his life in word and deed,
that all the world may know his power to change and save.
This we ask through Jesus Christ our Lord.

¶ Lent

Ash Wednesday *Purple or*
Principal Holy Day *Lent Array*

Collect

Almighty and everlasting God,
you hate nothing that you have made
and forgive the sins of all those who are penitent:
create and make in us new and contrite hearts
that we, worthily lamenting our sins
and acknowledging our wretchedness,
may receive from you, the God of all mercy,
perfect remission and forgiveness;
through Jesus Christ your Son our Lord,
who is alive and reigns with you,
in the unity of the Holy Spirit,
one God, now and for ever.

*This Collect may be used as the Post Communion on any day from the
First Sunday of Lent until the Saturday after the Fourth Sunday of Lent
instead of the Post Communion provided.*

Post Communion

Almighty God,
you have given your only Son to be for us
both a sacrifice for sin
and also an example of godly life:
give us grace
that we may always most thankfully receive
these his inestimable gifts,
and also daily endeavour
    to follow the blessed steps of his most holy life;
through Jesus Christ our Lord.

The First Sunday of Lent

Collect

Almighty God,
whose Son Jesus Christ fasted forty days in the wilderness,
and was tempted as we are, yet without sin:
give us grace to discipline ourselves in obedience to your Spirit;
and, as you know our weakness,
so may we know your power to save;
through Jesus Christ your Son our Lord,
who is alive and reigns with you,
in the unity of the Holy Spirit,
one God, now and for ever.

Post Communion

Lord God,
you have renewed us with the living bread from heaven;
by it you nourish our faith,
increase our hope,
and strengthen our love:
teach us always to hunger for him who is the true and living bread,
and enable us to live by every word
    that proceeds from out of your mouth;
through Jesus Christ our Lord.

The Second Sunday of Lent Purple or Lent Array

Collect

Almighty God,
you show to those who are in error the light of your truth,
that they may return to the way of righteousness:
grant to all those who are admitted
    into the fellowship of Christ's religion,
that they may reject those things
    that are contrary to their profession,
and follow all such things as are agreeable to the same;
through our Lord Jesus Christ,
who is alive and reigns with you,
in the unity of the Holy Spirit,
one God, now and for ever.

Post Communion

Almighty God,
you see that we have no power of ourselves to help ourselves:
keep us both outwardly in our bodies,
and inwardly in our souls;
that we may be defended from all adversities
    which may happen to the body,
and from all evil thoughts which may assault and hurt the soul;
through Jesus Christ our Lord.

The Third Sunday of Lent Purple or Lent Array

Collect

Almighty God,
whose most dear Son went not up to joy but first he suffered pain,
and entered not into glory before he was crucified:
mercifully grant that we, walking in the way of the cross,
may find it none other than the way of life and peace;
through Jesus Christ your Son our Lord,
who is alive and reigns with you,
in the unity of the Holy Spirit,
one God, now and for ever.

Post Communion

Merciful Lord,
grant your people grace to withstand the temptations
　　of the world, the flesh and the devil,
and with pure hearts and minds to follow you, the only God;
through Jesus Christ our Lord.

The Fourth Sunday of Lent　*Purple or*
Lent Array

*Mothering Sunday may be celebrated in preference to the provision
for the Fourth Sunday of Lent.*

Collect

Merciful Lord,
absolve your people from their offences,
that through your bountiful goodness
we may all be delivered from the chains of those sins
which by our frailty we have committed;
grant this, heavenly Father,
for Jesus Christ's sake, our blessed Lord and Saviour,
who is alive and reigns with you,
in the unity of the Holy Spirit,
one God, now and for ever.

Post Communion

Lord God,
whose blessed Son our Saviour
gave his back to the smiters
and did not hide his face from shame:
give us grace to endure the sufferings of this present time
with sure confidence in the glory that shall be revealed;
through Jesus Christ our Lord.

Mothering Sunday may be celebrated in preference to the provision
for the Fourth Sunday of Lent.

Collect

God of compassion,
whose Son Jesus Christ, the child of Mary,
shared the life of a home in Nazareth,
and on the cross drew the whole human family to himself:
strengthen us in our daily living
that in joy and in sorrow
we may know the power of your presence
    to bind together and to heal;
through Jesus Christ your Son our Lord,
who is alive and reigns with you,
in the unity of the Holy Spirit,
one God, now and for ever.

Post Communion

Loving God,
as a mother feeds her children at the breast
you feed us in this sacrament with the food and drink of eternal life:
help us who have tasted your goodness
to grow in grace within the household of faith;
through Jesus Christ our Lord.

The Fifth Sunday of Lent *Purple or*
Passiontide begins *Lent Array*

Collect

Most merciful God,
who by the death and resurrection of your Son Jesus Christ
delivered and saved the world:
grant that by faith in him who suffered on the cross
we may triumph in the power of his victory;
through Jesus Christ your Son our Lord,
who is alive and reigns with you,
in the unity of the Holy Spirit,
one God, now and for ever.

Post Communion

Lord Jesus Christ,
you have taught us
that what we do for the least of our brothers and sisters
we do also for you:
give us the will to be the servant of others
as you were the servant of all,
and gave up your life and died for us,
but are alive and reign, now and for ever.

Palm Sunday   *Red*

Collect

Almighty and everlasting God,
who in your tender love towards the human race
    sent your Son our Saviour Jesus Christ
to take upon him our flesh
and to suffer death upon the cross:
grant that we may follow the example of his patience and humility,
and also be made partakers of his resurrection;
through Jesus Christ your Son our Lord,
who is alive and reigns with you,
in the unity of the Holy Spirit,
one God, now and for ever.

Post Communion

Lord Jesus Christ,
you humbled yourself in taking the form of a servant,
and in obedience died on the cross for our salvation:
give us the mind to follow you
and to proclaim you as Lord and King,
to the glory of God the Father.

At Morning and Evening Prayer the Collect of Palm Sunday is used.
At Holy Communion this Collect is used.

Collect

God our Father,
you have invited us to share in the supper
which your Son gave to his Church
to proclaim his death until he comes:
may he nourish us by his presence,
and unite us in his love;
who is alive and reigns with you,
in the unity of the Holy Spirit,
one God, now and for ever.

Post Communion

Lord Jesus Christ,
we thank you that in this wonderful sacrament
you have given us the memorial of your passion:
grant us so to reverence the sacred mysteries
    of your body and blood
that we may know within ourselves
and show forth in our lives
the fruit of your redemption,
for you are alive and reign, now and for ever.

Good Friday
Principal Holy Day

Collect

Almighty Father,
look with mercy on this your family
for which our Lord Jesus Christ was content to be betrayed
    and given up into the hands of sinners
    and to suffer death upon the cross;
who is alive and glorified with you and the Holy Spirit,
one God, now and for ever.

Easter Eve

Collect

Grant, Lord,
that we who are baptized into the death
    of your Son our Saviour Jesus Christ
may continually put to death our evil desires
    and be buried with him;
and that through the grave and gate of death
we may pass to our joyful resurrection;
through his merits,
who died and was buried and rose again for us,
your Son Jesus Christ our Lord.

¶ Easter

Easter Day *Gold or*
Principal Feast *White*

Collect

Lord of all life and power,
who through the mighty resurrection of your Son
overcame the old order of sin and death
to make all things new in him:
grant that we, being dead to sin
and alive to you in Jesus Christ,
may reign with him in glory;
to whom with you and the Holy Spirit
be praise and honour, glory and might,
now and in all eternity.

Post Communion

God of Life,
who for our redemption gave your only-begotten Son
    to the death of the cross,
and by his glorious resurrection
have delivered us from the power of our enemy:
grant us so to die daily to sin,
that we may evermore live with him in the joy of his risen life;
through Jesus Christ our Lord.

The Second Sunday of Easter *White*

Collect

Almighty Father,
you have given your only Son to die for our sins
and to rise again for our justification:
grant us so to put away the leaven of malice and wickedness
that we may always serve you
in pureness of living and truth;
through the merits of your Son Jesus Christ our Lord,
who is alive and reigns with you,
in the unity of the Holy Spirit,
one God, now and for ever.

Post Communion

Lord God our Father,
through our Saviour Jesus Christ
you have assured your children of eternal life
and in baptism have made us one with him:
deliver us from the death of sin
and raise us to new life in your love,
in the fellowship of the Holy Spirit,
by the grace of our Lord Jesus Christ.

The Third Sunday of Easter   *White*

Collect

Almighty Father,
who in your great mercy gladdened the disciples
    with the sight of the risen Lord:
give us such knowledge of his presence with us,
that we may be strengthened and sustained by his risen life
and serve you continually in righteousness and truth;
through Jesus Christ your Son our Lord,
who is alive and reigns with you,
in the unity of the Holy Spirit,
one God, now and for ever.

Post Communion

Living God,
your Son made himself known to his disciples
in the breaking of bread:
open the eyes of our faith,
that we may see him in all his redeeming work;
who is alive and reigns, now and for ever.

The Fourth Sunday of Easter White

Collect

Almighty God,
whose Son Jesus Christ is the resurrection and the life:
raise us, who trust in him,
from the death of sin to the life of righteousness,
that we may seek those things which are above,
where he reigns with you
in the unity of the Holy Spirit,
one God, now and for ever.

Post Communion

Merciful Father,
you gave your Son Jesus Christ to be the good shepherd,
and in his love for us to lay down his life and rise again:
keep us always under his protection,
and give us grace to follow in his steps;
through Jesus Christ our Lord.

The Fifth Sunday of Easter White

Collect

Almighty God,
who through your only-begotten Son Jesus Christ
have overcome death and opened to us the gate of everlasting life:
grant that, as by your grace going before us
    you put into our minds good desires,
so by your continual help
we may bring them to good effect;
through Jesus Christ our risen Lord,
who is alive and reigns with you,
in the unity of the Holy Spirit,
one God, now and for ever.

Post Communion

Eternal God,
whose Son Jesus Christ is the way, the truth, and the life:
grant us to walk in his way,
to rejoice in his truth,
and to share his risen life;
who is alive and reigns, now and for ever.

The Sixth Sunday of Easter   *White*

This provision is not used on or after Ascension Day.

Collect

God our redeemer,
you have delivered us from the power of darkness
and brought us into the kingdom of your Son:
grant, that as by his death he has recalled us to life,
so by his continual presence in us he may raise us
    to eternal joy;
through Jesus Christ your Son our Lord,
who is alive and reigns with you,
in the unity of the Holy Spirit,
one God, now and for ever.

Post Communion

God our Father,
whose Son Jesus Christ gives the water of eternal life:
may we thirst for you,
the spring of life and source of goodness,
through him who is alive and reigns, now and for ever.

Ascension Day

Principal Feast

Gold or White

Collect

Grant, we pray, almighty God,
that as we believe your only-begotten Son our Lord Jesus Christ
to have ascended into the heavens,
so we in heart and mind may also ascend
and with him continually dwell;
who is alive and reigns with you,
in the unity of the Holy Spirit,
one God, now and for ever.

Post Communion

God our Father,
you have raised our humanity in Christ
and have fed us with the bread of heaven:
mercifully grant that, nourished with such spiritual blessings,
we may set our hearts in the heavenly places;
through Jesus Christ our Lord.

The Seventh Sunday of Easter

White

Sunday after Ascension Day

Collect

O God the King of glory,
you have exalted your only Son Jesus Christ
with great triumph to your kingdom in heaven:
we beseech you, leave us not comfortless,
but send your Holy Spirit to strengthen us
and exalt us to the place where our Saviour Christ is gone before,
who is alive and reigns with you,
in the unity of the Holy Spirit,
one God, now and for ever.

Post Communion

Eternal God, giver of love and power,
your Son Jesus Christ has sent us into all the world
to preach the gospel of his kingdom:
confirm us in this mission,
and help us to live the good news we proclaim;
through Jesus Christ our Lord.

Day of Pentecost   *Red*
Whit Sunday
Principal Feast

This provision is not used on the weekdays after the Day of Pentecost.

Collect

God, who as at this time
taught the hearts of your faithful people
by sending to them the light of your Holy Spirit:
grant us by the same Spirit
to have a right judgement in all things
and evermore to rejoice in his holy comfort;
through the merits of Christ Jesus our Saviour,
who is alive and reigns with you,
in the unity of the Holy Spirit,
one God, now and for ever.

Post Communion

Faithful God,
who fulfilled the promises of Easter
by sending us your Holy Spirit
and opening to every race and nation
the way of life eternal:
open our lips by your Spirit,
that every tongue may tell of your glory;
through Jesus Christ our Lord.

The Weekdays after the Day of Pentecost   *Green*

Collect

O Lord, from whom all good things come:
grant to us your humble servants,
that by your holy inspiration
we may think those things that are good,
and by your merciful guiding may perform the same;
through our Lord Jesus Christ,
who is alive and reigns with you,
in the unity of the Holy Spirit,
one God, now and for ever.

Post Communion

Gracious God, lover of all,
in this sacrament
we are one family in Christ your Son,
one in the sharing of his body and blood
and one in the communion of his Spirit:
help us to grow in love for one another
and come to the full maturity of the Body of Christ.
We make our prayer through your Son our Saviour.

Trinity Sunday   *Gold or*
Principal Feast   *White*

Collect

Almighty and everlasting God,
you have given us your servants grace,
by the confession of a true faith,
to acknowledge the glory of the eternal Trinity
and in the power of the divine majesty to worship the Unity:
keep us steadfast in this faith,
that we may evermore be defended from all adversities;
through Jesus Christ your Son our Lord,
who is alive and reigns with you,
in the unity of the Holy Spirit,
one God, now and for ever.

Post Communion

Almighty and eternal God,
you have revealed yourself as Father, Son and Holy Spirit,
and live and reign in the perfect unity of love:
hold us firm in this faith,
that we may know you in all your ways
and evermore rejoice in your eternal glory,
who are three Persons yet one God,
now and for ever.

The Thursday after Trinity Sunday may be observed as

The Day of Thanksgiving for the
Institution of Holy Communion *White*
(Corpus Christi)

Collect

Lord Jesus Christ,
we thank you that in this wonderful sacrament
you have given us the memorial of your passion:
grant us so to reverence the sacred mysteries
    of your body and blood
that we may know within ourselves
and show forth in our lives
the fruits of your redemption;
for you are alive and reign with the Father
in the unity of the Holy Spirit,
one God, now and for ever.

Post Communion

All praise to you, our God and Father,
for you have fed us with the bread of heaven
and quenched our thirst from the true vine:
hear our prayer that, being grafted into Christ,
we may grow together in unity
and feast with him in his kingdom;
through Jesus Christ our Lord.

The First Sunday after Trinity *Green*

Collect

O God,
the strength of all those who put their trust in you,
mercifully accept our prayers
and, because through the weakness of our mortal nature
we can do no good thing without you,
grant us the help of your grace,
that in the keeping of your commandments
we may please you both in will and deed;
through Jesus Christ your Son our Lord,
who is alive and reigns with you,
in the unity of the Holy Spirit,
one God, now and for ever.

Post Communion

Eternal Father,
we thank you for nourishing us
with these heavenly gifts:
may our communion strengthen us in faith,
build us up in hope,
and make us grow in love;
for the sake of Jesus Christ our Lord.

The Second Sunday after Trinity *Green*

Collect

Lord, you have taught us
that all our doings without love are nothing worth:
send your Holy Spirit
and pour into our hearts that most excellent gift of love,
the true bond of peace and of all virtues,
without which whoever lives is counted dead before you.
Grant this for your only Son Jesus Christ's sake,
who is alive and reigns with you,
in the unity of the Holy Spirit,
one God, now and for ever.

Post Communion

Loving Father,
we thank you for feeding us at the supper of your Son:
sustain us with your Spirit,
that we may serve you here on earth
until our joy is complete in heaven,
and we share in the eternal banquet
with Jesus Christ our Lord.

The Third Sunday after Trinity   *Green*

Collect

Almighty God,
you have broken the tyranny of sin
and have sent the Spirit of your Son into our hearts
    whereby we call you Father:
give us grace to dedicate our freedom to your service,
that we and all creation may be brought
    to the glorious liberty of the children of God;
through Jesus Christ your Son our Lord,
who is alive and reigns with you,
in the unity of the Holy Spirit,
one God, now and for ever.

Post Communion

O God, whose beauty is beyond our imagining
and whose power we cannot comprehend:
show us your glory as far as we can grasp it,
and shield us from knowing more than we can bear
until we may look upon you without fear;
through Jesus Christ our Saviour.

The Fourth Sunday after Trinity *Green*

Collect

O God, the protector of all who trust in you,
without whom nothing is strong, nothing is holy:
increase and multiply upon us your mercy;
that with you as our ruler and guide
we may so pass through things temporal
that we lose not our hold on things eternal;
grant this, heavenly Father,
for our Lord Jesus Christ's sake,
who is alive and reigns with you,
in the unity of the Holy Spirit,
one God, now and for ever.

Post Communion

Eternal God,
comfort of the afflicted and healer of the broken,
you have fed us at the table of life and hope:
teach us the ways of gentleness and peace,
that all the world may acknowledge
the kingdom of your Son Jesus Christ our Lord.

The Fifth Sunday after Trinity *Green*

Collect

Almighty and everlasting God,
by whose Spirit the whole body of the Church
    is governed and sanctified:
hear our prayer which we offer for all your faithful people,
that in their vocation and ministry
they may serve you in holiness and truth
to the glory of your name;
through our Lord and Saviour Jesus Christ,
who is alive and reigns with you,
in the unity of the Holy Spirit,
one God, now and for ever.

Post Communion

Grant, O Lord, we beseech you,
that the course of this world may be so peaceably ordered
    by your governance,
that your Church may joyfully serve you in all godly quietness;
through Jesus Christ our Lord.

The Sixth Sunday after Trinity *Green*

Collect

Merciful God,
you have prepared for those who love you
such good things as pass our understanding:
pour into our hearts such love toward you
that we, loving you in all things and above all things,
may obtain your promises,
which exceed all that we can desire;
through Jesus Christ your Son our Lord,
who is alive and reigns with you,
in the unity of the Holy Spirit,
one God, now and for ever.

Post Communion

God of our pilgrimage,
you have led us to the living water:
refresh and sustain us
as we go forward on our journey,
in the name of Jesus Christ our Lord.

The Seventh Sunday after Trinity Green

Collect

Lord of all power and might,
the author and giver of all good things:
graft in our hearts the love of your name,
increase in us true religion,
nourish us with all goodness,
and of your great mercy keep us in the same;
through Jesus Christ your Son our Lord,
who is alive and reigns with you,
in the unity of the Holy Spirit,
one God, now and for ever.

Post Communion

Lord God, whose Son is the true vine and the source of life,
ever giving himself that the world may live:
may we so receive within ourselves
    the power of his death and passion
that, in his saving cup,
    we may share his glory and be made perfect in his love;
for he is alive and reigns, now and for ever.

The Eighth Sunday after Trinity Green

Collect

Almighty Lord and everlasting God,
we beseech you to direct, sanctify and govern
    both our hearts and bodies
in the ways of your laws
    and the works of your commandments;
that through your most mighty protection, both here and ever,
we may be preserved in body and soul;
through our Lord and Saviour Jesus Christ,
who is alive and reigns with you,
in the unity of the Holy Spirit,
one God, now and for ever.

Post Communion

Strengthen for service, Lord,
the hands that have taken holy things;
may the ears which have heard your word
    be deaf to clamour and dispute;
may the tongues which have sung your praise be free from deceit;
may the eyes which have seen the tokens of your love
    shine with the light of hope;
and may the bodies which have been fed with your body
    be refreshed with the fullness of your life;
glory to you for ever.

The Ninth Sunday after Trinity   *Green*

Collect

Almighty God,
who sent your Holy Spirit
to be the life and light of your Church:
open our hearts to the riches of your grace,
that we may bring forth the fruit of the Spirit
in love and joy and peace;
through Jesus Christ your Son our Lord,
who is alive and reigns with you,
in the unity of the Holy Spirit,
one God, now and for ever.

Post Communion

Holy Father,
who gathered us here around the table of your Son
to share this meal with the whole household of God:
in that new world where you reveal the fullness of your peace,
gather people of every race and language
    to share in the eternal banquet of Jesus Christ our Lord.

The Tenth Sunday after Trinity

Collect

Let your merciful ears, O Lord,
be open to the prayers of your humble servants;
and that they may obtain their petitions
make them to ask such things as shall please you;
through Jesus Christ your Son our Lord,
who is alive and reigns with you,
in the unity of the Holy Spirit,
one God, now and for ever.

Post Communion

God of our pilgrimage,
you have willed that the gate of mercy
should stand open for those who trust in you:
look upon us with your favour
that we who follow the path of your will
may never wander from the way of life;
through Jesus Christ our Lord.

The Eleventh Sunday after Trinity

Collect

O God, you declare your almighty power
most chiefly in showing mercy and pity:
mercifully grant to us such a measure of your grace,
that we, running the way of your commandments,
may receive your gracious promises,
and be made partakers of your heavenly treasure;
through Jesus Christ your Son our Lord,
who is alive and reigns with you,
in the unity of the Holy Spirit,
one God, now and for ever.

Post Communion

Lord of all mercy,
we your faithful people have celebrated that one true sacrifice
    which takes away our sins and brings pardon and peace:
by our communion
keep us firm on the foundation of the gospel
and preserve us from all sin;
through Jesus Christ our Lord.

The Twelfth Sunday after Trinity   *Green*

Collect

Almighty and everlasting God,
you are always more ready to hear than we to pray
and to give more than either we desire or deserve:
pour down upon us the abundance of your mercy,
forgiving us those things of which our conscience is afraid
and giving us those good things
    which we are not worthy to ask
but through the merits and mediation
of Jesus Christ your Son our Lord,
who is alive and reigns with you,
in the unity of the Holy Spirit,
one God, now and for ever.

Post Communion

God of all mercy,
in this eucharist you have set aside our sins
and given us your healing:
grant that we who are made whole in Christ
may bring that healing to this broken world,
in the name of Jesus Christ our Lord.

The Thirteenth Sunday after Trinity Green

Collect

Almighty God,
who called your Church to bear witness
that you were in Christ reconciling the world to yourself:
help us to proclaim the good news of your love,
that all who hear it may be drawn to you;
through him who was lifted up on the cross,
and reigns with you in the unity of the Holy Spirit,
one God, now and for ever.

Post Communion

God our creator,
you feed your children with the true manna,
the living bread from heaven:
let this holy food sustain us through our earthly pilgrimage
until we come to that place
    where hunger and thirst are no more;
through Jesus Christ our Lord.

The Fourteenth Sunday after Trinity Green

Collect

Almighty God,
whose only Son has opened for us
a new and living way into your presence:
give us pure hearts and steadfast wills
to worship you in spirit and in truth;
through Jesus Christ your Son our Lord,
who is alive and reigns with you,
in the unity of the Holy Spirit,
one God, now and for ever.

Post Communion

Lord God, the source of truth and love,
keep us faithful to the apostles' teaching and fellowship,
united in prayer and the breaking of bread,
and one in joy and simplicity of heart,
in Jesus Christ our Lord.

The Fifteenth Sunday after Trinity

Green

Collect

God, who in generous mercy sent the Holy Spirit
    upon your Church in the burning fire of your love:
grant that your people may be fervent
    in the fellowship of the gospel
that, always abiding in you,
they may be found steadfast in faith and active in service;
through Jesus Christ your Son our Lord,
who is alive and reigns with you,
in the unity of the Holy Spirit,
one God, now and for ever.

Post Communion

Keep, O Lord, your Church, with your perpetual mercy;
and, because without you our human frailty cannot but fall,
keep us ever by your help from all things hurtful,
and lead us to all things profitable to our salvation;
through Jesus Christ our Lord.

The Sixteenth Sunday after Trinity

Collect

O Lord, we beseech you mercifully to hear the prayers
　　of your people who call upon you;
and grant that they may both perceive and know
　　what things they ought to do,
and also may have grace and power faithfully to fulfil them;
through Jesus Christ your Son our Lord,
who is alive and reigns with you,
in the unity of the Holy Spirit,
one God, now and for ever.

Post Communion

Almighty God,
you have taught us through your Son
that love is the fulfilling of the law:
grant that we may love you with our whole heart
and our neighbours as ourselves;
through Jesus Christ our Lord.

The Seventeenth Sunday after Trinity

Collect

Almighty God,
you have made us for yourself,
and our hearts are restless till they find their rest in you:
pour your love into our hearts and draw us to yourself,
and so bring us at last to your heavenly city
where we shall see you face to face;
through Jesus Christ your Son our Lord,
who is alive and reigns with you,
in the unity of the Holy Spirit,
one God, now and for ever.

Post Communion

Lord, we pray that your grace
    may always precede and follow us,
and make us continually to be given to all good works;
through Jesus Christ our Lord.

The Eighteenth Sunday after Trinity   *Green*

Collect

Almighty and everlasting God,
increase in us your gift of faith
that, forsaking what lies behind
and reaching out to that which is before,
we may run the way of your commandments
and win the crown of everlasting joy;
through Jesus Christ your Son our Lord,
who is alive and reigns with you,
in the unity of the Holy Spirit,
one God, now and for ever.

Post Communion

We praise and thank you, O Christ, for this sacred feast:
for here we receive you,
here the memory of your passion is renewed,
here our minds are filled with grace,
and here a pledge of future glory is given,
when we shall feast at that table where you reign
with all your saints for ever.

The Nineteenth Sunday after Trinity

Collect

O God, forasmuch as without you
we are not able to please you;
mercifully grant that your Holy Spirit
may in all things direct and rule our hearts;
through Jesus Christ your Son our Lord,
who is alive and reigns with you,
in the unity of the Holy Spirit,
one God, now and for ever.

Post Communion

Holy and blessed God,
you have fed us with the body and blood of your Son
and filled us with your Holy Spirit:
may we honour you,
not only with our lips
but in lives dedicated to the service
    of Jesus Christ our Lord.

The Twentieth Sunday after Trinity

Collect

God, the giver of life,
whose Holy Spirit wells up within your Church:
by the Spirit's gifts equip us to live the gospel of Christ
    and make us eager to do your will,
that we may share with the whole creation
    the joys of eternal life;
through Jesus Christ your Son our Lord,
who is alive and reigns with you,
in the unity of the Holy Spirit,
one God, now and for ever.

Post Communion

God our Father,
whose Son, the light unfailing,
has come from heaven to deliver the world
    from the darkness of ignorance:
let these holy mysteries open the eyes of our understanding
that we may know the way of life,
and walk in it without stumbling;
through Jesus Christ our Lord.

The Twenty-first Sunday after Trinity   *Green*

Collect

Grant, we beseech you, merciful Lord,
to your faithful people pardon and peace,
that they may be cleansed from all their sins
and serve you with a quiet mind;
through Jesus Christ your Son our Lord,
who is alive and reigns with you,
in the unity of the Holy Spirit,
one God, now and for ever.

Post Communion

Father of light,
in whom is no change or shadow of turning,
you give us every good and perfect gift
and have brought us to birth by your word of truth:
may we be a living sign of that kingdom
where your whole creation will be made perfect
    in Jesus Christ our Lord.

*If there are twenty-three Sundays after Trinity, the provision
for the Third Sunday before Lent (page 389) is used on the
Twenty-second Sunday after Trinity.*

The Last Sunday after Trinity   *Green*

Collect

Blessed Lord,
who caused all holy Scriptures to be written for our learning:
help us so to hear them,
to read, mark, learn and inwardly digest them
that, through patience, and the comfort of your holy word,
we may embrace and for ever hold fast
     the hope of everlasting life,
which you have given us in our Saviour Jesus Christ,
who is alive and reigns with you,
in the unity of the Holy Spirit,
one God, now and for ever.

Post Communion

God of all grace,
your Son Jesus Christ fed the hungry
with the bread of his life
and the word of his kingdom:
renew your people with your heavenly grace,
and in all our weakness
sustain us by your true and living bread;
who is alive and reigns, now and for ever.

1 November   **All Saints' Day**   *Gold or*
    Principal Feast   *White*

Collect

Almighty God,
you have knit together your elect
in one communion and fellowship
     in the mystical body of your Son Christ our Lord:
grant us grace so to follow your blessed saints
in all virtuous and godly living
that we may come to those inexpressible joys
that you have prepared for those who truly love you;
through Jesus Christ your Son our Lord,
who is alive and reigns with you,
in the unity of the Holy Spirit,
one God, now and for ever.

Post Communion

God, the source of all holiness and giver of all good things:
may we who have shared at this table
    as strangers and pilgrims here on earth
be welcomed with all your saints
    to the heavenly feast on the day of your kingdom;
through Jesus Christ our Lord.

The Fourth Sunday before Advent

*Red or
Green*

Collect

Almighty and eternal God,
you have kindled the flame of love
    in the hearts of the saints:
grant to us the same faith and power of love,
that, as we rejoice in their triumphs,
we may be sustained by their example and fellowship;
through Jesus Christ your Son our Lord,
who is alive and reigns with you,
in the unity of the Holy Spirit,
one God, now and for ever.

Post Communion

Lord of heaven,
in this eucharist you have brought us near
    to an innumerable company of angels
    and to the spirits of the saints made perfect:
as in this food of our earthly pilgrimage
    we have shared their fellowship,
so may we come to share their joy in heaven;
through Jesus Christ our Lord.

Collect

Almighty Father,
whose will is to restore all things
in your beloved Son, the King of all:
govern the hearts and minds of those in authority,
and bring the families of the nations,
divided and torn apart by the ravages of sin,
to be subject to his just and gentle rule;
who is alive and reigns with you,
in the unity of the Holy Spirit,
one God, now and for ever.

Post Communion

God of peace,
whose Son Jesus Christ proclaimed the kingdom
and restored the broken to wholeness of life:
look with compassion on the anguish of the world,
and by your healing power
make whole both people and nations;
through our Lord and Saviour Jesus Christ.

In years when Remembrance Sunday is observed on the Second Sunday
before Advent, the Collect and Post Communion for the Third Sunday
before Advent may be used on Remembrance Sunday and the Collect
and Post Communion for the Second Sunday before Advent may be
used on the Third Sunday before Advent.

The Second Sunday before Advent

Red or
Green

Collect

Heavenly Father,
whose blessed Son was revealed
    to destroy the works of the devil
and to make us the children of God and heirs of eternal life:
grant that we, having this hope,
may purify ourselves even as he is pure;
that when he shall appear in power and great glory
we may be made like him in his eternal and glorious kingdom;
where he is alive and reigns with you,
in the unity of the Holy Spirit,
one God, now and for ever.

Post Communion

Gracious Lord,
in this holy sacrament
you give substance to our hope:
bring us at the last
to that fullness of life for which we long;
through Jesus Christ our Saviour.

*In years when Remembrance Sunday is observed on the Second Sunday
before Advent, the Collect and Post Communion for the Third Sunday
before Advent may be used on Remembrance Sunday and the Collect
and Post Communion for the Second Sunday before Advent may be used
on the Third Sunday before Advent.*

Collect

Eternal Father,
whose Son Jesus Christ ascended to the throne of heaven
    that he might rule over all things as Lord and King:
keep the Church in the unity of the Spirit
and in the bond of peace,
and bring the whole created order to worship at his feet;
who is alive and reigns with you,
in the unity of the Holy Spirit,
one God, now and for ever.

Post Communion

Stir up, O Lord,
the wills of your faithful people;
that they, plenteously bringing forth the fruit of good works,
may by you be plenteously rewarded;
through Jesus Christ our Lord.

This Post Communion may be used as the Collect at Morning and
Evening Prayer during this week.

The Naming and Circumcision of Jesus   *White*

1 January

Collect

Almighty God,
whose blessed Son was circumcised
in obedience to the law for our sake
and given the Name that is above every name:
give us grace faithfully to bear his Name,
to worship him in the freedom of the Spirit,
and to proclaim him as the Saviour of the world;
who is alive and reigns with you,
in the unity of the Holy Spirit,
one God, now and for ever.

Post Communion

Eternal God,
whose incarnate Son was given the Name of Saviour:
grant that we who have shared
    in this sacrament of our salvation
may live out our years in the power
    of the Name above all other names,
Jesus Christ our Lord.

25 January   ## The Conversion of Paul   *White*

Collect

Almighty God,
who caused the light of the gospel
to shine throughout the world
through the preaching of your servant Saint Paul:
grant that we who celebrate his wonderful conversion
may follow him in bearing witness to your truth;
through Jesus Christ your Son our Lord,
who is alive and reigns with you,
in the unity of the Holy Spirit,
one God, now and for ever.

Post Communion
of Apostles and Evangelists

Almighty God,
who on the day of Pentecost
sent your Holy Spirit to the apostles
with the wind from heaven and in tongues of flame,
filling them with joy and boldness to preach the gospel:
by the power of the same Spirit
strengthen us to witness to your truth
and to draw everyone to the fire of your love;
through Jesus Christ our Lord.

(or)

Lord God, the source of truth and love,
keep us faithful to the apostles' teaching and fellowship,
united in prayer and the breaking of bread,
and one in joy and simplicity of heart,
in Jesus Christ our Lord.

19 March **Joseph of Nazareth** *White*

Collect

God our Father,
who from the family of your servant David
raised up Joseph the carpenter
to be the guardian of your incarnate Son
and husband of the Blessed Virgin Mary:
give us grace to follow him
in faithful obedience to your commands;
through Jesus Christ your Son our Lord,
who is alive and reigns with you,
in the unity of the Holy Spirit,
one God, now and for ever.

Post Communion

Heavenly Father,
whose Son grew in wisdom and stature
in the home of Joseph the carpenter of Nazareth
and on the wood of the cross
    perfected the work of the world's salvation:
help us, strengthened by this sacrament of his passion,
to count the wisdom of the world as foolishness,
and to walk with him in simplicity and trust;
through Jesus Christ our Lord.

25 March	**The Annunciation of Our Lord**	*Gold or*
	Principal Feast	*White*

Collect

We beseech you, O Lord,
pour your grace into our hearts,
that as we have known the incarnation of your Son Jesus Christ
    by the message of an angel,
so by his cross and passion
we may be brought to the glory of his resurrection;
through Jesus Christ your Son our Lord,
who is alive and reigns with you,
in the unity of the Holy Spirit,
one God, now and for ever.

Post Communion

God most high,
whose handmaid bore the Word made flesh:
we thank you that in this sacrament of our redemption
you visit us with your Holy Spirit
and overshadow us by your power;
strengthen us to walk with Mary the joyful path of obedience
and so to bring forth the fruits of holiness;
through Jesus Christ our Lord.

George

Collect

God of hosts,
who so kindled the flame of love
in the heart of your servant George
that he bore witness to the risen Lord
by his life and by his death:
give us the same faith and power of love
that we who rejoice in his triumphs
may come to share with him the fullness of the resurrection;
through Jesus Christ your Son our Lord,
who is alive and reigns with you,
in the unity of the Holy Spirit,
one God, now and for ever.

Post Communion

Eternal God,
who gave us this holy meal
in which we have celebrated the glory of the cross
and the victory of your martyr George:
by our communion with Christ
in his saving death and resurrection,
give us with all your saints the courage to conquer evil
and so to share the fruit of the tree of life;
through Jesus Christ our Lord.

(or)

God our redeemer,
whose Church was strengthened
    by the blood of your martyr George:
so bind us, in life and death, to Christ's sacrifice
that our lives, broken and offered with his,
may carry his death and proclaim his resurrection in the world;
through Jesus Christ our Lord.

Mark

Evangelist

Collect

Almighty God,
who enlightened your holy Church
through the inspired witness of your evangelist Saint Mark:
grant that we, being firmly grounded
    in the truth of the gospel,
may be faithful to its teaching both in word and deed;
through Jesus Christ your Son our Lord,
who is alive and reigns with you,
in the unity of the Holy Spirit,
one God, now and for ever.

Post Communion

One of the Post Communions of Apostles and Evangelists is used
(page 428).

Philip and James

Apostles

Collect

Almighty Father,
whom truly to know is eternal life:
teach us to know your Son Jesus Christ
as the way, the truth, and the life;
that we may follow the steps
    of your holy apostles Philip and James,
and walk steadfastly in the way that leads to your glory;
through Jesus Christ your Son our Lord,
who is alive and reigns with you,
in the unity of the Holy Spirit,
one God, now and for ever.

Post Communion

One of the Post Communions of Apostles and Evangelists is used
(page 428).

Matthias

Apostle

Collect

Almighty God,
who in the place of the traitor Judas
chose your faithful servant Matthias
to be of the number of the Twelve:
preserve your Church from false apostles
and, by the ministry of faithful pastors and teachers,
keep us steadfast in your truth;
through Jesus Christ your Son our Lord,
who is alive and reigns with you,
in the unity of the Holy Spirit,
one God, now and for ever.

Post Communion

One of the Post Communions of Apostles and Evangelists is used (page 428).

The Visit of the Blessed Virgin Mary to Elizabeth

Collect

Mighty God,
by whose grace Elizabeth rejoiced with Mary
and greeted her as the mother of the Lord:
look with favour on your lowly servants
that, with Mary, we may magnify your holy name
and rejoice to acclaim her Son our Saviour,
who is alive and reigns with you,
in the unity of the Holy Spirit,
one God, now and for ever.

Post Communion

Gracious God,
who gave joy to Elizabeth and Mary
as they recognized the signs of redemption
    at work within them:
help us, who have shared in the joy of this eucharist,
to know the Lord deep within us
and his love shining out in our lives,
that the world may rejoice in your salvation;
through Jesus Christ our Lord.

11 June   **Barnabas**   *Red*
                              Apostle

Collect

Bountiful God, giver of all gifts,
who poured your Spirit upon your servant Barnabas
and gave him grace to encourage others:
help us, by his example,
to be generous in our judgements
and unselfish in our service;
through Jesus Christ your Son our Lord,
who is alive and reigns with you,
in the unity of the Holy Spirit,
one God, now and for ever.

Post Communion

*One of the Post Communions of Apostles and Evangelists is used
(page 428).*

Collect

Almighty God,
by whose providence your servant John the Baptist
    was wonderfully born,
and sent to prepare the way of your Son our Saviour
by the preaching of repentance:
lead us to repent according to his preaching
and, after his example,
constantly to speak the truth, boldly to rebuke vice,
and patiently to suffer for the truth's sake;
through Jesus Christ your Son our Lord,
who is alive and reigns with you,
in the unity of the Holy Spirit,
one God, now and for ever.

Post Communion

Merciful Lord,
whose prophet John the Baptist
proclaimed your Son as the Lamb of God
    who takes away the sin of the world:
grant that we who in this sacrament
    have known your forgiveness and your life-giving love
may ever tell of your mercy and your peace;
through Jesus Christ our Lord.

Peter and Paul

Red

Apostles

Collect

Almighty God,
whose blessed apostles Peter and Paul
glorified you in their death as in their life:
grant that your Church,
inspired by their teaching and example,
and made one by your Spirit,
may ever stand firm upon the one foundation,
Jesus Christ your Son our Lord,
who is alive and reigns with you,
in the unity of the Holy Spirit,
one God, now and for ever.

or, where Peter is celebrated alone

Almighty God,
who inspired your apostle Saint Peter
to confess Jesus as Christ and Son of the living God:
build up your Church upon this rock,
that in unity and peace it may proclaim one truth
and follow one Lord, your Son our Saviour Christ,
who is alive and reigns with you,
in the unity of the Holy Spirit,
one God, now and for ever.

Post Communion

*One of the Post Communions of Apostles and Evangelists is used
(page 428).*

Thomas

Apostle

Collect

Almighty and eternal God,
who, for the firmer foundation of our faith,
allowed your holy apostle Thomas
      to doubt the resurrection of your Son
till word and sight convinced him:
grant to us, who have not seen, that we also may believe
and so confess Christ as our Lord and our God;
who is alive and reigns with you,
in the unity of the Holy Spirit,
one God, now and for ever.

Post Communion

One of the Post Communions of Apostles and Evangelists is used (page 428).

Mary Magdalene

Collect

Almighty God,
whose Son restored Mary Magdalene
      to health of mind and body
and called her to be a witness to his resurrection:
forgive our sins and heal us by your grace,
that we may serve you in the power of his risen life;
who is alive and reigns with you,
in the unity of the Holy Spirit,
one God, now and for ever.

Post Communion

God of life and love,
whose risen Son called Mary Magdalene by name
and sent her to tell of his resurrection to his apostles:
in your mercy, help us,
who have been united with him in this eucharist,
to proclaim the good news
    that he is alive and reigns, now and for ever.

25 July   **James**   *Red*
                                     Apostle

Collect

Merciful God,
whose holy apostle Saint James,
leaving his father and all that he had,
was obedient to the calling of your Son Jesus Christ
and followed him even to death:
help us, forsaking the false attractions of the world,
to be ready at all times to answer your call without delay;
through Jesus Christ your Son our Lord,
who is alive and reigns with you,
in the unity of the Holy Spirit,
one God, now and for ever.

Post Communion

*One of the Post Communions of Apostles and Evangelists is used
(page 428).*

The Transfiguration of Our Lord

Collect

Father in heaven,
whose Son Jesus Christ was wonderfully transfigured
before chosen witnesses upon the holy mountain,
and spoke of the exodus he would accomplish at Jerusalem:
give us strength so to hear his voice and bear our cross
that in the world to come we may see him as he is;
who is alive and reigns with you,
in the unity of the Holy Spirit,
one God, now and for ever.

Post Communion

Holy God,
we see your glory in the face of Jesus Christ:
may we who are partakers at his table
reflect his life in word and deed,
that all the world may know his power to change and save.
This we ask through Jesus Christ our Lord.

The Blessed Virgin Mary

Collect

Almighty God,
who looked upon the lowliness of the Blessed Virgin Mary
and chose her to be the mother of your only Son:
grant that we who are redeemed by his blood
may share with her in the glory of your eternal kingdom;
through Jesus Christ your Son our Lord,
who is alive and reigns with you,
in the unity of the Holy Spirit,
one God, now and for ever.

Post Communion

God most high,
whose handmaid bore the Word made flesh:
we thank you that in this sacrament of our redemption
you visit us with your Holy Spirit
and overshadow us by your power;
strengthen us to walk with Mary the joyful path of obedience
and so to bring forth the fruits of holiness;
through Jesus Christ our Lord.

24 August   **Bartholomew**   Red

Apostle

Collect

Almighty and everlasting God,
who gave to your apostle Bartholomew grace
     truly to believe and to preach your word:
grant that your Church
may love that word which he believed
and may faithfully preach and receive the same;
through Jesus Christ your Son our Lord,
who is alive and reigns with you,
in the unity of the Holy Spirit,
one God, now and for ever.

Post Communion

*One of the Post Communions of Apostles and Evangelists is used
(page 428).*

Collect

Almighty God,
who in the passion of your blessed Son
made an instrument of painful death
to be for us the means of life and peace:
grant us so to glory in the cross of Christ
that we may gladly suffer for his sake;
who is alive and reigns with you,
in the unity of the Holy Spirit,
one God, now and for ever.

Post Communion

Faithful God,
whose Son bore our sins in his body on the tree
and gave us this sacrament to show forth his death until he comes:
give us grace to glory in the cross of our Lord Jesus Christ,
for he is our salvation, our life and our hope,
who reigns as Lord, now and for ever.

Collect

O Almighty God,
whose blessed Son called Matthew the tax collector
to be an apostle and evangelist:
give us grace to forsake the selfish pursuit of gain
      and the possessive love of riches
that we may follow in the way of your Son Jesus Christ,
who is alive and reigns with you,
in the unity of the Holy Spirit,
one God, now and for ever.

Post Communion

*One of the Post Communions of Apostles and Evangelists is used
(page 428).*

Collect

Everlasting God,
you have ordained and constituted
    the ministries of angels and mortals in a wonderful order:
grant that as your holy angels always serve you in heaven,
so, at your command,
they may help and defend us on earth;
through Jesus Christ your Son our Lord,
who is alive and reigns with you,
in the unity of the Holy Spirit,
one God, now and for ever.

Post Communion

Lord of heaven,
in this eucharist you have brought us near
    to an innumerable company of angels
    and to the spirits of the saints made perfect:
as in this food of our earthly pilgrimage
    we have shared their fellowship,
so may we come to share their joy in heaven;
through Jesus Christ our Lord.

Luke

Evangelist

Collect

Almighty God,
you called Luke the physician,
whose praise is in the gospel,
to be an evangelist and physician of the soul:
by the grace of the Spirit
and through the wholesome medicine of the gospel,
give your Church the same love and power to heal;
through Jesus Christ your Son our Lord,
who is alive and reigns with you,
in the unity of the Holy Spirit,
one God, now and for ever.

Post Communion

One of the Post Communions of Apostles and Evangelists is used (page 428).

Simon and Jude

Apostles

Collect

Almighty God,
who built your Church upon the foundation
    of the apostles and prophets,
with Jesus Christ himself as the chief cornerstone:
so join us together in unity of spirit by their doctrine,
that we may be made a holy temple acceptable to you;
through Jesus Christ your Son our Lord,
who is alive and reigns with you,
in the unity of the Holy Spirit,
one God, now and for ever.

Post Communion

One of the Post Communions of Apostles and Evangelists is used (page 428).

Andrew *Red*

Apostle

Collect

Almighty God,
who gave such grace to your apostle Saint Andrew
that he readily obeyed the call of your Son Jesus Christ
   and brought his brother with him:
call us by your holy word,
and give us grace to follow you without delay
   and to tell the good news of your kingdom;
through Jesus Christ your Son our Lord,
who is alive and reigns with you,
in the unity of the Holy Spirit,
one God, now and for ever.

Post Communion

*One of the Post Communions of Apostles and Evangelists is used
(page 428).*

26 December **Stephen** *Red*

Deacon, First Martyr

Collect

Gracious Father,
who gave the first martyr Stephen
grace to pray for those who took up stones against him:
grant that in all our sufferings for the truth
we may learn to love even our enemies
and to seek forgiveness for those who desire our hurt,
looking up to heaven to him who was crucified for us,
Jesus Christ, our mediator and advocate,
who is alive and reigns with you,
in the unity of the Holy Spirit,
one God, now and for ever.

Post Communion

Merciful Lord,
we thank you for the signs of your mercy
revealed in birth and death:
save us by the coming of your Son,
and give us joy in honouring Stephen,
first martyr of the new Israel;
through Jesus Christ our Lord.

27 December   **John**   *White*
                        Apostle and Evangelist

Collect

Merciful Lord,
cast your bright beams of light upon the Church:
that, being enlightened by the teaching
    of your blessed apostle and evangelist Saint John,
we may so walk in the light of your truth
that we may at last attain to the light of everlasting life;
through Jesus Christ your incarnate Son our Lord,
who is alive and reigns with you,
in the unity of the Holy Spirit,
one God, now and for ever.

Post Communion

Grant, O Lord, we pray,
that the Word made flesh
proclaimed by your apostle John
may, by the celebration of these holy mysteries,
ever abide and live within us;
through Jesus Christ our Lord.

Collect

Heavenly Father,
whose children suffered at the hands of Herod,
though they had done no wrong:
by the suffering of your Son
and by the innocence of our lives
frustrate all evil designs
and establish your reign of justice and peace;
through Jesus Christ your Son our Lord,
who is alive and reigns with you,
in the unity of the Holy Spirit,
one God, now and for ever.

Post Communion

Lord Jesus Christ,
in your humility you have stooped to share our human life
with the most defenceless of your children:
may we who have received these gifts of your passion
rejoice in celebrating the witness of the Holy Innocents
    to the purity of your sacrifice
    made once for all upon the cross;
for you are alive and reign, now and for ever.

Collect

Almighty God,
to whose glory we celebrate the dedication
    of this house of prayer:
we praise you for the many blessings
you have given to those who worship you here:
and we pray that all who seek you in this place may find you,
and, being filled with the Holy Spirit,
may become a living temple acceptable to you;
through Jesus Christ your Son our Lord,
who is alive and reigns with you,
in the unity of the Holy Spirit,
one God, now and for ever.

Post Communion

Father in heaven,
whose Church on earth is a sign of your heavenly peace,
an image of the new and eternal Jerusalem:
grant to us in the days of our pilgrimage
that, fed with the living bread of heaven,
and united in the body of your Son,
we may be the temple of your presence,
the place of your glory on earth,
and a sign of your peace in the world;
through Jesus Christ our Lord.

¶ *Special Occasion*

Harvest Thanksgiving *Green*

Harvest Thanksgiving may be celebrated on a Sunday and may replace the provision for that day, provided it does not supersede any Principal Feast or Festival.

Collect

Eternal God,
you crown the year with your goodness
and you give us the fruits of the earth in their season:
grant that we may use them to your glory,
for the relief of those in need and for our own well-being;
through Jesus Christ your Son our Lord,
who is alive and reigns with you,
in the unity of the Holy Spirit,
one God, now and for ever.

Post Communion

Lord of the harvest,
with joy we have offered thanksgiving for your love in creation
and have shared in the bread and the wine of the kingdom:
by your grace plant within us a reverence for all that you give us
and make us generous and wise stewards
    of the good things we enjoy;
through Jesus Christ our Lord.

Collects and Post Communions for Sundays, Principal Holy Days and Festivals in Traditional Language

Notes

I   Collects and Post Communions for Lesser Festivals and Special Occasions, with Commons of the Saints, are published in the President's edition of *Common Worship*.

2   Normally on any occasion only one Collect is used.

3   The Collect for each Sunday is used on the following weekdays, except where other provision is made.

4   At Evening Prayer on Saturdays other than Easter Eve, Christmas Eve or Principal Feasts or Festivals, the Collect appointed for the ensuing Sunday shall be used. When Evening Prayer on the day before a Festival makes use of the lessons relating to that Festival, the Collect of that Festival shall be used.

5   Where a Collect ends 'Through Jesus Christ ... now and for ever', the minister may use the shorter ending, 'Through Jesus Christ our Lord' to which the people respond 'Amen' and omit the longer Trinitarian ending. The longer ending is to be preferred at Holy Communion.

For Rules, see page 525.

Contents

Much of this provision is taken from The Book of Common Prayer, *with slight adaptation. The original form may be used in place of the text provided here. A table showing where the original may be found is on page 522.*

For Collects and Post Communions in Contemporary Language, see page 375.

¶ *Advent*

The First Sunday of Advent *Purple*

Collect

Almighty God,
give us grace that we may cast away the works of darkness
and put upon us the armour of light,
now in the time of this mortal life,
in which thy Son Jesus Christ came to visit us in great humility;
that in the last day
when he shall come again in his glorious majesty
    to judge both the quick and the dead,
we may rise to the life immortal;
through him who liveth and reigneth with thee and the Holy Spirit,
now and for ever.

*This Collect may be used as the Post Communion on any day from
the Second Sunday of Advent until Christmas Eve instead of the
Post Communion provided.*

Post Communion

O Lord our God,
as we wait for the coming of thy Son our Lord,
preserve us in watchfulness and faith,
that when he shall appear
he may not find us asleep in sin
but active to serve him
and joyful to praise him;
through Jesus Christ our Lord.

The Second Sunday of Advent Purple

Collect

O Lord, raise up we pray thee thy power
and come among us,
and with great might succour us;
that whereas, through our sins and wickedness
we are sore let and hindered
in running the race that is set before us,
thy bountiful grace and mercy
may speedily help and deliver us;
through the satisfaction of thy Son our Lord,
to whom with thee and the Holy Spirit
be honour and glory, now and for ever.

Post Communion

Heavenly Father,
who didst send thy Son to redeem the world
and wilt send him again to be our judge:
give us grace so to imitate him
    in the humility and purity of his first coming
that when he shall come again,
we may be found ready to greet him
with joyful love and steadfast faith;
through Jesus Christ our Lord.

The Third Sunday of Advent Purple

Collect

O Lord Jesus Christ,
who at thy first coming didst send thy messenger
to prepare thy way before thee:
grant that the ministers and stewards of thy mysteries
may likewise so prepare and make ready thy way
by turning the hearts of the disobedient to the wisdom of the just,
that at thy second coming to judge the world
we may be found an acceptable people in thy sight;
who livest and reignest with the Father and the Holy Spirit,
one God, now and for ever.

Post Communion

We give thee thanks, O Lord, for these thy heavenly gifts;
kindle in us the fire of thy Spirit
that when our Saviour Christ shall come again
we may shine as lights before his face;
who liveth and reigneth now and for ever.

The Fourth Sunday of Advent   *Purple*

This provision is not used on weekdays after 23 December.

Collect

O God our redeemer,
who didst prepare the Blessed Virgin Mary
to be the mother of thy Son:
grant that, as she looked for his coming as our saviour,
so we may be ready to greet him
when he shall come again to be our judge;
who liveth and reigneth with thee
in the unity of the Holy Spirit,
one God, now and for ever.

Post Communion

Heavenly Father,
who didst choose the Blessed Virgin Mary
to be the mother of the promised saviour:
fill us thy servants with thy grace,
that in all things we may embrace thy holy will
and with her rejoice in thy salvation;
through Jesus Christ our Lord.

Collect

Almighty God,
who makest us glad with the yearly remembrance
    of the birth of thy only Son Jesus Christ:
grant that, as we joyfully receive him as our redeemer,
so we may with sure confidence behold him
when he shall come to be our judge;
who liveth and reigneth with thee
in the unity of the Holy Spirit,
one God, now and for ever.

Post Communion

Eternal God, for whom we wait,
who hast fed us with the bread of eternal life:
we pray that thou wilt keep us ever watchful
so that we may be ready to stand before the Son of man,
Jesus Christ our Lord.

¶ Christmas

Christmas Night
Principal Feast

Gold or
White

Collect

Eternal God,
who made this most holy night
to shine with the brightness of thy one true light:
bring us, who have known the revelation of that light on earth,
to see the radiance of thy heavenly glory;
through Jesus Christ thy Son our Lord,
who liveth and reigneth with thee,
in the unity of the Holy Spirit,
one God, now and for ever.

Post Communion

God our Father,
who in this night hast made known to us again
the coming of our Lord Jesus Christ:
confirm our faith and fix our eyes on him
until the dawning of the day
when Christ the Morning Star shall rise in our hearts;
to whom be glory both now and for ever.

Christmas Day

Principal Feast

Collect

Almighty God,
who hast given us thy only-begotten Son
to take our nature upon him
and as at this time to be born of a pure virgin:
grant that we, being regenerate
and made thy children by adoption and grace,
may daily be renewed by thy Holy Spirit;
through Jesus Christ thy Son our Lord,
who liveth and reigneth with thee and the same Spirit,
now and for ever.

Post Communion

O God our Father,
whose Word hath come among us
in the Holy Child of Bethlehem:
grant that the light of faith may illumine our hearts
and shine in all our words and deeds;
through him who is Christ the Lord.

The First Sunday of Christmas

This provision is not used on weekdays after 5 January.

Collect

Almighty God,
who hast wonderfully created us in thine own image
and hast yet more wonderfully restored us
through thy Son Jesus Christ:
grant that, as he came to share in our humanity,
so we may share the life of his divinity;
who liveth and reigneth with thee,
in the unity of the Holy Spirit,
one God, now and for ever.

Post Communion

Heavenly Father,
whose blessed Son shared at Nazareth the life of an earthly home:
grant to thy Church grace to live as one family,
united in love and obedience,
and at the last bring us all to our home in heaven;
through Jesus Christ our Lord.

The Second Sunday of Christmas   *White*

This provision is not used on weekdays after 5 January.

Collect

Almighty God,
who in the birth of thy Son
hast poured upon us the new light of thine incarnate Word
and revealed to us the fullness of thy love:
help us so to walk in his light and dwell in his love
that we may know the fullness of his joy;
who liveth and reigneth with thee,
in the unity of the Holy Spirit,
one God, now and for ever.

Post Communion

All praise to thee,
almighty God and heavenly king,
who hast sent thy Son into the world
to take our nature upon him
and to be born of a pure virgin:
grant that, as we are born again in him,
so he may continually dwell in us
and reign on earth as he reigneth in heaven,
now and for ever.

¶ Epiphany

6 January
The Epiphany
Principal Feast

Gold or White

Collect

O God,
who by the leading of a star
didst manifest thy only-begotten Son to the Gentiles:
mercifully grant that we,
who know thee now by faith,
may after this life have the fruition of thy glorious Godhead;
through Jesus Christ thy Son our Lord,
who liveth and reigneth with thee,
in the unity of the Holy Spirit,
one God, now and for ever.

Post Communion

O Lord our God,
the bright splendour whom the nations seek:
grant that we, who with the wise men
    have been drawn by thy light,
may discern the glory of thy presence in thy Son,
the Word made flesh, Jesus Christ our Lord.

The Baptism of Christ
The First Sunday of Epiphany

Gold or White

Collect

Eternal Father,
who at the baptism of Jesus
didst reveal him to be thy Son,
anointing him with the Holy Spirit:
grant that we, being born again by water and the Spirit,
may be faithful to our calling as thine adopted children;
through Jesus Christ thy Son our Lord,
who liveth and reigneth with thee,
in the unity of the Holy Spirit,
one God, now and for ever.

Post Communion

O Lord of all time and eternity,
who in the baptism of Jesus thy beloved Son
didst open the heavens
and didst reveal thyself as Father:
by the power of thy Spirit
make perfect the heavenly work of our rebirth
through the waters of the new creation;
through Jesus Christ our Lord.

The Second Sunday of Epiphany   *White*

Collect

Almighty God,
who in Christ makest all things new:
transform the poverty of our nature by the riches of thy grace,
and in the renewal of our lives
make known thy heavenly glory;
through Jesus Christ thy Son our Lord,
who liveth and reigneth with thee,
in the unity of the Holy Spirit,
one God, now and for ever.

Post Communion

God of glory,
as thou dost nourish us with thy Word
who is the bread of life:
fill us with thy Holy Spirit
that through us the light of thy glory
may shine in all the world;
through Jesus Christ our Lord.

The Third Sunday of Epiphany *White*

Collect

Almighty God,
whose Son revealed in signs and miracles
the wonder of thy saving presence:
renew thy people with thy heavenly grace,
and in all our weakness
sustain us by thy mighty power;
through Jesus Christ thy Son our Lord,
who liveth and reigneth with thee,
in the unity of the Holy Spirit,
one God, now and for ever.

Post Communion

Almighty God,
whose Son our Saviour Jesus Christ is the light of the world:
grant that thy people,
illumined by thy word and sacraments,
may shine with the radiance of his glory,
that he may be known, worshipped and obeyed
    to the ends of the earth,
who liveth and reigneth, now and for ever.

The Fourth Sunday of Epiphany *White*

Collect

Almighty God, creator of all things,
who in the beginning
didst command the light to shine out of darkness:
grant that the light of the glorious gospel of Christ
may dispel the darkness of ignorance and unbelief,
shine into the hearts of all thy people,
and reveal the knowledge of thy glory
    in the face of Jesus Christ thy Son our Lord,
who liveth and reigneth with thee,
in the unity of the Holy Spirit,
one God, now and for ever.

Post Communion

Gracious Lord,
by whose mercy we have proclaimed in word and sacrament
     the mystery of thy love:
help us so to live our lives
that we may show forth thy wonders in the world;
through Jesus Christ our Saviour.

<table>
<tr><td>2 February</td><td>The Presentation of Christ
in the Temple
Candlemas
Principal Feast</td><td>Gold or
White</td></tr>
</table>

Collect

Almighty and ever-living God,
we humbly beseech thy majesty,
that, as thy only-begotten Son
     was this day presented in the Temple,
in substance of our flesh,
so we may be presented unto thee
with pure and clean hearts,
by thy Son Jesus Christ our Lord,
who liveth and reigneth with thee,
in the unity of the Holy Spirit,
one God, now and for ever.

Post Communion

O Lord,
who didst fulfil the hope of Simeon and Anna
that they might live to greet the coming of the Messiah:
grant that we, who have received these inexpressible gifts,
may be prepared to meet Christ Jesus when he shall come
     to bring us to eternal life;
for he liveth and reigneth, now and for ever.

¶ Ordinary Time

The Fifth Sunday before Lent   *Green*

This provision is always used from the day after the Presentation of Christ in the Temple until the first of the Sundays before Lent.

Collect

Almighty God,
by whose grace alone we are accepted
    and called to thy service:
strengthen us by thy Holy Spirit
and make us worthy of our calling;
through Jesus Christ thy Son our Lord,
who liveth and reigneth with thee,
in the unity of the Holy Spirit,
one God, now and for ever.

Post Communion

O God of truth,
by whose grace we have seen with our eyes
    and touched with our hands the bread of life:
strengthen our faith
that we may grow in love for thee and for one another;
through Jesus Christ our Lord.

The Fourth Sunday before Lent

Collect

O God,
who knowest us to be set
in the midst of so many and great dangers,
that by reason of the frailty of our nature
we cannot always stand upright:
grant to us such strength and protection
as may support us in all dangers
and carry us through all temptations;
through Jesus Christ thy Son our Lord,
who liveth and reigneth with thee,
in the unity of the Holy Spirit,
one God, now and for ever.

Post Communion

Go before us, O Lord, in all our doings
with thy most gracious favour,
and further us with thy continual help,
that in all our works
begun, continued and ended in thee,
we may glorify thy holy name,
and finally by thy mercy obtain everlasting life;
through Jesus Christ our Lord.

The Third Sunday before Lent

Collect

O almighty God,
who alone canst order the unruly wills
    and affections of the sinful:
grant unto thy people
    that they may love the thing which thou commandest
and desire that which thou dost promise,
that so, among the sundry and manifold changes of the world,
our hearts may surely there be fixed
where true joys are to be found;
through Jesus Christ thy Son our Lord,
who liveth and reigneth with thee,
in the unity of the Holy Spirit,
one God, now and for ever.

Post Communion

Merciful Father,
who didst give thine only Son Jesus Christ
    to be for us the bread of life,
that those who come to him should never hunger:
draw us to him in faith and love,
that we may eat and drink with him
at his table in the kingdom,
where he liveth and reigneth, now and for ever.

The Second Sunday before Lent   *Green*

Collect

Almighty God,
who hast created the heavens and the earth
and hast made us in thine own image:
teach us to discern thy hand in all thy works
and thy likeness in all thy children;
through Jesus Christ thy Son our Lord,
who liveth and reigneth with thee,
in the unity of the Holy Spirit,
one God, now and for ever.

Post Communion

O God our creator,
by whose gift
the tree of life was set at the heart of the earthly paradise,
and the bread of life at the heart of thy Church:
may we who have been nourished at thy table on earth
be transformed by the glory of the Saviour's cross
and enjoy the delights of eternity;
through Jesus Christ our Lord.

The Sunday next before Lent   *Green*

This provision is not used on or after Ash Wednesday.

Collect

Almighty Father,
whose Son was revealed in majesty
before he suffered death upon the cross:
give us grace to perceive his glory,
that we may be strengthened to suffer with him
and be changed into his likeness, from glory to glory;
who liveth and reigneth with thee,
in the unity of the Holy Spirit,
one God, now and for ever.

Post Communion

O holy God,
we behold thy glory in the face of Jesus Christ:
grant that we who are partakers at his table
may reflect his life in word and deed,
that all the world may know his power to change and save;
through Jesus Christ our Lord.

¶ Lent

Collect

Almighty and everlasting God,
who hatest nothing that thou hast made
and dost forgive the sins of all them that are penitent:
create and make in us new and contrite hearts
that we, worthily lamenting our sins
and acknowledging our wretchedness,
may obtain of thee, the God of all mercy,
perfect remission and forgiveness;
through Jesus Christ thy Son our Lord,
who liveth and reigneth with thee,
in the unity of the Holy Spirit,
one God, now and for ever.

*This Collect may be used as the Post Communion on any day from the
First Sunday of Lent until the Saturday after the Fourth Sunday of Lent
instead of the Post Communion provided.*

Post Communion

Almighty God,
who hast given thine only Son to be unto us
both a sacrifice for sin
and also an example of godly life:
give us grace
that we may always most thankfully receive
that his inestimable benefit,
and also daily endeavour ourselves
    to follow the blessed steps of his most holy life;
through Jesus Christ our Lord.

The First Sunday of Lent

Collect

Almighty God,
whose Son Jesus Christ did fast forty days in the wilderness,
and was tempted as we are, yet without sin:
give us grace to discipline ourselves in obedience to thy Spirit;
and, as thou knowest our weakness,
so may we know thy power to save;
through Jesus Christ thy Son our Lord,
who liveth and reigneth with thee,
in the unity of the Holy Spirit,
one God, now and for ever.

Post Communion

O Lord our God,
who hast renewed us with the living bread from heaven,
and dost thereby nourish our faith,
increase our hope,
and strengthen our love:
incline our hearts always to hunger for him
    who is the true and living bread,
and give us grace to live by every word
    that proceedeth out of thy mouth;
through Jesus Christ our Lord.

The Second Sunday of Lent Purple or Lent Array

Collect

Almighty God,
who showest to them that be in error the light of thy truth,
to the intent that they may return into the way of righteousness:
grant unto all them that are admitted
    into the fellowship of Christ's religion,
that they may eschew those things
    that are contrary to their profession,
and follow all such things as are agreeable to the same;
through our Lord Jesus Christ,
who liveth and reigneth with thee,
in the unity of the Holy Spirit,
one God, now and for ever.

Post Communion

Almighty God,
who seest that we have no power of ourselves to help ourselves:
keep us both outwardly in our bodies,
and inwardly in our souls;
that we may be defended from all adversities
    which may happen to the body,
and from all evil thoughts which may assault and hurt the soul;
through Jesus Christ our Lord.

The Third Sunday of Lent Purple or Lent Array

Collect

Almighty God,
whose most dear Son went not up to joy but first he suffered pain,
and entered not into glory before he was crucified:
mercifully grant that we, walking in the way of the cross,
may find it none other than the way of life and peace;
through Jesus Christ thy Son our Lord,
who liveth and reigneth with thee,
in the unity of the Holy Spirit,
one God, now and for ever.

Post Communion

Lord, we beseech thee,
grant thy people grace to withstand the temptations
    of the world, the flesh and the devil,
and with pure hearts and minds to follow thee, the only God;
through Jesus Christ our Lord.

The Fourth Sunday of Lent *Purple or*
Lent Array

Mothering Sunday may be celebrated in preference to the provision
for the Fourth Sunday of Lent.

Collect

O Lord, we beseech thee,
absolve thy people from their offences,
that through thy bountiful goodness
we may all be delivered from the bands of those sins
which by our frailty we have committed;
grant this, O heavenly Father,
for Jesus Christ's sake, our blessed Lord and Saviour,
who liveth and reigneth with thee,
in the unity of the Holy Spirit,
one God, now and for ever.

Post Communion

Lord God,
whose blessed Son our Saviour
gave his back to the smiters
and hid not his face from shame:
give us grace to endure the sufferings of this present time
with sure confidence in the glory that shall be revealed;
through Jesus Christ our Lord.

Mothering Sunday may be celebrated in preference to the provision
for the Fourth Sunday of Lent.

Collect

Merciful God,
whose Son Jesus Christ, the child of Mary,
shared the life of a home in Nazareth
and on the cross drew the whole human family to himself:
strengthen us in our daily lives
that in joy and sorrow
we may know the power of thy presence
    to bind together and to heal;
through Jesus Christ thy Son our Lord,
who liveth and reigneth with thee,
in the unity of the Holy Spirit,
one God, now and for ever.

Post Communion

God of love,
who in this sacrament dost feed us
    with the food and drink of eternal life,
even as a mother feedeth her children at the breast:
mercifully grant that we who have tasted thy goodness
may grow in grace within the household of faith;
through Jesus Christ our Lord.

Collect

Most merciful God,
who by the death and resurrection of thy Son Jesus Christ
hast delivered and saved the world:
grant that by faith in him who suffered on the cross
we may triumph in the power of his victory;
through Jesus Christ thy Son our Lord,
who liveth and reigneth with thee,
in the unity of the Holy Spirit,
one God, now and for ever.

Post Communion

Lord Jesus Christ,
who hast taught us
that what we do for the least of our brothers and sisters
we do also for thee:
give us the will to be the servant of others
as thou wast the servant of all,
who gavest up thy life and didst die for us,
yet livest and reignest, now and for ever.

Collect

Almighty and everlasting God,
who of thy tender love towards the world
    hast sent thy Son our Saviour Jesus Christ
to take upon him our flesh
and to suffer death upon the cross:
grant that we may follow the example of his patience and humility,
and also be made partakers of his resurrection;
through Jesus Christ thy Son our Lord,
who liveth and reigneth with thee,
in the unity of the Holy Spirit,
one God, now and for ever.

Post Communion

Lord Jesus Christ,
who didst humble thyself by taking the form of a servant
and wast obedient even unto the death of the cross
    for our salvation:
grant us the mind to follow thee
and to proclaim thee as Lord and King,
to the glory of God the Father.

Maundy Thursday   *White*

Principal Holy Day

At Morning and Evening Prayer the Collect of Palm Sunday is used.
At Holy Communion this Collect is used.

Collect

God our Father,
who hast invited us to share in the supper
which thy Son hath given to his Church
that it may proclaim his death until he comes:
may he nourish us by his presence,
and unite us in his love;
who liveth and reigneth with thee,
in the unity of the Holy Spirit,
one God, now and for ever.

Post Communion

Lord Jesus Christ,
we thank thee that in this wonderful sacrament
thou hast given us a memorial of thy passion:
grant us so to reverence the sacred mysteries
    of thy body and blood
that we may know within ourselves
and show forth in our lives
the fruits of thy redemption;
for thou livest and reignest, now and for ever.

Good Friday

Principal Holy Day

Hangings
removed:
red for the
liturgy

Collect

Almighty God,
we beseech thee graciously to behold this thy family
for which our Lord Jesus Christ was contented to be betrayed
    and given up into the hands of sinners
    and to suffer death upon the cross;
who now liveth and reigneth with thee,
in the unity of the Holy Spirit,
one God, now and for ever.

Easter Eve

Hangings
removed

Collect

Grant, O Lord,
that as we are baptized into the death of thy blessed Son
    our Saviour Jesus Christ,
so by continually mortifying our corrupt affections
    we may be buried with him;
and that through the grave and gate of death
we may pass to our joyful resurrection;
for his merits, who died and was buried and rose again for us,
thy Son Jesus Christ our Lord.

¶ *Easter*

Easter Day *Gold or*
Principal Feast *White*

Collect

Lord of all life and power,
who through the mighty resurrection of thy Son
hast overcome the old order of sin and death
to make all things new in him:
grant that we, being dead to sin
and alive to thee in Jesus Christ,
may reign with him in glory;
to whom with thee and the Holy Spirit
be praise and honour, glory and might,
now and in all eternity.

Post Communion

God of Life,
who for our redemption didst give thine only-begotten Son
    to the death of the cross,
and by his glorious resurrection
hast delivered us from the power of our enemy:
grant us so to die daily unto sin
that we may evermore live with him in the joy of his risen life;
through Jesus Christ our Lord.

The Second Sunday of Easter *White*

Collect

Almighty Father,
who hast given thine only Son to die for our sins
and to rise again for our justification:
grant us so to put away the leaven of malice and wickedness
that we may alway serve thee
in pureness of living and truth;
through the merits of Jesus Christ thy Son our Lord,
who liveth and reigneth with thee,
in the unity of the Holy Spirit,
one God, now and for ever.

Post Communion

Lord God our Father,
who through our Saviour Jesus Christ
hast assured us of eternal life
and in baptism made us one with him:
deliver us from the death of sin
and raise us to new life in thy love,
in the fellowship of the Holy Spirit,
by the grace of our Lord Jesus Christ.

The Third Sunday of Easter *White*

Collect

Almighty Father,
who in thy great mercy gladdened the disciples
    with the sight of the risen Lord:
give us such knowledge of his presence with us,
that we may be strengthened and sustained by his risen life
and serve thee continually in righteousness and truth;
through Jesus Christ thy Son our Lord,
who liveth and reigneth with thee,
in the unity of the Holy Spirit,
one God, now and for ever.

Post Communion

O living God,
whose Son made himself known to his disciples
in the breaking of the bread:
open the eyes of our faith,
that we may see him in all his redeeming work;
who liveth and reigneth, now and for ever.

The Fourth Sunday of Easter *White*

Collect

Almighty God,
whose Son Jesus Christ is the resurrection and the life:
raise us, who trust in him,
from the death of sin unto the life of righteousness,
that we may seek those things which are above,
where he liveth and reigneth with thee,
in the unity of the Holy Spirit,
one God, now and for ever.

Post Communion

O merciful Father,
who gavest thy Son Jesus Christ to be the good shepherd,
and in his love for us to lay down his life and rise again:
keep us ever under his protection,
and give us grace to follow in his steps;
through Jesus Christ our Lord.

The Fifth Sunday of Easter *White*

Collect

Almighty God,
who through thine only-begotten Son Jesus Christ
hast overcome death and opened unto us the gate of everlasting life:
we humbly beseech thee that,
as by thy grace preceding us
    thou dost put into our minds good desires,
so by thy continual help
we may bring the same to good effect;
through Jesus Christ thy Son our Lord,
who liveth and reigneth with thee,
in the unity of the Holy Spirit,
one God, now and for ever.

Post Communion

Eternal God,
whose Son Jesus Christ is the way, the truth and the life:
grant us grace to walk in his way,
to rejoice in his truth,
and to share his risen life;
who liveth and reigneth, now and for ever.

The Sixth Sunday of Easter   *White*

This provision is not used on or after Ascension Day.

Collect

God our redeemer,
who hast delivered us from the power of darkness
and brought us into the kingdom of thy Son:
grant, that as by his death he hath recalled us to life,
so by his continual presence in us he may raise us to eternal joy;
through Jesus Christ thy Son our Lord,
who liveth and reigneth with thee,
in the unity of the Holy Spirit,
one God, now and for ever.

Post Communion

O God our Father,
whose Son Jesus Christ doth give the water of eternal life:
may we ever thirst for thee,
the spring of life and fountain of goodness,
through him who liveth and reigneth, now and for ever.

Ascension Day

Gold or
White

Collect

Grant, we beseech thee, almighty God,
that like as we do believe thy only-begotten Son
    our Lord Jesus Christ
to have ascended into the heavens;
so we may also in heart and mind thither ascend
and with him continually dwell,
who liveth and reigneth with thee,
in the unity of the Holy Spirit,
one God, now and for ever.

Post Communion

O God our Father,
who in Christ hast raised up our humanity
and fed us with the bread of heaven:
mercifully grant that, nourished with such spiritual blessings,
we may set our hearts in the heavenly places;
through Jesus Christ our Lord.

The Seventh Sunday of Easter

White

Sunday after Ascension Day

Collect

O God the King of glory,
who hast exalted thine only Son Jesus Christ
with great triumph unto thy kingdom in heaven:
we beseech thee, leave us not comfortless,
but send to us thine Holy Spirit to comfort us
and exalt us unto the same place
    whither our Saviour Christ is gone before;
who liveth and reigneth with thee,
in the unity of the Holy Spirit,
one God, now and for ever.

Post Communion

Eternal God, giver of love and power,
whose Son Jesus Christ hath sent us into all the world
to preach the gospel of his kingdom:
so confirm us in this mission
that our lives may show forth the good news which we proclaim;
through Jesus Christ our Lord.

Day of Pentecost *Red*
Whit Sunday
Principal Feast

This provision is not used on the weekdays after the Day of Pentecost.

Collect

God, who as at this time
didst teach the hearts of thy faithful people
by sending to them the light of thy Holy Spirit:
grant us by the same Spirit
to have a right judgement in all things
and evermore to rejoice in his holy comfort;
through the merits of Christ Jesus our Saviour,
who liveth and reigneth with thee,
in the unity of the same Spirit,
one God, now and for ever.

Post Communion

O faithful God,
who didst fulfil the promise of Easter
by sending to us thy Holy Spirit
and opening to every race and nation the way of eternal life:
open our lips by the same Spirit,
that every tongue may tell of thy glory;
through Jesus Christ our Lord.

The Weekdays after the Day of Pentecost   *Green*

Collect

O Lord, from whom all good things do come:
grant to us thy humble servants,
that by thy holy inspiration
we may think those things that be good
and, by thy merciful guiding may perform the same;
through Jesus Christ thy Son our Lord,
who liveth and reigneth with thee,
in the unity of the Holy Spirit,
one God, now and for ever.

Post Communion

O God of love,
who in this sacrament
dost make us one family in thy Son Jesus Christ,
one in the sharing of his body and blood
and one in the communion of his Spirit:
help us so to grow in love for one another
that we may come to the full maturity of the Body of Christ;
through Jesus Christ our Saviour.

Trinity Sunday   *Gold or*
Principal Feast   *White*

Collect

Almighty and everlasting God,
who hast given unto us thy servants grace,
by the confession of a true faith,
to acknowledge the glory of the eternal Trinity
and, in the power of the divine majesty, to worship the Unity:
we beseech thee that thou wouldest keep us steadfast
    in this faith
and evermore defend us from all adversities;
who livest and reignest, one God, now and for ever.

Post Communion

Almighty and eternal God,
who hast revealed thyself as Father, Son and Holy Spirit,
and dost ever live and reign in the perfect unity of love:
hold us firm in this faith,
that we may know thee in all thy ways
and evermore rejoice in thy eternal glory;
who art three Persons yet one God,
now and for ever.

The Thursday after Trinity Sunday may be observed as

The Day of Thanksgiving for the Institution of Holy Communion
(Corpus Christi)

White

Collect

Lord Jesus Christ,
we thank thee that in this wonderful sacrament
thou hast given us a memorial of thy passion:
grant us so to reverence the sacred mysteries
    of thy body and blood
that we may know within ourselves
and show forth in our lives
the fruits of thy redemption;
who livest and reignest with the Father
in the unity of the Holy Spirit,
one God, now and for ever.

Post Communion

All praise be to thee, our God and Father,
for that thou hast fed us with the bread of heaven
and hast quenched our thirst from the true vine:
grant that we, being grafted into Christ,
may grow together in unity
and be partakers of his heavenly feast;
through Jesus Christ our Lord.

The First Sunday after Trinity

Collect

O God,
the strength of all them that put their trust in thee,
mercifully accept our prayers
and, because through the weakness of our mortal nature
we can do no good thing without thee,
grant us the help of thy grace
that, in keeping of thy commandments,
we may please thee, both in will and deed;
through Jesus Christ thy Son our Lord,
who liveth and reigneth with thee,
in the unity of the Holy Spirit,
one God, now and for ever.

Post Communion

Everlasting Father,
we thank thee that thou dost nourish us
with these thy heavenly gifts:
by this sacrament strengthen us in faith,
build us up in hope
and make us grow in love;
for the sake of Jesus Christ our Lord.

The Second Sunday after Trinity

Collect

O Lord, who hast taught us
that all our doings without charity are nothing worth:
send thy Holy Spirit
and pour into our hearts that most excellent gift of charity,
the very bond of peace and of all virtues
without which whosoever liveth is counted dead before thee;
grant this for thine only Son Jesus Christ's sake,
who liveth and reigneth with thee,
in the unity of the Holy Spirit,
one God, now and for ever.

Post Communion

O loving Father,
we thank thee for feeding us at the supper of thy Son:
sustain us with thy Spirit
that we, serving thee here on earth,
may come at last to the fullness of thy joy in heaven
and be partakers of thine eternal banquet
with Jesus Christ our Lord.

The Third Sunday after Trinity   *Green*

Collect

Almighty God,
who hast broken the tyranny of sin
and hast sent the Spirit of thy Son into our hearts,
    whereby we call thee Father:
give us grace to dedicate our freedom to thy service,
that the whole world may be brought
    to the glorious liberty of the children of God;
through Jesus Christ thy Son our Lord,
who liveth and reigneth with thee,
in the unity of the Holy Spirit,
one God, now and for ever.

Post Communion

O God, whose beauty is beyond our imagining
and whose power we cannot comprehend:
show us thy glory as far as we can grasp it,
and shield us from knowing more than we can bear
until we may look upon thee without fear;
through Jesus Christ our Saviour.

The Fourth Sunday after Trinity

Collect

O God, the protector of all that trust in thee,
without whom nothing is strong, nothing is holy:
increase and multiply upon us thy mercy
that, thou being our ruler and guide,
we may so pass through things temporal
that we lose not our hold on things eternal;
grant this, O heavenly Father,
for Jesus Christ's sake our Lord,
who liveth and reigneth with thee,
in the unity of the Holy Spirit,
one God, now and for ever.

Post Communion

Everlasting God,
comforter to the afflicted and healer to the broken,
who hast nourished us at the table of life and hope:
teach us the ways of gentleness and peace
that all the world may acknowledge
the kingdom of thy Son Jesus Christ our Lord.

The Fifth Sunday after Trinity

Collect

Almighty and everlasting God,
by whose Spirit the whole body of the Church
    is governed and sanctified:
hear our prayer which we offer for all thy faithful people,
that in their vocation and ministry
they may serve thee in holiness and truth,
to the glory of thy name;
through our Lord and Saviour Jesus Christ,
who liveth and reigneth with thee,
in the unity of the Holy Spirit,
one God, now and for ever.

Post Communion

Grant, O Lord, we beseech thee,
that the course of this world may be so peaceably ordered
    by thy governance
that thy Church may joyfully serve thee in all godly quietness;
through Jesus Christ our Lord.

The Sixth Sunday after Trinity   *Green*

Collect

O God, who hast prepared for them that love thee
such good things as pass our understanding:
pour into our hearts such love toward thee
that we, loving thee in all things and above all things,
may obtain thy promises
which exceed all that we can desire;
through Jesus Christ thy Son our Lord,
who liveth and reigneth with thee,
in the unity of the Holy Spirit,
one God, now and for ever.

Post Communion

O God of our pilgrimage,
who hast led us to the living water:
refresh and sustain us
as we go forward on our journey,
in the name of Jesus Christ our Lord.

The Seventh Sunday after Trinity

Green

Collect

Lord of all power and might,
who art the author and giver of all good things:
graft in our hearts the love of thy name,
increase in us true religion,
nourish us with all goodness,
and of thy great mercy keep us in the same;
through Jesus Christ thy Son our Lord,
who liveth and reigneth with thee,
in the unity of the Holy Spirit,
one God, now and for ever.

Post Communion

Lord God, whose Son is the true vine,
the source of life, who ever giveth himself that the world may live:
may we so receive within ourselves
    the power of his death and passion
that in his cup of salvation we may partake of his glory
    and also be made perfect in his love;
who liveth and reigneth, now and for ever.

The Eighth Sunday after Trinity

Green

Collect

O almighty Lord and everlasting God,
vouchsafe, we beseech thee,
    to direct, sanctify and govern both our hearts and bodies
in the ways of thy laws and in the works of thy commandments,
that through thy most mighty protection,
both here and ever,
we may be preserved in body and soul;
through our Lord and Saviour Jesus Christ,
who liveth and reigneth with thee,
in the unity of the Holy Spirit,
one God, now and for ever.

Post Communion

Strengthen for service, Lord,
the hands that have taken holy things;
may the ears which have heard thy word
    be deaf to clamour and dispute;
may the tongues which have sung thy praise be free from deceit;
may the eyes which have seen the tokens of thy love
    shine with the light of hope;
and may the bodies which have been fed with thy body
    be refreshed with the fullness of thy life;
glory be to thee for ever.

The Ninth Sunday after Trinity *Green*

Collect

Almighty God,
who didst send thy Holy Spirit
to be the life and light of thy Church:
open our hearts to the riches of thy grace,
that we may bring forth the fruit of the Spirit
in love and joy and peace;
through Jesus Christ thy Son our Lord,
who liveth and reigneth with thee,
in the unity of the Holy Spirit,
one God, now and for ever.

Post Communion

Holy Father,
who didst gather us around the table of thy Son
that we, with all thy household,
might partake of this holy food:
in that new world wherein the fullness of thy peace is revealed,
gather people of every race and tongue
    to share in the eternal banquet of Jesus Christ our Lord.

The Tenth Sunday after Trinity

Collect

Let thy merciful ears, O Lord,
be open to the prayers of thy humble servants;
and that they may obtain their petitions
make them to ask such things as shall please thee;
through Jesus Christ thy Son our Lord,
who liveth and reigneth with thee,
in the unity of the Holy Spirit,
one God, now and for ever.

Post Communion

God of our pilgrimage,
who hast willed that the gate of mercy
should stand open for those who trust in thee:
look upon us with thy favour
that we, following in the path of thy will,
may never wander from the way of life;
through Jesus Christ our Lord.

The Eleventh Sunday after Trinity

Collect

O God,
who declarest thy almighty power
most chiefly in showing mercy and pity:
mercifully grant unto us such a measure of thy grace
that we, running the way of thy commandments,
may obtain thy gracious promises
and be made partakers of thy heavenly treasure;
through Jesus Christ thy Son our Lord,
who liveth and reigneth with thee,
in the unity of the Holy Spirit,
one God, now and for ever.

Post Communion

Merciful Lord,
whose faithful people have celebrated that one true sacrifice
    which taketh away our sins and bringeth pardon and peace:
by our communion
stablish us on the foundation of the gospel
and preserve us from all sin;
through Jesus Christ our Lord.

The Twelfth Sunday after Trinity   *Green*

Collect

Almighty and everlasting God,
who art always more ready to hear than we to pray,
and art wont to give more than either we desire or deserve:
pour down upon us the abundance of thy mercy,
forgiving us those things whereof our conscience is afraid
and giving us those good things
    which we are not worthy to ask,
but through the merits and mediation
of Jesus Christ thy Son our Lord,
who liveth and reigneth with thee,
in the unity of the Holy Spirit,
one God, now and for ever.

Post Communion

Merciful God,
who in this holy sacrament hast put away our sins
and given us thy healing;
grant that as we are made whole in Christ,
so we may bring thy healing to this broken world,
in the name of Jesus Christ our Lord.

The Thirteenth Sunday after Trinity

Collect

Almighty God,
who hast called thy Church to witness
that thou wast in Christ reconciling the world to thyself:
help us so to proclaim the good news of thy love
that all who hear it may be drawn unto thee;
through him who was lifted up on the cross,
and reigneth with thee and the Holy Spirit,
one God, now and for ever.

Post Communion

O God our creator,
who dost feed thy children with the true manna
which is the living bread from heaven:
grant that, by this holy food,
we may be sustained through our earthly pilgrimage
until we come to that place
    where hunger and thirst shall be no more;
through Jesus Christ our Lord.

The Fourteenth Sunday after Trinity

Collect

Almighty God,
whose only Son hath opened for us
a new and living way into thy presence:
grant that, with pure hearts and constant wills,
we may worship thee in spirit and in truth;
through Jesus Christ thy Son our Lord,
who liveth and reigneth with thee,
in the unity of the Holy Spirit,
one God, now and for ever.

Post Communion

O Lord God,
who art the source of all truth and love,
keep us faithful to the apostles' teaching and fellowship,
united in prayer and in the breaking of bread,
and one in joy and simplicity of heart,
in Jesus Christ our Lord.

The Fifteenth Sunday after Trinity   *Green*

Collect

God, who of thy generous mercy didst send the Holy Spirit
    upon thy Church in the burning fire of thy love:
grant that thy people may be fervent
    in the fellowship of the gospel
that, ever abiding in thee,
they may be found steadfast in faith and active in service;
through Jesus Christ thy Son our Lord,
who liveth and reigneth with thee,
in the unity of the Holy Spirit,
one God, now and for ever.

Post Communion

Keep, we beseech thee, O Lord,
    thy Church with thy perpetual mercy;
and, because our human frailty without thee cannot but fall,
keep us ever by thy help from all things hurtful
and lead us to all things profitable to our salvation;
through Jesus Christ our Lord.

The Sixteenth Sunday after Trinity *Green*

Collect

O Lord,
we beseech thee mercifully to receive the prayers
    of thy people which call upon thee;
and grant that they may both perceive and know
    what things they ought to do,
and also may have grace and power faithfully to fulfil the same;
through Jesus Christ thy Son our Lord,
who liveth and reigneth with thee,
in the unity of the Holy Spirit,
one God, now and for ever.

Post Communion

Almighty God,
who hast taught us through thy Son
that love is the fulfilling of the law:
grant that we may love thee with our whole heart
and our neighbours as ourselves;
through Jesus Christ our Lord.

The Seventeenth Sunday after Trinity *Green*

Collect

Almighty God,
thou hast made us for thyself
and our hearts are restless till they find their rest in thee:
pour thy love into our hearts and draw us to thyself,
and so bring us at the last to thy heavenly city
where we shall see thee face to face;
through Jesus Christ thy Son our Lord,
who liveth and reigneth with thee,
in the unity of the Holy Spirit,
one God, now and for ever.

Post Communion

Lord, we pray thee that thy grace
    may always precede and follow us,
and make us continually to be given to all good works;
through Jesus Christ our Lord.

The Eighteenth Sunday after Trinity   *Green*

Collect

Almighty and everlasting God,
increase in us thy gift of faith
that, forsaking that which is behind
and reaching out to that which is before,
we may run the way of thy commandments
and win the crown of everlasting joy;
through Jesus Christ thy Son our Lord,
who liveth and reigneth with thee,
in the unity of the Holy Spirit,
one God, now and for ever.

Post Communion

We give thee praise and thanks, Lord Jesus Christ,
for this sacred feast:
for here we receive thee,
here the memory of thy passion is renewed,
here our minds are filled with grace,
and here we are given a pledge of the glory to come,
when we shall feast at that table where thou reignest
with all thy saints for ever.

The Nineteenth Sunday after Trinity Green

Collect

O God, forasmuch as without thee
we are not able to please thee;
mercifully grant, that thy Holy Spirit
may in all things direct and rule our hearts;
through Jesus Christ thy Son our Lord,
who liveth and reigneth with thee,
in the unity of the Holy Spirit,
one God, now and for ever.

Post Communion

Holy and blessed God,
who dost vouchsafe to feed us
with the body and blood of thy Son
and hast filled us with thy Holy Spirit:
grant that we may honour thee
not only with our lips
but in lives dedicated to the service
    of Jesus Christ our Lord.

The Twentieth Sunday after Trinity Green

Collect

O God, giver of life,
whose Holy Spirit welleth up within thy Church:
fill us with the gifts of that same Spirit
    to live the gospel of Christ,
    and make us ready to do thy will,
that we may share with all thy whole creation
    the joys of eternal life;
through Jesus Christ thy Son our Lord,
who liveth and reigneth with thee,
in the unity of the Holy Spirit,
one God, now and for ever.

Post Communion

God our Father,
whose Son, the light unfailing,
hath come from heaven that he may deliver the world
    from the darkness of ignorance:
may the eyes of our understanding
be opened through these holy mysteries
that we, knowing the way of life,
may walk in it without stumbling;
through Jesus Christ our Lord.

The Twenty-first Sunday after Trinity   *Green*

Collect

Grant, we beseech thee, merciful Lord,
to thy faithful people pardon and peace,
that they may be cleansed from all their sins
and serve thee with a quiet mind;
through Jesus Christ thy Son our Lord,
who liveth and reigneth with thee,
in the unity of the Holy Spirit,
one God, now and for ever.

Post Communion

Father of light,
in whom is no change or shadow of turning,
who dost give us every good and perfect gift
and hast brought us to birth by thy word of truth:
grant that we may be a living sign of that kingdom
where thy whole creation will be made perfect
    in Jesus Christ our Lord.

*If there are twenty-three Sundays after Trinity, the provision
for the Third Sunday before Lent (page 462) is used on the
Twenty-second Sunday after Trinity.*

The Last Sunday after Trinity *Green*

Collect

Blessed Lord,
who hast caused all holy Scriptures to be written for our learning:
grant that we may in such wise hear them,
read, mark, learn and inwardly digest them,
that by patience and comfort of thy holy word,
we may embrace and ever hold fast
    the blessed hope of everlasting life,
which thou hast given us in our Saviour Jesus Christ,
who liveth and reigneth with thee,
in the unity of the Holy Spirit,
one God, now and for ever.

Post Communion

Most gracious God,
whose Son Jesus Christ fed the hungry
with the bread of his life
and the word of his kingdom:
renew thy people with thy heavenly grace
and in all our weakness
sustain us by thy true and living bread;
who liveth and reigneth, now and for ever.

---

1 November   **All Saints' Day**   *Gold or*
                  Principal Feast   *White*

Collect

O almighty God,
who hast knit together thine elect
in one communion and fellowship
    in the mystical body of thy Son Christ our Lord:
grant us grace so to follow thy blessed saints
in all virtuous and godly living
that we may come to those inexpressible joys
which thou hast prepared for them that unfeignedly love thee;
through Jesus Christ thy Son our Lord,
who liveth and reigneth with thee,
in the unity of the Holy Spirit,
one God, now and for ever.

Post Communion

O God,
the source of all holiness and giver of all good things:
grant that we, who have shared at this table
    as strangers and pilgrims here on earth,
may with all thy saints
    be welcomed to the heavenly feast
    in the day of thy kingdom;
through Jesus Christ our Lord.

The Fourth Sunday before Advent
Red or Green

Collect

Almighty and everlasting God,
who hast kindled the flame of love
    in the hearts of thy saints:
grant to us, we beseech thee,
the same faith and power of love
that we, rejoicing in their triumphs,
may be sustained by their example and fellowship;
through Jesus Christ thy Son our Lord,
who liveth and reigneth with thee,
in the unity of the Holy Spirit,
one God, now and for ever.

Post Communion

O Lord of heaven,
who in this sacrament hast brought us near
    to an innumerable company of angels
    and to the spirits of the saints made perfect:
grant that, as in this food of our earthly pilgrimage
    we have shared their fellowship,
so we may come to share their heavenly joy;
through Jesus Christ our Lord.

The Third Sunday before Advent

Collect

Almighty Father,
whose will is to restore all things
    in thy beloved Son, the King of all:
govern the hearts and minds of those in authority
and bring the families of the nations,
divided and torn apart by the ravages of sin,
to be subject to his just and gentle rule;
who liveth and reigneth with thee,
in the unity of the Holy Spirit,
one God, now and for ever.

Post Communion

O God of peace,
whose Son Jesus Christ proclaimed the kingdom
and restored the broken to wholeness of life:
look with compassion upon the anguish of the world
and, by thy healing power,
make whole both people and nations;
through our Lord and Saviour Jesus Christ.

*In years when Remembrance Sunday is observed on the Second Sunday
before Advent, the Collect and Post Communion for the Third Sunday
before Advent may be used on Remembrance Sunday and the Collect
and Post Communion for the Second Sunday before Advent may be
used on the Third Sunday before Advent.*

The Second Sunday before Advent

Collect

O God,
whose blessed Son was manifested
    that he might destroy the works of the devil
and make us the children of God and heirs of eternal life:
grant us, we beseech thee, that, having this hope,
we may purify ourselves, even as he is pure,
that when he shall appear again with power and great glory
we may be made like unto him in his eternal and glorious kingdom;
where with thee, O Father, and thee, O Holy Spirit,
he liveth and reigneth, one God, now and for ever.

Post Communion

Gracious Lord,
who in this holy sacrament
dost give substance to our hope:
bring us at the last
to that fullness of life for which we long;
through Jesus Christ our Saviour.

*In years when Remembrance Sunday is observed on the Second Sunday
before Advent, the Collect and Post Communion for the Third Sunday
before Advent may be used on Remembrance Sunday and the Collect
and Post Communion for the Second Sunday before Advent may be
used on the Third Sunday before Advent.*

Collect

Eternal Father,
whose Son Jesus Christ ascended to the throne of heaven
      that he might rule over all things as Lord and King:
keep the Church in the unity of the Spirit
and in the bond of peace,
and bring the whole created order to worship at his feet;
who liveth and reigneth with thee,
in the unity of the Holy Spirit,
one God, now and for ever.

Post Communion

Stir up, we beseech thee, O Lord,
the wills of thy faithful people;
that they, plenteously bringing forth the fruit of good works,
may of thee be plenteously rewarded;
through Jesus Christ our Lord.

*This Post Communion may be used as the Collect at Morning and
Evening Prayer during this week.*

¶ *Festivals*

The Naming and Circumcision of Jesus   *White*

1 January

Collect

Almighty God,
whose blessed Son was circumcised
in obedience to the law for our sake
and given the Name that is above every name:
give us grace faithfully to bear his Name,
to worship him in the freedom of the Spirit
and to proclaim him as the Saviour of the world;
who liveth and reigneth with thee,
in the unity of the Holy Spirit,
one God, now and for ever.

Post Communion

Almighty and everlasting God,
whose incarnate Son was given the Name of Saviour:
grant that we who have shared
    in this sacrament of our salvation
may live out our lives in this world
    in the power of the Name that is above every name,
Jesus Christ our Lord.

Collect

O God,
who through the preaching of the blessed apostle Saint Paul,
hast caused the light of the gospel
    to shine throughout the world:
grant, we beseech thee, that we,
having his wonderful conversion in remembrance,
may show forth our thankfulness unto thee for the same,
by following the holy doctrine which he taught;
through Jesus Christ thy Son our Lord,
who liveth and reigneth with thee,
in the unity of the Holy Spirit,
one God, now and for ever.

Post Communion
of Apostles and Evangelists

Almighty God,
who on the day of Pentecost
didst send thy Holy Spirit to the apostles
with the wind from heaven and in tongues of flame,
filling them with joy and boldness to preach the gospel:
by the power of the same Spirit
strengthen us to bear witness to thy truth
and to draw everyone to the fire of thy love;
through Jesus Christ our Lord.

(or)

O Lord God, the source of truth and love,
keep us faithful to the apostles' teaching and fellowship,
united in prayer and the breaking of bread,
and one in joy and simplicity of heart,
in Jesus Christ our Lord.

Collect

O God our Father,
who from the house of thy servant David
didst raise up Joseph the carpenter
to be the guardian of thine incarnate Son
and husband of the Blessed Virgin Mary:
give us grace to follow him
in faithful obedience to thy commands;
through Jesus Christ thy Son our Lord,
who liveth and reigneth with thee,
in the unity of the Holy Spirit,
one God, now and for ever.

Post Communion

Heavenly Father,
whose Son grew in wisdom and stature
in the home of Joseph the carpenter in Nazareth
and on the wood of the cross
    perfected the work of the world's salvation:
grant us, strengthened by this sacrament of his passion,
to count the wisdom of this world as foolishness,
and to walk with him in simplicity and faith;
through Jesus Christ thy Son our Lord.

The Annunciation of Our Lord *Gold or*

Collect

We beseech thee, O Lord,
pour thy grace into our hearts;
that, as we have known the incarnation of thy Son Jesus Christ
    by the message of an angel,
so by his cross and passion
we may be brought unto the glory of his resurrection;
through Jesus Christ thy Son our Lord,
who liveth and reigneth with thee,
in the unity of the Holy Spirit,
one God, now and for ever.

Post Communion

O God most high,
whose handmaid bore the Word made flesh:
we give thee thanks that in this sacrament of our redemption
thou dost visit us with thy Holy Spirit
and dost overshadow us by thy power;
strengthen us to walk with Mary the joyful path of obedience
and so to bring forth the fruits of holiness;
through Jesus Christ our Lord.

George

Martyr, Patron of England, c.304

Collect

O God of hosts,
who didst so kindle the flame of love
in the heart of thy servant George
that he bore witness to the risen Lord
by his life and by his death:
grant us the same faith and power of love
that we, who rejoice in his triumphs,
may come to share with him the fullness of the resurrection;
through Jesus Christ thy Son our Lord,
who liveth and reigneth with thee,
in the unity of the Holy Spirit,
one God, now and for ever.

Post Communion

O eternal God,
who hast given us this holy meal
in which we have celebrated the glory of the cross
and the victory of thy martyr George:
by our communion with Christ
in his saving death and resurrection,
grant us with all thy saints the courage to overcome evil
and so to partake of the fruit of the tree of life;
through Jesus Christ our Lord.

(or)

O God our redeemer,
whose Church was strengthened
    by the blood of thy martyr George:
so bind us, in life and in death,
to the sacrifice of Christ
that, our lives being broken and offered with his,
we may carry his death
and proclaim his resurrection in the world;
through Jesus Christ our Lord.

Mark

Evangelist

Collect

Almighty God,
who hast enlightened thy holy Church
through the inspired witness of thine evangelist Saint Mark:
grant that we, being rooted and grounded
    in the truth of the gospel,
may be faithful to its teaching both in word and deed;
through Jesus Christ thy Son our Lord,
who liveth and reigneth with thee,
in the unity of the Holy Spirit,
one God, now and for ever.

Post Communion

*One of the Post Communions of Apostles and Evangelists is used
(page 500).*

Philip and James

Apostles

Collect

O almighty God,
whom truly to know is everlasting life:
grant us perfectly to know thy Son Jesus Christ
to be the way, the truth and the life;
that, following the steps of thy holy apostles,
    Saint Philip and Saint James,
we may steadfastly walk
    in the way that leadeth to eternal life;
through Jesus Christ thy Son our Lord,
who liveth and reigneth with thee,
in the unity of the Holy Spirit,
one God, now and for ever.

Post Communion

*One of the Post Communions of Apostles and Evangelists is used
(page 500).*

Matthias *Red*

Apostle

Collect

O almighty God,
who into the place of the traitor Judas
didst choose thy faithful servant Matthias
to be of the number of the twelve apostles:
grant that thy Church,
being alway preserved from false apostles,
may be ordered and guided by faithful and true pastors;
through Jesus Christ thy Son our Lord,
who liveth and reigneth with thee,
in the unity of the Holy Spirit,
one God, now and for ever.

Post Communion

*One of the Post Communions of Apostles and Evangelists is used
(page 500).*

31 May **The Visit of** *White*
**the Blessed Virgin Mary
to Elizabeth**

Collect

Almighty God,
by whose grace Elizabeth rejoiced with Mary
and greeted her as the mother of the Lord:
look with favour, we beseech thee, on thy lowly servants,
that, with Mary, we may magnify thy holy name
and rejoice to acclaim her Son our Saviour,
who liveth and reigneth with thee,
in the unity of the Holy Spirit,
one God, now and for ever.

Post Communion

O gracious God,
who gavest to Elizabeth and Mary
joy in recognizing the signs of redemption
    at work within them:
grant us, who have shared in the joy of this communion,
knowledge of the Lord deep within us,
and of his love shining forth in our lives,
that the world may rejoice in thy salvation;
through Jesus Christ our Lord.

11 June   **Barnabas**   *Red*
Apostle

Collect

O God, the giver of all good gifts,
who didst pour out thy Spirit upon thy servant Barnabas
and gavest him grace to strengthen others:
grant us, by his example,
to be generous in our judgements
and faithful in our service;
through Jesus Christ thy Son our Lord,
who liveth and reigneth with thee,
in the unity of the Holy Spirit,
one God, now and for ever.

Post Communion

*One of the Post Communions of Apostles and Evangelists is used
(page 500).*

The Birth of John the Baptist

Collect

Almighty God,
by whose providence thy servant John Baptist
    was wonderfully born,
and sent to prepare the way of thy Son our Saviour,
by preaching of repentance:
make us so to follow his doctrine and holy life,
that we may truly repent according to his preaching
and, after his example,
constantly speak the truth,
boldly rebuke vice
and patiently suffer for the truth's sake;
through Jesus Christ thy Son our Lord,
who liveth and reigneth with thee,
in the unity of the Holy Spirit,
one God, now and for ever.

Post Communion

O merciful Lord,
whose prophet John the Baptist
proclaimed thy Son to be the Lamb of God
    who taketh away the sin of the world:
grant that we, who in this sacrament
    have known thy pardon and thy life-giving love,
may ever tell of thy mercy and thy peace;
through Jesus Christ our Lord.

Peter and Paul

Apostles

Collect

Almighty God,
whose blessed apostles Peter and Paul
glorified thee in their death as in their life:
grant that thy Church,
inspired by their teaching and example,
and made one by thy Spirit,
may ever stand firm on the one foundation
which is thy Son, Jesus Christ our Lord;
who liveth and reigneth with thee,
in the unity of the Holy Spirit,
one God, now and for ever.

or, where Peter is celebrated alone

Almighty God,
who didst inspire thy apostle Saint Peter
to confess Jesus as Christ and Son of the living God:
build up thy Church upon this rock,
that in unity and peace it may proclaim one truth
and follow one Lord, thy Son our Saviour Jesus Christ,
who liveth and reigneth with thee,
in the unity of the Holy Spirit,
one God, now and for ever.

Post Communion

*One of the Post Communions of Apostles and Evangelists is used
(page 500).*

Thomas *Red*
Apostle

Collect

Almighty and eternal God,
who, for the greater confirmation of the faith,
didst allow thy holy apostle Thomas
    to doubt the resurrection of thy Son
till word and sight convinced him:
grant to us, who have not seen, that we also may believe,
and so confess Christ as our Lord and our God;
who liveth and reigneth with thee,
in the unity of the Holy Spirit,
one God, now and for ever.

Post Communion

*One of the Post Communions of Apostles and Evangelists is used
(page 500).*

Mary Magdalene *White*

Collect

Almighty God,
whose Son restored Mary Magdalene
    to health of mind and body
and called her to be a witness to his resurrection:
forgive us our sins, we beseech thee,
and heal us by thy grace,
that we may serve thee in the power of his risen life;
who liveth and reigneth with thee,
in the unity of the Holy Spirit,
one God, now and for ever.

Post Communion

Almighty God,
from whom all life and love proceed,
whose risen Son called Mary Magdalene by her name,
sending her to tell his apostles of his resurrection:
we pray thee in thy mercy to assist us,
who have been united with him in this holy communion,
to proclaim the good news
that he liveth and reigneth, now and for ever.

25 July   **James**   *Red*
Apostle

Collect

Grant, O merciful God,
that as thine holy apostle Saint James,
leaving his father and all that he had,
without delay was obedient unto the calling
of thy Son Jesus Christ, and followed him:
so we, forsaking all worldly and carnal affections,
may be evermore ready to follow thy holy commandments;
through Jesus Christ thy Son our Lord,
who liveth and reigneth with thee,
in the unity of the Holy Spirit,
one God, now and for ever.

Post Communion

*One of the Post Communions of Apostles and Evangelists is used
(page 500).*

The Transfiguration of Our Lord *Gold or*
White

Collect

Heavenly Father,
whose Son Jesus Christ was wonderfully transfigured
before chosen witnesses upon the holy mountain,
and spoke of the exodus he would accomplish at Jerusalem:
grant us strength so to hear his voice and bear our cross
that in the world to come we may behold him as he is;
who liveth and reigneth with thee,
in the unity of the Holy Spirit,
one God, now and for ever.

Post Communion

O holy God,
we behold thy glory in the face of Jesus Christ:
grant that we who are partakers at his table
may reflect his life in word and deed,
that all the world may know his power to change and save;
through Jesus Christ our Lord.

15 August **The Blessed Virgin Mary** *White*

Collect

Almighty God,
who didst look upon the lowliness of the Blessed Virgin Mary
and didst choose her to be the mother of thy only Son:
grant that we who are redeemed by his blood
may share with her in the glory of thine eternal kingdom;
through Jesus Christ thy Son our Lord,
who liveth and reigneth with thee,
in the unity of the Holy Spirit,
one God, now and for ever.

Post Communion

O God most high,
whose handmaid bore the Word made flesh:
we give thee thanks that in this sacrament of our redemption
thou dost visit us with thy Holy Spirit
and dost overshadow us with thy power;
strengthen us to walk with Mary in the joyful path of obedience,
that we may bring forth the fruits of holiness;
through Jesus Christ our Lord.

24 August   **Bartholomew**   *Red*
Apostle

Collect

O almighty and everlasting God,
who didst give to thine apostle Bartholomew grace
    truly to believe and to preach thy word:
grant, we beseech thee, unto thy Church,
to love that word which he believed,
and both to preach and receive the same;
through Jesus Christ thy Son our Lord,
who liveth and reigneth with thee,
in the unity of the Holy Spirit,
one God, now and for ever.

Post Communion

*One of the Post Communions of Apostles and Evangelists is used
(page 500).*

Collect

Almighty God,
who in the passion of thy blessed Son
hast made an instrument of painful death
to be for us the means of life and peace:
grant us so to glory in the cross of Christ
that we may gladly suffer for his sake;
who liveth and reigneth with thee,
in the unity of the Holy Spirit,
one God, now and for ever.

Post Communion

O faithful God,
whose Son bore our sins in his body on the tree
and gave us this sacrament to show forth his death until he comes:
give us grace to glory in the cross of our Lord Jesus Christ,
for he is our salvation, our life and our hope,
who reigneth as Lord, now and for ever.

21 September   **Matthew**   *Red*
Apostle and Evangelist

Collect

O almighty God,
who by thy blessed Son
didst call Matthew from the receipt of custom
to be an apostle and evangelist:
grant us grace to forsake all covetous desires
    and inordinate love of riches,
and to follow the same thy Son Jesus Christ,
who liveth and reigneth with thee,
in the unity of the Holy Spirit,
one God, now and for ever.

Post Communion

One of the Post Communions of Apostles and Evangelists is used
(page 500).

Collect

O everlasting God,
who hast ordained and constituted
    the services of angels and mortals in a wonderful order:
mercifully grant that,
    as thy holy angels alway do thee service in heaven,
so by thy appointment
they may succour and defend us on earth;
through Jesus Christ thy Son our Lord,
who liveth and reigneth with thee,
in the unity of the Holy Spirit,
one God, now and for ever.

Post Communion

O Lord of heaven,
in this sacrament thou hast brought us near
    to an innumerable company of angels
    and to the spirits of the saints made perfect:
as in this food of our earthly pilgrimage
    we have shared their fellowship,
so may we come to share their joy in heaven;
through Jesus Christ thy Son our Lord.

Luke *Red*

Evangelist

Collect

Almighty God,
who calledst Luke the physician,
whose praise is in the gospel,
to be an evangelist and physician of the soul:
may it please thee that,
by the wholesome medicines of the doctrine delivered by him,
all the diseases of our souls may be healed;
through the merits of thy Son Jesus Christ our Lord,
who liveth and reigneth with thee,
in the unity of the Holy Spirit,
one God, now and for ever.

Post Communion

*One of the Post Communions of Apostles and Evangelists is used
(page 500).*

28 October **Simon and Jude** *Red*

Apostles

Collect

O almighty God,
who hast built thy Church upon the foundation
    of the apostles and prophets,
Jesus Christ himself being the head cornerstone:
grant us so to be joined together in unity of spirit
    by their doctrine,
that we may be made an holy temple acceptable unto thee;
through Jesus Christ thy Son our Lord,
who liveth and reigneth with thee,
in the unity of the Holy Spirit,
one God, now and for ever.

Post Communion

*One of the Post Communions of Apostles and Evangelists is used
(page 500).*

Collect

Almighty God,
who didst give such grace unto thy apostle Saint Andrew
that he readily obeyed the calling of thy Son Jesus Christ
  and followed him without delay:
grant unto us all that we, being called by thy holy word,
may forthwith give up ourselves obediently
  to fulfil thy holy commandments;
through Jesus Christ thy Son our Lord,
who liveth and reigneth with thee,
in the unity of the Holy Spirit,
one God, now and for ever.

Post Communion

One of the Post Communions of Apostles and Evangelists is used (page 500).

Stephen *Red*
Deacon, First Martyr

Collect

Gracious Father,
who gavest to the first martyr Stephen
grace to pray for those who took up stones against him:
grant that in all our sufferings for the truth
we may learn to love even our enemies
and to seek forgiveness for those who desire our hurt,
looking up to heaven to him who was crucified for us,
Jesus Christ, our mediator and advocate,
who liveth and reigneth with thee,
in the unity of the Holy Spirit,
one God, now and for ever.

Post Communion

Merciful Lord,
we give thee thanks for the signs of thy mercy
revealed in birth and death:
save us, we beseech thee, by the coming of thy Son,
and grant us joy in honouring Stephen,
first martyr of the new Israel;
through Jesus Christ our Lord.

John

Apostle and Evangelist

Collect

Merciful Lord,
we beseech thee to cast thy bright beams of light upon thy Church,
that it being enlightened by the doctrine
    of thy blessed apostle and evangelist Saint John
may so walk in the light of thy truth,
that it may at length attain to the light of everlasting life;
through Jesus Christ thy Son our Lord,
who liveth and reigneth with thee,
in the unity of the Holy Spirit,
one God, now and for ever.

Post Communion

Grant, O Lord God, we beseech thee,
that the Word made flesh
proclaimed by thine apostle John
may, by the celebration of these holy mysteries,
ever abide and live within us;
through Jesus Christ our Lord.

Collect

Heavenly Father,
whose children suffered at the hands of Herod,
though they had done no wrong:
by the suffering of thy Son
and by the innocence of our lives
frustrate, we beseech thee, all evil designs
and establish thy reign of justice and peace;
through Jesus Christ thy Son our Lord,
who liveth and reigneth with thee,
in the unity of the Holy Spirit,
one God, now and for ever.

Post Communion

Lord Jesus Christ,
who in thy humility stooped to share our human life
even with the most defenceless of thy children:
grant that we who have received these gifts of thy passion
may rejoice in celebrating the witness of the Holy Innocents
    to the purity of thy sacrifice
    made once for all upon the cross;
for thou livest and reignest, now and for ever.

Collect

Almighty God,
to whose glory we celebrate the dedication
   of this house of prayer:
we praise thee for the many blessings
thou hast given to those who worship thee here:
and we pray that all who seek thee in this place
   may find thee,
and, being filled with the Holy Spirit,
may become a living temple acceptable to thee;
through Jesus Christ thy Son our Lord,
who liveth and reigneth with thee,
in the unity of the Holy Spirit,
one God, now and for ever.

Post Communion

Father in heaven,
whose Church on earth is a sign of thy heavenly peace,
an image of the new and eternal Jerusalem:
grant to us in the days of our pilgrimage
that, fed with the living bread of heaven,
and united in the body of thy Son,
we may be the temple of thy presence,
the place of thy glory on earth,
and a sign of thy peace in the world;
through Jesus Christ our Lord.

¶ Special Occasion

Harvest Thanksgiving *Green*

Harvest Thanksgiving may be celebrated on a Sunday and may replace the provision for that day, provided it does not supersede any Principal Feast or Festival.

Collect

O eternal God,
who crownest the year with thy goodness
and dost give us the fruits of the earth in their season:
give us grace that we may use them to thy glory,
for the relief of those in need and for our own well-being;
through Jesus Christ thy Son our Lord,
who liveth and reigneth with thee,
in the unity of the Holy Spirit,
one God, now and for ever.

Post Communion

Lord of the harvest,
as with joy we have offered our thanksgiving
    for thy love shown in creation
and have shared in the bread and the wine of the kingdom:
so by thy grace plant within us
a reverence for all that thou hast given us
and make us generous and wise stewards
    of those good things which we enjoy;
through Jesus Christ our Lord.

¶ A Table of Collects and Post Communions taken from The Book of Common Prayer

Many of the Collects and some Post Communions in *Common Worship* are based on Collects in *The Book of Common Prayer*. This table indicates the *Book of Common Prayer* originals of the *Common Worship* Collects and Post Communions.

The *Book of Common Prayer* original listed in the right hand column may be used in place of the corresponding *Common Worship* Collect or Post Communion in the first column.

 C = Collect
PC = Post Communion

Common Worship Collect/Post Communion		BCP original
First Sunday of Advent	C	Advent 1
Second Sunday of Advent	C	Advent 4
Third Sunday of Advent	C	Advent 3
Christmas Day	C	Christmas Day
Epiphany	C	Epiphany
Presentation of Christ in the Temple	C	Presentation of Christ in the Temple
Fourth Sunday before Lent	C PC	Epiphany 4 Holy Communion
Third Sunday before Lent	C	Easter 4
Ash Wednesday	C PC	Ash Wednesday Easter 2
Second Sunday of Lent	C PC	Easter 3 Lent 2
Third Sunday of Lent	PC	Trinity 18
Fourth Sunday of Lent	C	Trinity 24
Palm Sunday	C	Sunday next before Easter
Good Friday	C	Good Friday (1)
Easter Eve	C	Easter Even
Second Sunday of Easter	C	Easter 1
Fifth Sunday of Easter	C	Easter Day
Ascension Day	C	Ascension Day
Seventh Sunday of Easter	C	Sunday after Ascension Day

Common Worship Collect/Post Communion		BCP original
Day of Pentecost	C	Whit-Sunday
Weekdays after the Day of Pentecost	C	Easter 5
Trinity Sunday	C	Trinity Sunday
First Sunday after Trinity	C	Trinity 1
Second Sunday after Trinity	C	Quinquagesima
Fourth Sunday after Trinity	C	Trinity 4
Fifth Sunday after Trinity	C PC	Good Friday (2) Trinity 5
Sixth Sunday after Trinity	C	Trinity 6
Seventh Sunday after Trinity	C	Trinity 7
Eighth Sunday after Trinity	C	Holy Communion
Tenth Sunday after Trinity	C	Trinity 10
Eleventh Sunday after Trinity	C	Trinity 11
Twelfth Sunday after Trinity	C	Trinity 12
Fifteenth Sunday after Trinity	PC	Trinity 15
Sixteenth Sunday after Trinity	C	Epiphany 1
Seventeenth Sunday after Trinity	PC	Trinity 17
Nineteenth Sunday after Trinity	C	Trinity 19
Twenty-first Sunday after Trinity	C	Trinity 21
Last Sunday after Trinity	C	Advent 2
All Saints' Day	C	All Saints' Day
Second Sunday before Advent	C	Epiphany 6
Christ the King	PC	Trinity 25
Conversion of Paul	C	Conversion of St Paul
Annunciation of Our Lord	C	Annunciation
Philip and James	C	St Philip and St James
Matthias	C	St Matthias
Birth of John the Baptist	C	St John Baptist
James	C	St James
Bartholomew	C	St Bartholomew
Matthew	C	St Matthew
Michael and All Angels	C	St Michael and All Angels
Luke	C	St Luke
Simon and Jude	C	St Simon and St Jude
Andrew	C	St Andrew
John	C	St John the Evangelist

Rules for Regulating
Authorized Forms of Service

¶ *General*

1   Any reference in authorized provision to the use of hymns shall be construed as including the use of texts described as songs, chants, canticles.

2   If occasion requires, hymns may be sung at points other than those indicated in particular forms of service. Silence may be kept at points other than those indicated in particular forms of service.

3   Where rubrics indicate that a text is to be 'said' this must be understood to include 'or sung' and vice versa.

4   Where parts of a service make use of well-known and traditional texts, other translations or versions, particularly when used in musical compositions, may be used.

5   Local custom may be established and followed in respect of posture but regard should be had to indications in Notes attached to authorized forms of service that a particular posture is appropriate for some parts of that form of service.

6   On any occasion when the text of an alternative service authorized under the provisions of Canon B 2 provides for the Lord's Prayer to be said or sung, it may be used in the form included in *The Book of Common Prayer* or in either of the two other forms included in services in *Common Worship*. The further text included in Prayers for Various Occasions (page 106) may be used on suitable occasions.

7   Normally on any occasion only one Collect is used.

8   At Baptisms, Confirmations, Ordinations and Marriages which take place on Principal Feasts, other Principal Holy Days and on Sundays of Advent, Lent and Easter, within the Celebration of the Holy Communion, the Readings of the day are used and the Collect of the Day is said, unless the bishop directs otherwise.

9   The Collects and Lectionary in *Common Worship* may, optionally, be used in conjunction with the days included in the Calendar of *The Book of Common Prayer*, notwithstanding any difference in the title or name of a Sunday, Holy Day or other observance included in both Calendars.

¶ Rules to Order the Christian Year

For a Table of Transferences see page 534.

Sundays

All Sundays celebrate the paschal mystery of the death and resurrection of the Lord. Nevertheless, they also reflect the character of the seasons in which they are set.

At Evening Prayer on Saturdays other than Easter Eve, Christmas Eve or Principal Feasts or Festivals, the Collect appointed for the ensuing Sunday shall be used.

When a Festival occurs on the First or Second Sunday of Christmas, a Sunday of Epiphany, a Sunday before Lent, a Sunday after Trinity or on the Fourth, Third or Second Sundays before Advent, it is always to be observed but may be celebrated either on the Sunday or on the first available day thereafter. Festivals may not be celebrated on Sundays in Advent, Lent or Eastertide.

In a year when there are 23 Sundays after Trinity before the Fourth Sunday before Advent, the Collect and Post Communion for the Last Sunday after Trinity shall be used on the 23rd Sunday after Trinity and the Collect and Post Communion for the 3rd Sunday before Lent shall be used on the 22nd Sunday after Trinity.

Principal Feasts

The Principal Feasts which are to be observed are:
> Christmas Day
> The Epiphany
> The Presentation of Christ in the Temple
> The Annunciation of Our Lord to the Blessed Virgin Mary
> Easter Day
> Ascension Day
> Pentecost (Whit Sunday)
> Trinity Sunday
> All Saints' Day

On these days the Holy Communion is celebrated in every cathedral and parish church, and this celebration, required by Canon B 14, may only be dispensed with in accordance with the provision of Canon B 14A.

These days, and the liturgical provision for them, may not be displaced by any other celebration, except that the Annunciation, falling on a Sunday, is transferred to the Monday following or, falling between Palm Sunday and the Second Sunday of Easter inclusive, is transferred to the Monday after the Second Sunday of Easter.

Except in the case of Christmas Day and Easter Day, the celebration of the Feast begins with Evening Prayer on the day before the Feast, and the Collect at that Evening Prayer is that of the Feast. In the case of Christmas Eve and Easter Eve, there is proper liturgical provision, including a Collect, for the Eve, and this is used at both Morning and Evening Prayer.

In any year when there is a Second Sunday of Christmas, the Epiphany (6 January) may, for pastoral reasons, be celebrated on that Sunday.

The Presentation of Christ in the Temple (Candlemas) is celebrated either on 2 February or on the Sunday falling between 28 January and 3 February.

All Saints' Day is celebrated on either 1 November or the Sunday falling between 30 October and 5 November; if the latter there may be a secondary celebration on 1 November.

Other Principal Holy Days

Ash Wednesday, Maundy Thursday and Good Friday are Principal Holy Days. These days, and the liturgical provision for them, may not be displaced by any other celebration.

On Ash Wednesday and Maundy Thursday the Holy Communion is celebrated in every cathedral and parish church, except where there is dispensation under Canon B 14A.

Eastertide

The paschal character of the Great Fifty Days of Easter, from Easter Day to Pentecost, should be celebrated throughout the season, and should not be displaced by other celebrations. Except for a Patronal or Dedication Festival, no Festival may displace the celebration of Sunday as a memorial of the resurrection, and no saint's day may be celebrated in Easter Week.

The paschal character of the season should be retained on those weekdays when saints' days are celebrated.

Rogation Days are the three days before Ascension Day, when prayer is offered for God's blessing on the fruits of the earth and on human labour.

The nine days after Ascension Day until Pentecost are days of prayer and preparation to celebrate the outpouring of the Spirit.

Festivals

The Festivals are:

The Naming and Circumcision of Jesus *(1 January)*
The Baptism of Christ
    (Epiphany 1 or, when 6 January is a Sunday, on 7 January)
The Conversion of Paul *(25 January)*
Joseph of Nazareth *(19 March)*
George, Martyr, Patron of England *(23 April)*
Mark the Evangelist *(25 April)*
Philip and James, Apostles *(1 May)*
Matthias the Apostle *(14 May)*
The Visit of the Blessed Virgin Mary to Elizabeth *(31 May)*
Barnabas the Apostle *(11 June)*
The Birth of John the Baptist *(24 June)*
Peter and Paul, Apostles *(29 June)*
Thomas the Apostle *(3 July)*
Mary Magdalene *(22 July)*
James the Apostle *(25 July)*
The Transfiguration of Our Lord *(6 August)*
The Blessed Virgin Mary *(15 August)*
Bartholomew the Apostle *(24 August)*
Holy Cross Day *(14 September)*
Matthew, Apostle and Evangelist *(21 September)*
Michael and All Angels *(29 September)*
Luke the Evangelist *(18 October)*
Simon and Jude, Apostles *(28 October)*
Christ the King *(Sunday next before Advent)*
Andrew the Apostle *(30 November)*
Stephen, Deacon, First Martyr *(26 December)*
John, Apostle and Evangelist *(27 December)*
The Holy Innocents *(28 December)*

These days, and the liturgical provision for them, are not usually displaced. For each day there is full liturgical provision for the Holy Communion and for Morning and Evening Prayer.

Provision is also made for a first Evening Prayer on the day before the Festival where this is required. When Evening Prayer on the day before a Festival makes use of the lessons relating to that Festival, the Collect of that Festival shall be used.

Festivals falling on a Sunday are to be kept on that day or transferred to the Monday (or, at the discretion of the minister, to the next suitable weekday). But a Festival may not be celebrated on Sundays in Advent, Lent or Eastertide. Festivals coinciding with a Principal Feast or Principal Holy Day are transferred to the first available day.

The Baptism of Christ is transferred only when 6 January is a Sunday.

When St Joseph's Day falls between Palm Sunday and the Second Sunday of Easter inclusive, it is transferred to the Monday after the Second Sunday of Easter or, if the Annunciation has already been moved to that date, to the first available day thereafter.

When St George's Day or St Mark's Day falls between Palm Sunday and the Second Sunday of Easter inclusive, it is transferred to the Monday after the Second Sunday of Easter. If both fall in this period, St George's Day is transferred to the Monday and St Mark's Day to the Tuesday. When the Festivals of George and Mark both occur in the week following Easter and are transferred in accordance with these Rules in a place where the calendar of *The Book of Common Prayer* is followed, the Festival of Mark shall be observed on the second available day so that it will be observed on the same day as in places following alternative authorized Calendars, where George will have been transferred to the first available free day.

The Thursday after Trinity Sunday may be observed as the Day of Thanksgiving for the Holy Communion (sometimes known as Corpus Christi), and may be kept as a Festival. Where the Thursday following Trinity Sunday is observed as a Festival to commemorate the Institution of the Holy Communion and that day falls on a date which is also a Festival, the commemoration of the Institution of Holy Communion shall be observed on that Thursday and the other occurring Festival shall be transferred to the first available day.

The Festival of the Blessed Virgin Mary (15 August) may, for pastoral reasons, be celebrated instead on 8 September.

Christ the King is never transferred.

Local Celebrations

The celebration of the patron saint or the title of a church is kept either as a Festival or as a Principal Feast.

The Dedication Festival of a church is the anniversary of the date of its dedication or consecration. This is kept either as a Festival or as a Principal Feast.

When the date of dedication is unknown, the Dedication Festival may be observed on the first Sunday in October, or on the Last Sunday after Trinity, or on a suitable date chosen locally.

When kept as Principal Feasts, the Patronal and Dedication Festivals may be transferred to the nearest Sunday, unless that day is already a Principal Feast or one of the following days: the First Sunday of Advent, the Baptism of Christ, the First Sunday of Lent, the Fifth Sunday of Lent or Palm Sunday.

Harvest Thanksgiving may be celebrated on a Sunday and may replace the provision for that day, provided it does not supersede any Principal Feast or Festival.

In the Calendar of the Saints, diocesan and other local provision may be made to supplement the national Calendar.

Lesser Festivals

Lesser Festivals, which are listed in the Calendar, are observed at the level appropriate to a particular church. Each is provided with a Collect, Psalm and Readings, which may supersede the Collect of the week and the daily eucharistic lectionary. The daily Psalms and Readings at Morning and Evening Prayer are not usually superseded by those for Lesser Festivals, but at the minister's discretion Psalms and Readings provided on these days for the Holy Communion may be used at Morning and Evening Prayer.

The minister may be selective in the Lesser Festivals that are observed, and may also keep some or all of them as commemorations.

When a Lesser Festival falls on a Principal Feast or Holy Day or on a Festival, its celebration is normally omitted for that year, but, where there is sufficient reason, it may, at the discretion of the minister, be celebrated on the nearest available day.

Commemorations

Commemorations, which are listed in the Calendar, are made by a mention in prayers of intercession and thanksgiving. They are not provided with Collect, Psalm and Readings, and do not replace the usual weekday provision at either the Holy Communion or Morning and Evening Prayer.

The minister may be selective in the Commemorations that are made.

A Commemoration may be observed as a Lesser Festival, with liturgical provision from the common material for holy men and women, only where there is an established celebration in the wider church or where the day has a special local significance. In designating a Commemoration as a Lesser Festival, the minister must remember the need not to lose the spirit of the season, especially of Advent and Lent, by too many celebrations that detract from its character.

Days of Discipline and Self Denial

The weekdays of Lent and every Friday in the year are days of discipline and self denial, except all Principal Feasts and Festivals outside Lent and Fridays from Easter Day to Pentecost.

The eves of Principal Feasts are also appropriately kept as days of discipline and self denial in preparation for the Feast.

Ember Days

Ember Days should be kept, under the bishop's directions, in the week before an ordination as days of prayer for those to be made deacon or priest.

Ember Days may also be kept even when there is no ordination in the diocese as more general days of prayer for those who serve the Church in its various ministries, both ordained and lay, and for vocations.

Traditionally they have been observed on the Wednesdays, Fridays and Saturdays within the weeks before the Third Sunday of Advent, the Second Sunday of Lent and the Sundays nearest to 29 June and 29 September.

Ordinary Time

Ordinary Time is the period after the Feast of the Presentation of Christ until Shrove Tuesday, and from the day after the Feast of Pentecost until the day before the First Sunday of Advent. During Ordinary Time there is no seasonal emphasis, except that the period between All Saints' Day and the First Sunday of Advent is observed as a time to celebrate and reflect upon the reign of Christ in earth and heaven.

Liturgical Colours

Appropriate liturgical colours are suggested (adjacent to each Collect on pages 376–521): they are not mandatory and traditional or local use may be followed. The colour for a particular service should reflect the predominant theme. If the Collect, Readings, etc. on a Lesser Festival are those of the saint, then either red (for a martyr) or white is used; otherwise, the colour of the season is retained.

White is the colour for the festal periods from Christmas Day to the Presentation and from Easter Day to the Eve of Pentecost, for Trinity Sunday, for Festivals of Our Lord and the Blessed Virgin Mary, for All Saints' Day, and for the Festivals of those saints not venerated as martyrs, for the Feast of Dedication of a church, at Holy Communion on Maundy Thursday and in thanksgiving for Holy Communion and Holy Baptism. It is used for Marriages, and is suitable for Baptism, Confirmation and Ordination, though red may be preferred. It may be used in preference to purple or black for Funerals, and should be used at the Funeral of a child. Where a church has two sets of white, one may be kept for great Festivals indicated as 'gold or white'.

Red is used during Holy Week (except at Holy Communion on Maundy Thursday), on the Feast of Pentecost, may be used between All Saints' Day and the First Sunday of Advent (except where other provision is made) and is used for the Feasts of those saints venerated as martyrs. It is appropriate for any services which focus on the gift of the Holy Spirit, and is therefore suitable for Baptism, Confirmation and Ordination. Coloured hangings are traditionally removed for Good Friday and Easter Eve, but red is the colour for the liturgy on Good Friday.

Purple   (which may vary from 'Roman purple' to violet, with blue as an alternative) is the colour for Advent and from Ash Wednesday until the day before Palm Sunday. It is recommended for Funerals and for the Commemoration of the Faithful Departed, although either black or white may be preferred. A Lent array of unbleached linen is sometimes used as an alternative to purple, but only from Ash Wednesday until the day before Palm Sunday. Rose-colour is sometimes used as an alternative on the Third Sunday of Advent and the Fourth Sunday of Lent.

Green   is used from the day after the Presentation until Shrove Tuesday, and from the day after Pentecost until the eve of All Saints' Day, except when other provision is made. It may also be used, rather than red, between All Saints' Day and the First Sunday of Advent.

¶ A Table of Transferences
required, permitted or excluded by the Rules

Principal Feasts and Principal Holy Days

Epiphany	may be celebrated on the Second Sunday of Christmas (if any)
Candlemas	may be celebrated on the Sunday falling between 28 January and 3 February
The Annunciation	falling on a Sunday must be transferred
All Saints' Day	may be celebrated on the Sunday falling between 30 October and 5 November
All other Principal Feasts and Principal Holy Days	may not be transferred

Festivals

The Baptism of Christ	falling on 6 January must be transferred but otherwise may not be transferred
St Joseph, St George or St Mark	falling between Palm Sunday and the Second Sunday of Easter inclusive must be transferred
A Festival	falling on the Thursday after Trinity Sunday is transferred if Corpus Christi is celebrated as a Festival
Christ the King	may not be transferred
A Festival	falling on a Sunday in Advent, Lent or Eastertide must be transferred
A Festival (except the Baptism of Christ and Christ the King)	falling on another Sunday may be transferred
A Festival	falling on a Principal Feast or Principal Holy Day must be transferred

Local Celebrations

The Dedication or Patronal Festival of a church, kept as a Principal Feast or Festival	falling on a Principal Feast or Principal Holy Day or the First Sunday of Advent, Baptism of Christ, First Sunday of Lent, Fifth Sunday of Lent, or Palm Sunday must be transferred
The Dedication or Patronal Festival of a church, kept as a Principal Feast or Festival	falling on any other Sunday is observed as a Principal Feast or may be transferred as a Festival
Harvest Thanksgiving	may not be observed on a Sunday so as to displace a Principal Feast or Festival

Lectionary

for Sundays,
Principal Feasts and Holy Days,
and Festivals

¶ The Lectionary Years

Church Year (Advent to Advent)	Sunday Lectionary Year	Weekday Lectionary Year
2000 / 2001	C	1
2001 / 2002	A	2
2002 / 2003	B	1
2003 / 2004	C	2
2004 / 2005	A	1
2005 / 2006	B	2
2006 / 2007	C	1
2007 / 2008	A	2
2008 / 2009	B	1
2009 / 2010	C	2
2010 / 2011	A	1
2011 / 2012	B	2
2012 / 2013	C	1
2013 / 2014	A	2
2014 / 2015	B	1
2015 / 2016	C	2
2016 / 2017	A	1
2017 / 2018	B	2
2018 / 2019	C	1
2019 / 2020	A	2
2020 / 2021	B	1
2021 / 2022	C	2
2022 / 2023	A	1
2023 / 2024	B	2
2024 / 2025	C	1
2025 / 2026	A	2
2026 / 2027	B	1
2027 / 2028	C	2
2028 / 2029	A	1
2029 / 2030	B	2

The weekday lectionary is published separately.

¶ Rules to order how the Psalter and the rest of Holy Scripture are appointed to be read

1 In the reading of psalms and other portions of Holy Scripture any version of Holy Scripture which is not prohibited by lawful authority may be used.

2 The references in the following tables, except those to the psalms, are to the *New Revised Standard Version* of the Bible. References to the psalms are to the *Common Worship* psalter (pages 593–773). When other versions are used, such adaptations are made as necessary.

   The references in the following tables, including those to the psalms, state book, chapter and verse in that order. Where optional additional verses or psalms are set, the references are placed in square parentheses [. . .]. A simple choice between two alternative readings is indicated by an italicized *or*, placed between references.

   Longer psalms, which are starred thus*, have optional shorter alternatives given in the tables on pages 589–590.

3 When a reading begins with a personal pronoun, the reader may substitute the appropriate noun.

4 In these tables, verses are stated inclusively. The letter *a* after the number of a verse signifies the first part of that verse; the letter *b* the second part.

5 In a compact cycle of readings such as these, some passages have necessarily been abbreviated. When opportunity allows, the passages may be read in full. Verses in brackets may be included or omitted, as desired.

6   When there are only two readings at the principal service and that service is Holy Communion, the second reading is always the Gospel reading.

If there are only two readings at the principal service on Ascension Day, Pentecost, the Conversion of Paul or the Festivals of Matthias, Barnabas, James and Stephen, the reading from the Acts of the Apostles must always be used.

In the choice of readings other than the Gospel reading, the minister should ensure that, in any year, a balance is maintained between readings from the Old and New Testaments and that, where a particular biblical book is appointed to be read over several weeks, the choice ensures that this continuity of one book is not lost.

When the Principal Service Lectionary is used at a service other than Holy Communion, the Gospel reading need not always be chosen.

7   During the period from the First Sunday of Advent to the Presentation of Christ in the Temple, during the period from Ash Wednesday to Trinity Sunday, and on All Saints' Day, the readings shall come from an authorized lectionary. During Ordinary Time (i.e. between the Presentation and Ash Wednesday and between Trinity Sunday and Advent Sunday), authorized lectionary provision remains the norm but, after due consultation with the Parochial Church Council, the minister may, from time to time, depart from the lectionary provision for pastoral reasons or preaching or teaching purposes.

8   Three sets of psalms and readings are provided for each Sunday. The Principal Service Lectionary (which is drawn from the Revised Common Lectionary) is intended for use at the principal service of the day (whether this service is Holy Communion or some other authorized form). In most church communities, this is likely to be the mid-morning service, but the minister is free to decide which service time normally constitutes the principal service of the day.

The Second Service Lectionary is intended for a second main service. In many churches, this lectionary will be the appropriate provision for a Sunday afternoon or evening service. A Gospel reading is always provided so that this lectionary can, if necessary, be used at Holy Communion.

The Third Service Lectionary, with shorter readings, is intended for use when a third set of psalms and readings is needed. It is most appropriate for use at an office.

On Principal Feasts and Festivals the psalms are appropriate either for morning use or for evening use. They are therefore shown separately from the readings for the Second and Third Services.

9   On the Sundays between the Presentation of Christ in the Temple and the Second Sunday before Lent, and again on the Sundays after Trinity, the readings and Collects follow independent courses. The Collects and Post Communions are attached to the Sunday title (the Fifth/Fourth/Third Sunday before Lent, the First/Second/Third Sunday after Trinity, etc.), but the sets of proper readings (Propers 4, 5, 6) belong to particular calendar dates (i.e. the Sunday between two dates).

10   On the Sundays after Trinity, the Principal Service Lectionary provides alternative Old Testament readings and psalms. Those under the heading 'Continuous' allow the Old Testament reading and its complementary psalm to stand independently of the other readings. Those under the heading 'Related' relate the Old Testament reading and the psalm to the Gospel reading. It is unhelpful to move from week to week from one column to another. One column should be followed for the whole sequence of Sundays after Trinity.

An asterisk against a reference indicates that a shorter optional alternative
is given in the tables on pages 589 and 590.*

¶ Advent

The First Sunday of Advent

	Year A	Year B	Year C
Principal Service	Isaiah 2.1-5 Psalm 122 Romans 13.11-14 Matthew 24.36-44	Isaiah 64.1-9 Psalm 80.1-8,18-20* 1 Corinthians 1.3-9 Mark 13.24-37	Jeremiah 33.14-16 Psalm 25.1-9 1 Thessalonians 3.9-13 Luke 21.25-36
Second Service	Psalm 9* Isaiah 52.1-12 Matthew 24.15-28	Psalm 25* Isaiah 1.1-20 Matthew 21.1-13	Psalm 9* Joel 3.9-21 Revelation 14.13 – 15.4 Gospel at Holy Communion: John 3.1-17
Third Service	Psalm 44 Micah 4.1-7 1 Thessalonians 5.1-11	Psalm 44 Isaiah 2.1-5 Luke 12.35-48	Psalm 44 Isaiah 51.4-11 Romans 13.11-14

The Second Sunday of Advent

	Year A	Year B	Year C
Principal Service	Isaiah 11.1-10 Psalm 72.1-7,18,19* Romans 15.4-13 Matthew 3.1-12	Isaiah 40.1-11 Psalm 85.1-2,8-13* 2 Peter 3.8-15a Mark 1.1-8	Baruch 5.1-9 *or* Malachi 3.1-4 *Canticle:* Benedictus Philippians 1.3-11 Luke 3.1-6
Second Service	Psalms 11 [28] 1 Kings 18.17-39 John 1.19-28	Psalm 40* 1 Kings 22.1-28 Romans 15.4-13 Gospel at Holy Communion: Matthew 11.2-11	Psalms 75 [76] Isaiah 40.1-11 Luke 1.1-25
Third Service	Psalm 80 Amos 7 Luke 1.5-20	Psalm 80 Baruch 5.1-9 *or* Zephaniah 3.14-20 Luke 1.5-20	Psalm 80 Isaiah 64.1-7 Matthew 11.2-11

The Third Sunday of Advent

	Year A	Year B	Year C
Principal Service	Isaiah 35.1-10 Psalm 146.4-10 *or* *Canticle*: Magnificat James 5.7-10 Matthew 11.2-11	Isaiah 61.1-4,8-11 Psalm 126 *or* *Canticle*: Magnificat 1 Thessalonians 5.16-24 John 1.6-8,19-28	Zephaniah 3.14-20 *Canticle*: Isaiah 12.2-6* Philippians 4.4-7 Luke 3.7-18
Second Service	Psalms 12 [14] Isaiah 5.8-30 Acts 13.13-41 Gospel at Holy Communion: John 5.31-40	Psalm 68.1-19* Malachi 3.1-4; 4 Philippians 4.4-7 Gospel at Holy Communion: Matthew 14.1-12	Psalms 50.1-6 [62] Isaiah 35 Luke 1.57-66[67-80]
Third Service	Psalm 68.1-19 Zephaniah 3.14-20 Philippians 4.4-7	Psalms 50.1-6, 62 Isaiah 12 Luke 1.57-66	Psalms 12, 14 Isaiah 25.1-9 1 Corinthians 4.1-5

The Fourth Sunday of Advent

	Year A	Year B	Year C
Principal Service	Isaiah 7.10-16 Psalm 80.1-8,18-20* Romans 1.1-7 Matthew 1.18-25	2 Samuel 7.1-11,16 *Canticle*: Magnificat *or* Psalm 89.1-4,19-26* Romans 16.25-27 Luke 1.26-38	Micah 5.2-5a *Canticle*: Magnificat *or* Psalm 80.1-8 Hebrews 10.5-10 Luke 1.39-45[46-55]
Second Service	Psalms 113 [126] 1 Samuel 1.1-20 Revelation 22.6-21 Gospel at Holy Communion: Luke 1.39-45	Psalms 113 [131] Zechariah 2.10-13 Luke 1.39-55	Psalms 123 [131] Isaiah 10.33 – 11.10 Matthew 1.18-25
Third Service	Psalm 144 Micah 5.2-5a Luke 1.26-38	Psalm 144 Isaiah 7.10-16 Romans 1.1-7	Psalm 144 Isaiah 32.1-8 Revelation 22.6-21

Christmas Eve *24 December*

Morning Eucharist Years A, B, C	2 Samuel 7.1-5,8-11,16 Psalm 89.2,19-27 Acts 13.16-26 Luke 1.67-79
Evening Prayer Years A, B, C	Psalm 85 Zechariah 2 Revelation 1.1-8

¶ Christmas

Christmas Day 25 December

Principal Feast

Any of the following sets of readings may be used on Christmas Night and on Christmas Day. Set III should be used at some service during the celebration.

	I	II	III
Principal	Isaiah 9.2-7	Isaiah 62.6-12	Isaiah 52.7-10
Service	Psalm 96	Psalm 97	Psalm 98
Years	Titus 2.11-14	Titus 3.4-7	Hebrews 1.1-4[5-12]
A, B, C	Luke 2.1-14[15-20]	Luke 2.[1-7]8-20	John 1.1-14

Second	Isaiah 65.17-25
Service	Philippians 2.5-11
Years	*or* Luke 2.1-20
A, B, C	if it has not been used
	at the principal service
	of the day
	Evening Psalm
	Psalm 8

Third	Isaiah 62.1-5
Service	Matthew 1.18-25
Years	**Morning Psalms**
A, B, C	Psalms 110, 117

The First Sunday of Christmas

	Year A	Year B	Year C
Principal	Isaiah 63.7-9	Isaiah 61.10 – 62.3	1 Samuel 2.18-20,26
Service	Psalm 148*	Psalm 148*	Psalm 148*
	Hebrews 2.10-18	Galatians 4.4-7	Colossians 3.12-17
	Matthew 2.13-23	Luke 2.15-21	Luke 2.41-52
Second	Psalm 132	Psalm 132	Psalm 132
Service	Isaiah 49.7-13	Isaiah 35	Isaiah 61
	Philippians 2.1-11	Colossians 1.9-20 *or*	Galatians 3.27 – 4.7
	Gospel at Holy Communion:	Luke 2.41-52	Gospel at Holy Communion:
	Luke 2.41-52		Luke 2.15-21
Third	Psalm 105.1-11	Psalm 105.1-11	Psalm 105.1-11
Service	Isaiah 35.1-6	Isaiah 63.7-9	Isaiah 41.21 – 42.1
	Galatians 3.23-29	Ephesians 3.5-12	1 John 1.1-7

The Second Sunday of Christmas

	Year A	Year B	Year C
Principal Service (Readings for Years A, B, C are the same)	Jeremiah 31.7-14 Psalm 147.13-21 Ephesians 1.3-14 John 1.[1-9]10-18	Jeremiah 31.7-14 Psalm 147.13-21 Ephesians 1.3-14 John 1.[1-9]10-18	Jeremiah 31.7-14 Psalm 147.13-21 Ephesians 1.3-14 John 1.[1-9]10-18
	(or)	*(or)*	*(or)*
	Ecclesiasticus 24.1-12 *Canticle:* Wisdom of Solomon 10.15-21 Ephesians 1.3-14 John 1.[1-9]10-18	Ecclesiasticus 24.1-12 *Canticle:* Wisdom of Solomon 10.15-21 Ephesians 1.3-14 John 1.[1-9]10-18	Ecclesiasticus 24.1-12 *Canticle:* Wisdom of Solomon 10.15-21 Ephesians 1.3-14 John 1.[1-9]10-18
Second Service	Psalm 135* Isaiah 41.21 – 42.4 Colossians 1.1-14 Gospel at Holy Communion: Matthew 2.13-23	Psalm 135* Isaiah 46.3-13 Romans 12.1-8 Gospel at Holy Communion: Matthew 2.13-23	Psalm 135* 1 Samuel 1.20-28 1 John 4.7-16 Gospel at Holy Communion: Matthew 2.13-23
Third Service	Psalm 87 Jeremiah 31.15-17 2 Corinthians 1.3-12	Psalm 87 Zechariah 8.1-8 Luke 2.41-52	Psalm 87 Isaiah 12 1 Thessalonians 2.1-8

¶ *Epiphany*

The Epiphany 6 January
Principal Feast

Evening Prayer on the Eve Years A, B, C	Psalms 96, 97 Isaiah 49.1-13 John 4.7-26
Principal Service Years A, B, C	Isaiah 60.1-6 Psalm 72.[1-9]10-15 Ephesians 3.1-12 Matthew 2.1-12
Second Service Years A, B, C	Baruch 4.36 – 5.9 *or* Isaiah 60.1-9 John 2.1-11 **Evening Psalms** Psalms 98, 100
Third Service Years A, B, C	Jeremiah 31.7-14 John 1.29-34 **Morning Psalms** Psalms 132, 113

The Baptism of Christ The First Sunday of Epiphany

Evening Prayer on the Eve (if required)

Psalm 36
Isaiah 61
Titus 2.11-14; 3.4-7

	Year A	Year B	Year C
Principal Service	Isaiah 42.1-9 Psalm 29 Acts 10.34-43 Matthew 3.13-17	Genesis 1.1-5 Psalm 29 Acts 19.1-7 Mark 1.4-11	Isaiah 43.1-7 Psalm 29 Acts 8.14-17 Luke 3.15-17,21,22
Second Service	Psalms 46, 47 Joshua 3.1-8,14-17 Hebrews 1.1-12 Gospel at Holy Communion: Luke 3.15-22	Psalms 46 [47] Isaiah 42.1-9 Ephesians 2.1-10 Gospel at Holy Communion: Matthew 3.13-17	Psalms 46, 47 Isaiah 55.1-11 Romans 6.1-11 Gospel at Holy Communion: Mark 1.4-11
Third Service	Psalm 89.19-29 Exodus 14.15-22 1 John 5.6-9	Psalm 89.19-29 1 Samuel 16.1-3,13 John 1.29-34	Psalm 89.19-29 Isaiah 42.1-9 Acts 19.1-7

The Second Sunday of Epiphany

	Year A	Year B	Year C
Principal Service	Isaiah 49.1-7 Psalm 40.1-12 1 Corinthians 1.1-9 John 1.29-42	1 Samuel 3.1-10[11-20] Psalm 139.1-5,12-18* Revelation 5.1-10 John 1.43-51	Isaiah 62.1-5 Psalm 36.5-10 1 Corinthians 12.1-11 John 2.1-11
Second Service	Psalm 96 Ezekiel 2.1 – 3.4 Galatians 1.11-24 Gospel at Holy Communion: John 1.43-51	Psalm 96 Isaiah 60.9-22 Hebrews 6.17 – 7.10 Gospel at Holy Communion: Matthew 8.5-13	Psalm 96 1 Samuel 3.1-20 Ephesians 4.1-16 Gospel at Holy Communion: John 1.29-42
Third Service	Psalm 145.1-12 Jeremiah 1.4-10 Mark 1.14-20	Psalm 145.1-12 Isaiah 62.1-5 1 Corinthians 6.11-20	Psalm 145.1-13 Isaiah 49.1-7 Acts 16.11-15

The Third Sunday of Epiphany

	Year A	Year B	Year C
Principal Service	Isaiah 9.1-4 Psalm 27.1,4-12* 1 Corinthians 1.10-18 Matthew 4.12-23	Genesis 14.17-20 Psalm 128 Revelation 19.6-10 John 2.1-11	Nehemiah 8.1-3,5-6,8-10 Psalm 19* 1 Corinthians 12.12-31a Luke 4.14-21
Second Service	Psalm 33* Ecclesiastes 3.1-11 1 Peter 1.3-12 Gospel at Holy Communion: Luke 4.14-21	Psalm 33* Jeremiah 3.21 – 4.2 Titus 2.1-8,11-14 Gospel at Holy Communion: Matthew 4.12-23	Psalm 33 Numbers 9.15-23 1 Corinthians 7.17-24 Gospel at Holy Communion: Mark 1.21-28
Third Service	Psalm 113 Amos 3.1-8 1 John 1.1-4	Psalm 113 Jonah 3.1-5,10 John 3.16-21	Psalm 113 Deuteronomy 30.11-15 3 John 1,5-8

The Fourth Sunday of Epiphany

	Year A	Year B	Year C
Principal Service	1 Kings 17.8-16 Psalm 36.5-10 1 Corinthians 1.18-31 John 2.1-11	Deuteronomy 18.15-20 Psalm 111 Revelation 12.1-5a Mark 1.21-28	Ezekiel 43.27 – 44.4 Psalm 48 1 Corinthians 13.1-13 Luke 2.22-40
Second Service	Psalm 34* Genesis 28.10-22 Philemon 1-16 Gospel at Holy Communion: Mark 1.21-28	Psalm 34* 1 Samuel 3.1-20 1 Corinthians 14.12-20 Gospel at Holy Communion: Matthew 13.10-17	Psalm 34 1 Chronicles 29.6-19 Acts 7.44-50 Gospel at Holy Communion: John 4.19-29a
Third Service	Psalm 71.1-6,15-17 Haggai 2.1-9 1 Corinthians 3.10-17	Psalm 71.1-6,15-17 Jeremiah 1.4-10 Mark 1.40-45	Psalm 71.1-6,15-17 Micah 6.1-8 1 Corinthians 6.12-20

The Presentation of Christ in the Temple

(Candlemas) *2 February*

Principal Feast

Evening Prayer on the Eve Years A, B, C	Psalm 118 1 Samuel 1.19b-28 Hebrews 4.11-16
Principal Service Years A, B, C	Malachi 3.1-5 Psalm 24.[1-6]7-10 Hebrews 2.14-18 Luke 2.22-40
Second Service Years A, B, C	Haggai 2.1-9 John 2.18-22 **Evening Psalms** Psalms 122, 132
Third Service Years A, B, C	Exodus 13.1-16 Romans 12.1-5 **Morning Psalms** Psalms 48, 146

¶ *Ordinary Time*

Proper 1

Sunday between 3 and 9 February inclusive

(if earlier than the Second Sunday before Lent)

	Year A	Year B	Year C
Principal Service	Isaiah 58.1-9a[b-12] Psalm 112.1-9[10] 1 Corinthians 2.1-12[13-16] Matthew 5.13-20	Isaiah 40.21-31 Psalm 147.1-12,21c* 1 Corinthians 9.16-23 Mark 1.29-39	Isaiah 6.1-8[9-13] Psalm 138 1 Corinthians 15.1-11 Luke 5.1-11
Second Service	Psalms [1, 3] 4 Amos 2.4-16 Ephesians 4.17-32 Gospel at Holy Communion: Mark 1.29-39	Psalm 5 Numbers 13.1-2,27-33 Philippians 2.12-28 Gospel at Holy Communion: Luke 5.1-11	Psalms [1] 2 Wisdom 6.1-21 *or* Hosea 1 Colossians 3.1-22 Gospel at Holy Communion: Matthew 5.13-20
Third Service	Psalms 5, 6 Jeremiah 26.1-16 Acts 3.1-10	Psalms 2, 3 Jeremiah 26.1-16 Acts 3.1-10	Psalms 3, 4 Jeremiah 26.1-16 Acts 3.1-10

Sunday between 10 and 16 February inclusive

(if earlier than the Second Sunday before Lent)

	Year A	Year B	Year C
Principal Service	Deuteronomy 30.15-20 *or* Ecclesiasticus 15.15-20 Psalm 119.1-8 1 Corinthians 3.1-9 Matthew 5.21-37	2 Kings 5.1-14 Psalm 30 1 Corinthians 9.24-27 Mark 1.40-45	Jeremiah 17.5-10 Psalm 1 1 Corinthians 15.12-20 Luke 6.17-26
Second Service	Psalms [7] 13 Amos 3.1-8 Ephesians 5.1-17 Gospel at Holy Communion: Mark 1.40-45	Psalm 6 Numbers 20.2-13 Philippians 3.7-21 Gospel at Holy Communion: Luke 6.17-26	Psalms [5] 6 Wisdom 11.21 – 12.11 *or* Hosea 10.1-8,12 Galatians 4.8-20 Gospel at Holy Communion: Matthew 5.21-37
Third Service	Psalm 10 Jeremiah 30.1-3,10-22 Acts 6	Psalm 7 Jeremiah 30.1-3,10-22 Acts 6	Psalm 7 Jeremiah 30.1-3,10-22 Acts 6

Sunday between 17 and 23 February inclusive

(if earlier than the Second Sunday before Lent)

	Year A	Year B	Year C
Principal Service	Leviticus 19.1-2,9-18 Psalm 119.33-40 1 Corinthians 3.10-11,16-23 Matthew 5.38-48	Isaiah 43.18-25 Psalm 41 2 Corinthians 1.18-22 Mark 2.1-12	Genesis 45.3-11,15 Psalm 37.1-11,40,41* 1 Corinthians 15.35-38, 42-50 Luke 6.27-38
Second Service	Psalm 18.1-20 *or* 18.21-30 Amos 9.5-15 Ephesians 6.1-20 Gospel at Holy Communion: Mark 2.1-12	Psalm 10 Numbers 22.21 – 23.12 Philippians 4.10-20 Gospel at Holy Communion: Luke 6.27-38	Psalms [11] 13 Hosea 14 Galatians 5.2-10 Gospel at Holy Communion: Matthew 6.1-8
Third Service	Psalms 21, 23 Jeremiah 33.1-11 Acts 8.4-25	Psalm 9 Jeremiah 33.1-11 Acts 8.4-25	Psalm 10 Jeremiah 33.1-11 Acts 8.4-25

The Second Sunday before Lent

	Year A	Year B	Year C
Principal Service	Genesis 1.1 – 2.3 Psalm 136 or Psalm 136.1-9,23-26 Romans 8.18-25 Matthew 6.25-34	Proverbs 8.1,22-31 Psalm 104.26-37 Colossians 1.15-20 John 1.1-14	Genesis 2.4b-9,15-25 Psalm 65 Revelation 4 Luke 8.22-25
Second Service	Psalm 148 Proverbs 8.1,22-31 Revelation 4 Gospel at Holy Communion: Luke 12.16-31	Psalm 65 Genesis 2.4b-25 Luke 8.22-35	Psalm 147* Genesis 1.1 – 2.3 Matthew 6.25-34
Third Service	Psalms 100, 150 Job 38.1-21 Colossians 1.15-20	Psalms 29, 67 Deuteronomy 8.1-10 Matthew 6.25-34	Psalm 104.1-26 Job 28.1-11 Acts 14.8-17

The Sunday next before Lent

	Year A	Year B	Year C
Principal Service	Exodus 24.12-18 Psalm 2 or Psalm 99 2 Peter 1.16-21 Matthew 17.1-9	2 Kings 2.1-12 Psalm 50.1-6 2 Corinthians 4.3-6 Mark 9.2-9	Exodus 34.29-35 Psalm 99 2 Corinthians 3.12 – 4.2 Luke 9.28-36[37-43a]
Second Service	Psalm 84 Ecclesiasticus 48.1-10 or 2 Kings 2.1-12 Matthew 17.9-23 (or 1-23)	Psalms 2 [99] 1 Kings 19.1-16 2 Peter 1.16-21 Gospel at Holy Communion: Mark 9.[2-8]9-13	Psalm 89.1-18* Exodus 3.1-6 John 12.27-36a
Third Service	Psalm 72 Exodus 34.29-35 2 Corinthians 4.3-6	Psalms 27, 150 Exodus 24.12-18 2 Corinthians 3.12-18	Psalm 2 Exodus 33.17-23 1 John 3.1-3

¶ *Lent*

Ash Wednesday
Principal Holy Day

Principal	Joel 2.1-2,12-17 *or*
Service	Isaiah 58.1-12
Years	Psalm 51.1-18
A, B, C	2 Corinthians 5.20b – 6.10
	Matthew 6.1-6,16-21
	or John 8.1-11

Second	Isaiah 1.10-18
Service	Luke 15.11-32
Years	**Evening Psalm**
A, B, C	Psalm 102*

Third	Daniel 9.3-6,17-19
Service	I Timothy 6.6-19
Years	**Morning Psalm**
A, B, C	Psalm 38

The First Sunday of Lent

	Year A	Year B	Year C
Principal	Genesis 2.15-17; 3.1-7	Genesis 9.8-17	Deuteronomy 26.1-11
Service	Psalm 32	Psalm 25.1-9	Psalm 91.1-2,9-16*
	Romans 5.12-19	I Peter 3.18-22	Romans 10.8b-13
	Matthew 4.1-11	Mark 1.9-15	Luke 4.1-13
Second	Psalm 50.1-15	Psalm 119.17-32	Psalm 119.73-88
Service	Deuteronomy 6.4-9,16-25	Genesis 2.15-17; 3.1-7	Jonah 3
	Luke 15.1-10	Romans 5.12-19 *or*	Luke 18.9-14
		Luke 13.31-35	
Third	Psalm 119.1-16	Psalm 77	Psalm 50.1-15
Service	Jeremiah 18.1-11	Exodus 34.1-10	Micah 6.1-8
	Luke 18.9-14	Romans 10.8b-13	Luke 5.27-39

The Second Sunday of Lent

	Year A	Year B	Year C
Principal Service	Genesis 12.1-4a Psalm 121 Romans 4.1-5,13-17 John 3.1-17	Genesis 17.1-7,15,16 Psalm 22.23-31 Romans 4.13-25 Mark 8.31-38	Genesis 15.1-12,17-18 Psalm 27 Philippians 3.17 – 4.1 Luke 13.31-35
Second Service	Psalm 135* Numbers 21.4-9 Luke 14.27-33	Psalm 135* Genesis 12.1-9 Hebrews 11.1-3,8-16 Gospel at Holy Communion: John 8.51-59	Psalm 135* Jeremiah 22.1-9,13-17 Luke 14.27-33
Third Service	Psalm 74 Jeremiah 22.1-9 Matthew 8.1-13	Psalm 105.1-6,37-45 Isaiah 51.1-11 Galatians 3.1-9,23-29	Psalm 119.161-176 Genesis 17.1-7,15,16 Romans 11.13-24

The Third Sunday of Lent

	Year A	Year B	Year C
Principal Service	Exodus 17.1-7 Psalm 95 Romans 5.1-11 John 4.5-42	Exodus 20.1-17 Psalm 19* 1 Corinthians 1.18-25 John 2.13-22	Isaiah 55.1-9 Psalm 63.1-9 1 Corinthians 10.1-13 Luke 13.1-9
Second Service	Psalm 40 Joshua 1.1-9 Ephesians 6.10-20 Gospel at Holy Communion: John 2.13-22	Psalms 11, 12 Exodus 5.1 – 6.1 Philippians 3.4b-14 *or* Matthew 10.16-22	Psalms 12, 13 Genesis 28.10-19a John 1.35-51
Third Service	Psalm 46 Amos 7.10-17 2 Corinthians 1.1-11	Psalm 18.1-25 Jeremiah 38 Philippians 1.1-26	Psalms 26, 28 Deuteronomy 6.4-9 John 17.1a,11b-19

The Fourth Sunday of Lent

	Year A	Year B	Year C
Principal Service	1 Samuel 16.1-13 Psalm 23 Ephesians 5.8-14 John 9.1-41	Numbers 21.4-9 Psalm 107.1-3,17-22* Ephesians 2.1-10 John 3.14-21	Joshua 5.9-12 Psalm 32 2 Corinthians 5.16-21 Luke 15.1-3,11b-32
Second Service	*If the Principal Service readings have been displaced by Mothering Sunday provisions, they may be used at the Second Service.*		
	Psalm 31.1-16 or 31.1-8 Micah 7 or Prayer of Manasseh James 5 Gospel at Holy Communion: John 3.14-21	Psalms 13, 14 Exodus 6.2-13 Romans 5.1-11 Gospel at Holy Communion: John 12.1-8	Psalm 30 Prayer of Manasseh or Isaiah 40.27 – 41.13 2 Timothy 4.1-18 Gospel at Holy Communion: John 11.17-44
Third Service	Psalm 19 Isaiah 43.1-7 Ephesians 2.8-14	Psalm 27 1 Samuel 16.1-13 John 9.1-25	Psalms 84, 85 Genesis 37.3-4,12-36 1 Peter 2.16-25

Mothering Sunday

Principal Service **Years** **A, B, C**	Exodus 2.1-10 or 1 Samuel 1.20-28 Psalm 34.11-20 or Psalm 127.1-4 2 Corinthians 1.3-7 or Colossians 3.12-17 Luke 2.33-35 or John 19.25-27

The Fifth Sunday of Lent

Passiontide begins

	Year A	Year B	Year C
Principal Service	Ezekiel 37.1-14 Psalm 130 Romans 8.6-11 John 11.1-45	Jeremiah 31.31-34 Psalm 51.1-13 or Psalm 119.9-16 Hebrews 5.5-10 John 12.20-33	Isaiah 43.16-21 Psalm 126 Philippians 3.4b-14 John 12.1-8
Second Service	Psalm 30 Lamentations 3.19-33 Matthew 20.17-34	Psalm 34* Exodus 7.8-24 Romans 5.12-21 Gospel at Holy Communion: Luke 22.1-13	Psalm 35* 2 Chronicles 35.1-6,10-16 Luke 22.1-13
Third Service	Psalm 86 Jeremiah 31.27-37 John 12.20-33	Psalm 107.1-22 Exodus 24.3-8 Hebrews 12.18-29	Psalms 111, 112 Isaiah 35.1-10 Romans 7.21 – 8.4

Palm Sunday

	Year A	Year B	Year C
Principal Service	**Liturgy of the Palms:** Matthew 21.1-11 Psalm 118.1-2,19-29*	**Liturgy of the Palms:** Mark 11.1-11 *or* John 12.12-16 Psalm 118.1-2,19-24*	**Liturgy of the Palms:** Luke 19.28-40 Psalm 118.1-2,19-29*
	Liturgy of the Passion: Isaiah 50.4-9a Psalm 31.9-16* Philippians 2.5-11 Matthew 26.14 – 27.66 *or* Matthew 27.11-54	**Liturgy of the Passion:** Isaiah 50.4-9a Psalm 31.9-16* Philippians 2.5-11 Mark 14.1 – 15.47 *or* Mark 15.1-39[40-47]	**Liturgy of the Passion:** Isaiah 50.4-9a Psalm 31.9-16* Philippians 2.5-11 Luke 22.14 – 23.56 *or* Luke 23.1-49
Second Service	Psalm 80 Isaiah 5.1-7 Matthew 21.33-46	Psalm 69.1-20 Isaiah 5.1-7 Mark 12.1-12	Psalm 69.1-20 Isaiah 5.1-7 Luke 20.9-19
Third Service	Psalms 61, 62 Zechariah 9.9-12 Luke 16.19-31	Psalms 61, 62 Zechariah 9.9-12 1 Corinthians 2.1-12	Psalms 61, 62 Zechariah 9.9-12 1 Corinthians 2.1-12

Monday of Holy Week

Principal Service Years A, B, C	Isaiah 42.1-9 Psalm 36.5-11 Hebrews 9.11-15 John 12.1-11
Second Service Years A, B, C	Psalm 41 Lamentations 1.1-12a Luke 22.1-23
Third Service Years A, B, C	Psalm 25 Lamentations 2.8-19 Colossians 1.18-23

Tuesday of Holy Week

Principal	Isaiah 49.1-7
Service	Psalm 71.1-14*
Years	1 Corinthians 1.18-31
A, B, C	John 12.20-36

Second	Psalm 27
Service	Lamentations 3.1-18
Years	Luke 22.24-53 (or 39-53)
A, B, C	

Third	Psalm 55.13-24
Service	Lamentations 3.40-51
Years	Galatians 6.11-18
A, B, C	

Wednesday of Holy Week

Principal	Isaiah 50.4-9a
Service	Psalm 70
Years	Hebrews 12.1-3
A, B, C	John 13.21-32

Second	Psalm 102*
Service	Wisdom 1.16 – 2.1;
Years	2.12-22 or
A, B, C	Jeremiah 11.18-20
	Luke 22.54-71

Third	Psalm 88
Service	Isaiah 63.1-9
Years	Revelation 14.18 – 15.4
A, B, C	

Maundy Thursday
Principal Holy Day

Principal	Exodus 12.1-4[5-10] 11-14
Service	Psalm 116.1,10-17*
Years	1 Corinthians 11.23-26
A, B, C	John 13.1-17,31b-35

Second	Leviticus 16.2-24
Service	Luke 23.1-25
Years	**Evening Psalm**
A, B, C	Psalm 39

Third	Exodus 11
Service	Ephesians 2.11-18
Years	**Morning Psalms**
A, B, C	Psalms 42, 43

Good Friday

Principal Holy Day

Principal	Isaiah 52.13 – 53.12
Service	Psalm 22*
Years	Hebrews 10.16-25 *or*
A, B, C	Hebrews 4.14-16; 5.7-9
	John 18.1 – 19.42

Second	Genesis 22.1-18
Service	A part of John 18 – 19
Years	if not used at the Principal Service
A, B, C	especially in the evening,
	John 19.38-42 *or*
	Colossians 1.18-23
	Evening Psalms
	Psalms 130, 143

Third	Lamentations 5.15-22
Service	A part of John 18 – 19
Years	if not used at the Principal Service
A, B, C	*or* Hebrews 10.1-10
	Morning Psalm
	Psalm 69

Easter Eve

These readings are for use at services other than the Easter Vigil.

Principal	Job 14.1-14 *or* Lamentations 3.1-9,19-24
Service	Psalm 31.1-4,15,16*
Years	1 Peter 4.1-8
A, B, C	Matthew 27.57-66 *or*
	John 19.38-42

Second	Psalm 142
Service	Hosea 6.1-6
Years	John 2.18-22
A, B, C	

Third	Psalm 116
Service	Job 19.21-27
Years	1 John 5.5-12
A, B, C	

¶ Easter

Easter Vigil

Year A

A minimum of three Old Testament readings should be chosen.
The reading from Exodus 14 should always be used.

Genesis 1.1 – 2.4a	Psalm 136.1-9,23-26
Genesis 7.1-5,11-18; 8.6-18; 9.8-13	Psalm 46
Genesis 22.1-18	Psalm 16
Exodus 14.10-31; 15.20,21	***Canticle*: Exodus 15.1b-13,17,18**
Isaiah 55.1-11	*Canticle*: Isaiah 12.2-6
Baruch 3.9-15,32 – 4.4	
or Proverbs 8.1-8,19-21; 9.4b-6	Psalm 19
Ezekiel 36.24-28	Psalms 42, 43
Ezekiel 37.1-14	Psalm 143
Zephaniah 3.14-20	Psalm 98
Romans 6.3-11	**Psalm 114**
Matthew 28.1-10	

Year B

A minimum of three Old Testament readings should be chosen.
The reading from Exodus 14 should always be used.

Genesis 1.1 – 2.4a	Psalm 136.1-9,23-26
Genesis 7.1-5,11-18; 8.6-18; 9.8-13	Psalm 46
Genesis 22.1-18	Psalm 16
Exodus 14.10-31; 15.20,21	***Canticle*: Exodus 15.1b-13,17,18**
Isaiah 55.1-11	*Canticle*: Isaiah 12.2-6
Baruch 3.9-15,32 – 4.4	
or Proverbs 8.1-8,19-21; 9.4b-6	Psalm 19
Ezekiel 36.24-28	Psalms 42, 43
Ezekiel 37.1-14	Psalm 143
Zephaniah 3.14-20	Psalm 98
Romans 6.3-11	**Psalm 114**
Mark 16.1-8	

Year C

A minimum of three Old Testament readings should be chosen.
The reading from Exodus 14 should always be used.

Genesis 1.1 – 2.4a	Psalm 136.1-9,23-26
Genesis 7.1-5,11-18; 8.6-18; 9.8-13	Psalm 46
Genesis 22.1-18	Psalm 16
Exodus 14.10-31; 15.20,21	***Canticle*: Exodus 15.1b-13,17,18**
Isaiah 55.1-11	*Canticle*: Isaiah 12.2-6
Baruch 3.9-15,32 – 4.4	
or Proverbs 8.1-8,19-21; 9.4b-6	Psalm 19
Ezekiel 36.24-28	Psalms 42, 43
Ezekiel 37.1-14	Psalm 143
Zephaniah 3.14-20	Psalm 98
Romans 6.3-11	**Psalm 114**
Luke 24.1-12	

Easter Day

Principal Feast

	Year A	Year B	Year C
Principal Service	Acts 10.34-43 *or* Jeremiah 31.1-6 Psalm 118.1-2,14-24* Colossians 3.1-4 *or* Acts 10.34-43 John 20.1-18 *or* Matthew 28.1-10	Acts 10.34-43 *or* Isaiah 25.6-9 Psalm 118.1-2,14-24* 1 Corinthians 15.1-11 *or* Acts 10.34-43 John 20.1-18 *or* Mark 16.1-8	Acts 10.34-43 *or* Isaiah 65.17-25 Psalm 118.1-2,14-24* 1 Corinthians 15.19-26 *or* Acts 10.34-43 John 20.1-18 *or* Luke 24.1-12
Second Service	Song of Solomon 3.2-5; 8.6,7 John 20.11-18 if not used at the Principal Service *or* Revelation 1.12-18 **Evening Psalms** Psalms 105 *or* 66.1-11	Ezekiel 37.1-14 Luke 24.13-35 **Evening Psalms** Psalms 105 *or* 66.1-11	Isaiah 43.1-21 1 Corinthians 15.1-11 *or* John 20.19-23 **Evening Psalms** Psalms 105 *or* 66.1-11
Third Service	Exodus 14.10-18,26 – 15.2 Revelation 15.2-4 **Morning Psalms** Psalms 114, 117	Genesis 1.1-5,26-31 2 Corinthians 5.14 – 6.2 **Morning Psalms** Psalms 114, 117	Ezekiel 47.1-12 John 2.13-22 **Morning Psalms** Psalms 114, 117

Old Testament Readings for Sundays of Easter

For those who require an Old Testament reading on the Sundays of Easter, provision is made in this table. If an Old Testament reading is used, the reading from Acts must be used as the second reading.

Principal Service

Year A	The Second Sunday of Easter	Exodus 14.10-31; 15.20,21
	The Third Sunday of Easter	Zephaniah 3.14-20
	The Fourth Sunday of Easter	Genesis 7
	The Fifth Sunday of Easter	Genesis 8.1-19
	The Sixth Sunday of Easter	Genesis 8.20 – 9.17
	The Seventh Sunday of Easter	Ezekiel 36.24-28
Year B	The Second Sunday of Easter	Exodus 14.10-31; 15.20,21
	The Third Sunday of Easter	Zephaniah 3.14-20
	The Fourth Sunday of Easter	Genesis 7.1-5,11-18; 8.6-18; 9.8-13
	The Fifth Sunday of Easter	Baruch 3.9-15,32 – 4.4 *or* Genesis 22.1-18
	The Sixth Sunday of Easter	Isaiah 55.1-11
	The Seventh Sunday of Easter	Ezekiel 36.24-28
Year C	The Second Sunday of Easter	Exodus 14.10-31; 15.20,21
	The Third Sunday of Easter	Zephaniah 3.14-20
	The Fourth Sunday of Easter	Genesis 7.1-5,11-18; 8.6-18; 9.8-13
	The Fifth Sunday of Easter	Baruch 3.9-15,32 – 4.4 *or* Genesis 22.1-18
	The Sixth Sunday of Easter	Ezekiel 37.1-14
	The Seventh Sunday of Easter	Ezekiel 36.24-28

The Second Sunday of Easter

	Year A	Year B	Year C
Principal Service	Acts 2.14a,22-32 Psalm 16 1 Peter 1.3-9 John 20.19-31	Acts 4.32-35 Psalm 133 1 John 1.1 – 2.2 John 20.19-31	Acts 5.27-32 Psalm 118.14-29 or Psalm 150 Revelation 1.4-8 John 20.19-31
Second Service	Psalm 30.1-5 Daniel 6.1-23 or 6.6-23 Mark 15.46 – 16.8	Psalm 143.1-11 Isaiah 26.1-9,19 Luke 24.1-12	Psalm 16 Isaiah 52.13 – 53.12 or 53.1-6,9-12 Luke 24.13-35
Third Service	Psalm 81.1-10 Exodus 12.1-17 1 Corinthians 5.6b-8	Psalm 22.20-31 Isaiah 53.6-12 Romans 4.13-25	Psalm 136.1-16 Exodus 12.1-13 1 Peter 1.3-12

The Third Sunday of Easter

	Year A	Year B	Year C
Principal Service	Acts 2.14a,36-41 Psalm 116.1-3,10-17* 1 Peter 1.17-23 Luke 24.13-35	Acts 3.12-19 Psalm 4 1 John 3.1-7 Luke 24.36b-48	Acts 9.1-6 [7-20] Psalm 30 Revelation 5.11-14 John 21.1-19
Second Service	Psalm 48 Haggai 1.13 – 2.9 1 Corinthians 3.10-17 Gospel at Holy Communion: John 2.13-22	Psalm 142 Deuteronomy 7.7-13 Revelation 2.1-11 Gospel at Holy Communion: Luke 16.19-31	Psalm 86 Isaiah 38.9-20 John 11.[17-26]27-44
Third Service	Psalm 23 Isaiah 40.1-11 1 Peter 5.1-11	Psalm 77.11-20 Isaiah 63.7-15 1 Corinthians 10.1-13	Psalm 80.1-8 Exodus 15.1-2,9,18 John 10.1-19

The Fourth Sunday of Easter

	Year A	Year B	Year C
Principal Service	Acts 2.42-47 Psalm 23 1 Peter 2.19-25 John 10.1-10	Acts 4.5-12 Psalm 23 1 John 3.16-24 John 10.11-18	Acts 9.36-43 Psalm 23 Revelation 7.9-17 John 10.22-30
Second Service	Psalm 29.1-10 Ezra 3.1-13 Ephesians 2.11-22 Gospel at Holy Communion: Luke 19.37-48	Psalm 81.8-16 Exodus 16.4-15 Revelation 2.12-17 Gospel at Holy Communion: John 6.30-40	Psalms 113, 114 Isaiah 63.7-14 Luke 24.36-49
Third Service	Psalm 106.6-24 Nehemiah 9.6-15 1 Corinthians 10.1-13	Psalm 119.89-96 Nehemiah 7.73b – 8.12 Luke 24.25-32	Psalm 146 1 Kings 17.17-24 Luke 7.11-23

The Fifth Sunday of Easter

	Year A	Year B	Year C
Principal Service	Acts 7.55-60 Psalm 31.1-5,15-16* 1 Peter 2.2-10 John 14.1-14	Acts 8.26-40 Psalm 22.25-31 1 John 4.7-21 John 15.1-8	Acts 11.1-18 Psalm 148* Revelation 21.1-6 John 13.31-35
Second Service	Psalm 147.1-12 Zechariah 4.1-10 Revelation 21.1-14 Gospel at Holy Communion: Luke 2.25-32[33-38]	Psalm 96 Isaiah 60.1-14 Revelation 3.1-13 Gospel at Holy Communion: Mark 16.9-16	Psalm 98 Daniel 6.[1-5]6-23 Mark 15.46 – 16.8
Third Service	Psalm 30 Ezekiel 37.1-12 John 5.19-29	Psalm 44.16-27 2 Maccabees 7.7-14 or Daniel 3.16-28 Hebrews 11.32 – 12.2	Psalm 16 2 Samuel 7.4-13 Acts 2.14a,22-32[33-36]

The Sixth Sunday of Easter

	Year A	**Year B**	**Year C**
Principal Service	Acts 17.22-31	Acts 10.44-48	Acts 16.9-15
	Psalm 66.7-18	Psalm 98	Psalm 67
	1 Peter 3.13-22	1 John 5.1-6	Revelation 21.10,22 – 22.5
	John 14.15-21	John 15.9-17	John 14.23-29 or
			John 5.1-9
Second Service	Psalms 87, 36.5-10	Psalm 45	Psalms 126, 127
	Zechariah 8.1-13	Song of Solomon	Zephaniah 3.14-20
	Revelation 21.22 – 22.5	4.16 – 5.2; 8.6,7	Matthew 28.1-10,16-20
	Gospel at Holy Communion:	Revelation 3.14-22	
	John 21.1-14	Gospel at Holy Communion:	
		Luke 22.24-30	
Third Service	Psalm 73.21-28	Psalm 104.28-34	Psalm 40.1-9
	Job 14.1-2,7-15; 19.23-27a	Ezekiel 47.1-12	Genesis 1.26-28 [29-31]
	1 Thessalonians 4.13-18	John 21.1-19	Colossians 3.1-11

Ascension Day

Principal Feast

Evening Prayer on the Eve Years A, B, C	Psalms 15, 24
	2 Samuel 23.1-5
	Colossians 2.20 – 3.4

	Year A	**Year B**	**Year C**

The reading from Acts must be used as either the first or second reading.

	Year A	**Year B**	**Year C**
Principal Service (Readings for Years A, B, C are the same)	Acts 1.1-11 or Daniel 7.9-14	Acts 1.1-11 or Daniel 7.9-14	Acts 1.1-11 or Daniel 7.9-14
	Psalm 47 or Psalm 93	Psalm 47 or Psalm 93	Psalm 47 or Psalm 93
	Ephesians 1.15-23 or	Ephesians 1.15-23 or	Ephesians 1.15-23 or
	Acts 1.1-11	Acts 1.1-11	Acts 1.1-11
	Luke 24.44-53	Luke 24.44-53	Luke 24.44-53
Second Service	Song of the Three	Song of the Three	Song of the Three 29-37
	29-37 or 2 Kings 2.1-15	29-37 or 2 Kings 2.1-15	or 2 Kings 2.1-15
	Revelation 5	Revelation 5	Revelation 5
	Gospel at Holy Communion:	Gospel at Holy Communion:	Gospel at Holy Communion:
	Mark 16.14-20	Matthew 28.16-20	Matthew 28.16-20
	Evening Psalm	**Evening Psalm**	**Evening Psalm**
	Psalm 8	Psalm 8	Psalm 8
Third Service	Isaiah 52.7-15	Isaiah 52.7-15	Isaiah 52.7-15
	Hebrews 7.[11-25] 26-28	Hebrews 7.[11-25] 26-28	Hebrews 7.[11-25] 26-28
	Morning Psalm	**Morning Psalm**	**Morning Psalm**
	Psalm 110	Psalm 110	Psalm 110

The Seventh Sunday of Easter

Sunday after Ascension Day

	Year A	Year B	Year C
Principal Service	Acts 1.6-14 Psalm 68.1-10,32-35* 1 Peter 4.12-14; 5.6-11 John 17.1-11	Acts 1.15-17,21-26 Psalm 1 1 John 5.9-13 John 17.6-19	Acts 16.16-34 Psalm 97 Revelation 22.12-14, 16,17,20,21 John 17.20-26
Second Service	Psalm 47 2 Samuel 23.1-5 Ephesians 1.15-23 Gospel at Holy Communion: Mark 16.14-20	Psalm 147.1-12 Isaiah 61 Luke 4.14-21	Psalm 68* Isaiah 44.1-8 Ephesians 4.7-16 Gospel at Holy Communion: Luke 24.44-53
Third Service	Psalm 104.26-35 Isaiah 65.17-25 Revelation 21.1-8	Psalm 76 Isaiah 14.3-15 Revelation 14.1-13	Psalm 99 Deuteronomy 34 Luke 24.44-53 or Acts 1.1-8

Day of Pentecost (Whit Sunday)

Principal Feast

	Year A	Year B	Year C
Evening Prayer on the Eve	Psalm 48 Deuteronomy 16.9-15 John 15.26 – 16.15	Psalm 48 Deuteronomy 16.9-15 John 7.37-39	Psalm 48 Deuteronomy 16.9-15 John 7.37-39

	Year A	Year B	Year C
	The reading from Acts must be used as either the first or second reading.		
Principal Service	Acts 2.1-21 or Numbers 11.24-30 Psalm 104.26-36,37b* 1 Corinthians 12.3b-13 or Acts 2.1-21 John 20.19-23 or John 7.37-39	Acts 2.1-21 or Ezekiel 37.1-14 Psalm 104.26-36,37b* Romans 8.22-27 or Acts 2.1-21 John 15.26-27; 16.4b-15	Acts 2.1-21 or Genesis 11.1- Psalm 104.26-36,37b* Romans 8.14-17 or Acts 2.1-21 John 14.8-17[25-27]
Second Service	Joel 2.21-32 Acts 2.14-21[22-38] Gospel at Holy Communion: Luke 24.44-53 **Evening Psalms** Psalms 67, 133	Ezekiel 36.22-28 Acts 2.22-38 Gospel at Holy Communion: John 20.19-23 **Evening Psalm** Psalm 139.1-11 [13-18,23-24]	Exodus 33.7-20 2 Corinthians 3.4-18 Gospel at Holy Communion: John 16.4b-15 **Evening Psalm** Psalm 33.1-12
Third Service	Genesis 11.1-9 Acts 10.34-48 **Morning Psalm** Psalm 87	Isaiah 11.1-9 or Wisdom 7.15-23 [24-27] 1 Corinthians 12.4-13 **Morning Psalm** Psalm 145	Isaiah 40.12-23 or Wisdom 9.9-17 1 Corinthians 2.6-16 **Morning Psalms** Psalms 36.5-10; 150

¶ *Ordinary Time*

Trinity Sunday
Principal Feast

	Year A	**Year B**	**Year C**
Evening Prayer on the Eve	Psalms 97, 98 Exodus 34.1-10 Mark 1.1-13	Psalms 97, 98 Isaiah 40.12-31 Mark 1.1-13	Psalms 97, 98 Isaiah 40.12-31 Mark 1.1-13

	Year A	**Year B**	**Year C**
Principal Service	Isaiah 40.12-17,27-31 Psalm 8 2 Corinthians 13.11-13 Matthew 28.16-20	Isaiah 6.1-8 Psalm 29 Romans 8.12-17 John 3.1-17	Proverbs 8.1-4,22-31 Psalm 8 Romans 5.1-5 John 16.12-15
Second Service	Isaiah 6.1-8 John 16.5-15 **Evening Psalms** Psalms 93, 150	Ezekiel 1.4-10,22-28a Revelation 4 Gospel at Holy Communion: Mark 1.1-13 **Evening Psalm** Psalm 104.1-10	Exodus 3.1-15 John 3.1-17 **Evening Psalm** Psalm 73.1-3,16-28
Third Service	Exodus 3.1-6,13-15 John 17.1-11 **Morning Psalm** Psalm 86.8-13	Proverbs 8.1-4,22-31 2 Corinthians 13.[5-10]11-13 **Morning Psalm** Psalm 33.1-12	Isaiah 6.1-8 Revelation 4 **Morning Psalm** Psalm 29

Thursday after Trinity Sunday *if observed as*
Day of Thanksgiving for Holy Communion
(Corpus Christi)

Evening Prayer on the Eve (if required)	Psalms 110, 111 Exodus 16.2-15 John 6.22-35
Principal Service	Genesis 14.18-20 Psalm 116.10-17 1 Corinthians 11.23-26 John 6.51-58
Second Service	Proverbs 9.1-5 Luke 9.11-17 **Evening Psalms** Psalms 23, 42, 43
Third Service	Deuteronomy 8.2-16 1 Corinthians 10.1-17 **Morning Psalm** Psalm 147

Sunday between 24 and 28 May inclusive

If this follows Trinity Sunday, Proper 3 (page 549) is used.

Proper 4

Sunday between 29 May and 4 June inclusive

(if after Trinity Sunday)

	Year A	Year B	Year C
Principal Service	**Continuous**	**Continuous**	**Continuous**
	Genesis 6.9-22; 7.24; 8.14-19	1 Samuel 3.1-10 [11-20]	1 Kings 18.20,21
	Psalm 46	Psalm 139.1-5,12-18	[22-29]30-39
	Romans 1.16,17;	2 Corinthians 4.5-12	Psalm 96
	3.22b-28[29-31]	Mark 2.23 – 3.6	Galatians 1.1-12
(or)	Matthew 7.21-29		Luke 7.1-10
	Related	**Related**	**Related**
	Deuteronomy 11.18-21,26-28	Deuteronomy 5.12-15	1 Kings 8.22-23,41-43
	Psalm 31.1-5,19-24*	Psalm 81.1-10	Psalm 96.1-9
	Romans 1.16,17;	2 Corinthians 4.5-12	Galatians 1.1-12
	3.22b-28[29-31]	Mark 2.23 – 3.6	Luke 7.1-10
	Matthew 7.21-29		
Second Service	Psalm 33*	Psalm 35*	Psalm 39
	Ruth 2.1-20a	Jeremiah 5.1-19	Genesis 4.1-16
	Luke 8.4-15	Romans 7.7-25	Mark 3.7-19
		Gospel at Holy Communion:	
		Luke 7.1-10	
Third Service	Psalm 37.1-18	Psalms 28, 32	Psalm 41
	Deuteronomy 5.1-21	Deuteronomy 5.1-21	Deuteronomy 5.1-21
	Acts 21.17-39a	Acts 21.17-39a	Acts 21.17-39a

Proper 5

Sunday between 5 and 11 June inclusive

(if after Trinity Sunday)

	Year A	Year B	Year C
Principal Service	**Continuous**	**Continuous**	**Continuous**
	Genesis 12.1-9	1 Samuel 8.4-11[12-15]	1 Kings 17.8-16[17-24]
	Psalm 33.1-12	16-20 [11.14-15]	Psalm 146
	Romans 4.13-25	Psalm 138	Galatians 1.11-24
	Matthew 9.9-13,18-26	2 Corinthians 4.13 – 5.1	Luke 7.11-17
(or)		Mark 3.20-35	
	Related	**Related**	**Related**
	Hosea 5.15 – 6.6	Genesis 3.8-15	1 Kings 17.17-24
	Psalm 50.7-15	Psalm 130	Psalm 30
	Romans 4.13-25	2 Corinthians 4.13 – 5.1	Galatians 1.11-24
	Matthew 9.9-13,18-26	Mark 3.20-35	Luke 7.11-17
Second Service	Psalms [39] 41	Psalm 37.1-11[12-17]	Psalm 44*
	1 Samuel 18.1-16	Jeremiah 6.16-21	Genesis 8.15 – 9.17
	Luke 8.41-56	Romans 9.1-13	Mark 4.1-20
		Gospel at Holy Communion:	
		Luke 7.11-17	
Third Service	Psalm 38	Psalm 36	Psalm 45
	Deuteronomy 6.10-25	Deuteronomy 6.10-25	Deuteronomy 6.10-25
	Acts 22.22 – 23.11	Acts 22.22 – 23.11	Acts 22.22 – 23.11

Sunday between 12 and 18 June inclusive

(if after Trinity Sunday)

	Year A	Year B	Year C
Principal Service	**Continuous**	**Continuous**	**Continuous**
	Genesis 18.1-15 [21.1-7]	1 Samuel 15.34 – 16.13	1 Kings 21.1-10[11-14] 15-21a
	Psalm 116.1,10-17*	Psalm 20	Psalm 5.1-8
	Romans 5.1-8	2 Corinthians 5.6-10	Galatians 2.15-21
	Matthew 9.35 – 10.8 [9-23]	[11-13]14-17	Luke 7.36 – 8.3
		Mark 4.26-34	
(or)			
	Related	**Related**	**Related**
	Exodus 19.2-8a	Ezekiel 17.22-24	2 Samuel 11.26 – 12.10,13-15
	Psalm 100	Psalm 92.1-4,12-15*	Psalm 32
	Romans 5.1-8	2 Corinthians 5.6-10	Galatians 2.15-21
	Matthew 9.35 – 10.8 [9-23]	[11-13]14-17	Luke 7.36 – 8.3
		Mark 4.26-34	
Second Service	Psalms [42] 43	Psalm 39	Psalms 52 [53]
	1 Samuel 21.1-15	Jeremiah 7.1-16	Genesis 13
	Luke 11.14-28	Romans 9.14-26	Mark 4.21-41
		Gospel at Holy Communion:	
		Luke 7.36 – 8.3	
Third Service	Psalm 45	Psalms 42, 43	Psalm 49
	Deuteronomy 10.12 – 11.1	Deuteronomy 10.12 – 11.1	Deuteronomy 10.12 – 11.1
	Acts 23.12-35	Acts 23.12-35	Acts 23.12-35

Sunday between 19 and 25 June inclusive

(if after Trinity Sunday)

	Year A	Year B	Year C
Principal Service	**Continuous**	**Continuous**	**Continuous**
	Genesis 21.8-21	1 Samuel 17.[1a,4-11,	1 Kings 19.1-4[5-7]
	Psalm 86.1-10,16-17*	19-23]32-49	8-15a
	Romans 6.1b-11	Psalm 9.9-20 or	Psalms 42, 43*
	Matthew 10.24-39	1 Samuel 17.57 – 18.5,	Galatians 3.23-29
		10-16	Luke 8.26-39
		Psalm 133	
		2 Corinthians 6.1-13	
		Mark 4.35-41	
(or)			
	Related	**Related**	**Related**
	Jeremiah 20.7-13	Job 38.1-11	Isaiah 65.1-9
	Psalm 69.8-11[12-17]18-20*	Psalm 107.1-3,23-32*	Psalm 22.19-28
	Romans 6.1b-11	2 Corinthians 6.1-13	Galatians 3.23-29
	Matthew 10.24-39	Mark 4.35-41	Luke 8.26-39
Second Service	Psalms 46 [48]	Psalm 49	Psalms [50] 57
	1 Samuel 24.1-17	Jeremiah 10.1-16	Genesis 24.1-27
	Luke 14.12-24	Romans 11.25-36	Mark 5.21-43
		Gospel at Holy Communion:	
		Luke 8.26-39	
Third Service	Psalm 49	Psalm 48	Psalm 55.1-16,18-21
	Deuteronomy 11.1-15	Deuteronomy 11.1-15	Deuteronomy 11.1-15
	Acts 27.1-12	Acts 27.1-12	Acts 27.1-12

Sunday between 26 June and 2 July inclusive

	Year A	Year B	Year C
Principal Service	**Continuous**	**Continuous**	**Continuous**
	Genesis 22.1-14	2 Samuel 1.1,17-27	2 Kings 2.1-2,6-14
	Psalm 13	Psalm 130	Psalm 77.1-2,11-20*
	Romans 6.12-23	2 Corinthians 8.7-15	Galatians 5.1,13-25
	Matthew 10.40-42	Mark 5.21-43	Luke 9.51-62
(or)			
	Related	**Related**	**Related**
	Jeremiah 28.5-9	Wisdom of Solomon	1 Kings 19.5-16,19-21
	Psalm 89.1-4,15-18*	1.13-15; 2.23,24	Psalm 16
	Romans 6.12-23	*Canticle*: Lamentations	Galatians 5.1,13-25
	Matthew 10.40-42	3.23-33 *or* Psalm 30	Luke 9.51-62
		2 Corinthians 8.7-15	
		Mark 5.21-43	
		Lamentations 3.23-33 may be	
		read as the first reading in place	
		of Wisdom 1.13-15; 2.23,24	
Second Service	Psalm 50*	Psalms [52] 53	Psalms [59.1-6,18-20] 60
	1 Samuel 28.3-19	Jeremiah 11.1-14	Genesis 27.1-40
	Luke 17.20-37	Romans 13.1-10	Mark 6.1-6
		Gospel at Holy Communion:	
		Luke 9.51-62	
Third Service	Psalms 52, 53	Psalm 56	Psalm 64
	Deuteronomy 15.1-11	Deuteronomy 15.1-11	Deuteronomy 15.1-11
	Acts 27.[13-32]33-44	Acts 27.[13-32]33-44	Acts 27.[13-32]33-44

Sunday between 3 and 9 July inclusive

	Year A	Year B	Year C
Principal Service	**Continuous**	**Continuous**	**Continuous**
	Genesis 24.34-38,42-49,	2 Samuel 5.1-5,9-10	2 Kings 5.1-14
	58-67	Psalm 48	Psalm 30
	Psalm 45.10-17 *or Canticle*:	2 Corinthians 12.2-10	Galatians 6.[1-6]7-16
	Song of Solomon 2.8-13	Mark 6.1-13	Luke 10.1-11,16-20
	Romans 7.15-25a		
	Matthew 11.16-19,25-30		
(or)			
	Related	**Related**	**Related**
	Zechariah 9.9-12	Ezekiel 2.1-5	Isaiah 66.10-14
	Psalm 145.8-15	Psalm 123	Psalm 66.1-8
	Romans 7.15-25a	2 Corinthians 12.2-10	Galatians 6.[1-6]7-16
	Matthew 11.16-19,25-30	Mark 6.1-13	Luke 10.1-11,16-20
Second Service	Psalms 56 [57]	Psalms [63] 64	Psalms 65 [70]
	2 Samuel 2.1-11; 3.1	Jeremiah 20.1-11a	Genesis 29.1-20
	Luke 18.31 – 19.10	Romans 14.1-17	Mark 6.7-29
		Gospel at Holy Communion:	
		Luke 10.1-11,16-20	
Third Service	Psalm 55.1-15,18-22	Psalm 57	Psalm 74
	Deuteronomy 24.10-22	Deuteronomy 24.10-22	Deuteronomy 24.10-22
	Acts 28.1-16	Acts 28.1-16	Acts 28.1-16

Sunday between 10 and 16 July inclusive

	Year A	Year B	Year C
Principal Service	**Continuous**	**Continuous**	**Continuous**
	Genesis 25.19-34	2 Samuel 6.1-5,12b-19	Amos 7.7-17
	Psalm 119.105-112	Psalm 24	Psalm 82
	Romans 8.1-11	Ephesians 1.3-14	Colossians 1.1-14
(or)	Matthew 13.1-9,18-23	Mark 6.14-29	Luke 10.25-37
	Related	**Related**	**Related**
	Isaiah 55.10-13	Amos 7.7-15	Deuteronomy 30.9-14
	Psalm 65.[1-7]8-13*	Psalm 85.8-13	Psalm 25.1-10
	Romans 8.1-11	Ephesians 1.3-14	Colossians 1.1-14
	Matthew 13.1-9,18-23	Mark 6.14-29	Luke 10.25-37
Second Service	Psalms 60 [63]	Psalm 66*	Psalm 77*
	2 Samuel 7.18-29	Job 4.1; 5.6-27 *or*	Genesis 32.9-30
	Luke 19.41 – 20.8	Ecclesiasticus 4.11-31	Mark 7.1-23
		Romans 15.14-29	
		Gospel at Holy Communion:	
		Luke 10.25-37	
Third Service	Psalms 64, 65	Psalm 65	Psalm 76
	Deuteronomy 28.1-14	Deuteronomy 28.1-14	Deuteronomy 28.1-14
	Acts 28.17-31	Acts 28.17-31	Acts 28.17-31

Sunday between 17 and 23 July inclusive

	Year A	Year B	Year C
Principal Service	**Continuous**	**Continuous**	**Continuous**
	Genesis 28.10-19a	2 Samuel 7.1-14a	Amos 8.1-12
	Psalm 139.1-11,23,24*	Psalm 89.20-37	Psalm 52
	Romans 8.12-25	Ephesians 2.11-22	Colossians 1.15-28
(or)	Matthew 13.24-30,36-43	Mark 6.30-34,53-56	Luke 10.38-42
	Related	**Related**	**Related**
	Wisdom of Solomon	Jeremiah 23.1-6	Genesis 18.1-10a
	12.13,16-19 *or* Isaiah 44.6-8	Psalm 23	Psalm 15
	Psalm 86.11-17	Ephesians 2.11-22	Colossians 1.15-28
	Romans 8.12-25	Mark 6.30-34,53-56	Luke 10.38-42
	Matthew 13.24-30,36-43		
Second Service	Psalms 67 [70]	Psalm 73*	Psalm 81
	1 Kings 2.10-12; 3.16-28	Job 13.13 – 14.6 *or*	Genesis 41.1-16,25-37
	Acts 4.1-22	Ecclesiasticus 18.1-14	1 Corinthians 4.8-13
	Gospel at Holy Communion:	Hebrews 2.5-18	Gospel at Holy Communion:
	Mark 6.30-34,53-56	Gospel at Holy Communion:	John 4.31-35
		Luke 10.38-42	
Third Service	Psalm 71	Psalms 67, 70	Psalms 82, 100
	Deuteronomy 30.1-10	Deuteronomy 30.1-10	Deuteronomy 30.1-10
	1 Peter 3.8-18	1 Peter 3.8-18	1 Peter 3.8-18

Sunday between 24 and 30 July inclusive

	Year A	Year B	Year C
Principal Service	**Continuous**	**Continuous**	**Continuous**
	Genesis 29.15-28	2 Samuel 11.1-15	Hosea 1.2-10
	Psalm 105.1-11,45b* or	Psalm 14	Psalm 85*
	Psalm 128	Ephesians 3.14-21	Colossians 2.6-15[16-19]
	Romans 8.26-39	John 6.1-21	Luke 11.1-13
(or)	Matthew 13.31-33,44-52		
	Related	**Related**	**Related**
	1 Kings 3.5-12	2 Kings 4.42-44	Genesis 18.20-32
	Psalm 119.129-136	Psalm 145.10-19	Psalm 138
	Romans 8.26-39	Ephesians 3.14-21	Colossians 2.6-15[16-19]
	Matthew 13.31-33,44-52	John 6.1-21	Luke 11.1-13
Second Service	Psalms 75 [76]	Psalm 74*	Psalm 88*
	1 Kings 6.11-14,23-38	Job 19.1-27a or	Genesis 42.1-25
	Acts 12.1-17	Ecclesiasticus 38.24-34	1 Corinthians 10.1-24
	Gospel at Holy Communion:	Hebrews 8	Gospel at Holy Communion:
	John 6.1-21	Gospel at Holy Communion:	Matthew 13.24-30[31-43]
		Luke 11.1-13	
Third Service	Psalm 77	Psalm 75	Psalm 95
	Song of Solomon 2 or	Song of Solomon 2 or	Song of Solomon 2 or
	1 Maccabees 2.[1-14]15-22	1 Maccabees 2.[1-14]15-22	1 Maccabees 2.[1-14]15-22
	1 Peter 4.7-14	1 Peter 4.7-14	1 Peter 4.7-14

Sunday between 31 July and 6 August inclusive

	Year A	Year B	Year C
Principal Service	**Continuous**	**Continuous**	**Continuous**
	Genesis 32.22-31	2 Samuel 11.26 – 12.13a	Hosea 11.1-11
	Psalm 17.1-7,16*	Psalm 51.1-13	Psalm 107.1-9,43*
	Romans 9.1-5	Ephesians 4.1-16	Colossians 3.1-11
(or)	Matthew 14.13-21	John 6.24-35	Luke 12.13-21
	Related	**Related**	**Related**
	Isaiah 55.1-5	Exodus 16.2-4,9-15	Ecclesiastes 1.2,12-14; 2.18-
	Psalm 145.8-9,15-22*	Psalm 78.23-29	Psalm 49.1-12*
	Romans 9.1-5	Ephesians 4.1-16	Colossians 3.1-11
	Matthew 14.13-21	John 6.24-35	Luke 12.13-21
Second Service	Psalm 80*	Psalm 88*	Psalm 107.1-32*
	1 Kings 10.1-13	Job 28 or	Genesis 50.4-26
	Acts 13.1-13	Ecclesiasticus 42.15-25	1 Corinthians 14.1-19
	Gospel at Holy Communion:	Hebrews 11.17-31	Gospel at Holy Communion:
	John 6.24-35	Gospel at Holy Communion:	Mark 6.45-52
		Luke 12.13-21	
Third Service	Psalm 85	Psalm 86	Psalm 106.1-10
	Song of Solomon 5.2-16 or	Song of Solomon 5.2-16 or	Song of Solomon 5.2-16 or
	1 Maccabees 3.1-12	1 Maccabees 3.1-12	1 Maccabees 3.1-12
	2 Peter 1.1-15	2 Peter 1.1-15	2 Peter 1.1-15

Sunday between 7 and 13 August inclusive

	Year A	Year B	Year C
Principal Service	**Continuous**	**Continuous**	**Continuous**
	Genesis 37.1-4,12-28	2 Samuel 18.5-9,15,31-33	Isaiah 1.1,10-20
	Psalm 105.1-6,16-22,45b*	Psalm 130	Psalm 50.1-8, 23,24*
	Romans 10.5-15	Ephesians 4.25 – 5.2	Hebrews 11.1-3,8-16
(or)	Matthew 14.22-33	John 6.35,41-51	Luke 12.32-40
	Related	**Related**	**Related**
	1 Kings 19.9-18	1 Kings 19.4-8	Genesis 15.1-6
	Psalm 85.8-13	Psalm 34.1-8	Psalm 33.12-22*
	Romans 10.5-15	Ephesians 4.25 – 5.2	Hebrews 11.1-3,8-16
	Matthew 14.22-33	John 6.35,41-51	Luke 12.32-40
Second Service	Psalm 86	Psalm 91*	Psalms 108 [116]
	1 Kings 11.41 – 12.20	Job 39.1 – 40.4 *or*	Isaiah 11.10 – 12.6
	Acts 14.8-20	Ecclesiasticus 43.13-33	2 Corinthians 1.1-22
	Gospel at Holy Communion:	Hebrews 12.1-17	Gospel at Holy Communion:
	John 6.35,41-51	Gospel at Holy Communion:	Mark 7.24-30
		Luke 12.32-40	
Third Service	Psalm 88	Psalm 90	Psalm 115
	Song of Solomon 8.5-7	Song of Solomon 8.5-7	Song of Solomon 8.5-7
	or 1 Maccabees 14.4-15	*or* 1 Maccabees 14.4-15	*or* 1 Maccabees 14.4-15
	2 Peter 3.8-13	2 Peter 3.8-13	2 Peter 3.8-13

Sunday between 14 and 20 August inclusive

	Year A	Year B	Year C
Principal Service	**Continuous**	**Continuous**	**Continuous**
	Genesis 45.1-15	1 Kings 2.10-12; 3.3-14	Isaiah 5.1-7
	Psalm 133	Psalm 111	Psalm 80.1-2,9-20*
	Romans 11.1-2a, 29-32	Ephesians 5.15-20	Hebrews 11.29 – 12.2
(or)	Matthew 15.[10-20]21-28	John 6.51-58	Luke 12.49-56
	Related	**Related**	**Related**
	Isaiah 56.1,6-8	Proverbs 9.1-6	Jeremiah 23.23-29
	Psalm 67	Psalm 34.9-14	Psalm 82
	Romans 11.1-2a,29-32	Ephesians 5.15-20	Hebrews 11.29 – 12.2
	Matthew 15.[10-20]21-28	John 6.51-58	Luke 12.49-56
Second Service	Psalm 90*	Psalms [92] 100	Psalm 119.17-32*
	2 Kings 4.1-37	Exodus 2.23 – 3.10	Isaiah 28.9-22
	Acts 16.1-15	Hebrews 13.1-15	2 Corinthians 8.1-9
	Gospel at Holy Communion:	Gospel at Holy Communion:	Gospel at Holy Communion:
	John 6.51-58	Luke 12.49-56	Matthew 20.1-16
Third Service	Psalm 92	Psalm 106.1-10	Psalm 119.33-48
	Jonah 1 *or*	Jonah 1 *or*	Jonah 1 *or*
	Ecclesiasticus 3.1-15	Ecclesiasticus 3.1-15	Ecclesiasticus 3.1-15
	2 Peter 3.14-18	2 Peter 3.14-18	2 Peter 3.14-18

Sunday between 21 and 27 August inclusive

	Year A	Year B	Year C
Principal Service	**Continuous**	**Continuous**	**Continuous**
	Exodus 1.8 – 2.10	1 Kings 8.[1,6,10-11]	Jeremiah 1.4-10
	Psalm 124	22-30,41-43	Psalm 71.1-6
	Romans 12.1-8	Psalm 84	Hebrews 12.18-29
	Matthew 16.13-20	Ephesians 6.10-20	Luke 13.10-17
		John 6.56-69	
(or)			
	Related	**Related**	**Related**
	Isaiah 51.1-6	Joshua 24.1-2a,14-18	Isaiah 58.9b-14
	Psalm 138	Psalm 34.15-22	Psalm 103.1-8
	Romans 12.1-8	Ephesians 6.10-20	Hebrews 12.18-29
	Matthew 16.13-20	John 6.56-69	Luke 13.10-17
Second Service	Psalm 95	Psalm 116*	Psalm 119.49-72*
	2 Kings 6.8-23	Exodus 4.27 – 5.1	Isaiah 30.8-21
	Acts 17.15-34	Hebrews 13.16-21	2 Corinthians 9
	Gospel at Holy Communion:	Gospel at Holy Communion:	Gospel at Holy Communion:
	John 6.56-69	Luke 13.10-17	Matthew 21.28-32
Third Service	Psalm 104.1-25	Psalm 115	Psalm 119.73-88
	Jonah 2 *or*	Jonah 2 *or*	Jonah 2 *or*
	Ecclesiasticus 3.17-29	Ecclesiasticus 3.17-29	Ecclesiasticus 3.17-29
	Revelation 1	Revelation 1	Revelation 1

Sunday between 28 August and 3 September inclusive

	Year A	Year B	Year C
Principal Service	**Continuous**	**Continuous**	**Continuous**
	Exodus 3.1-15	Song of Solomon 2.8-13	Jeremiah 2.4-13
	Psalm 105.1-6,23-26,45b*	Psalm 45.1-2,6-9*	Psalm 81.1,10-16*
	Romans 12.9-21	James 1.17-27	Hebrews 13.1-8,15,16
	Matthew 16.21-28	Mark 7.1-8,14,15,21-23	Luke 14.1,7-14
(or)			
	Related	**Related**	**Related**
	Jeremiah 15.15-21	Deuteronomy 4.1-2,6-9	Ecclesiasticus 10.12-18
	Psalm 26.1-8	Psalm 15	or Proverbs 25.6-7
	Romans 12.9-21	James 1.17-27	Psalm 112
	Matthew 16.21-28	Mark 7.1-8,14,15,21-23	Hebrews 13.1-8,15,16
			Luke 14.1,7-14
Second Service	Psalm 105.1-15	Psalm 119.1-16*	Psalm 119.81-96*
	2 Kings 6.24-25; 7.3-20	Exodus 12.21-27	Isaiah 33.13-22
	Acts 18.1-16	Matthew 4.23 – 5.20	John 3.22-36
	Gospel at Holy Communion:		
	Mark 7.1-8,14,15, 21-23		
Third Service	Psalm 107.1-32	Psalm 119.17-40	Psalm 119.161-176
	Jonah 3.1-9 *or*	Jonah 3.1-9 *or*	Jonah 3.1-9 *or*
	Ecclesiasticus 11.7-28	Ecclesiasticus 11.7-28	Ecclesiasticus 11.[7-17]18-28
	(*or* 19-28)	(*or* 19-28)	Revelation 3.14-22
	Revelation 3.14-22	Revelation 3.14-22	

Sunday between 4 and 10 September inclusive

	Year A	Year B	Year C
Principal Service	**Continuous**	**Continuous**	**Continuous**
	Exodus 12.1-14	Proverbs 22.1-2,8,9,22,23	Jeremiah 18.1-11
	Psalm 149	Psalm 125	Psalm 139.1-5,12-18*
	Romans 13.8-14	James 2.1-10[11-13] 14-17	Philemon 1-21
(or)	Matthew 18.15-20	Mark 7.24-37	Luke 14.25-33
	Related	**Related**	**Related**
	Ezekiel 33.7-11	Isaiah 35.4-7a	Deuteronomy 30.15-20
	Psalm 119.33-40	Psalm 146	Psalm 1
	Romans 13.8-14	James 2.1-10[11-13] 14-17	Philemon 1-21
	Matthew 18.15-20	Mark 7.24-37	Luke 14.25-33
Second Service	Psalm 108 [115]	Psalm 119.41-56*	Psalms [120] 121
	Ezekiel 12.21 – 13.16	Exodus 14.5-31	Isaiah 43.14 – 44.5
	Acts 19.1-20	Matthew 6.1-18	John 5.30-47
	Gospel at Holy Communion:		
	Mark 7.24-37		
Third Service	Psalm 119.17-32	Psalm 119.57-72	Psalms 122, 123
	Jonah 3.10 – 4.11 *or*	Jonah 3.10 – 4.11 *or*	Jonah 3.10 – 4.11 *or*
	Ecclesiasticus 27.30 – 28.9	Ecclesiasticus 27.30 – 28.9	Ecclesiasticus 27.30 – 28.9
	Revelation 8.1-5	Revelation 8.1-5	Revelation 8.1-5

Sunday between 11 and 17 September inclusive

	Year A	Year B	Year C
Principal Service	**Continuous**	**Continuous**	**Continuous**
	Exodus 14.19-31	Proverbs 1.20-33	Jeremiah 4.11-12,22-28
	Psalm 114 *or*	Psalm 19* *or*	Psalm 14
	Canticle: Exodus	*Canticle*: Wisdom of	1 Timothy 1.12-17
	15.1b-11, 20,21	Solomon 7.26 – 8.1	Luke 15.1-10
	Romans 14.1-12	James 3.1-12	
(or)	Matthew 18.21-35	Mark 8.27-38	
	Related	**Related**	**Related**
	Genesis 50.15-21	Isaiah 50.4-9a	Exodus 32.7-14
	Psalm 103.[1-7]8-13*	Psalm 116.1-8	Psalm 51.1-11
	Romans 14.1-12	James 3.1-12	1 Timothy 1.12-17
	Matthew 18.21-35	Mark 8.27-38	Luke 15.1-10
Second Service	Psalm 119.41-48[49-64]	Psalm 119.73-88*	Psalms 124, 125
	Ezekiel 20.1-8,33-44	Exodus 18.13-26	Isaiah 60
	Acts 20.17-38	Matthew 7.1-14	John 6.51-69
	Gospel at Holy Communion:		
	Mark 8.27-38		
Third Service	Psalm 119.65-88	Psalm 119.105-120	Psalms 126, 127
	Isaiah 44.24 – 45.8	Isaiah 44.24 – 45.8	Isaiah 44.24 – 45.8
	Revelation 12.1-12	Revelation 12.1-12	Revelation 12.1-12

Sunday between 18 and 24 September inclusive

	Year A	Year B	Year C
Principal Service	**Continuous**	**Continuous**	**Continuous**
	Exodus 16.2-15	Proverbs 31.10-31	Jeremiah 8.18 – 9.1
	Psalm 105.1-6,37-45*	Psalm 1	Psalm 79.1-9
	Philippians 1.21-30	James 3.13 – 4.3,7-8a	1 Timothy 2.1-7
(or)	Matthew 20.1-16	Mark 9.30-37	Luke 16.1-13
	Related	**Related**	**Related**
	Jonah 3.10 – 4.11	Wisdom of Solomon	Amos 8.4-7
	Psalm 145.1-8	1.16 – 2.1,12-22 *or*	Psalm 113
	Philippians 1.21-30	Jeremiah 11.18-20	1 Timothy 2.1-7
	Matthew 20.1-16	Psalm 54	Luke 16.1-13
		James 3.13 – 4.3,7-8a	
		Mark 9.30-37	
Second Service	Psalm 119.113-136*	Psalm 119.137-152*	Psalms [128] 129
	Ezekiel 33.23,30 – 34.10	Exodus 19.10-25	Ezra 1
	Acts 26.1,9-25	Matthew 8.23-34	John 7.14-36
	Gospel at Holy Communion:		
	Mark 9.30-37		
Third Service	Psalm 119.153-176	Psalm 119.153-176	Psalms 130, 131
	Isaiah 45.9-22	Isaiah 45.9-22	Isaiah 45.9-22
	Revelation 14.1-5	Revelation 14.1-5	Revelation 14.1-5

Sunday between 25 September and 1 October inclusive

	Year A	Year B	Year C
Principal Service	**Continuous**	**Continuous**	**Continuous**
	Exodus 17.1-7	Esther 7.1-6,9,10; 9.20-22	Jeremiah 32.1-3a,6-15
	Psalm 78.1-4,12-16*	Psalm 124	Psalm 91.1-6,14-16*
	Philippians 2.1-13	James 5.13-20	1 Timothy 6.6-19
(or)	Matthew 21.23-32	Mark 9.38-50	Luke 16.19-31
	Related	**Related**	**Related**
	Ezekiel 18.1-4,25-32	Numbers 11.4-6,10-16,24-29	Amos 6.1a,4-7
	Psalm 25.1-8	Psalm 19.7-14	Psalm 146
	Philippians 2.1-13	James 5.13-20	1 Timothy 6.6-19
	Matthew 21.23-32	Mark 9.38-50	Luke 16.19-31
Second Service	Psalms [120, 123] 124	Psalms 120, 121	Psalms 134, 135*
	Ezekiel 37.15-28	Exodus 24	Nehemiah 2
	1 John 2.22-29	Matthew 9.1-8	John 8.31-38,48-59
	Gospel at Holy Communion:		
	Mark 9.38-50		
Third Service	Psalms 125, 126, 127	Psalm 122	Psalm 132
	Isaiah 48.12-21	Isaiah 48.12-22	Isaiah 48.12-22
	Luke 11.37-54	Luke 11.37-54	Luke 11.37-54

Sunday between 2 and 8 October inclusive

	Year A	Year B	Year C
Principal Service	**Continuous**	**Continuous**	**Continuous**
	Exodus 20.1-4,7-9,12-20	Job 1.1; 2.1-10	Lamentations 1.1-6
	Psalm 19*	Psalm 26	*Canticle*: Lamentations 3.19-26
	Philippians 3.4b-14	Hebrews 1.1-4; 2.5-12	*or* Psalm 137*
	Matthew 21.33-46	Mark 10.2-16	2 Timothy 1.1-14
			Luke 17.5-10
(or)	**Related**	**Related**	**Related**
	Isaiah 5.1-7	Genesis 2.18-24	Habakkuk 1.1-4; 2.1-4
	Psalm 80.8-16	Psalm 8	Psalm 37.1-9
	Philippians 3.4b-14	Hebrews 1.1-4; 2.5-12	2 Timothy 1.1-14
	Matthew 21.33-46	Mark 10.2-16	Luke 17.5-10
Second Service	Psalm 136*	Psalms 125, 126	Psalm 142
	Proverbs 2.1-11	Joshua 3.7-17	Nehemiah 5.1-13
	1 John 2.1-17	Matthew 10.1-22	John 9
	Gospel at Holy Communion:		
	Mark 10.2-16		
Third Service	Psalms 128, 129, 134	Psalms 123, 124	Psalm 141
	Isaiah 49.13-23	Isaiah 49.13-23	Isaiah 49.13-23
	Luke 12.1-12	Luke 12.1-12	Luke 12.1-12

Sunday between 9 and 15 October inclusive

	Year A	Year B	Year C
Principal Service	**Continuous**	**Continuous**	**Continuous**
	Exodus 32.1-14	Job 23.1-9,16,17	Jeremiah 29.1,4-7
	Psalm 106.1-6,19-23*	Psalm 22.1-15	Psalm 66.1-11
	Philippians 4.1-9	Hebrews 4.12-16	2 Timothy 2.8-15
	Matthew 22.1-14	Mark 10.17-31	Luke 17.11-19
(or)	**Related**	**Related**	**Related**
	Isaiah 25.1-9	Amos 5.6-7,10-15	2 Kings 5.1-3,7-15c
	Psalm 23	Psalm 90.12-17	Psalm 111
	Philippians 4.1-9	Hebrews 4.12-16	2 Timothy 2.8-15
	Matthew 22.1-14	Mark 10.17-31	Luke 17.11-19
Second Service	Psalm 139.1-18*	Psalms 127 [128]	Psalm 144
	Proverbs 3.1-18	Joshua 5.13 – 6.20	Nehemiah 6.1-16
	1 John 3.1-15	Matthew 11.20-30	John 15.12-27
	Gospel at Holy Communion:		
	Mark 10.17-31		
Third Service	Psalms 138, 141	Psalms 129, 130	Psalm 143
	Isaiah 50.4-10	Isaiah 50.4-10	Isaiah 50.4-10
	Luke 13.22-30	Luke 13.22-30	Luke 13.22-30

Sunday between 16 and 22 October inclusive

	Year A	Year B	Year C
Principal Service	**Continuous**	**Continuous**	**Continuous**
	Exodus 33.12-23	Job 38.1-7[34-41]	Jeremiah 31.27-34
	Psalm 99*	Psalm 104.1-10,26,35c*	Psalm 119.97-104
	1 Thessalonians 1.1-10	Hebrews 5.1-10	2 Timothy 3.14 – 4.5
(or)	Matthew 22.15-22	Mark 10.35-45	Luke 18.1-8
	Related	**Related**	**Related**
	Isaiah 45.1-7	Isaiah 53.4-12	Genesis 32.22-31
	Psalm 96.1-9[10-13]	Psalm 91.9-16	Psalm 121
	1 Thessalonians 1.1-10	Hebrews 5.1-10	2 Timothy 3.14 – 4.5
	Matthew 22.15-22	Mark 10.35-45	Luke 18.1-8
Second Service	Psalms 142 [143.1-11]	Psalm 141	Psalms [146] 149
	Proverbs 4.1-18	Joshua 14.6-14	Nehemiah 8.9-18
	1 John 3.16 – 4.6	Matthew 12.1-21	John 16.1-11
	Gospel at Holy Communion:		
	Mark 10.35-45		
Third Service	Psalms 145, 149	Psalms 133, 134, 137.1-6	Psalm 147
	Isaiah 54.1-14	Isaiah 54.1-14	Isaiah 54.1-14
	Luke 13.31-35	Luke 13.31-35	Luke 13.31-35

Sunday between 23 and 29 October inclusive

	Year A	Year B	Year C
Principal Service	**Continuous**	**Continuous**	**Continuous**
	Deuteronomy 34.1-12	Job 42.1-6,10-17	Joel 2.23-32
	Psalm 90.1-6,13-17*	Psalm 34.1-8,19-22*	Psalm 65*
	1 Thessalonians 2.1-8	Hebrews 7.23-28	2 Timothy 4.6-8,16-18
(or)	Matthew 22.34-46	Mark 10.46-52	Luke 18.9-14
	Related	**Related**	**Related**
	Leviticus 19.1-2,15-18	Jeremiah 31.7-9	Ecclesiasticus 35.12-17
	Psalm 1	Psalm 126	*or* Jeremiah 14.7-10, 19-22
	1 Thessalonians 2.1-8	Hebrews 7.23-28	Psalm 84.1-7
	Matthew 22.34-46	Mark 10.46-52	2 Timothy 4.6-8,16-18
			Luke 18.9-14
Second Service	Psalms 119.89-104	Psalm 119.121-136	Psalm 119.1-16
	Ecclesiastes 11, 12	Ecclesiastes 11, 12	Ecclesiastes 11, 12
	2 Timothy 2.1-7	2 Timothy 2.1-7	2 Timothy 2.1-7
	Gospel at Holy Communion:	Gospel at Holy Communion:	Gospel at Holy Communion:
	Mark 12.28-34	Luke 18.9-14	Matthew 22.34-46
Third Service	Psalm 119.137-152	Psalm 119.89-104	Psalm 119.105-128
	Isaiah 59.9-20	Isaiah 59.9-20	Isaiah 59.9-20
	Luke 14.1-14	Luke 14.1-14	Luke 14.1-14

The Last Sunday after Trinity *if observed as*
Bible Sunday

	Year A	Year B	Year C
Principal Service	Nehemiah 8.1-4a[5-6] 8-12 Psalm 119.9-16 Colossians 3.12-17 Matthew 24.30-35	Isaiah 55.1-11 Psalm 19.7-14 2 Timothy 3.14 – 4.5 John 5.36b-47	Isaiah 45.22-25 Psalm 119.129-136 Romans 15.1-6 Luke 4.16-24
Second Service	Psalm 119.89-104 Isaiah 55.1-11 Luke 4.14-30	Psalm 119.1-16 2 Kings 22 Colossians 3.12-17 Gospel at Holy Communion: Luke 4.14-30	Psalm 119.1-16 Jeremiah 36.9-32 Romans 10.5-17 Gospel at Holy Communion: Matthew 22.34-40
Third Service	Psalm 119.137-152 Deuteronomy 17.14-15, 18-20 John 5.36b-47	Psalm 119.89-104 Isaiah 45.22-25 Matthew 24.30-35 *or* Luke 14.1-14	Psalm 119.105-128 1 Kings 22.1-17 Romans 15.4-13 *or* Luke 14.1-14

All Saints' Day *1 November*

Principal Feast

Sunday between 30 October and 5 November if this is kept as All Saints' Sunday

Evening Prayer on the Eve	Psalms 1, 5 Ecclesiasticus 44.1-15 *or* Isaiah 40.27-31 Revelation 19.6-10		

	Year A	**Year B**	**Year C**
Principal Service	Revelation 7.9-17 Psalm 34.1-10 1 John 3.1-3 Matthew 5.1-12	Wisdom 3.1-9 *or* Isaiah 25.6-9 Psalm 24.1-6 Revelation 21.1-6a John 11.32-44	Daniel 7.1-3,15-18 Psalm 149 Ephesians 1.11-23 Luke 6.20-31

Second Service. Years A, B, C	Isaiah 65.17-25 Hebrews 11.32 – 12.2 **Evening Psalms** Psalms 148, 150

Third Service, Years A, B, C	Isaiah 35.1-9 Luke 9.18-27 **Morning Psalms** Psalms 15, 84, 149

On 1 November if the material above is used on the Sunday:

Principal Service	Isaiah 56.3-8 *or* 2 Esdras 2.42-48 Psalm 33.1-5 Hebrews 12.18-24 Matthew 5.1-12

Second Service	Isaiah 66.20-23 Colossians 1.9-14 **Evening Psalm** Psalm 145

Third Service	Wisdom 5.1-16 *or* Jeremiah 31.31-34 2 Corinthians 4.5-12 **Morning Psalms** Psalms 111, 112, 117

The Fourth Sunday before Advent

Sunday between 30 October and 5 November inclusive

For use if the Feast of All Saints is celebrated on 1 November

	Year A	Year B	Year C
Principal Service	Micah 3.5-12 Psalm 43* 1 Thessalonians 2.9-13 Matthew 24.1-14	Deuteronomy 6.1-9 Psalm 119.1-8 Hebrews 9.11-14 Mark 12.28-34	Isaiah 1.10-18 Psalm 32.1-8 2 Thessalonians 1.1-12 Luke 19.1-10
Second Service	Psalms 111, 117 Daniel 7.1-18 Luke 6.17-31	Psalm 145* Daniel 2.1-48 (or 1-11, 25-48) Revelation 7.9-17 Gospel at Holy Communion: Matthew 5.1-12	Psalm 145* Lamentations 3.22-33 John 11.[1-31]32-44
Third Service	Psalm 33 Isaiah 66.20-23 Ephesians 1.11-23	Psalms 112, 149 Jeremiah 31.31-34 1 John 3.1-3	Psalm 87 Job 26 Colossians 1.9-14

The Third Sunday before Advent

Sunday between 6 and 12 November inclusive

	Year A	Year B	Year C
Principal Service *(or)*	Wisdom of Solomon 6.12-16 *Canticle:* Wisdom of Solomon 6.17-20 1 Thessalonians 4.13-18 Matthew 25.1-13 Amos 5.18-24 Psalm 70 1 Thessalonians 4.13-18 Matthew 25.1-13	Jonah 3.1-5, 10 Psalm 62.5-12 Hebrews 9.24-28 Mark 1.14-20	Job 19.23-27a Psalm 17.1-9* 2 Thessalonians 2.1-5, 13-17 Luke 20.27-38
Second Service	Psalms [20] 82 Judges 7.2-22 John 15.9-17	Psalms 46 [82] Isaiah 10.33 – 11.9 John 14.1-29 (or 23-29)	Psalm 40 1 Kings 3.1-15 Romans 8.31-39 Gospel at Holy Communion: Matthew 22.15-22
Third Service	Psalm 91 Deuteronomy 17.14-20 1 Timothy 2.1-7	Psalm 136 Micah 4.1-5 Philippians 4.6-9	Psalms 20, 90 Isaiah 2.1-5 James 3.13-18

The Second Sunday before Advent

Sunday between 13 and 19 November inclusive

	Year A	Year B	Year C
Principal Service	Zephaniah 1.7,12-18 Psalm 90.1-8[9-11]12* 1 Thessalonians 5.1-11 Matthew 25.14-30	Daniel 12.1-3 Psalm 16 Hebrews 10.11-14 [15-18]19-25 Mark 13.1-8	Malachi 4.1-2a Psalm 98 2 Thessalonians 3.6-13 Luke 21.5-19
Second Service	Psalm 89.19-37* 1 Kings 1.15-40 (or 1-40) Revelation 1.4-18 Gospel at Holy Communion: Luke 9.1-6	Psalm 95 Daniel 3 (or 3.13-30) Matthew 13.24-30,36-43	Psalms [93] 97 Daniel 6 Matthew 13.1-9,18-23
Third Service	Psalm 98 Daniel 10.19-21 Revelation 4	Psalm 96 1 Samuel 9.27 – 10.2a; 10.17-26 Matthew 13.31-35	Psalm 132 1 Samuel 16.1-13 Matthew 13.44-52

Christk the King The Sunday next before Advent

Sunday between 20 and 26 November inclusive

Evening Prayer on the Eve Years A,B,C (if required)	Psalms 99, 100 Isaiah 10.33 – 11.9 1 Timothy 6.11-16		

	Year A	Year B	Year C
Principal Service	Ezekiel 34.11-16,20-24 Psalm 95.1-7* Ephesians 1.15-23 Matthew 25.31-46	Daniel 7.9-10,13,14 Psalm 93 Revelation 1.4b-8 John 18.33-37	Jeremiah 23.1-6 Psalm 46 Colossians 1.11-20 Luke 23.33-43
Second Service	2 Samuel 23.1-7 or 1 Maccabees 2.15-29 Matthew 28.16-20 **Evening Psalms** Psalms 93 [97]	Daniel 5 John 6.1-15 **Evening Psalm** Psalm 72*	1 Samuel 8.4-20 John 18.33-37 **Evening Psalm** Psalm 72*
Third Service	Isaiah 4.2 – 5.7 Luke 19.29-38 **Morning Psalms** Psalms 29, 110	Isaiah 32.1-8 Revelation 3.7-22 **Morning Psalms** Psalms 29, 110	Zechariah 6.9-15 Revelation 11.15-18 **Morning Psalms** Psalms 29, 110

¶ *Festivals*

For Lesser Festivals, the Commons of Saints and special occasions, see the complete Common Worship Lectionary published separately.

The Naming and Circumcision of Jesus *1 January*

Evening Prayer on the Eve (if required)
Psalm 148
Jeremiah 23.1-6
Colossians 2.8-15

Principal Service	Second Service	Third Service
Numbers 6.22-27	Deuteronomy 30.[1-10]11-20	Genesis 17.1-13
Psalm 8	Acts 3.1-16	Romans 2.17-29
Galatians 4.4-7	**Evening Psalm**	**Morning Psalms**
Luke 2.15-21	Psalm 115	Psalms 103, 150

The Conversion of Paul *25 January*

Evening Prayer on the Eve (if required)
Psalm 149
Isaiah 49.1-13
Acts 22.3-16

Principal Service	Second Service	Third Service
Jeremiah 1.4-10	Ecclesiasticus 39.1-10 *or*	Ezekiel 3.22-27
Psalm 67	Isaiah 56.1-8	Philippians 3.1-14
Acts 9.1-22	Colossians 1.24 – 2.7	**Morning Psalms**
Matthew 19.27-30	**Evening Psalm**	Psalms 66, 147.13-21
	Psalm 119.41-56	

(or)

Acts 9.1-22
Psalm 67
Galatians 1.11-16a
Matthew 19.27-30

Joseph of Nazareth *19 March*

Evening Prayer on the Eve (if required)
Psalm 132
Hosea 11.1-9
Luke 2.41-52

Principal Service	Second Service	Third Service
2 Samuel 7.4-16	Genesis 50.22-26	Isaiah 11.1-10
Psalm 89.26-36	Matthew 2.13-23	Matthew 13.54-58
Romans 4.13-18	**Evening Psalms**	**Morning Psalms**
Matthew 1.18-25	Psalms 1, 112	Psalms 25, 147.1-12

The Annunciation of Our Lord 25 March

Principal Feast

Evening Psalm 85
Prayer Wisdom 9.1-12 *or* Genesis 3.8-15
on the Eve Galatians 4.1-5

Principal Service	**Second Service**	**Third Service**
Isaiah 7.10-14	Isaiah 52.1-12	I Samuel 2.1-10
Psalm 40.5-10	Hebrews 2.5-18	Romans 5.12-21
Hebrews 10.4-10	**Evening Psalms**	**Morning Psalms**
Luke 1.26-38	Psalms 131, 146	Psalms 111, 113

George 23 April

Evening Psalms 111, 116
Prayer Jeremiah 15.15-21
on the Eve Hebrews 11.32 – 12.2
(if required)

Principal Service	**Second Service**	**Third Service**
I Maccabees 2.59-64 *or*	Isaiah 43.1-7	Joshua 1.1-9
Revelation 12.7-12	John 15.1-8	Ephesians 6.10-20
Psalm 126	**Evening Psalms**	**Morning Psalms**
2 Timothy 2.3-13	Psalms 3, 11	Psalms 5, 146
John 15.18-21		

Mark 25 April

Evening Psalm 19
Prayer Isaiah 52.7-10
on the Eve Mark 1.1-15
(if required)

Principal Service	**Second Service**	**Third Service**
Proverbs 15.28-33 *or*	Ezekiel 1.4-14	Isaiah 62.6-10 *or*
Acts 15.35-41	2 Timothy 4.1-11	Ecclesiasticus 51.13-30
Psalm 119.9-16	**Evening Psalm**	Acts 12.25 – 13.13
Ephesians 4.7-16	Psalm 45	**Morning Psalms**
Mark 13.5-13		Psalms 37.23-41, 148

Philip and James 1 May

Evening Psalm 25
Prayer Isaiah 40.27-31
on the Eve John 12.20-26
(if required)

Principal Service	**Second Service**	**Third Service**
Isaiah 30.15-21	Job 23.1-12	Proverbs 4.10-18
Psalm 119.1-8	John 1.43-51	James 1.1-12
Ephesians 1.3-10	**Evening Psalm**	**Morning Psalms**
John 14.1-14	Psalm 149	Psalms 139, 146

Matthias *14 May*

Evening
Prayer
on the Eve
(if required)

Psalm 147
Isaiah 22.15-22
Philippians 3.13b – 4.1

Principal Service	**Second Service**	**Third Service**
Principal Service	1 Samuel 16.1-13a	1 Samuel 2.27-35
Isaiah 22.15-25	Matthew 7.15-27	Acts 2.37-47
Psalm 15	**Evening Psalm**	**Morning Psalms**
Acts 1.15-26	Psalm 80	Psalms 16, 147.1-12
John 15.9-17		

(or)

Acts 1.15-26
Psalm 15
1 Corinthians 4.1-7
John 15.9-17

The Visit of the Blessed Virgin Mary to Elizabeth *31 May*

Evening
Prayer
on the Eve
(if required)

Psalm 45
Song of Solomon 2.8-14
Luke 1.26-38

Principal Service	**Second Service**	**Third Service**
Zephaniah 3.14-18	Zechariah 2.10-13	1 Samuel 2.1-10
Psalm 113	John 3.25-30	Mark 3.31-35
Romans 12.9-16	**Evening Psalms**	**Morning Psalms**
Luke 1.39-49[50-56]	Psalms 122, 127, 128	Psalms 85, 150

Barnabas *11 June*

Evening
Prayer
on the Eve
(if required)

Psalms 1, 15
Isaiah 42.5-12
Acts 14.8-28

Principal Service	**Second Service**	**Third Service**
Job 29.11-16	Ecclesiastes 12.9-14 *or*	Jeremiah 9.23,24
Psalm 112	Tobit 4.5-11	Acts 4.32-37
Acts 11.19-30	Acts 9.26-31	**Morning Psalms**
John 15.12-17	**Evening Psalm**	Psalms 100, 101, 117
	Psalm 147	

(or)

Acts 11.19-30
Psalm 112
Galatians 2.1-10
John 15.12-17

The Birth of John the Baptist 24 June

Evening Prayer on the Eve (if required)
Psalm 71
Judges 13.2-7,24-25
Luke 1.5-25

Principal Service	Second Service	Third Service
Isaiah 40.1-11	Malachi 4	Ecclesiasticus 48.1-10
Psalm 85.7-13	Matthew 11.2-19	or Malachi 3.1-6
Acts 13.14b-26 or	**Evening Psalms**	Luke 3.1-17
Galatians 3.23-29	Psalms 80, 82	**Morning Psalms**
Luke 1.57-66,80		Psalms 50, 149

Peter and Paul 29 June

Evening Prayer on the Eve (if required)
Psalms 66, 67
Ezekiel 3.4-11
Galatians 1.13 – 2.8

Principal Service	Second Service	Third Service
Zechariah 4.1-6a,10b-14	Ezekiel 34.11-16	Isaiah 49.1-6
Psalm 125	John 21.15-22	Acts 11.1-18
Acts 12.1-11	**Evening Psalms**	**Morning Psalms**
Matthew 16.13-19	Psalms 124, 138	Psalms 71, 113

(or)

Acts 12.1-11
Psalm 125
2 Timothy 4.6-8,17,18
Matthew 16.13-19

or, Peter, *where celebrated alone*

Evening Prayer on the Eve (if required)
Psalms 66, 67
Ezekiel 3.4-11
Acts 9.32-43

Principal Service	Second Service	Third Service
Ezekiel 3.22-27	Ezekiel 34.11-16	Isaiah 49.1-6
Psalm 125	John 21.15-22	Acts 11.1-18
Acts 12.1-11	**Evening Psalms**	**Morning Psalms**
Matthew 16.13-19	Psalms 124, 138	Psalms 71, 113

(or)

Acts 12.1-11
Psalm 125
1 Peter 2.19-25
Matthew 16.13-19

Thomas *3 July*

Evening
Prayer
on the Eve
(if required)

Psalm 27
Isaiah 35
Hebrews 10.35 – 11.1

Principal Service	**Second Service**	**Third Service**
Habakkuk 2.1-4	Job 42.1-6	2 Samuel 15.17-21 *or*
Psalm 31.1-6	1 Peter 1.3-12	Ecclesiasticus 2
Ephesians 2.19-22	**Evening Psalm**	John 11.1-16
John 20.24-29	Psalm 139	**Morning Psalms**
		Psalms 92, 146

Mary Magdalene *22 July*

Evening
Prayer
on the Eve
(if required)

Psalm 139
Isaiah 25.1-9
2 Corinthians 1.3-7

Principal Service	**Second Service**	**Third Service**
Song of Solomon 3.1-4	Zephaniah 3.14-20	1 Samuel 16.14-23
Psalm 42.1-10	Mark 15.40 – 16.7	Luke 8.1-3
2 Corinthians 5.14-17	**Evening Psalm**	**Morning Psalms**
John 20.1-2,11-18	Psalm 63	Psalms 30, 32, 150

James *25 July*

Evening
Prayer
on the Eve
(if required)

Psalm 144
Deuteronomy 30.11-20
Mark 5.21-43

Principal Service	**Second Service**	**Third Service**
Jeremiah 45.1-5	Jeremiah 26.1-15	2 Kings 1.9-15
Psalm 126	Mark 1.14-20	Luke 9.46-56
Acts 11.27 – 12.2	**Evening Psalm**	**Morning Psalms**
Matthew 20.20-28	Psalm 94	Psalms 7, 29, 117

(or)

Acts 11.27 – 12.2
Psalm 126
2 Corinthians 4.7-15
Matthew 20.20-28

The Transfiguration of Our Lord 6 August

Evening
Prayer
on the Eve
(if required)

Psalms 99, 110
Exodus 24.12-18
John 12.27-36a

Principal Service	Second Service	Third Service
Daniel 7.9,10,13,14	Exodus 34.29-35	Ecclesiasticus 48.1-10 or
Psalm 97	2 Corinthians 3	1 Kings 19.1-16
2 Peter 1.16-19	**Evening Psalm**	1 John 3.1-3
Luke 9.28-36	Psalm 72	**Morning Psalms**
		Psalms 27, 150

The Blessed Virgin Mary 15 August

Evening
Prayer
on the Eve
(if required)

Psalm 72
Proverbs 8.22-31
John 19.23-27

Principal Service	Second Service	Third Service
Isaiah 61.10,11 or	Song of Solomon 2.1-7	Isaiah 7.10-15
Revelation 11.19 – 12.6,10	Acts 1.6-14	Luke 11.27,28
Psalm 45.10-17	**Evening Psalm**	**Morning Psalms**
Galatians 4.4-7	Psalm 132	Psalms 98, 138, 147.1-12
Luke 1.46-55		

Bartholomew 24 August

Evening
Prayer
on the Eve
(if required)

Psalm 97
Isaiah 61.1-9
2 Corinthians 6.1-10

Principal Service	Second Service	Third Service
Isaiah 43.8-13	Ecclesiasticus 39.1-10	Genesis 28.10-17
Psalm 145.1-7	or Deuteronomy 18.15-19	John 1.43-51
Acts 5.12-16	Matthew 10.1-22	**Morning Psalms**
Luke 22.24-30	**Evening Psalms**	Psalms 86, 117
	Psalms 91, 116	

(or)

Acts 5.12-16
Psalm 145.1-7
1 Corinthians 4.9-15
Luke 22.24-30

Holy Cross Day *14 September*

Evening
Prayer
on the Eve
(if required)

Psalm 66
Isaiah 52.13 – 53.12
Ephesians 2.11-22

Principal Service	**Second Service**	**Third Service**
Numbers 21.4-9	Isaiah 63.1-16	Genesis 3.1-15
Psalm 22.23-28	1 Corinthians 1.18-25	John 12.27-36a
Philippians 2.6-11	**Evening Psalms**	**Morning Psalms**
John 3.13-17	Psalms 110, 150	Psalms 2, 8, 146

Matthew *21 September*

Evening
Prayer
on the Eve
(if required)

Psalm 34
Isaiah 33.13-17
Matthew 6.19-34

Principal Service	**Second Service**	**Third Service**
Proverbs 3.13-18	Ecclesiastes 5.4-12	1 Kings 19.15-21
Psalm 119.65-72	Matthew 19.16-30	2 Timothy 3.14-17
2 Corinthians 4.1-6	**Evening Psalm**	**Morning Psalms**
Matthew 9.9-13	Psalm 119.33-40, 89-96	Psalms 49, 117

Michael and All Angels *29 September*

Evening
Prayer
on the Eve
(if required)

Psalm 91
2 Kings 6.8-17
Matthew 18.1-6, 10

Principal Service	**Second Service**	**Third Service**
Genesis 28.10-17	Daniel 10.4-21	Tobit 12.6-22 *or*
Psalm 103.19-22	Revelation 5	Daniel 12.1-4
Revelation 12.7-12	**Evening Psalms**	Acts 12.1-11
John 1.47-51	Psalms 138, 148	**Morning Psalms**
		Psalms 34, 150

(or)

Revelation 12.7-12
Psalm 103.19-22
Hebrews 1.5-14
John 1.47-51

Luke *18 October*

Evening
Prayer
on the Eve
(if required)
Psalm 33
Hosea 6.1-3
2 Timothy 3.10-17

Principal Service	Second Service	Third Service
Isaiah 35.3-6 *or*	Ecclesiasticus 38.1-14	Isaiah 55
Acts 16.6-12a	*or* Isaiah 61.1-6	Luke 1.1-4
Psalm 147.1-7	Colossians 4.7-18	**Morning Psalms**
2 Timothy 4.5-17	**Evening Psalm**	Psalms 145, 146
Luke 10.1-9	Psalm 103	

Simon and Jude *28 October*

Evening
Prayer
on the Eve
(if required)
Psalms 124, 125, 126
Deuteronomy 32.1-4
John 14.15-26

Principal Service	Second Service	Third Service
Isaiah 28.14-16	1 Maccabees 2.42-66	Wisdom 5.1-16 *or*
Psalm 119.89-96	*or* Jeremiah 3.11-18	Isaiah 45.18-26
Ephesians 2.19-22	Jude 1-4, 17-25	Luke 6.12-16
John 15.17-27	**Evening Psalm**	**Morning Psalms**
	Psalm 119.1-16	Psalms 116, 117

Andrew *30 November*

Evening
Prayer
on the Eve
(if required)
Psalm 48
Isaiah 49.1-9a
1 Corinthians 4.9-16

Principal Service	Second Service	Third Service
Isaiah 52.7-10	Zechariah 8.20-23	Ezekiel 47.1-12 *or*
Psalm 19.1-6	John 1.35-42	Ecclesiasticus 14.20-27
Romans 10.12-18	**Evening Psalms**	John 12.20-32
Matthew 4.18-22	Psalms 87, 96	**Morning Psalms**
		Psalms 47, 147.1-12

Stephen *26 December*

Principal Service	Second Service	Third Service
2 Chronicles 24.20-22	Genesis 4.1-10	Jeremiah 26.12-15
Psalm 119.161-168	Matthew 23.34-39	Acts 6
Acts 7.51-60	**Evening Psalms**	**Morning Psalms**
Matthew 10.17-22	Psalms 57, 86	Psalms 13, 31.1-8, 150

(or)

Acts 7.51-60
Psalm 119.161-168
Galatians 2.16b-20
Matthew 10.17-22

586 *Lectionary*

John *27 December*

Principal Service	Second Service	Third Service
Exodus 33.7-11a	Isaiah 6.1-8	Exodus 33.12-23
Psalm 117	1 John 5.1-12	1 John 2.1-11
1 John 1	**Evening Psalm**	**Morning Psalms**
John 21.19b-25	Psalm 97	Psalms 21, 147.13-21

The Holy Innocents *28 December*

Principal Service	Second Service	Third Service
Jeremiah 31.15-17	Isaiah 49.14-25	Baruch 4.21-27 *or*
Psalm 124	Mark 10.13-16	Genesis 37.13-20
1 Corinthians 1.26-29	**Evening Psalms**	Matthew 18.1-10
Matthew 2.13-18	Psalms 123, 128	**Morning Psalms**
		Psalms 36, 146

Dedication Festival

If date not known, observe on the First Sunday in October or Last Sunday after Trinity.

Evening Prayer on the Eve Years A, B, C	Psalm 24
	2 Chronicles 7.11-16
	John 4.19-29

	Year A	Year B	Year C
Principal Service	1 Kings 8.22-30 *or*	Genesis 28.11-18 *or*	1 Chronicles 29.6-19
	Revelation 21.9-14	Revelation 21.9-14	Psalm 122
	Psalm 122	Psalm 122	Ephesians 2.19-22
	Hebrews 12.18-24	1 Peter 2.1-10	John 2.13-22
	Matthew 21.12-16	John 10.22-29	
Second Service	Jeremiah 7.1-11	Jeremiah 7.1-11	Jeremiah 7.1-11
	1 Corinthians 3.9-17	Luke 19.1-10	Luke 19.1-10
	Gospel at Holy Communion:	**Evening Psalm**	**Evening Psalm**
	Luke 19.1-10	Psalm 132	Psalm 132
	Evening Psalm		
	Psalm 132		
Third Service (Readings for Years A,B,C are the same)	Haggai 2.6-9	Haggai 2.6-9	Haggai 2.6-9
	Hebrews 10.19-25	Hebrews 10.19-25	Hebrews 10.19-25
	Morning Psalms	**Morning Psalms**	**Morning Psalms**
	Psalms 48, 150	Psalms 48, 150	Psalms 48, 150

¶ *Special Occasion*

Harvest Thanksgiving

Year A

Deuteronomy 8.7-18 *or*
Deuteronomy 28.1-14
Psalm 65
2 Corinthians 9.6-15
Luke 12.16-30 *or*
Luke 17.11-19

Year B

Joel 2.21-27
Psalm 126
1 Timothy 2.1-7 *or*
1 Timothy 6.6-10
Matthew 6.25-33

Year C

Deuteronomy 26.1-11
Psalm 100
Philippians 4.4-9 *or*
Revelation 14.14-18
John 6.25-35

Alternative Psalmody
for the Principal Service Lectionary

The purpose of this Alternative Psalmody is, in some cases, to reduce the number of verses of a particular provision and, in others, to simplify the reading. Psalms which are starred * have alternatives listed in this table.

	Year A	Year B	Year C
Advent 1		80.1-8	
Advent 2	72.1-7	85.8-13	
Advent 3			146.4-10
Advent 4	80.1-8	89.1-8	
Christmas 1	148.7-14	148.7-14	148.7-14
Epiphany 2		139.1-9	
Epiphany 3	27.1-11		19.1-6
Proper 1		147.1-12	
Proper 3			37.1-7
Lent 1			91.1-11
Lent 3		19.7-14	
Lent 4		107.1-9	
Palm Sunday	118.19-24	118.19-24	118.19-24
	31.9-18	31.9-18	31.9-18
Tuesday in Holy Week	71.1-8	71.1-8	71.1-8
Maundy Thursday	116.9-17	116.9-17	116.9-17
Good Friday	22.1-11 or 1-21	22.1-11 or 1-21	22.1-11 or 1-21
Easter Eve	31.1-5	31.1-5	31.1-5
Easter Day	118.14-24	118.14-24	118.14-24
Easter 3	116.1-7		
Easter 5	31.1-5		148.1-6
Easter 7	68.1-10		
Pentecost	104.26-37	104.26-37	104.26-37
Proper 4	31.19-24		
Proper 6	116.9-17	92.1-8	
Proper 7	86.1-10		42 or 43
	69.14-20	107.23-32	
Proper 8	89.8-18		77.11-20
Proper 10	65.8-13		
Proper 11	139.1-11		
Proper 12	105.1-11		85.1-7
Proper 13	17.1-7		107.1-9
	145.15-22		49.1-9
Proper 14	105.1-10		50.1-7
			33.12-22
Proper 15			80.9-20
Proper 17	115	45.1-7	81.1-11
Proper 18			139.1-7
Proper 19	103.8-13	19.1-6	
Proper 20	105.37-45		
Proper 21	78.1-7		91.11-16
Proper 22	19.7-14		137.1-6
Proper 23	106.1-6		
Proper 24	99	104.1-10	
Proper 25	90.1-6	34.1-8	65.1-7
4 before Advent	107.1-8		
3 before Advent			17.1-8
2 before Advent	90.1-8		
Christ the King	95.1-7		

Alternative Psalmody
for the Second Service Lectionary

The purpose of this Alternative Psalmody is to reduce the number of verses of a particular provision. Psalms which are starred * have alternatives listed in this table.

	Year A	Year B	Year C
Advent 1	9.1-8	25.1-9	9.1-8
Advent 2		40.12-19	
Advent 3		68.1-8	
Christmas 2	135.1-14	135.1-14	135.1-14
Epiphany 3	33.1-12	33.1-12	33.1-12
Epiphany 4	34.1-10	34.1-10	34.1-10
2 before Lent			147.13-21
1 before Lent			89.5-12
Ash Wednesday	102.1-18	102.1-18	102.1-18
Lent 2	135.1-14	135.1-14	135.1-14
Lent 5		34.1-10	35.1-9
Wednesday in Holy Week	102.1-18	102.1-18	102.1-18
Easter 7			68.1-13,18-19
Proper 4	33.12-22	35.1-10	
Proper 5			44.1-9
Proper 8	50.1-15		
Proper 10		66.1-8	77.1-12
Proper 11		73.21-28	
Proper 12		74.11-16	88.1-10
Proper 13	80.1-8	88.1-10	107.1-12
Proper 14		91.1-12	
Proper 15	90.1-12		119.17-24
Proper 16		116.10-17	119.49-56
Proper 17		119.9-16	119.81-88
Proper 18		119.49-56	
Proper 19		119.73-80	
Proper 20	119.121-128	119.137-144	
Proper 21			135.1-14
Proper 22	136.1-9		
Proper 23	139.1-11		
4 before Advent		145.1-9	145.1-9
2 before Advent	89.19-29		
Christ the King		72.1-7	72.1-7

The Psalter

¶ *When saying a psalm aloud, the word 'blessed' is to be pronounced as two syllables: 'bless - ed'. Where spelled 'blest', the word is pronounced as one syllable.*

¶ *A diamond ♦ marks the mid-point in each psalm verse where, traditionally, a pause is observed.*

¶ *Each psalm or group of psalms may end with*

Glory to the Father and to the Son
and to the Holy Spirit;
as it was in the beginning is now
and shall be for ever. Amen.

Psalm 1

1   Blessed are they who have not walked
        in the counsel of the wicked, ♦
nor lingered in the way of sinners,
        nor sat in the assembly of the scornful.

2   Their delight is in the law of the Lord ♦
and they meditate on his law day and night.

3   Like a tree planted by streams of water
        bearing fruit in due season, with leaves that do not wither, ♦
whatever they do, it shall prosper.

4   As for the wicked, it is not so with them; ♦
they are like chaff which the wind blows away.

5   Therefore the wicked shall not be able to stand in the judgement, ♦
nor the sinner in the congregation of the righteous.

6   For the Lord knows the way of the righteous, ♦
but the way of the wicked shall perish.

Psalm 2

1   Why are the nations in tumult, ♦
and why do the peoples devise a vain plot?

2   The kings of the earth rise up,
        and the rulers take counsel together, ♦
against the Lord and against his anointed:

3   'Let us break their bonds asunder ♦
and cast away their cords from us.'

4   He who dwells in heaven shall laugh them to scorn; ♦
the Lord shall have them in derision.

5   Then shall he speak to them in his wrath ♦
and terrify them in his fury:

6   'Yet have I set my king ♦
upon my holy hill of Zion.'

7   I will proclaim the decree of the Lord; ♦
       he said to me: 'You are my Son; this day have I begotten you.

8   'Ask of me and I will give you the nations for your inheritance ♦
       and the ends of the earth for your possession.

9   'You shall break them with a rod of iron ♦
       and dash them in pieces like a potter's vessel.'

10   Now therefore be wise, O kings; ♦
       be prudent, you judges of the earth.

11   Serve the Lord with fear, and with trembling kiss his feet, ♦
       lest he be angry and you perish from the way,
          for his wrath is quickly kindled.

12   Happy are all they ♦
       who take refuge in him.

Psalm 3

1   Lord, how many are my adversaries; ♦
       many are they who rise up against me.

2   Many are they who say to my soul, ♦
       'There is no help for you in your God.'

3   But you, Lord, are a shield about me; ♦
       you are my glory, and the lifter up of my head.

4   When I cry aloud to the Lord, ♦
       he will answer me from his holy hill;

5   I lie down and sleep and rise again, ♦
       because the Lord sustains me.

6   I will not be afraid of hordes of the peoples ♦
       that have set themselves against me all around.

7   Rise up, O Lord, and deliver me, O my God, ♦
       for you strike all my enemies on the cheek
          and break the teeth of the wicked.

8   Salvation belongs to the Lord: ♦
       may your blessing be upon your people.

Psalm 4

1   Answer me when I call, O God of my righteousness; ♦
    you set me at liberty when I was in trouble;
        have mercy on me and hear my prayer.

2   How long will you nobles dishonour my glory; ♦
    how long will you love vain things and seek after falsehood?

3   But know that the Lord has shown me his marvellous kindness; ♦
    when I call upon the Lord, he will hear me.

4   Stand in awe, and sin not; ♦
    commune with your own heart upon your bed, and be still.

5   Offer the sacrifices of righteousness ♦
    and put your trust in the Lord.

6   There are many that say, 'Who will show us any good?' ♦
    Lord, lift up the light of your countenance upon us.

7   You have put gladness in my heart, ♦
    more than when their corn and wine and oil increase.

8   In peace I will lie down and sleep, ♦
    for it is you Lord, only, who make me dwell in safety.

Psalm 5

1   Give ear to my words, O Lord; ♦
    consider my lamentation.

2   Hearken to the voice of my crying, my King and my God, ♦
    for to you I make my prayer.

3   In the morning, Lord, you will hear my voice; ♦
    early in the morning I make my appeal to you, and look up.

4   For you are the God who takes no pleasure in wickedness; ♦
    no evil can dwell with you.

5   The boastful cannot stand in your sight; ♦
    you hate all those that work wickedness.

6   You destroy those who speak lies; ♦
    the bloodthirsty and deceitful the Lord will abhor.

7   But as for me, through the greatness of your mercy,
        I will come into your house; ♦
    I will bow down towards your holy temple in awe of you.

8   Lead me, Lord, in your righteousness,
        because of my enemies; ♦
    make your way straight before my face.

9   For there is no truth in their mouth,
        in their heart is destruction, ♦
    their throat is an open sepulchre,
        and they flatter with their tongue.

10 Punish them, O God; ♦
    let them fall through their own devices.

11 Because of their many transgressions cast them out, ♦
    for they have rebelled against you.

12 But let all who take refuge in you be glad; ♦
    let them sing out their joy for ever.

13 You will shelter them, ♦
    so that those who love your name may exult in you.

14 For you, O Lord, will bless the righteous; ♦
    and with your favour you will defend them as with a shield.

Psalm 6

1   O Lord, rebuke me not in your wrath; ♦
    neither chasten me in your fierce anger.

2   Have mercy on me, Lord, for I am weak; ♦
    Lord, heal me, for my bones are racked.

3   My soul also shakes with terror; ♦
    how long, O Lord, how long?

4   Turn again, O Lord, and deliver my soul; ♦
    save me for your loving mercy's sake.

5   For in death no one remembers you; ♦
    and who can give you thanks in the grave?

6   I am weary with my groaning; ♦
    every night I drench my pillow
        and flood my bed with my tears.

7   My eyes are wasted with grief ♦
    and worn away because of all my enemies.

8   Depart from me, all you that do evil, ♦
    for the Lord has heard the voice of my weeping.

9   The Lord has heard my supplication; ♦
    the Lord will receive my prayer.

10 All my enemies shall be put to shame and confusion; ♦
    they shall suddenly turn back in their shame.

Psalm 7

1   O Lord my God, in you I take refuge; ♦
    save me from all who pursue me, and deliver me,

2   Lest they rend me like a lion and tear me in pieces ♦
    while there is no one to help me.

3   O Lord my God, if I have done these things: ♦
    if there is any wickedness in my hands,

4   If I have repaid my friend with evil, ♦
    or plundered my enemy without a cause,

5   Then let my enemy pursue me and overtake me, ♦
    trample my life to the ground,
        and lay my honour in the dust.

6   Rise up, O Lord, in your wrath;
        lift yourself up against the fury of my enemies. ♦
    Awaken, my God, the judgement that you have commanded.

7   Let the assembly of the peoples gather round you; ♦
    be seated high above them: O Lord, judge the nations.

8   Give judgement for me
        according to my righteousness, O Lord, ♦
    and according to the innocence that is in me.

9   Let the malice of the wicked come to an end,
        but establish the righteous; ♦
    for you test the mind and heart, O righteous God.

10   God is my shield that is over me; ♦
      he saves the true of heart.

11   God is a righteous judge; ♦
      he is provoked all day long.

12   If they will not repent, God will whet his sword; ♦
      he has bent his bow and made it ready.

13   He has prepared the weapons of death; ♦
      he makes his arrows shafts of fire.

14   Behold those who are in labour with wickedness, ♦
      who conceive evil and give birth to lies.

15   They dig a pit and make it deep ♦
      and fall into the hole that they have made for others.

16   Their mischief rebounds on their own head; ♦
      their violence falls on their own scalp.

17   I will give thanks to the Lord for his righteousness, ♦
      and I will make music to the name of the Lord Most High.

                                                    Psalm 8

      First version

1   *O Lord our governor,* ♦
      how glorious is your name in all the world!

2   Your majesty above the heavens is praised ♦
      out of the mouths of babes at the breast.

3   You have founded a stronghold against your foes, ♦
      that you might still the enemy and the avenger.

4   When I consider your heavens, the work of your fingers, ♦
      the moon and the stars that you have ordained,

5   What is man, that you should be mindful of him; ♦
      the son of man, that you should seek him out?

6   You have made him little lower than the angels ♦
      and crown him with glory and honour.

7   You have given him dominion over the works of your hands ♦
      and put all things under his feet,

8   All sheep and oxen, ♦
even the wild beasts of the field,

9   The birds of the air, the fish of the sea ♦
and whatsoever moves in the paths of the sea.

10   *O Lord our governor, ♦*
how glorious is your name in all the world!

Psalm 8

Second version

1   *O Lord our governor, ♦*
how glorious is your name in all the world!

2   Your majesty above the heavens is praised ♦
out of the mouths of babes at the breast.

3   You have founded a stronghold against your foes, ♦
that you might still the enemy and the avenger.

4   When I consider your heavens, the work of your fingers, ♦
the moon and the stars that you have ordained,

5   What are mortals, that you should be mindful of them; ♦
mere human beings, that you should seek them out?

6   You have made them little lower than the angels ♦
and crown them with glory and honour.

7   You have given them dominion over the works of your hands ♦
and put all things under their feet,

8   All sheep and oxen, ♦
even the wild beasts of the field,

9   The birds of the air, the fish of the sea ♦
and whatsoever moves in the paths of the sea.

10   *O Lord our governor, ♦*
how glorious is your name in all the world!

1 I will give thanks to you, Lord, with my whole heart; ♦
  I will tell of all your marvellous works.

2 I will be glad and rejoice in you; ♦
  I will make music to your name, O Most High.

3 When my enemies are driven back, ♦
  they stumble and perish at your presence.

4 For you have maintained my right and my cause; ♦
  you sat on your throne giving righteous judgement.

5 You have rebuked the nations and destroyed the wicked; ♦
  you have blotted out their name for ever and ever.

6 The enemy was utterly laid waste. ♦
  You uprooted their cities;
      their very memory has perished.

7 But the Lord shall endure for ever; ♦
  he has made fast his throne for judgement.

8 For he shall rule the world with righteousness ♦
  and govern the peoples with equity.

9 Then will the Lord be a refuge for the oppressed, ♦
  a refuge in the time of trouble.

10 And those who know your name will put their trust in you, ♦
  for you, Lord, have never failed those who seek you.

11 Sing praises to the Lord who dwells in Zion; ♦
  declare among the peoples the things he has done.

12 The avenger of blood has remembered them; ♦
  he did not forget the cry of the oppressed.

13 Have mercy upon me, O Lord; ♦
  consider the trouble I suffer from those who hate me,
      you that lift me up from the gates of death;

14 That I may tell all your praises in the gates of the city of Zion ♦
  and rejoice in your salvation.

15   The nations shall sink into the pit of their making ♦
        and in the snare which they set will their own foot be taken.

16   The Lord makes himself known by his acts of justice; ♦
        the wicked are snared in the works of their own hands.

17   They shall return to the land of darkness, ♦
        all the nations that forget God.

18   For the needy shall not always be forgotten ♦
        and the hope of the poor shall not perish for ever.

19   Arise, O Lord, and let not mortals have the upper hand; ♦
        let the nations be judged before your face.

20   Put them in fear, O Lord, ♦
        that the nations may know themselves to be but mortal.

Psalm 10

1   Why stand so far off, O Lord? ♦
        Why hide yourself in time of trouble?

2   The wicked in their pride persecute the poor; ♦
        let them be caught in the schemes they have devised.

3   The wicked boast of their heart's desire; ♦
        the covetous curse and revile the Lord.

4   The wicked in their arrogance say, 'God will not avenge it'; ♦
        in all their scheming God counts for nothing.

5   They are stubborn in all their ways,
          for your judgements are far above out of their sight; ♦
        they scoff at all their adversaries.

6   They say in their heart, 'I shall not be shaken; ♦
        no harm shall ever happen to me.'

7   Their mouth is full of cursing, deceit and fraud; ♦
        under their tongue lie mischief and wrong.

8   They lurk in the outskirts
          and in dark alleys they murder the innocent; ♦
        their eyes are ever watching for the helpless.

9   They lie in wait, like a lion in his den;
         they lie in wait to seize the poor; ✦
     they seize the poor when they get them into their net.

10   The innocent are broken and humbled before them; ✦
     the helpless fall before their power.

11   They say in their heart, 'God has forgotten; ✦
     he hides his face away; he will never see it.'

12   Arise, O Lord God, and lift up your hand; ✦
     forget not the poor.

13   Why should the wicked be scornful of God? ✦
     Why should they say in their hearts, 'You will not avenge it'?

14   Surely, you behold trouble and misery; ✦
     you see it and take it into your own hand.

15   The helpless commit themselves to you, ✦
     for you are the helper of the orphan.

16   Break the power of the wicked and malicious; ✦
     search out their wickedness until you find none.

17   The Lord shall reign for ever and ever; ✦
     the nations shall perish from his land.

18   Lord, you will hear the desire of the poor; ✦
     you will incline your ear to the fullness of their heart,

19   To give justice to the orphan and oppressed, ✦
     so that people are no longer driven in terror from the land.

Psalm 11

1   In the Lord have I taken refuge; ✦
     how then can you say to me,
         'Flee like a bird to the hills,

2   'For see how the wicked bend the bow
         and fit their arrows to the string, ✦
     to shoot from the shadows at the true of heart.

3   'When the foundations are destroyed, ✦
     what can the righteous do?'

4   The Lord is in his holy temple; ♦
    the Lord's throne is in heaven.

5   His eyes behold, ♦
    his eyelids try every mortal being.

6   The Lord tries the righteous as well as the wicked, ♦
    but those who delight in violence his soul abhors.

7   Upon the wicked he shall rain coals of fire
        and burning sulphur; ♦
    scorching wind shall be their portion to drink.

8   For the Lord is righteous;
        he loves righteous deeds, ♦
    and those who are upright shall behold his face.

Psalm 12

1   Help me, Lord, for no one godly is left; ♦
    the faithful have vanished from the whole human race.

2   They all speak falsely with their neighbour; ♦
    they flatter with their lips, but speak from a double heart.

3   O that the Lord would cut off all flattering lips ♦
    and the tongue that speaks proud boasts!

4   Those who say, 'With our tongue will we prevail; ♦
    our lips we will use; who is lord over us?'

5   'Because of the oppression of the needy,
        and the groaning of the poor, ♦
    I will rise up now,' says the Lord,
        'and set them in the safety that they long for.'

6   The words of the Lord are pure words, ♦
    like silver refined in the furnace
        and purified seven times in the fire.

7   You, O Lord, will watch over us ♦
    and guard us from this generation for ever.

8   The wicked strut on every side, ♦
    when what is vile is exalted by the whole human race.

Psalm 13

1 How long will you forget me, O Lord; for ever? ♦
How long will you hide your face from me?

2 How long shall I have anguish in my soul
and grief in my heart, day after day? ♦
How long shall my enemy triumph over me?

3 Look upon me and answer, O Lord my God; ♦
lighten my eyes, lest I sleep in death;

4 Lest my enemy say, 'I have prevailed against him,' ♦
and my foes rejoice that I have fallen.

5 But I put my trust in your steadfast love; ♦
my heart will rejoice in your salvation.

6 I will sing to the Lord, ♦
for he has dealt so bountifully with me.

Psalm 14

1 The fool has said in his heart, 'There is no God.' ♦
Corrupt are they, and abominable in their wickedness;
there is no one that does good.

2 The Lord has looked down from heaven
upon the children of earth, ♦
to see if there is anyone who is wise
and seeks after God.

3 But every one has turned back;
all alike have become corrupt: ♦
there is none that does good; no, not one.

4 Have they no knowledge, those evildoers, ♦
who eat up my people as if they ate bread
and do not call upon the Lord?

5 There shall they be in great fear; ♦
for God is in the company of the righteous.

6   Though they would confound the counsel of the poor, ♦
     yet the Lord shall be their refuge.

7   O that Israel's salvation would come out of Zion! ♦
     When the Lord restores the fortunes of his people,
        then will Jacob rejoice and Israel be glad.

Psalm 15

1   Lord, who may dwell in your tabernacle? ♦
     Who may rest upon your holy hill?

2   Whoever leads an uncorrupt life ♦
     and does the thing that is right;

3   Who speaks the truth from the heart ♦
     and bears no deceit on the tongue;

4   Who does no evil to a friend ♦
     and pours no scorn on a neighbour;

5   In whose sight the wicked are not esteemed, ♦
     but who honours those who fear the Lord.

6   Whoever has sworn to a neighbour ♦
     and never goes back on that word;

7   Who does not lend money in hope of gain, ♦
     nor takes a bribe against the innocent;

8   Whoever does these things ♦
     shall never fall.

Psalm 16

1   Preserve me, O God, for in you have I taken refuge; ♦
     I have said to the Lord, 'You are my lord,
        all my good depends on you.'

2   All my delight is upon the godly that are in the land, ♦
     upon those who are noble in heart.

3   Though the idols are legion
     that many run after, ♦
     their drink offerings of blood I will not offer,
     neither make mention of their names upon my lips.

4   The Lord himself is my portion and my cup; ♦
in your hands alone is my fortune.

5   My share has fallen in a fair land; ♦
indeed, I have a goodly heritage.

6   I will bless the Lord who has given me counsel, ♦
and in the night watches he instructs my heart.

7   I have set the Lord always before me; ♦
he is at my right hand; I shall not fall.

8   Wherefore my heart is glad and my spirit rejoices; ♦
my flesh also shall rest secure.

9   For you will not abandon my soul to Death, ♦
nor suffer your faithful one to see the Pit.

10   You will show me the path of life;
in your presence is the fullness of joy ♦
and in your right hand are pleasures for evermore.

Psalm 17

1   Hear my just cause, O Lord; consider my complaint; ♦
listen to my prayer, which comes not from lying lips.

2   Let my vindication come forth from your presence; ♦
let your eyes behold what is right.

3   Weigh my heart, examine me by night, ♦
refine me, and you will find no impurity in me.

4   My mouth does not trespass for earthly rewards; ♦
I have heeded the words of your lips.

5   My footsteps hold fast in the ways of your commandments; ♦
my feet have not stumbled in your paths.

6   I call upon you, O God, for you will answer me; ♦
incline your ear to me, and listen to my words.

7   Show me your marvellous loving-kindness, ♦
O Saviour of those who take refuge at your right hand
from those who rise up against them.

8   Keep me as the apple of your eye; ♦
hide me under the shadow of your wings,

9   From the wicked who assault me, ♦
from my enemies who surround me to take away my life.

10   They have closed their heart to pity ♦
and their mouth speaks proud things.

11   They press me hard, they surround me on every side, ♦
watching how they may cast me to the ground,

12   Like a lion that is greedy for its prey, ♦
like a young lion lurking in secret places.

13   Arise, Lord; confront them and cast them down; ♦
deliver me from the wicked by your sword.

14   Deliver me, O Lord, by your hand ♦
from those whose portion in life is unending,

15   Whose bellies you fill with your treasure, ♦
who are well supplied with children
      and leave their wealth to their little ones.

16   As for me, I shall see your face in righteousness; ♦
when I awake and behold your likeness, I shall be satisfied.

Psalm 18

1   I love you, O Lord my strength. ♦
The Lord is my crag, my fortress and my deliverer,

2   My God, my rock in whom I take refuge, ♦
my shield, the horn of my salvation and my stronghold.

3   I cried to the Lord in my anguish ♦
and I was saved from my enemies.

4   The cords of death entwined me ♦
and the torrents of destruction overwhelmed me.

5   The cords of the Pit fastened about me ♦
and the snares of death entangled me.

6   In my distress I called upon the Lord ♦
and cried out to my God for help.

7   He heard my voice in his temple ♦
and my cry came to his ears.

8   The earth trembled and quaked; ♦
the foundations of the mountains shook;
    they reeled because he was angry.

9   Smoke rose from his nostrils
    and a consuming fire went out of his mouth; ♦
burning coals blazed forth from him.

10   He parted the heavens and came down ♦
and thick darkness was under his feet.

11   He rode upon the cherubim and flew; ♦
he came flying on the wings of the wind.

12   He made darkness his covering round about him, ♦
dark waters and thick clouds his pavilion.

13   From the brightness of his presence, through the clouds ♦
burst hailstones and coals of fire.

14   The Lord also thundered out of heaven; ♦
the Most High uttered his voice
    with hailstones and coals of fire.

15   He sent out his arrows and scattered them; ♦
he hurled down lightnings and put them to flight.

16   The springs of the ocean were seen,
    and the foundations of the world uncovered ♦
at your rebuke, O Lord,
    at the blast of the breath of your displeasure.

17   He reached down from on high and took me; ♦
he drew me out of the mighty waters.

18   He delivered me from my strong enemy, ♦
from foes that were too mighty for me.

19   They came upon me in the day of my trouble; ♦
but the Lord was my upholder.

20   He brought me out into a place of liberty; ♦
he rescued me because he delighted in me.

21   The Lord rewarded me after my righteous dealing; ♦
according to the cleanness of my hands he recompensed me,

22   Because I had kept the ways of the Lord ♦
and had not gone wickedly away from my God,

23   For I had an eye to all his laws, ♦
       and did not cast out his commandments from me.

24   I was also wholehearted before him ♦
       and kept myself from iniquity;

25   Therefore the Lord rewarded me
          after my righteous dealing, ♦
       and according to the cleanness of my hands in his sight.

26   With the faithful you show yourself faithful; ♦
       with the true you show yourself true;

27   With the pure you show yourself pure, ♦
       but with the crooked you show yourself perverse.

28   For you will save a lowly people ♦
       and bring down the high looks of the proud.

29   You also shall light my candle; ♦
       the Lord my God shall make my darkness to be bright.

30   By your help I shall run at an enemy host; ♦
       with the help of my God I can leap over a wall.

31   As for God, his way is perfect;
          the word of the Lord is tried in the fire; ♦
       he is a shield to all who trust in him.

32   For who is God but the Lord, ♦
       and who is the rock except our God?

33   It is God who girds me about with strength ♦
       and makes my way perfect.

34   He makes my feet like hinds' feet ♦
       so that I tread surely on the heights.

35   He teaches my hands to fight ♦
       and my arms to bend a bow of bronze.

36   You have given me the shield of your salvation; ♦
       your right hand upholds me
          and your grace has made me great.

37   You enlarge my strides beneath me, ♦
       yet my feet do not slide.

38   I will pursue my enemies and overtake them, ♦
       nor turn again until I have destroyed them.

39 I will smite them down so they cannot rise; ♦
they shall fall beneath my feet.

40 You have girded me with strength for the battle; ♦
you will cast down my enemies under me;

41 You will make my foes turn their backs upon me ♦
and I shall destroy them that hate me.

42 They will cry out, but there shall be none to help them; ♦
they will cry to the Lord, but he will not answer.

43 I shall beat them as small as the dust on the wind; ♦
I will cast them out as the mire in the streets.

44 You will deliver me from the strife of the peoples; ♦
you will make me the head of the nations.

45 A people I have not known shall serve me;
as soon as they hear me, they shall obey me; ♦
strangers will humble themselves before me.

46 The foreign peoples will lose heart ♦
and come trembling out of their strongholds.

47 The Lord lives, and blessed be my rock! ♦
Praised be the God of my salvation,

48 Even the God who vindicates me ♦
and subdues the peoples under me!

49 You that deliver me from my enemies,
you will set me up above my foes; ♦
from the violent you will deliver me;

50 Therefore will I give you thanks, O Lord, among the nations ♦
and sing praises to your name,

51 To the one who gives great victory to his king ♦
and shows faithful love to his anointed,
to David and his seed for ever.

Psalm 19

1   The heavens are telling the glory of God ♦
    and the firmament proclaims his handiwork.

2   One day pours out its song to another ♦
    and one night unfolds knowledge to another.

3   They have neither speech nor language ♦
    and their voices are not heard,

4   Yet their sound has gone out into all lands ♦
    and their words to the ends of the world.

5   In them has he set a tabernacle for the sun, ♦
    that comes forth as a bridegroom out of his chamber
        and rejoices as a champion to run his course.

6   It goes forth from the end of the heavens
        and runs to the very end again, ♦
    and there is nothing hidden from its heat.

7   The law of the Lord is perfect, reviving the soul; ♦
    the testimony of the Lord is sure
        and gives wisdom to the simple.

8   The statutes of the Lord are right and rejoice the heart; ♦
    the commandment of the Lord is pure
        and gives light to the eyes.

9   The fear of the Lord is clean and endures for ever; ♦
    the judgements of the Lord are true
        and righteous altogether.

10   More to be desired are they than gold,
        more than much fine gold, ♦
    sweeter also than honey,
        dripping from the honeycomb.

11   By them also is your servant taught ♦
    and in keeping them there is great reward.

12   Who can tell how often they offend? ♦
    O cleanse me from my secret faults!

13   Keep your servant also from presumptuous sins
        lest they get dominion over me; ♦
    so shall I be undefiled,
        and innocent of great offence.

14   Let the words of my mouth and the meditation of my heart
        be acceptable in your sight, ♦
    O Lord, my strength and my redeemer.

Psalm 20

1   May the Lord hear you in the day of trouble, ♦
    the name of the God of Jacob defend you;

2   Send you help from his sanctuary ♦
    and strengthen you out of Zion;

3   Remember all your offerings ♦
    and accept your burnt sacrifice;

4   Grant you your heart's desire ♦
    and fulfil all your mind.

5   May we rejoice in your salvation
        and triumph in the name of our God; ♦
    may the Lord perform all your petitions.

6   Now I know that the Lord will save his anointed; ♦
    he will answer him from his holy heaven,
        with the mighty strength of his right hand.

7   Some put their trust in chariots and some in horses, ♦
    but we will call only on the name of the Lord our God.

8   They are brought down and fallen, ♦
    but we are risen and stand upright.

9   O Lord, save the king ♦
    and answer us when we call upon you.

1   The king shall rejoice in your strength, O Lord; ♦
    how greatly shall he rejoice in your salvation!

2   You have given him his heart's desire ♦
    and have not denied the request of his lips.

3   For you come to meet him with blessings of goodness ♦
    and set a crown of pure gold upon his head.

4   He asked of you life and you gave it him, ♦
    length of days, for ever and ever.

5   His honour is great because of your salvation; ♦
    glory and majesty have you laid upon him.

6   You have granted him everlasting felicity ♦
    and will make him glad with joy in your presence.

7   For the king puts his trust in the Lord; ♦
    because of the loving-kindness of the Most High,
        he shall not be overthrown.

8   Your hand shall mark down all your enemies; ♦
    your right hand will find out those who hate you.

9   You will make them like a fiery oven
        in the time of your wrath; ♦
    the Lord will swallow them up in his anger
        and the fire will consume them.

10 Their fruit you will root out of the land ♦
    and their seed from among its inhabitants.

11 Because they intend evil against you ♦
        and devise wicked schemes
    which they cannot perform,

12 You will put them to flight ♦
    when you aim your bow at their faces.

13 Be exalted, O Lord, in your own might; ♦
    we will make music and sing of your power.

29   How can those who sleep in the earth
          bow down in worship, ♦
      or those who go down to the dust kneel before him?

30   He has saved my life for himself;
          my descendants shall serve him; ♦
      this shall be told of the Lord for generations to come.

31   They shall come and make known his salvation,
          to a people yet unborn, ♦
      declaring that he, the Lord, has done it.

Psalm 23

1   The Lord is my shepherd; ♦
     therefore can I lack nothing.

2   He makes me lie down in green pastures ♦
     and leads me beside still waters.

3   He shall refresh my soul ♦
     and guide me in the paths of righteousness for his name's sake.

4   Though I walk through the valley of the shadow of death,
          I will fear no evil; ♦
     for you are with me;
          your rod and your staff, they comfort me.

5   You spread a table before me
          in the presence of those who trouble me; ♦
     you have anointed my head with oil
          and my cup shall be full.

6   Surely goodness and loving mercy shall follow me
          all the days of my life, ♦
     and I will dwell in the house of the Lord for ever.

1   The earth is the Lord's and all that fills it, ♦
       the compass of the world and all who dwell therein.

2   For he has founded it upon the seas ♦
       and set it firm upon the rivers of the deep.

3   'Who shall ascend the hill of the Lord, ♦
       or who can rise up in his holy place?'

4   'Those who have clean hands and a pure heart, ♦
       who have not lifted up their soul to an idol,
          nor sworn an oath to a lie;

5   'They shall receive a blessing from the Lord, ♦
       a just reward from the God of their salvation.'

6   Such is the company of those who seek him, ♦
       of those who seek your face, O God of Jacob.

7   Lift up your heads, O gates;
          be lifted up, you everlasting doors; ♦
       and the King of glory shall come in.

8   'Who is the King of glory?' ♦
       'The Lord, strong and mighty,
          the Lord who is mighty in battle.'

9   Lift up your heads, O gates;
          be lifted up, you everlasting doors; ♦
       and the King of glory shall come in.

10   'Who is this King of glory?' ♦
       'The Lord of hosts,
          he is the King of glory.'

1   To you, O Lord, I lift up my soul;
        O my God, in you I trust; ♦
    let me not be put to shame;
        let not my enemies triumph over me.

2   Let none who look to you be put to shame, ♦
    but let the treacherous be shamed and frustrated.

3   Make me to know your ways, O Lord, ♦
    and teach me your paths.

4   Lead me in your truth and teach me, ♦
    for you are the God of my salvation;
        for you have I hoped all the day long.

5   Remember, Lord, your compassion and love, ♦
    for they are from everlasting.

6   Remember not the sins of my youth
        or my transgressions, ♦
    but think on me in your goodness, O Lord,
        according to your steadfast love.

7   Gracious and upright is the Lord; ♦
    therefore shall he teach sinners in the way.

8   He will guide the humble in doing right ♦
    and teach his way to the lowly.

9   All the paths of the Lord are mercy and truth ♦
    to those who keep his covenant and his testimonies.

10   For your name's sake, O Lord, ♦
    be merciful to my sin, for it is great.

11   Who are those who fear the Lord? ♦
    Them will he teach in the way that they should choose.

12   Their soul shall dwell at ease ♦
    and their offspring shall inherit the land.

13   The hidden purpose of the Lord is for those who fear him ♦
    and he will show them his covenant.

14   My eyes are ever looking to the Lord, ♦
    for he shall pluck my feet out of the net.

15   Turn to me and be gracious to me, ♦
    for I am alone and brought very low.

16   The sorrows of my heart have increased; ♦
       O bring me out of my distress.

17   Look upon my adversity and misery ♦
       and forgive me all my sin.

18   Look upon my enemies, for they are many ♦
       and they bear a violent hatred against me.

19   O keep my soul and deliver me; ♦
       let me not be put to shame, for I have put my trust in you.

20   Let integrity and uprightness preserve me, ♦
       for my hope has been in you.

21   Deliver Israel, O God, ♦
       out of all his troubles.

Psalm 26

1   Give judgement for me, O Lord,
       for I have walked with integrity; ♦
       I have trusted in the Lord and have not faltered.

2   Test me, O Lord, and try me; ♦
       examine my heart and my mind.

3   For your love is before my eyes; ♦
       I have walked in your truth.

4   I have not joined the company of the false, ♦
       nor consorted with the deceitful.

5   I hate the gathering of evildoers ♦
       and I will not sit down with the wicked.

6   I will wash my hands in innocence, O Lord, ♦
       that I may go about your altar,

7   To make heard the voice of thanksgiving ♦
       and tell of all your wonderful deeds.

8   Lord, I love the house of your habitation ♦
       and the place where your glory abides.

9   Sweep me not away with sinners, ♦
       nor my life with the bloodthirsty,

10   Whose hands are full of wicked schemes ♦
      and their right hand full of bribes.

11   As for me, I will walk with integrity; ♦
      redeem me, Lord, and be merciful to me.

12   My foot stands firm; ♦
      in the great congregation I will bless the Lord.

Psalm 27

1   The Lord is my light and my salvation;
          whom then shall I fear? ♦
      The Lord is the strength of my life;
          of whom then shall I be afraid?

2   When the wicked, even my enemies and my foes,
          came upon me to eat up my flesh, ♦
      they stumbled and fell.

3   Though a host encamp against me,
          my heart shall not be afraid, ♦
      and though there rise up war against me,
          yet will I put my trust in him.

4   One thing have I asked of the Lord
          and that alone I seek: ♦
      that I may dwell in the house of the Lord
          all the days of my life,

5   To behold the fair beauty of the Lord ♦
      and to seek his will in his temple.

6   For in the day of trouble
          he shall hide me in his shelter; ♦
      in the secret place of his dwelling shall he hide me
          and set me high upon a rock.

7   And now shall he lift up my head ♦
      above my enemies round about me;

8   Therefore will I offer in his dwelling an oblation
          with great gladness; ♦
      I will sing and make music to the Lord.

9   Hear my voice, O Lord, when I call; ♦
      have mercy upon me and answer me.

10   My heart tells of your word, 'Seek my face.' ♦
      Your face, Lord, will I seek.

11   Hide not your face from me, ♦
      nor cast your servant away in displeasure.

12   You have been my helper; ♦
      leave me not, neither forsake me, O God of my salvation.

13   Though my father and my mother forsake me, ♦
      the Lord will take me up.

14   Teach me your way, O Lord; ♦
      lead me on a level path,
         because of those who lie in wait for me.

15   Deliver me not into the will of my adversaries, ♦
      for false witnesses have risen up against me,
         and those who breathe out violence.

16   I believe that I shall see the goodness of the Lord ♦
      in the land of the living.

17   Wait for the Lord;
         be strong and he shall comfort your heart; ♦
      wait patiently for the Lord.

Psalm 28

1   To you I call, O Lord my rock;
         be not deaf to my cry, ♦
      lest, if you do not hear me,
         I become like those who go down to the Pit.

2   Hear the voice of my prayer when I cry out to you, ♦
      when I lift up my hands to your holy of holies.

3   Do not snatch me away with the wicked,
         with the evildoers, ♦
      who speak peaceably with their neighbours,
         while malice is in their hearts.

4   Repay them according to their deeds ♦
      and according to the wickedness of their devices.

5   Reward them according to the work of their hands ♦
and pay them their just deserts.

6   They take no heed of the Lord's doings,
       nor of the works of his hands; ♦
therefore shall he break them down
       and not build them up.

7   Blessed be the Lord, ♦
for he has heard the voice of my prayer.

8   The Lord is my strength and my shield; ♦
my heart has trusted in him and I am helped;

9   Therefore my heart dances for joy ♦
and in my song will I praise him.

10   The Lord is the strength of his people, ♦
a safe refuge for his anointed.

11   Save your people and bless your inheritance; ♦
shepherd them and carry them for ever.

Psalm 29

1   Ascribe to the Lord, you powers of heaven, ♦
ascribe to the Lord glory and strength.

2   Ascribe to the Lord the honour due to his name; ♦
worship the Lord in the beauty of holiness.

3   The voice of the Lord is upon the waters;
       the God of glory thunders; ♦
the Lord is upon the mighty waters.

4   The voice of the Lord is mighty in operation; ♦
the voice of the Lord is a glorious voice.

5   The voice of the Lord breaks the cedar trees; ♦
the Lord breaks the cedars of Lebanon;

6   He makes Lebanon skip like a calf ♦
and Sirion like a young wild ox.

7   The voice of the Lord splits the flash of lightning;
       the voice of the Lord shakes the wilderness; ♦
the Lord shakes the wilderness of Kadesh.

8   The voice of the Lord makes the oak trees writhe
         and strips the forests bare; ♦
     in his temple all cry, 'Glory!'

9   The Lord sits enthroned above the water flood; ♦
     the Lord sits enthroned as king for evermore.

10   The Lord shall give strength to his people; ♦
     the Lord shall give his people the blessing of peace.

Psalm 30

1   I will exalt you, O Lord,
         because you have raised me up ♦
     and have not let my foes triumph over me.

2   O Lord my God, I cried out to you ♦
     and you have healed me.

3   You brought me up, O Lord, from the dead; ♦
     you restored me to life from among those that go down to the Pit.

4   Sing to the Lord, you servants of his; ♦
     give thanks to his holy name.

5   For his wrath endures but the twinkling of an eye,
         his favour for a lifetime. ♦
     Heaviness may endure for a night,
         but joy comes in the morning.

6   In my prosperity I said,
         'I shall never be moved. ♦
     You, Lord, of your goodness,
         have made my hill so strong.'

7   Then you hid your face from me ♦
     and I was utterly dismayed.

8   To you, O Lord, I cried; ♦
     to the Lord I made my supplication:

9   'What profit is there in my blood,
         if I go down to the Pit? ♦
     Will the dust praise you or declare your faithfulness?

10   'Hear, O Lord, and have mercy upon me; ♦
     O Lord, be my helper.'

11   You have turned my mourning into dancing; ♦
you have put off my sackcloth and girded me with gladness;

12   Therefore my heart sings to you without ceasing; ♦
O Lord my God, I will give you thanks for ever.

Psalm 31

1   In you, O Lord, have I taken refuge;
        let me never be put to shame; ♦
    deliver me in your righteousness.

2   Incline your ear to me; ♦
    make haste to deliver me.

3   Be my strong rock, a fortress to save me,
        for you are my rock and my stronghold; ♦
    guide me, and lead me for your name's sake.

4   Take me out of the net
        that they have laid secretly for me, ♦
    for you are my strength.

5   Into your hands I commend my spirit, ♦
    for you have redeemed me, O Lord God of truth.

6   I hate those who cling to worthless idols; ♦
    I put my trust in the Lord.

7   I will be glad and rejoice in your mercy, ♦
    for you have seen my affliction
        and known my soul in adversity.

8   You have not shut me up in the hand of the enemy; ♦
    you have set my feet in an open place.

9   Have mercy on me, Lord, for I am in trouble; ♦
    my eye is consumed with sorrow,
        my soul and my body also.

10   For my life is wasted with grief,
        and my years with sighing; ♦
    my strength fails me because of my affliction,
        and my bones are consumed.

11 I have become a reproach to all my enemies
and even to my neighbours,
an object of dread to my acquaintances; ♦
when they see me in the street they flee from me.

12 I am forgotten like one that is dead, out of mind; ♦
I have become like a broken vessel.

13 For I have heard the whispering of the crowd;
fear is on every side; ♦
they scheme together against me,
and plot to take my life.

14 But my trust is in you, O Lord. ♦
I have said, 'You are my God.

15 'My times are in your hand; ♦
deliver me from the hand of my enemies,
and from those who persecute me.

16 'Make your face to shine upon your servant, ♦
and save me for your mercy's sake.'

17 Lord, let me not be confounded
for I have called upon you; ♦
but let the wicked be put to shame;
let them be silent in the grave.

18 Let the lying lips be put to silence ♦
that speak against the righteous
with arrogance, disdain and contempt.

19 How abundant is your goodness, O Lord,
which you have laid up for those who fear you; ♦
which you have prepared in the sight of all
for those who put their trust in you.

20 You hide them in the shelter of your presence
from those who slander them; ♦
you keep them safe in your refuge from the strife of tongues.

21 Blessed be the Lord! ♦
For he has shown me his steadfast love
when I was as a city besieged.

22   I had said in my alarm,
        'I have been cut off from the sight of your eyes.' ♦
    Nevertheless, you heard the voice of my prayer
        when I cried out to you.

23   Love the Lord, all you his servants; ♦
    for the Lord protects the faithful,
        but repays to the full the proud.

24   Be strong and let your heart take courage, ♦
    all you who wait in hope for the Lord.

Psalm 32

1   Happy the one whose transgression is forgiven, ♦
    and whose sin is covered.

2   Happy the one to whom the Lord imputes no guilt, ♦
    and in whose spirit there is no guile.

3   For I held my tongue; ♦
    my bones wasted away
        through my groaning all the day long.

4   Your hand was heavy upon me day and night; ♦
    my moisture was dried up like the drought in summer.

5   Then I acknowledged my sin to you ♦
    and my iniquity I did not hide.

6   I said, 'I will confess my transgressions to the Lord,' ♦
    and you forgave the guilt of my sin.

7   Therefore let all the faithful make their prayers to you
        in time of trouble; ♦
    in the great water flood, it shall not reach them.

8   You are a place for me to hide in;
        you preserve me from trouble; ♦
    you surround me with songs of deliverance.

9   'I will instruct you and teach you
        in the way that you should go; ♦
    I will guide you with my eye.

10 'Be not like horse and mule which have no understanding; ♦
whose mouths must be held with bit and bridle,
or else they will not stay near you.'

11 Great tribulations remain for the wicked, ♦
but mercy embraces those who trust in the Lord.

12 Be glad, you righteous, and rejoice in the Lord; ♦
shout for joy, all who are true of heart.

Psalm 33

1 Rejoice in the Lord, O you righteous, ♦
for it is good for the just to sing praises.

2 Praise the Lord with the lyre; ♦
on the ten-stringed harp sing his praise.

3 Sing for him a new song; ♦
play skilfully, with shouts of praise.

4 For the word of the Lord is true ♦
and all his works are sure.

5 He loves righteousness and justice; ♦
the earth is full of the loving-kindness of the Lord.

6 By the word of the Lord were the heavens made ♦
and all their host by the breath of his mouth.

7 He gathers up the waters of the sea as in a waterskin ♦
and lays up the deep in his treasury.

8 Let all the earth fear the Lord; ♦
stand in awe of him, all who dwell in the world.

9 For he spoke, and it was done; ♦
he commanded, and it stood fast.

10 The Lord brings the counsel of the nations to naught; ♦
he frustrates the designs of the peoples.

11 But the counsel of the Lord shall endure for ever ♦
and the designs of his heart from generation to generation.

12 Happy the nation whose God is the Lord ♦
and the people he has chosen for his own.

13 The Lord looks down from heaven ♦
and beholds all the children of earth.

14 From where he sits enthroned he turns his gaze ♦
on all who dwell on the earth.

15 He fashions all the hearts of them ♦
and understands all their works.

16 No king is saved by the might of his host; ♦
no warrior delivered by his great strength.

17 A horse is a vain hope for deliverance; ♦
for all its strength it cannot save.

18 Behold, the eye of the Lord
is upon those who fear him, ♦
on those who wait in hope for his steadfast love,

19 To deliver their soul from death ♦
and to feed them in time of famine.

20 Our soul waits longingly for the Lord; ♦
he is our help and our shield.

21 Indeed, our heart rejoices in him; ♦
in his holy name have we put our trust.

22 Let your loving-kindness, O Lord, be upon us, ♦
as we have set our hope on you.

Psalm 34

1 I will bless the Lord at all times; ♦
his praise shall ever be in my mouth.

2 My soul shall glory in the Lord; ♦
let the humble hear and be glad.

3 O magnify the Lord with me; ♦
let us exalt his name together.

4 I sought the Lord and he answered me ♦
and delivered me from all my fears.

5 Look upon him and be radiant ♦
and your faces shall not be ashamed.

6   This poor soul cried, and the Lord heard me ♦
and saved me from all my troubles.

7   The angel of the Lord encamps around those who fear him ♦
and delivers them.

8   O taste and see that the Lord is gracious; ♦
blessed is the one who trusts in him.

9   Fear the Lord, all you his holy ones, ♦
for those who fear him lack nothing.

10   Lions may lack and suffer hunger, ♦
but those who seek the Lord
    lack nothing that is good.

11   Come, my children, and listen to me; ♦
I will teach you the fear of the Lord.

12   Who is there who delights in life ♦
and longs for days to enjoy good things?

13   Keep your tongue from evil ♦
and your lips from lying words.

14   Turn from evil and do good; ♦
seek peace and pursue it.

15   The eyes of the Lord are upon the righteous ♦
and his ears are open to their cry.

16   The face of the Lord is against those who do evil, ♦
to root out the remembrance of them from the earth.

17   The righteous cry and the Lord hears them ♦
and delivers them out of all their troubles.

18   The Lord is near to the brokenhearted ♦
and will save those who are crushed in spirit.

19   Many are the troubles of the righteous; ♦
from them all will the Lord deliver them.

20   He keeps all their bones, ♦
so that not one of them is broken.

21   But evil shall slay the wicked ♦
and those who hate the righteous will be condemned.

22   The Lord ransoms the life of his servants ♦
and will condemn none who seek refuge in him.

1   Contend, O Lord, with those that contend with me; ♦
    fight against those that fight against me.

2   Take up shield and buckler ♦
    and rise up to help me.

3   Draw the spear and bar the way
        against those who pursue me; ♦
    say to my soul, 'I am your salvation.'

4   Let those who seek after my life be shamed and disgraced; ♦
    let those who plot my ruin fall back and be put to confusion.

5   Let them be as chaff before the wind, ♦
    with the angel of the Lord thrusting them down.

6   Let their way be dark and slippery, ♦
    with the angel of the Lord pursuing them.

7   For they have secretly spread a net for me without a cause; ♦
    without any cause they have dug a pit for my soul.

8   Let ruin come upon them unawares; ♦
    let them be caught in the net they laid;
        let them fall in it to their destruction.

9   Then will my soul be joyful in the Lord ♦
    and glory in his salvation.

10 My very bones will say, 'Lord, who is like you? ♦
    You deliver the poor from those that are too strong for them,
        the poor and needy from those who would despoil them.'

11 False witnesses rose up against me; ♦
    they charged me with things I knew not.

12 They rewarded me evil for good, ♦
    to the desolation of my soul.

13 But as for me, when they were sick I put on sackcloth ♦
    and humbled myself with fasting;

14 When my prayer returned empty to my bosom, ♦
        it was as though I grieved for my friend or brother;

15 I behaved as one who mourns for his mother, ♦
    bowed down and brought very low.

16   But when I stumbled, they gathered in delight;
       they gathered together against me; ♦
    as if they were strangers I did not know
       they tore at me without ceasing.

17   When I fell they mocked me; ♦
    they gnashed at me with their teeth.

18   O Lord, how long will you look on? ♦
    Rescue my soul from their ravages,
       and my poor life from the young lions.

19   I will give you thanks in the great congregation; ♦
    I will praise you in the mighty throng.

20   Do not let my treacherous foes rejoice over me, ♦
    or those who hate me without a cause
       mock me with their glances.

21   For they do not speak of peace, ♦
    but invent deceitful schemes against those that are quiet in the land.

22   They opened wide their mouths and derided me, saying ♦
    'We have seen it with our very eyes.'

23   This you have seen, O Lord; do not keep silent; ♦
    go not far from me, O Lord.

24   Awake, arise, to my cause, ♦
    to my defence, my God and my Lord!

25   Give me justice, O Lord my God,
       according to your righteousness; ♦
    let them not triumph over me.

26   Let them not say to themselves,
       'Our heart's desire!' ♦
    Let them not say, 'We have swallowed him up.'

27   Let all who rejoice at my trouble be put to shame and confusion; ♦
    let those who boast against me
       be clothed with shame and dishonour.

28   Let those who favour my cause rejoice and be glad; ♦
    let them say always,
       'Great is the Lord, who delights in his servant's well-being.'

29   So shall my tongue be talking of your righteousness ♦
    and of your praise all the day long.

1   Sin whispers to the wicked, in the depths of their heart; ♦
there is no fear of God before their eyes.

2   They flatter themselves in their own eyes ♦
that their abominable sin will not be found out.

3   The words of their mouth are unrighteous and full of deceit; ♦
they have ceased to act wisely and to do good.

4   They think out mischief upon their beds
and have set themselves in no good way; ♦
nor do they abhor that which is evil.

5   Your love, O Lord, reaches to the heavens ♦
and your faithfulness to the clouds.

6   Your righteousness stands like the strong mountains,
your justice like the great deep; ♦
you, Lord, shall save both man and beast.

7   How precious is your loving mercy, O God! ♦
All mortal flesh shall take refuge
under the shadow of your wings.

8   They shall be satisfied with the abundance of your house; ♦
they shall drink from the river of your delights.

9   For with you is the well of life ♦
and in your light shall we see light.

10   O continue your loving-kindness to those who know you ♦
and your righteousness to those who are true of heart.

11   Let not the foot of pride come against me, ♦
nor the hand of the ungodly thrust me away.

12   There are they fallen, all who work wickedness. ♦
They are cast down and shall not be able to stand.

1   Fret not because of evildoers; ♦
be not jealous of those who do wrong.

2   For they shall soon wither like grass ♦
and like the green herb fade away.

3   Trust in the Lord and be doing good; ♦
dwell in the land and be nourished with truth.

4   Let your delight be in the Lord ♦
and he will give you your heart's desire.

5   Commit your way to the Lord and put your trust in him, ♦
and he will bring it to pass.

6   He will make your righteousness as clear as the light ♦
and your just dealing as the noonday.

7   Be still before the Lord and wait for him; ♦
do not fret over those that prosper
     as they follow their evil schemes.

8   Refrain from anger and abandon wrath; ♦
do not fret, lest you be moved to do evil.

9   For evildoers shall be cut off, ♦
but those who wait upon the Lord shall possess the land.

10   Yet a little while and the wicked shall be no more; ♦
you will search for their place and find them gone.

11   But the lowly shall possess the land ♦
and shall delight in abundance of peace.

12   The wicked plot against the righteous ♦
and gnash at them with their teeth.

13   The Lord shall laugh at the wicked, ♦
for he sees that their day is coming.

14   The wicked draw their sword and bend their bow
     to strike down the poor and needy, ♦
to slaughter those who walk in truth.

15   Their sword shall go through their own heart ♦
and their bows shall be broken.

16   The little that the righteous have ♦
is better than great riches of the wicked.

17   For the arms of the wicked shall be broken, ♦
       but the Lord upholds the righteous.

18   The Lord knows the days of the godly, ♦
       and their inheritance shall stand for ever.

19   They shall not be put to shame in the perilous time, ♦
       and in days of famine they shall have enough.

20   But the wicked shall perish;
         like the glory of the meadows
         the enemies of the Lord shall vanish; ♦
       they shall vanish like smoke.

21   The wicked borrow and do not repay, ♦
       but the righteous are generous in giving.

22   For those who are blest by God shall possess the land, ♦
       but those who are cursed by him shall be rooted out.

23   When your steps are guided by the Lord ♦
       and you delight in his way,

24   Though you stumble, you shall not fall headlong, ♦
       for the Lord holds you fast by the hand.

25   I have been young and now am old, ♦
       yet never have I seen the righteous forsaken,
         or their children begging their bread.

26   All the day long they are generous in lending, ♦
       and their children also shall be blest.

27   Depart from evil and do good ♦
       and you shall abide for ever.

28   For the Lord loves the thing that is right ♦
       and will not forsake his faithful ones.

29   The unjust shall be destroyed for ever, ♦
       and the offspring of the wicked shall be rooted out.

30   The righteous shall possess the land ♦
       and dwell in it for ever.

31   The mouth of the righteous utters wisdom, ♦
       and their tongue speaks the thing that is right.

32   The law of their God is in their heart ♦
       and their footsteps shall not slide.

33 The wicked spy on the righteous ♦
and seek occasion to slay them.

34 The Lord will not leave them in their hand, ♦
nor let them be condemned when they are judged.

35 Wait upon the Lord and keep his way; ♦
he will raise you up to possess the land,
and when the wicked are uprooted, you shall see it.

36 I myself have seen the wicked in great power ♦
and flourishing like a tree in full leaf.

37 I went by and lo, they were gone; ♦
I sought them, but they could nowhere be found.

38 Keep innocence and heed the thing that is right, ♦
for that will bring you peace at the last.

39 But the sinners shall perish together, ♦
and the posterity of the wicked shall be rooted out.

40 The salvation of the righteous comes from the Lord; ♦
he is their stronghold in the time of trouble.

41 The Lord shall stand by them and deliver them; ♦
he shall deliver them from the wicked and shall save them,
because they have put their trust in him.

Psalm 38

1 Rebuke me not, O Lord, in your anger, ♦
neither chasten me in your heavy displeasure.

2 For your arrows have stuck fast in me ♦
and your hand presses hard upon me.

3 There is no health in my flesh
because of your indignation; ♦
there is no peace in my bones because of my sin.

4 For my iniquities have gone over my head; ♦
their weight is a burden too heavy to bear.

5 My wounds stink and fester ♦
because of my foolishness.

6 I am utterly bowed down and brought very low; ♦
I go about mourning all the day long.

7   My loins are filled with searing pain; ♦
there is no health in my flesh.

8   I am feeble and utterly crushed; ♦
I roar aloud because of the disquiet of my heart.

9   O Lord, you know all my desires ♦
and my sighing is not hidden from you.

10   My heart is pounding, my strength has failed me; ♦
the light of my eyes is gone from me.

11   My friends and companions stand apart from my affliction; ♦
my neighbours stand afar off.

12   Those who seek after my life lay snares for me; ♦
and those who would harm me whisper evil
    and mutter slander all the day long.

13   But I am like one who is deaf and hears not, ♦
like one that is dumb, who does not open his mouth.

14   I have become like one who does not hear ♦
and from whose mouth comes no retort.

15   For in you, Lord, have I put my trust; ♦
you will answer me, O Lord my God.

16   For I said, 'Let them not triumph over me, ♦
those who exult over me when my foot slips.'

17   Truly, I am on the verge of falling ♦
and my pain is ever with me.

18   I will confess my iniquity ♦
and be sorry for my sin.

19   Those that are my enemies without any cause are mighty, ♦
and those who hate me wrongfully are many in number.

20   Those who repay evil for good are against me, ♦
because the good is what I seek.

21   Forsake me not, O Lord; ♦
be not far from me, O my God.

22   Make haste to help me, ♦
O Lord of my salvation.

1   I said, 'I will keep watch over my ways, ♦
     so that I offend not with my tongue.

2   'I will guard my mouth with a muzzle, ♦
     while the wicked are in my sight.'

3   So I held my tongue and said nothing; ♦
     I kept silent but to no avail.

4   My distress increased, my heart grew hot within me; ♦
     while I mused, the fire was kindled
        and I spoke out with my tongue:

5   'Lord, let me know my end and the number of my days, ♦
     that I may know how short my time is.

6   'You have made my days but a handsbreadth,
        and my lifetime is as nothing in your sight; ♦
     truly, even those who stand upright are but a breath.

7   'We walk about like a shadow
        and in vain we are in turmoil; ♦
     we heap up riches and cannot tell who will gather them.

8   'And now, what is my hope? ♦
     Truly my hope is even in you.

9   'Deliver me from all my transgressions ♦
     and do not make me the taunt of the fool.'

10   I fell silent and did not open my mouth, ♦
     for surely it was your doing.

11   Take away your plague from me; ♦
     I am consumed by the blows of your hand.

12   With rebukes for sin you punish us;
        like a moth you consume our beauty; ♦
     truly, everyone is but a breath.

13   Hear my prayer, O Lord, and give ear to my cry; ♦
     hold not your peace at my tears.

14   For I am but a stranger with you, ♦
     a wayfarer, as all my forebears were.

15   Turn your gaze from me, that I may be glad again, ♦
     before I go my way and am no more.

1   I waited patiently for the Lord; ♦
    he inclined to me and heard my cry.

2   He brought me out of the roaring pit,
        out of the mire and clay; ♦
    he set my feet upon a rock and made my footing sure.

3   He has put a new song in my mouth,
        a song of praise to our God; ♦
    many shall see and fear
        and put their trust in the Lord.

4   Blessed is the one who trusts in the Lord, ♦
    who does not turn to the proud that follow a lie.

5   Great are the wonders you have done, O Lord my God.
        How great your designs for us! ♦
    There is none that can be compared with you.

6   If I were to proclaim them and tell of them ♦
    they would be more than I am able to express.

7   Sacrifice and offering you do not desire ♦
    but my ears you have opened;

8   Burnt offering and sacrifice for sin you have not required; ♦
    then said I: 'Lo, I come.

9   'In the scroll of the book it is written of me
        that I should do your will, O my God; ♦
    I delight to do it: your law is within my heart.'

10 I have declared your righteousness in the great congregation; ♦
    behold, I did not restrain my lips,
        and that, O Lord, you know.

11 Your righteousness I have not hidden in my heart;
        I have spoken of your faithfulness and your salvation; ♦
    I have not concealed your loving-kindness and truth
        from the great congregation.

12 Do not withhold your compassion from me, O Lord; ♦
    let your love and your faithfulness always preserve me,

13   For innumerable troubles have come about me;
        my sins have overtaken me so that I cannot look up; ♦
    they are more in number than the hairs of my head,
        and my heart fails me.

14   Be pleased, O Lord, to deliver me; ♦
    O Lord, make haste to help me.

15   Let them be ashamed and altogether dismayed
        who seek after my life to destroy it; ♦
    let them be driven back and put to shame
        who wish me evil.

16   Let those who heap insults upon me ♦
    be desolate because of their shame.

17   Let all who seek you rejoice in you and be glad; ♦
    let those who love your salvation say always,
        'The Lord is great.'

18   Though I am poor and needy, ♦
    the Lord cares for me.

19   You are my helper and my deliverer; ♦
    O my God, make no delay.

Psalm 41

1   Blessed are those who consider the poor and needy; ♦
    the Lord will deliver them in the time of trouble.

2   The Lord preserves them and restores their life,
        that they may be happy in the land; ♦
    he will not hand them over to the will of their enemies.

3   The Lord sustains them on their sickbed; ♦
    their sickness, Lord, you will remove.

4   And so I said, 'Lord, be merciful to me; ♦
    heal me, for I have sinned against you.'

5   My enemies speak evil about me, ♦
    asking when I shall die and my name perish.

6   If they come to see me, they utter empty words; ◆
their heart gathers mischief;
      when they go out, they tell it abroad.

7   All my enemies whisper together against me, ◆
against me they devise evil,

8   Saying that a deadly thing has laid hold on me, ◆
and that I will not rise again from where I lie.

9   Even my bosom friend, whom I trusted,
      who ate of my bread, ◆
has lifted up his heel against me.

10   But you, O Lord, be merciful to me ◆
and raise me up, that I may reward them.

11   By this I know that you favour me, ◆
that my enemy does not triumph over me.

12   Because of my integrity you uphold me ◆
and will set me before your face for ever.

13   Blessed be the Lord God of Israel, ◆
from everlasting to everlasting. Amen and Amen.

Psalm 42

1   As the deer longs for the water brooks, ◆
so longs my soul for you, O God.

2   My soul is athirst for God, even for the living God; ◆
when shall I come before the presence of God?

3   My tears have been my bread day and night, ◆
while all day long they say to me, 'Where is now your God?'

4   Now when I think on these things, I pour out my soul: ◆
how I went with the multitude
      and led the procession to the house of God,

5   With the voice of praise and thanksgiving, ◆
among those who kept holy day.

6   *Why are you so full of heaviness, O my soul, ◆*
and why are you so disquieted within me?

7   *O put your trust in God;* ♦
      for I will yet give him thanks,
           who is the help of my countenance, and my God.

8   My soul is heavy within me; ♦
      therefore I will remember you from the land of Jordan,
           and from Hermon and the hill of Mizar.

9   Deep calls to deep in the thunder of your waterfalls; ♦
      all your breakers and waves have gone over me.

10   The Lord will grant his loving-kindness in the daytime; ♦
      through the night his song will be with me,
           a prayer to the God of my life.

11   I say to God my rock,
           'Why have you forgotten me, ♦
      and why go I so heavily, while the enemy oppresses me?'

12   As they crush my bones, my enemies mock me; ♦
      while all day long they say to me, 'Where is now your God?'

13   *Why are you so full of heaviness, O my soul,* ♦
      and why are you so disquieted within me?

14   *O put your trust in God;* ♦
      for I will yet give him thanks,
           who is the help of my countenance, and my God.

Psalm 43

1   Give judgement for me, O God,
           and defend my cause against an ungodly people; ♦
      deliver me from the deceitful and the wicked.

2   For you are the God of my refuge;
           why have you cast me from you, ♦
      and why go I so heavily, while the enemy oppresses me?

3   O send out your light and your truth, that they may lead me, ♦
      and bring me to your holy hill and to your dwelling,

4   That I may go to the altar of God,
           to the God of my joy and gladness; ♦
      and on the lyre I will give thanks to you, O God my God.

5   *Why are you so full of heaviness, O my soul,* ♦
    and why are you so disquieted within me?

6   *O put your trust in God;* ♦
    for I will yet give him thanks,
        who is the help of my countenance, and my God.

Psalm 44

1   We have heard with our ears, O God, our forebears have told us, ♦
    all that you did in their days, in time of old;

2   How with your hand you drove out nations and planted us in, ♦
    and broke the power of peoples and set us free.

3   For not by their own sword did our ancestors take the land ♦
    nor did their own arm save them,

4   But your right hand, your arm, and the light of your countenance, ♦
    because you were gracious to them.

5   You are my King and my God, ♦
    who commanded salvation for Jacob.

6   Through you we drove back our adversaries; ♦
    through your name we trod down our foes.

7   For I did not trust in my bow; ♦
    it was not my own sword that saved me;

8   It was you that saved us from our enemies ♦
    and put our adversaries to shame.

9   We gloried in God all the day long, ♦
    and were ever praising your name.

10   But now you have rejected us and brought us to shame, ♦
    and go not out with our armies.

11   You have made us turn our backs on our enemies, ♦
    and our enemies have despoiled us.

12   You have made us like sheep to be slaughtered, ♦
    and have scattered us among the nations.

13   You have sold your people for a pittance ♦
    and made no profit on their sale.

14   You have made us the taunt of our neighbours, ♦
       the scorn and derision of those that are round about us.

15   You have made us a byword among the nations; ♦
       among the peoples they wag their heads.

16   My confusion is daily before me, ♦
       and shame has covered my face,

17   At the taunts of the slanderer and reviler, ♦
       at the sight of the enemy and avenger.

18   All this has come upon us,
       though we have not forgotten you ♦
       and have not played false to your covenant.

19   Our hearts have not turned back, ♦
       nor our steps gone out of your way,

20   Yet you have crushed us in the haunt of jackals, ♦
       and covered us with the shadow of death.

21   If we have forgotten the name of our God, ♦
       or stretched out our hands to any strange god,

22   Will not God search it out? ♦
       For he knows the secrets of the heart.

23   But for your sake are we killed all the day long, ♦
       and are counted as sheep for the slaughter.

24   Rise up! Why sleep, O Lord? ♦
       Awake, and do not reject us for ever.

25   Why do you hide your face ♦
       and forget our grief and oppression?

26   Our soul is bowed down to the dust; ♦
       our belly cleaves to the earth.

27   Rise up, O Lord, to help us ♦
       and redeem us for the sake of your steadfast love.

1   My heart is astir with gracious words; ♦
as I make my song for the king,
      my tongue is the pen of a ready writer.

2   You are the fairest of men; ♦
full of grace are your lips,
      for God has blest you for ever.

3   Gird your sword upon your thigh, O mighty one; ♦
gird on your majesty and glory.

4   Ride on and prosper in the cause of truth ♦
and for the sake of humility and righteousness.

5   Your right hand will teach you terrible things; ♦
your arrows will be sharp in the heart of the king's enemies,
      so that peoples fall beneath you.

6   Your throne is God's throne, for ever; ♦
the sceptre of your kingdom is the sceptre of righteousness.

7   You love righteousness and hate iniquity; ♦
therefore God, your God, has anointed you
      with the oil of gladness above your fellows.

8   All your garments are fragrant with myrrh, aloes and cassia; ♦
from ivory palaces the music of strings makes you glad.

9   Kings' daughters are among your honourable women; ♦
at your right hand stands the queen in gold of Ophir.

10   Hear, O daughter; consider and incline your ear; ♦
forget your own people and your father's house.

11   So shall the king have pleasure in your beauty; ♦
he is your lord, so do him honour.

12   The people of Tyre shall bring you gifts; ♦
the richest of the people shall seek your favour.

13   The king's daughter is all glorious within; ♦
her clothing is embroidered cloth of gold.

14   She shall be brought to the king in raiment of needlework; ♦
after her the virgins that are her companions.

15   With joy and gladness shall they be brought ♦
    and enter into the palace of the king.

16   'Instead of your fathers you shall have sons, ♦
    whom you shall make princes over all the land.

17   'I will make your name to be remembered through all generations; ♦
    therefore shall the peoples praise you for ever and ever.'

Psalm 46

1   God is our refuge and strength, ♦
    a very present help in trouble;

2   Therefore we will not fear, though the earth be moved, ♦
    and though the mountains tremble in the heart of the sea;

3   Though the waters rage and swell, ♦
    and though the mountains quake at the towering seas.

4   There is a river whose streams make glad the city of God, ♦
    the holy place of the dwelling of the Most High.

5   God is in the midst of her;
        therefore shall she not be removed; ♦
    God shall help her at the break of day.

6   The nations are in uproar and the kingdoms are shaken, ♦
    but God utters his voice and the earth shall melt away.

7   *The Lord of hosts is with us; ♦*
    the God of Jacob is our stronghold.

8   Come and behold the works of the Lord, ♦
    what destruction he has wrought upon the earth.

9   He makes wars to cease in all the world; ♦
    he shatters the bow and snaps the spear
        and burns the chariots in the fire.

10   'Be still, and know that I am God; ♦
    I will be exalted among the nations;
        I will be exalted in the earth.'

11   *The Lord of hosts is with us; ♦*
    the God of Jacob is our stronghold.

Psalm 47

1 Clap your hands together, all you peoples; ♦
O sing to God with shouts of joy.

2 For the Lord Most High is to be feared; ♦
he is the great King over all the earth.

3 He subdued the peoples under us ♦
and the nations under our feet.

4 He has chosen our heritage for us, ♦
the pride of Jacob, whom he loves.

5 God has gone up with a merry noise, ♦
the Lord with the sound of the trumpet.

6 O sing praises to God, sing praises; ♦
sing praises to our King, sing praises.

7 For God is the King of all the earth; ♦
sing praises with all your skill.

8 God reigns over the nations; ♦
God has taken his seat upon his holy throne.

9 The nobles of the peoples are gathered together ♦
with the people of the God of Abraham.

10 For the powers of the earth belong to God ♦
and he is very highly exalted.

Psalm 48

1 Great is the Lord and highly to be praised, ♦
in the city of our God.

2 His holy mountain is fair and lifted high, ♦
the joy of all the earth.

3 On Mount Zion, the divine dwelling place, ♦
stands the city of the great king.

4 In her palaces God has shown himself ♦
to be a sure refuge.

5 For behold, the kings of the earth assembled ♦
and swept forward together.

6   They saw, and were dumbfounded; ♦
     dismayed, they fled in terror.

7   Trembling seized them there;
          they writhed like a woman in labour, ♦
     as when the east wind shatters the ships of Tarshish.

8   As we had heard, so have we seen
          in the city of the Lord of hosts, the city of our God: ♦
     God has established her for ever.

9   We have waited on your loving-kindness, O God, ♦
     in the midst of your temple.

10   As with your name, O God,
          so your praise reaches to the ends of the earth; ♦
     your right hand is full of justice.

11   Let Mount Zion rejoice and the daughters of Judah be glad, ♦
     because of your judgements, O Lord.

12   Walk about Zion and go round about her;
          count all her towers; ♦
     consider well her bulwarks; pass through her citadels,

13   That you may tell those who come after
          that such is our God for ever and ever. ♦
     It is he that shall be our guide for evermore.

Psalm 49

1   Hear this, all you peoples; ♦
     listen, all you that dwell in the world,

2   You of low or high degree, ♦
     both rich and poor together.

3   My mouth shall speak of wisdom ♦
     and my heart shall meditate on understanding.

4   I will incline my ear to a parable; ♦
     I will unfold my riddle with the lyre.

5   Why should I fear in evil days, ♦
     when the malice of my foes surrounds me,

6   Such as trust in their goods ♦
       and glory in the abundance of their riches?

7   For no one can indeed ransom another ♦
       or pay to God the price of deliverance.

8   To ransom a soul is too costly; ♦
       there is no price one could pay for it,

9   So that they might live for ever, ♦
       and never see the grave.

10   For we see that the wise die also;
       with the foolish and ignorant they perish ♦
       and leave their riches to others.

11   Their tomb is their home for ever,
       their dwelling through all generations, ♦
       though they call their lands after their own names.

12   Those who have honour, but lack understanding, ♦
       are like the beasts that perish.

13   Such is the way of those who boast in themselves, ♦
       the end of those who delight in their own words.

14   Like a flock of sheep they are destined to die;
       death is their shepherd; ♦
       they go down straight to the Pit.

15   Their beauty shall waste away, ♦
       and the land of the dead shall be their dwelling.

16   But God shall ransom my soul; ♦
       from the grasp of death will he take me.

17   Be not afraid if some grow rich ♦
       and the glory of their house increases,

18   For they will carry nothing away when they die, ♦
       nor will their glory follow after them.

19   Though they count themselves happy while they live ♦
       and praise you for your success,

20   They shall enter the company of their ancestors ♦
       who will nevermore see the light.

21   Those who have honour, but lack understanding, ♦
       are like the beasts that perish.

1   The Lord, the most mighty God, has spoken ♦
    and called the world from the rising of the sun to its setting.

2   Out of Zion, perfect in beauty, God shines forth; ♦
    our God comes and will not keep silence.

3   Consuming fire goes out before him ♦
    and a mighty tempest stirs about him.

4   He calls the heaven above, ♦
    and the earth, that he may judge his people:

5   'Gather to me my faithful, ♦
    who have sealed my covenant with sacrifice.'

6   Let the heavens declare his righteousness, ♦
    for God himself is judge.

7   Hear, O my people, and I will speak: ♦
    'I will testify against you, O Israel;
        for I am God, your God.

8   'I will not reprove you for your sacrifices, ♦
    for your burnt offerings are always before me.

9   'I will take no bull out of your house, ♦
    nor he-goat out of your folds,

10 'For all the beasts of the forest are mine, ♦
    the cattle upon a thousand hills.

11 'I know every bird of the mountains ♦
    and the insect of the field is mine.

12 'If I were hungry, I would not tell you, ♦
    for the whole world is mine and all that fills it.

13 'Do you think I eat the flesh of bulls, ♦
    or drink the blood of goats?

14 'Offer to God a sacrifice of thanksgiving ♦
    and fulfil your vows to God Most High.

15 'Call upon me in the day of trouble; ♦
    I will deliver you and you shall honour me.'

16   But to the wicked, says God: ♦
      'Why do you recite my statutes
            and take my covenant upon your lips,

17   'Since you refuse to be disciplined ♦
      and have cast my words behind you?

18   'When you saw a thief, you made friends with him ♦
      and you threw in your lot with adulterers.

19   'You have loosed your lips for evil ♦
      and harnessed your tongue to deceit.

20   'You sit and speak evil of your brother; ♦
      you slander your own mother's son.

21   'These things have you done, and should I keep silence? ♦
      Did you think that I am even such a one as yourself?

22   'But no, I must reprove you, ♦
      and set before your eyes the things that you have done.

23   'You that forget God, consider this well, ♦
      lest I tear you apart and there is none to deliver you.

24   'Whoever offers me the sacrifice of thanksgiving honours me ♦
      and to those who keep my way
            will I show the salvation of God.'

Psalm 51

1   Have mercy on me, O God, in your great goodness; ♦
      according to the abundance of your compassion
            blot out my offences.

2   Wash me thoroughly from my wickedness ♦
      and cleanse me from my sin.

3   For I acknowledge my faults ♦
      and my sin is ever before me.

4   Against you only have I sinned ♦
      and done what is evil in your sight,

5   So that you are justified in your sentence ♦
      and righteous in your judgement.

6   I have been wicked even from my birth, ♦
      a sinner when my mother conceived me.

7   Behold, you desire truth deep within me ♦
and shall make me understand wisdom
    in the depths of my heart.

8   Purge me with hyssop and I shall be clean; ♦
wash me and I shall be whiter than snow.

9   Make me hear of joy and gladness, ♦
that the bones you have broken may rejoice.

10   Turn your face from my sins ♦
and blot out all my misdeeds.

11   Make me a clean heart, O God, ♦
and renew a right spirit within me.

12   Cast me not away from your presence ♦
and take not your holy spirit from me.

13   Give me again the joy of your salvation ♦
and sustain me with your gracious spirit;

14   Then shall I teach your ways to the wicked ♦
and sinners shall return to you.

15   Deliver me from my guilt, O God,
    the God of my salvation, ♦
and my tongue shall sing of your righteousness.

16   O Lord, open my lips ♦
and my mouth shall proclaim your praise.

17   For you desire no sacrifice, else I would give it; ♦
you take no delight in burnt offerings.

18   The sacrifice of God is a broken spirit; ♦
a broken and contrite heart, O God, you will not despise.

19   O be favourable and gracious to Zion; ♦
build up the walls of Jerusalem.

20   Then you will accept sacrifices offered in righteousness,
    the burnt offerings and oblations; ♦
then shall they offer up bulls on your altar.

1   Why do you glory in evil, you tyrant, ✦
    while the goodness of God endures continually?

2   You plot destruction, you deceiver; ✦
    your tongue is like a sharpened razor.

3   You love evil rather than good, ✦
    falsehood rather than the word of truth.

4   You love all words that hurt, ✦
    O you deceitful tongue.

5   Therefore God shall utterly bring you down; ✦
    he shall take you and pluck you out of your tent
        and root you out of the land of the living.

6   The righteous shall see this and tremble; ✦
    they shall laugh you to scorn, and say:

7   'This is the one who did not take God for a refuge, ✦
    but trusted in great riches and relied upon wickedness.'

8   But I am like a spreading olive tree in the house of God; ✦
    I trust in the goodness of God for ever and ever.

9   I will always give thanks to you for what you have done; ✦
    I will hope in your name,
        for your faithful ones delight in it.

Psalm 53

1   The fool has said in his heart, 'There is no God.' ✦
    Corrupt are they, and abominable in their wickedness;
        there is no one that does good.

2   God has looked down from heaven upon the children of earth, ✦
    to see if there is anyone who is wise and seeks after God.

3   They are all gone out of the way;
        all alike have become corrupt; ✦
    there is no one that does good, no not one.

4   Have they no knowledge, those evildoers, ♦
       who eat up my people as if they ate bread,
          and do not call upon God?

5   There shall they be in great fear,
          such fear as never was; ♦
       for God will scatter the bones of the ungodly.

6   They will be put to shame, ♦
       because God has rejected them.

7   O that Israel's salvation would come out of Zion! ♦
       When God restores the fortunes of his people
          then will Jacob rejoice and Israel be glad.

Psalm 54

1   Save me, O God, by your name ♦
       and vindicate me by your power.

2   Hear my prayer, O God; ♦
       give heed to the words of my mouth.

3   For strangers have risen up against me,
          and the ruthless seek after my life; ♦
       they have not set God before them.

4   Behold, God is my helper; ♦
       it is the Lord who upholds my life.

5   May evil rebound on those who lie in wait for me; ♦
       destroy them in your faithfulness.

6   An offering of a free heart will I give you ♦
       and praise your name, O Lord, for it is gracious.

7   For he has delivered me out of all my trouble, ♦
       and my eye has seen the downfall of my enemies.

1   Hear my prayer, O God; ♦
    hide not yourself from my petition.

2   Give heed to me and answer me; ♦
    I am restless in my complaining.

3   I am alarmed at the voice of the enemy ♦
    and at the clamour of the wicked;

4   For they would bring down evil upon me ♦
    and are set against me in fury.

5   My heart is disquieted within me, ♦
    and the terrors of death have fallen upon me.

6   Fearfulness and trembling are come upon me, ♦
    and a horrible dread has overwhelmed me.

7   And I said: 'O that I had wings like a dove, ♦
    for then would I fly away and be at rest.

8   'Then would I flee far away ♦
    and make my lodging in the wilderness.

9   'I would make haste to escape ♦
    from the stormy wind and tempest.'

10   Confuse their tongues, O Lord, and divide them, ♦
    for I have seen violence and strife in the city.

11   Day and night they go about on her walls; ♦
    mischief and trouble are in her midst.

12   Wickedness walks in her streets; ♦
    oppression and guile never leave her squares.

13   For it was not an open enemy that reviled me, ♦
    for then I could have borne it;

14   Nor was it my adversary that puffed himself up against me, ♦
    for then I would have hid myself from him.

15   But it was even you, one like myself, ♦
    my companion and my own familiar friend.

16   We took sweet counsel together ♦
    and walked with the multitude in the house of God.

17   Let death come suddenly upon them;
          let them go down alive to the Pit; ♦
      for wickedness inhabits their dwellings, their very hearts.

18   As for me, I will call upon God ♦
      and the Lord will deliver me.

19   In the evening and morning and at noonday
          I will pray and make my supplication, ♦
      and he shall hear my voice.

20   He shall redeem my soul in peace
          from the battle waged against me, ♦
      for many have come upon me.

21   God, who is enthroned of old,
          will hear and bring them down; ♦
      they will not repent, for they have no fear of God.

22   My companion stretched out his hands against his friend ♦
      and has broken his covenant;

23   His speech was softer than butter, though war was in his heart; ♦
      his words were smoother than oil, yet are they naked swords.

24   Cast your burden upon the Lord and he will sustain you, ♦
      and will not let the righteous fall for ever.

25   But those that are bloodthirsty and deceitful, O God, ♦
      you will bring down to the pit of destruction.

26   They shall not live out half their days, ♦
      but my trust shall be in you, O Lord.

1   Have mercy on me, O God, for they trample over me; ♦
    all day long they assault and oppress me.

2   My adversaries trample over me all the day long; ♦
    many are they that make proud war against me.

3   In the day of my fear I put my trust in you, ♦
    in God whose word I praise.

4   In God I trust, and will not fear, ♦
    for what can flesh do to me?

5   All day long they wound me with words; ♦
    their every thought is to do me evil.

6   They stir up trouble; they lie in wait; ♦
    marking my steps, they seek my life.

7   Shall they escape for all their wickedness? ♦
    In anger, O God, cast the peoples down.

8   You have counted up my groaning;
        put my tears into your bottle; ♦
    are they not written in your book?

9   Then shall my enemies turn back
        on the day when I call upon you; ♦
    this I know, for God is on my side.

10 In God whose word I praise,
        in the Lord whose word I praise, ♦
    in God I trust and will not fear:
        what can flesh do to me?

11 To you, O God, will I fulfil my vows; ♦
    to you will I present my offerings of thanks,

12 For you will deliver my soul from death
        and my feet from falling, ♦
    that I may walk before God in the light of the living.

1   Be merciful to me, O God, be merciful to me, ♦
      for my soul takes refuge in you;

2   In the shadow of your wings will I take refuge ♦
      until the storm of destruction has passed by.

3   I will call upon the Most High God, ♦
      the God who fulfils his purpose for me.

4   He will send from heaven and save me
         and rebuke those that would trample upon me; ♦
      God will send forth his love and his faithfulness.

5   I lie in the midst of lions, ♦
      people whose teeth are spears and arrows,
         and their tongue a sharp sword.

6   *Be exalted, O God, above the heavens,* ♦
      and your glory over all the earth.

7   They have laid a net for my feet;
         my soul is pressed down; ♦
      they have dug a pit before me
         and will fall into it themselves.

8   My heart is ready, O God, my heart is ready; ♦
      I will sing and give you praise.

9   Awake, my soul; awake, harp and lyre, ♦
      that I may awaken the dawn.

10   I will give you thanks, O Lord, among the peoples; ♦
      I will sing praise to you among the nations.

11   For your loving-kindness is as high as the heavens, ♦
      and your faithfulness reaches to the clouds.

12   *Be exalted, O God, above the heavens,* ♦
      and your glory over all the earth.

1   Do you indeed speak justly, you mighty? ♦
      Do you rule the peoples with equity?

2   With unjust heart you act throughout the land; ♦
      your hands mete out violence.

3   The wicked are estranged, even from the womb; ♦
      those who speak falsehood go astray from their birth.

4   They are as venomous as a serpent; ♦
      they are like the deaf adder which stops its ears,

5   Which does not heed the voice of the charmers, ♦
      and is deaf to the skilful weaver of spells.

6   Break, O God, their teeth in their mouths; ♦
      smash the fangs of these lions, O Lord.

7   Let them vanish like water that runs away; ♦
      let them wither like trodden grass.

8   Let them be as the slimy track of the snail, ♦
      like the untimely birth that never sees the sun.

9   Before ever their pots feel the heat of the thorns, ♦
      green or blazing, let them be swept away.

10   The righteous will be glad when they see God's vengeance; ♦
      they will bathe their feet in the blood of the wicked.

11   So that people will say,
        'Truly, there is a harvest for the righteous; ♦
      truly, there is a God who judges in the earth.'

Psalm 59

1   Rescue me from my enemies, O my God; ♦
      set me high above those that rise up against me.

2   Save me from the evildoers ♦
      and from murderous foes deliver me.

3   For see how they lie in wait for my soul ♦
      and the mighty stir up trouble against me.

4   Not for any fault or sin of mine, O Lord; ♦
      for no offence, they run and prepare themselves for war.

5   Rouse yourself, come to my aid and see; ♦
     for you are the Lord of hosts, the God of Israel.

6   Awake, and judge all the nations; ♦
     show no mercy to the evil traitors.

7   They return at nightfall and snarl like dogs ♦
     and prowl about the city.

8   They pour out evil words with their mouths;
          swords are on their lips; ♦
     'For who', they say, 'can hear us?'

9   But you laugh at them, O Lord; ♦
     you hold all the nations in derision.

10   For you, O my strength, will I watch; ♦
     you, O God, are my strong tower.

11   My God in his steadfast love will come to me; ♦
     he will let me behold the downfall of my enemies.

12   Slay them not, lest my people forget; ♦
     send them reeling by your might
          and bring them down, O Lord our shield.

13   For the sins of their mouth, for the words of their lips, ♦
     let them be taken in their pride.

14   For the cursing and falsehood they have uttered, ♦
     consume them in wrath, consume them till they are no more.

15   And they shall know that God rules in Jacob, ♦
     and to the ends of the earth.

16   And still they return at nightfall and snarl like dogs ♦
     and prowl about the city.

17   Though they forage for something to devour, ♦
     and howl if they are not filled,

18   Yet will I sing of your strength ♦
     and every morning praise your steadfast love;

19   For you have been my stronghold, ♦
     my refuge in the day of my trouble.

20   To you, O my strength, will I sing; ♦
     for you, O God, are my refuge,
          my God of steadfast love.

1   O God, you have cast us off and broken us; ♦
    you have been angry; restore us to yourself again.

2   You have shaken the earth and torn it apart; ♦
    heal its wounds, for it trembles.

3   You have made your people drink bitter things; ♦
    we reel from the deadly wine you have given us.

4   You have made those who fear you to flee, ♦
    to escape from the range of the bow.

5   That your beloved may be delivered, ♦
    save us by your right hand and answer us.

6   God has spoken in his holiness: ♦
    'I will triumph and divide Shechem,
        and share out the valley of Succoth.

7   'Gilead is mine and Manasseh is mine; ♦
    Ephraim is my helmet and Judah my sceptre.

8   'Moab shall be my washpot;
        over Edom will I cast my sandal; ♦
    across Philistia will I shout in triumph.'

9   Who will lead me into the strong city? ♦
    Who will bring me into Edom?

10 Have you not cast us off, O God? ♦
    Will you no longer go forth with our troops?

11 Grant us your help against the enemy, ♦
    for earthly help is in vain.

12 Through God will we do great acts, ♦
    for it is he that shall tread down our enemies.

Psalm 61

1   Hear my crying, O God, ♦
     and listen to my prayer.

2   From the end of the earth I call to you with fainting heart; ♦
     O set me on the rock that is higher than I.

3   For you are my refuge, ♦
     a strong tower against the enemy.

4   Let me dwell in your tent for ever ♦
     and take refuge under the cover of your wings.

5   For you, O God, will hear my vows; ♦
     you will grant the request of those who fear your name.

6   You will add length of days to the life of the king, ♦
     that his years may endure throughout all generations.

7   May he sit enthroned before God for ever; ♦
     may steadfast love and truth watch over him.

8   So will I always sing praise to your name, ♦
     and day by day fulfil my vows.

Psalm 62

1   On God alone my soul in stillness waits; ♦
     from him comes my salvation.

2   He alone is my rock and my salvation, ♦
     my stronghold, so that I shall never be shaken.

3   How long will all of you assail me to destroy me, ♦
     as you would a tottering wall or a leaning fence?

4   They plot only to thrust me down from my place of honour;
         lies are their chief delight; ♦
     they bless with their mouth, but in their heart they curse.

5   Wait on God alone in stillness, O my soul; ♦
     for in him is my hope.

6   He alone is my rock and my salvation, ♦
     my stronghold, so that I shall not be shaken.

7   In God is my strength and my glory; ♦
     God is my strong rock; in him is my refuge.

8   Put your trust in him always, my people; ♦
     pour out your hearts before him, for God is our refuge.

9   The peoples are but a breath,
        the whole human race a deceit; ♦
    on the scales they are altogether lighter than air.

10   Put no trust in oppression; in robbery take no empty pride; ♦
    though wealth increase, set not your heart upon it.

11   God spoke once, and twice have I heard the same, ♦
    that power belongs to God.

12   Steadfast love belongs to you, O Lord, ♦
    for you repay everyone according to their deeds.

Psalm 63

1   O God, you are my God; eagerly I seek you; ♦
    my soul is athirst for you.

2   My flesh also faints for you, ♦
    as in a dry and thirsty land where there is no water.

3   So would I gaze upon you in your holy place, ♦
    that I might behold your power and your glory.

4   Your loving-kindness is better than life itself ♦
    and so my lips shall praise you.

5   I will bless you as long as I live ♦
    and lift up my hands in your name.

6   My soul shall be satisfied, as with marrow and fatness, ♦
    and my mouth shall praise you with joyful lips,

7   When I remember you upon my bed ♦
    and meditate on you in the watches of the night.

8   For you have been my helper ♦
    and under the shadow of your wings will I rejoice.

9   My soul clings to you; ♦
    your right hand shall hold me fast.

10   But those who seek my soul to destroy it ♦
    shall go down to the depths of the earth;

11   Let them fall by the edge of the sword ♦
    and become a portion for jackals.

12   But the king shall rejoice in God;
        all those who swear by him shall be glad, ♦
    for the mouth of those who speak lies shall be stopped.

1   Hear my voice, O God, in my complaint; ♦
       preserve my life from fear of the enemy.

2   Hide me from the conspiracy of the wicked, ♦
       from the gathering of evildoers.

3   They sharpen their tongue like a sword ♦
       and aim their bitter words like arrows,

4   That they may shoot at the blameless from hiding places; ♦
       suddenly they shoot, and are not seen.

5   They hold fast to their evil course; ♦
       they talk of laying snares, saying, 'Who will see us?'

6   They search out wickedness and lay a cunning trap, ♦
       for deep are the inward thoughts of the heart.

7   But God will shoot at them with his swift arrow, ♦
       and suddenly they shall be wounded.

8   Their own tongues shall make them fall, ♦
       and all who see them shall wag their heads in scorn.

9   All peoples shall fear and tell what God has done, ♦
       and they will ponder all his works.

10   The righteous shall rejoice in the Lord
         and put their trust in him, ♦
       and all that are true of heart shall exult.

Psalm 65

1   Praise is due to you, O God, in Zion; ♦
       to you that answer prayer shall vows be paid.

2   To you shall all flesh come to confess their sins; ♦
       when our misdeeds prevail against us,
         you will purge them away.

3   Happy are they whom you choose
         and draw to your courts to dwell there. ♦
       We shall be satisfied with the blessings of your house,
         even of your holy temple.

4   With wonders you will answer us in your righteousness,
       O God of our salvation, ♦
    O hope of all the ends of the earth
       and of the farthest seas.

5   In your strength you set fast the mountains ♦
    and are girded about with might.

6   You still the raging of the seas, ♦
    the roaring of their waves
       and the clamour of the peoples.

7   Those who dwell at the ends of the earth
       tremble at your marvels; ♦
    the gates of the morning and evening sing your praise.

8   You visit the earth and water it; ♦
    you make it very plenteous.

9   The river of God is full of water; ♦
    you prepare grain for your people,
       for so you provide for the earth.

10   You drench the furrows and smooth out the ridges; ♦
    you soften the ground with showers and bless its increase.

11   You crown the year with your goodness, ♦
    and your paths overflow with plenty.

12   May the pastures of the wilderness flow with goodness ♦
    and the hills be girded with joy.

13   May the meadows be clothed with flocks of sheep ♦
    and the valleys stand so thick with corn
       that they shall laugh and sing.

Psalm 66

1   Be joyful in God, all the earth; ♦
    sing the glory of his name;
       sing the glory of his praise.

2   Say to God, 'How awesome are your deeds! ♦
    Because of your great strength
       your enemies shall bow before you.

3   'All the earth shall worship you, ♦
    sing to you, sing praise to your name.'

4   Come now and behold the works of God, ♦
    how wonderful he is in his dealings with humankind.

5   He turned the sea into dry land;
        the river they passed through on foot; ♦
    there we rejoiced in him.

6   In his might he rules for ever;
        his eyes keep watch over the nations; ♦
    let no rebel rise up against him.

7   Bless our God, O you peoples; ♦
    make the voice of his praise to be heard,

8   Who holds our souls in life ♦
    and suffers not our feet to slip.

9   For you, O God, have proved us; ♦
    you have tried us as silver is tried.

10 You brought us into the snare; ♦
    you laid heavy burdens upon our backs.

11 You let enemies ride over our heads;
        we went through fire and water; ♦
    but you brought us out into a place of liberty.

12 I will come into your house with burnt offerings
        and will pay you my vows, ♦
    which my lips uttered
        and my mouth promised when I was in trouble.

13 I will offer you fat burnt sacrifices
        with the smoke of rams; ♦
    I will sacrifice oxen and goats.

14 Come and listen, all you who fear God, ♦
    and I will tell you what he has done for my soul.

15 I called out to him with my mouth ♦
    and his praise was on my tongue.

16 If I had nursed evil in my heart, ♦
  the Lord would not have heard me,

17 But in truth God has heard me; ♦
  he has heeded the voice of my prayer.

18 Blessed be God, who has not rejected my prayer, ♦
  nor withheld his loving mercy from me.

Psalm 67

1 God be gracious to us and bless us ♦
  and make his face to shine upon us,

2 That your way may be known upon earth, ♦
  your saving power among all nations.

3 *Let the peoples praise you, O God; ♦*
  let all the peoples praise you.

4 O let the nations rejoice and be glad, ♦
  for you will judge the peoples righteously
   and govern the nations upon earth.

5 *Let the peoples praise you, O God; ♦*
  let all the peoples praise you.

6 Then shall the earth bring forth her increase, ♦
  and God, our own God, will bless us.

7 God will bless us, ♦
  and all the ends of the earth shall fear him.

Psalm 68

1 Let God arise and let his enemies be scattered; ♦
  let those that hate him flee before him.

2 As the smoke vanishes, so may they vanish away; ♦
  as wax melts at the fire,
   so let the wicked perish at the presence of God.

3 But let the righteous be glad and rejoice before God; ♦
  let them make merry with gladness.

4   Sing to God, sing praises to his name;
        exalt him who rides on the clouds. ♦
    The Lord is his name; rejoice before him.

5   Father of the fatherless, defender of widows, ♦
    God in his holy habitation!

6   God gives the solitary a home
        and brings forth prisoners to songs of welcome, ♦
    but the rebellious inhabit a burning desert.

7   O God, when you went forth before your people, ♦
    when you marched through the wilderness,

8   The earth shook and the heavens dropped down rain,
        at the presence of God, the Lord of Sinai, ♦
    at the presence of God, the God of Israel.

9   You sent down a gracious rain, O God; ♦
    you refreshed your inheritance when it was weary.

10 Your people came to dwell there; ♦
    in your goodness, O God, you provide for the poor.

11 The Lord gave the word;
        great was the company of women who bore the tidings: ♦
    'Kings and their armies they flee, they flee!'
        and women at home are dividing the spoil.

12 Though you stayed among the sheepfolds, ♦
    see now a dove's wings covered with silver
        and its feathers with green gold.

13 When the Almighty scattered the kings, ♦
    it was like snowflakes falling on Zalmon.

14 You mighty mountain, great mountain of Bashan! ♦
    You towering mountain, great mountain of Bashan!

15 Why look with envy, you towering mountains,
        at the mount which God has desired for his dwelling, ♦
    the place where the Lord will dwell for ever?

16 The chariots of God are twice ten thousand,
        even thousands upon thousands; ♦
    the Lord is among them, the Lord of Sinai in holy power.

17   You have gone up on high and led captivity captive; ♦
you have received tribute,
      even from those who rebelled,
      that you may reign as Lord and God.

18   Blessed be the Lord who bears our burdens day by day, ♦
for God is our salvation.

19   God is for us the God of our salvation; ♦
God is the Lord who can deliver from death.

20   God will smite the head of his enemies, ♦
the hairy scalp of those who walk in wickedness.

21   The Lord has said, 'From the heights of Bashan, ♦
from the depths of the sea will I bring them back,

22   'Till you dip your foot in blood ♦
and the tongue of your dogs has a taste of your enemies.'

23   We see your solemn processions, O God, ♦
your processions into the sanctuary, my God and my King.

24   The singers go before, the musicians follow after, ♦
in the midst of maidens playing on timbrels.

25   In your companies, bless your God; ♦
bless the Lord, you that are of the fount of Israel.

26   At the head there is Benjamin, least of the tribes,
      the princes of Judah in joyful company, ♦
the princes of Zebulun and Naphtali.

27   Send forth your strength, O God; ♦
establish, O God, what you have wrought in us.

28   For your temple's sake in Jerusalem ♦
kings shall bring their gifts to you.

29   Drive back with your word the wild beast of the reeds, ♦
the herd of the bull-like, the brutish hordes.

30   Trample down those who lust after silver; ♦
scatter the peoples that delight in war.

31   Vessels of bronze shall be brought from Egypt; ♦
Ethiopia will stretch out her hands to God.

32 Sing to God, you kingdoms of the earth; ♦
   make music in praise of the Lord;

33 He rides on the ancient heaven of heavens ♦
   and sends forth his voice, a mighty voice.

34 Ascribe power to God, whose splendour is over Israel, ♦
   whose power is above the clouds.

35 How terrible is God in his holy sanctuary, ♦
   the God of Israel, who gives power and strength to his people!
      Blessed be God.

Psalm 69

1 Save me, O God, ♦
   for the waters have come up, even to my neck.

2 I sink in deep mire where there is no foothold; ♦
   I have come into deep waters and the flood sweeps over me.

3 I have grown weary with crying; my throat is raw; ♦
   my eyes have failed from looking so long for my God.

4 Those who hate me without any cause ♦
   are more than the hairs of my head;

5 Those who would destroy me are mighty; ♦
   my enemies accuse me falsely:
      must I now give back what I never stole?

6 O God, you know my foolishness, ♦
   and my faults are not hidden from you.

7 Let not those who hope in you
      be put to shame through me, Lord God of hosts; ♦
   let not those who seek you be disgraced because of me,
      O God of Israel.

8 For your sake have I suffered reproach; ♦
   shame has covered my face.

9 I have become a stranger to my kindred, ♦
   an alien to my mother's children.

10 Zeal for your house has eaten me up; ♦
   the scorn of those who scorn you has fallen upon me.

11   I humbled myself with fasting, ♦
      but that was turned to my reproach.

12   I put on sackcloth also ♦
      and became a byword among them.

13   Those who sit at the gate murmur against me, ♦
      and the drunkards make songs about me.

14   But as for me, I make my prayer to you, O Lord; ♦
      at an acceptable time, O God.

15   Answer me, O God, in the abundance of your mercy ♦
      and with your sure salvation.

16   Draw me out of the mire, that I sink not; ♦
      let me be rescued from those who hate me
            and out of the deep waters.

17   Let not the water flood drown me,
            neither the deep swallow me up; ♦
      let not the Pit shut its mouth upon me.

18   Answer me, Lord, for your loving-kindness is good; ♦
      turn to me in the multitude of your mercies.

19   Hide not your face from your servant; ♦
      be swift to answer me, for I am in trouble.

20   Draw near to my soul and redeem me; ♦
      deliver me because of my enemies.

21   You know my reproach, my shame and my dishonour; ♦
      my adversaries are all in your sight.

22   Reproach has broken my heart; I am full of heaviness. ♦
      I looked for some to have pity, but there was no one,
            neither found I any to comfort me.

23   They gave me gall to eat, ♦
      and when I was thirsty, they gave me vinegar to drink.

24   Let the table before them be a trap ♦
      and their sacred feasts a snare.

25   Let their eyes be darkened, that they cannot see, ♦
      and give them continual trembling in their loins.

26   Pour out your indignation upon them, ♦
       and let the heat of your anger overtake them.

27   Let their camp be desolate, ♦
       and let there be no one to dwell in their tents.

28   For they persecute the one whom you have stricken, ♦
       and increase the sorrows of him whom you have pierced.

29   Lay to their charge guilt upon guilt, ♦
       and let them not receive your vindication.

30   Let them be wiped out of the book of the living ♦
       and not be written among the righteous.

31   As for me, I am poor and in misery; ♦
       your saving help, O God, will lift me up.

32   I will praise the name of God with a song; ♦
       I will proclaim his greatness with thanksgiving.

33   This will please the Lord more than an offering of oxen, ♦
       more than bulls with horns and hooves.

34   The humble shall see and be glad; ♦
       you who seek God, your heart shall live.

35   For the Lord listens to the needy, ♦
       and his own who are imprisoned he does not despise.

36   Let the heavens and the earth praise him, ♦
       the seas and all that moves in them;

37   For God will save Zion and rebuild the cities of Judah; ♦
       they shall live there and have it in possession.

38   The children of his servants shall inherit it, ♦
       and they that love his name shall dwell therein.

Psalm 70

1   O God, make speed to save me; ♦
       O Lord, make haste to help me.

2   Let those who seek my life
          be put to shame and confusion; ♦
       let them be turned back and disgraced
          who wish me evil.

3   Let those who mock and deride me ♦
    turn back because of their shame.

4   But let all who seek you rejoice and be glad in you; ♦
    let those who love your salvation say always, 'Great is the Lord!'

5   As for me, I am poor and needy; ♦
    come to me quickly, O God.

6   You are my help and my deliverer; ♦
    O Lord, do not delay.

Psalm 71

1   In you, O Lord, do I seek refuge; ♦
    let me never be put to shame.

2   In your righteousness, deliver me and set me free; ♦
    incline your ear to me and save me.

3   Be for me a stronghold to which I may ever resort; ♦
    send out to save me, for you are my rock and my fortress.

4   Deliver me, my God, from the hand of the wicked, ♦
    from the grasp of the evildoer and the oppressor.

5   For you are my hope, O Lord God, ♦
    my confidence, even from my youth.

6   Upon you have I leaned from my birth,
        when you drew me from my mother's womb; ♦
    my praise shall be always of you.

7   I have become a portent to many, ♦
    but you are my refuge and my strength.

8   Let my mouth be full of your praise ♦
    and your glory all the day long.

9   Do not cast me away in the time of old age; ♦
    forsake me not when my strength fails.

10 For my enemies are talking against me, ♦
    and those who lie in wait for my life take counsel together.

11 They say, 'God has forsaken him;
        pursue him and take him, ♦
    because there is none to deliver him.'

12 O God, be not far from me; ♦
come quickly to help me, O my God.

13 Let those who are against me
   be put to shame and disgrace; ♦
   let those who seek to do me evil
   be covered with scorn and reproach.

14 But as for me I will hope continually ♦
   and will praise you more and more.

15 My mouth shall tell of your righteousness
   and salvation all the day long, ♦
   for I know no end of the telling.

16 I will begin with the mighty works of the Lord God; ♦
   I will recall your righteousness, yours alone.

17 O God, you have taught me since I was young, ♦
   and to this day I tell of your wonderful works.

18 Forsake me not, O God,
   when I am old and grey-headed, ♦
   till I make known your deeds to the next generation
   and your power to all that are to come.

19 Your righteousness, O God, reaches to the heavens; ♦
   in the great things you have done, who is like you, O God?

20 What troubles and adversities you have shown me, ♦
   and yet you will turn and refresh me
   and bring me from the deep of the earth again.

21 Increase my honour; ♦
   turn again and comfort me.

22 Therefore will I praise you upon the harp
   for your faithfulness, O my God; ♦
   I will sing to you with the lyre, O Holy One of Israel.

23 My lips will sing out as I play to you, ♦
   and so will my soul, which you have redeemed.

24 My tongue also will tell of your righteousness all the day long, ♦
   for they shall be shamed and disgraced
   who sought to do me evil.

1   Give the king your judgements, O God, ♦
     and your righteousness to the son of a king.

2   Then shall he judge your people righteously ♦
     and your poor with justice.

3   May the mountains bring forth peace, ♦
     and the little hills righteousness for the people.

4   May he defend the poor among the people, ♦
     deliver the children of the needy and crush the oppressor.

5   May he live as long as the sun and moon endure, ♦
     from one generation to another.

6   May he come down like rain upon the mown grass, ♦
     like the showers that water the earth.

7   In his time shall righteousness flourish, ♦
     and abundance of peace
          till the moon shall be no more.

8   May his dominion extend from sea to sea ♦
     and from the River to the ends of the earth.

9   May his foes kneel before him ♦
     and his enemies lick the dust.

10   The kings of Tarshish and of the isles shall pay tribute; ♦
     the kings of Sheba and Seba shall bring gifts.

11   All kings shall fall down before him; ♦
     all nations shall do him service.

12   For he shall deliver the poor that cry out, ♦
     the needy and those who have no helper.

13   He shall have pity on the weak and poor; ♦
     he shall preserve the lives of the needy.

14   He shall redeem their lives from oppression and violence, ♦
     and dear shall their blood be in his sight.

15   Long may he live;
          unto him may be given gold from Sheba; ♦
     may prayer be made for him continually
          and may they bless him all the day long.

16 May there be abundance of grain on the earth,
  standing thick upon the hilltops; ♦
 may its fruit flourish like Lebanon
  and its grain grow like the grass of the field.

17 May his name remain for ever
  and be established as long as the sun endures; ♦
 may all nations be blest in him
  and call him blessed.

18 Blessed be the Lord, the God of Israel, ♦
 who alone does wonderful things.

19 And blessed be his glorious name for ever. ♦
 May all the earth be filled with his glory.
  Amen. Amen.

Psalm 73

1 Truly, God is loving to Israel, ♦
 to those who are pure in heart.

2 Nevertheless, my feet were almost gone; ♦
 my steps had well-nigh slipped.

3 For I was envious of the proud; ♦
 I saw the wicked in such prosperity;

4 For they suffer no pains ♦
 and their bodies are sleek and sound;

5 They come to no misfortune like other folk; ♦
 nor are they plagued as others are;

6 Therefore pride is their necklace ♦
 and violence wraps them like a cloak.

7 Their iniquity comes from within; ♦
 the conceits of their hearts overflow.

8 They scoff, and speak only of evil; ♦
 they talk of oppression from on high.

9 They set their mouth against the heavens, ♦
 and their tongue ranges round the earth;

10   And so the people turn to them ♦
      and find in them no fault.

11   They say, 'How should God know? ♦
      Is there knowledge in the Most High?'

12   Behold, these are the wicked; ♦
      ever at ease, they increase their wealth.

13   Is it in vain that I cleansed my heart ♦
      and washed my hands in innocence?

14   All day long have I been stricken ♦
      and chastened every morning.

15   If I had said, 'I will speak as they do,' ♦
      I should have betrayed the generation of your children.

16   Then thought I to understand this, ♦
      but it was too hard for me,

17   Until I entered the sanctuary of God ♦
      and understood the end of the wicked:

18   How you set them in slippery places; ♦
      you cast them down to destruction.

19   How suddenly do they come to destruction, ♦
      perish and come to a fearful end!

20   As with a dream when one awakes, ♦
      so, Lord, when you arise you will despise their image.

21   When my heart became embittered ♦
      and I was pierced to the quick,

22   I was but foolish and ignorant; ♦
      I was like a brute beast in your presence.

23   Yet I am always with you; ♦
      you hold me by my right hand.

24   You will guide me with your counsel ♦
      and afterwards receive me with glory.

25   Whom have I in heaven but you? ♦
      And there is nothing upon earth that I desire
         in comparison with you.

26   Though my flesh and my heart fail me, ♦
      God is the strength of my heart and my portion for ever.

27   Truly, those who forsake you will perish; ♦
       you will put to silence the faithless who betray you.

28   But it is good for me to draw near to God; ♦
       in the Lord God have I made my refuge,
          that I may tell of all your works.

Psalm 74

1   O God, why have you utterly disowned us? ♦
       Why does your anger burn
          against the sheep of your pasture?

2   Remember your congregation that you purchased of old, ♦
       the tribe you redeemed for your own possession,
          and Mount Zion where you dwelt.

3   Hasten your steps towards the endless ruins, ♦
       where the enemy has laid waste all your sanctuary.

4   Your adversaries roared in the place of your worship; ♦
       they set up their banners as tokens of victory.

5   Like men brandishing axes on high in a thicket of trees, ♦
       all her carved work they smashed down with hatchet and hammer.

6   They set fire to your holy place; ♦
       they defiled the dwelling place of your name
          and razed it to the ground.

7   They said in their heart, 'Let us make havoc of them altogether,' ♦
       and they burned down all the sanctuaries of God in the land.

8   There are no signs to see, not one prophet left, ♦
       not one among us who knows how long.

9   How long, O God, will the adversary scoff? ♦
       Shall the enemy blaspheme your name for ever?

10   Why have you withheld your hand ♦
       and hidden your right hand in your bosom?

11   Yet God is my king from of old, ♦
       who did deeds of salvation in the midst of the earth.

12   It was you that divided the sea by your might ♦
       and shattered the heads of the dragons on the waters;

13   You alone crushed the heads of Leviathan ♦
       and gave him to the beasts of the desert for food.

14   You cleft the rock for fountain and flood; ♦
       you dried up ever-flowing rivers.

15   Yours is the day, yours also the night; ♦
       you established the moon and the sun.

16   You set all the bounds of the earth; ♦
       you fashioned both summer and winter.

17   Remember now, Lord, how the enemy scoffed, ♦
       how a foolish people despised your name.

18   Do not give to wild beasts the soul of your turtle dove; ♦
       forget not the lives of your poor for ever.

19   Look upon your creation,
         for the earth is full of darkness, ♦
       full of the haunts of violence.

20   Let not the oppressed turn away ashamed, ♦
       but let the poor and needy praise your name.

21   Arise, O God, maintain your own cause; ♦
       remember how fools revile you all the day long.

22   Forget not the clamour of your adversaries, ♦
       the tumult of your enemies that ascends continually.

Psalm 75

1   We give you thanks, O God, we give you thanks, ♦
       for your name is near, as your wonderful deeds declare.

2   'I will seize the appointed time; ♦
       I, the Lord, will judge with equity.

3   'Though the earth reels and all that dwell in her, ♦
       it is I that hold her pillars steady.

4   'To the boasters I say, "Boast no longer," ♦
       and to the wicked, "Do not lift up your horn.

5   ' "Do not lift up your horn on high; ♦
       do not speak with a stiff neck." '

6   For neither from the east nor from the west, ♦
       nor yet from the wilderness comes exaltation.

7   But God alone is judge; ♦
       he puts down one and raises up another.

8   For in the hand of the Lord there is a cup, ♦
       well mixed and full of foaming wine.

9   He pours it out for all the wicked of the earth; ♦
       they shall drink it, and drain the dregs.

10   But I will rejoice for ever ♦
       and make music to the God of Jacob.

11   All the horns of the wicked will I break, ♦
       but the horns of the righteous shall be exalted.

Psalm 76

1   In Judah God is known; ♦
       his name is great in Israel.

2   At Salem is his tabernacle, ♦
       and his dwelling place in Zion.

3   There broke he the flashing arrows of the bow, ♦
       the shield, the sword and the weapons of war.

4   In the light of splendour you appeared, ♦
       glorious from the eternal mountains.

5   The boastful were plundered; they have slept their sleep; ♦
       none of the warriors can lift their hand.

6   At your rebuke, O God of Jacob, ♦
       both horse and chariot fell stunned.

7   Terrible are you in majesty: ♦
       who can stand before your face when you are angry?

8   You caused your judgement to be heard from heaven; ♦
       the earth trembled and was still,

9   When God arose to judgement, ♦
       to save all the meek upon earth.

10   You crushed the wrath of the peoples ♦
       and bridled the wrathful remnant.

11   Make a vow to the Lord your God and keep it; ♦
       let all who are round about him bring gifts
           to him that is worthy to be feared.

12   He breaks down the spirit of princes ♦
       and strikes terror in the kings of the earth.

Psalm 77

1   I cry aloud to God; ♦
       I cry aloud to God and he will hear me.

2   In the day of my trouble I have sought the Lord; ♦
       by night my hand is stretched out and does not tire;
           my soul refuses comfort.

3   I think upon God and I groan; ♦
       I ponder, and my spirit faints.

4   You will not let my eyelids close; ♦
       I am so troubled that I cannot speak.

5   I consider the days of old; ♦
       I remember the years long past;

6   I commune with my heart in the night; ♦
       my spirit searches for understanding.

7   Will the Lord cast us off for ever? ♦
       Will he no more show us his favour?

8   Has his loving mercy clean gone for ever? ♦
       Has his promise come to an end for evermore?

9   Has God forgotten to be gracious? ♦
       Has he shut up his compassion in displeasure?

10   And I said, 'My grief is this: ♦
       that the right hand of the Most High has lost its strength.'

11   I will remember the works of the Lord ♦
       and call to mind your wonders of old time.

12   I will meditate on all your works ♦
       and ponder your mighty deeds.

13   Your way, O God, is holy; ♦
       who is so great a god as our God?

14 You are the God who worked wonders ◆
and declared your power among the peoples.

15 With a mighty arm you redeemed your people, ◆
the children of Jacob and Joseph.

16 The waters saw you, O God;
the waters saw you and were afraid; ◆
the depths also were troubled.

17 The clouds poured out water; the skies thundered; ◆
your arrows flashed on every side;

18 The voice of your thunder was in the whirlwind;
your lightnings lit up the ground; ◆
the earth trembled and shook.

19 Your way was in the sea, and your paths in the great waters, ◆
but your footsteps were not known.

20 You led your people like sheep ◆
by the hand of Moses and Aaron.

Psalm 78

1 Hear my teaching, O my people; ◆
incline your ears to the words of my mouth.

2 I will open my mouth in a parable; ◆
I will pour forth mysteries from of old,

3 Such as we have heard and known, ◆
which our forebears have told us.

4 We will not hide from their children,
but will recount to generations to come, ◆
the praises of the Lord and his power
and the wonderful works he has done.

5 He laid a solemn charge on Jacob
and made it a law in Israel, ◆
which he commanded them to teach their children,

6 That the generations to come might know,
and the children yet unborn, ◆
that they in turn might tell it to their children;

7   So that they might put their trust in God ♦
    and not forget the deeds of God,
        but keep his commandments,

8   And not be like their forebears,
        a stubborn and rebellious generation, ♦
    a generation whose heart was not steadfast,
        and whose spirit was not faithful to God.

9   The people of Ephraim, armed with the bow, ♦
    turned back in the day of battle;

10   They did not keep the covenant of God ♦
    and refused to walk in his law;

11   They forgot what he had done ♦
    and the wonders he had shown them.

12   For he did marvellous things in the sight of their forebears, ♦
    in the land of Egypt, in the field of Zoan.

13   He divided the sea and let them pass through; ♦
    he made the waters stand still in a heap.

14   He led them with a cloud by day ♦
    and all the night through with a blaze of fire.

15   He split the hard rocks in the wilderness ♦
    and gave them drink as from the great deep.

16   He brought streams out of the rock ♦
    and made water gush out like rivers.

17   Yet for all this they sinned more against him ♦
    and defied the Most High in the wilderness.

18   They tested God in their hearts ♦
    and demanded food for their craving.

19   They spoke against God and said, ♦
    'Can God prepare a table in the wilderness?

20   'He struck the rock indeed, so that the waters gushed out
        and the streams overflowed, ♦
    but can he give bread or provide meat for his people?'

21   When the Lord heard this, he was full of wrath; ♦
    a fire was kindled against Jacob
        and his anger went out against Israel,

22 For they had no faith in God ♦
and put no trust in his saving help.

23 So he commanded the clouds above ♦
and opened the doors of heaven.

24 He rained down upon them manna to eat ♦
and gave them the grain of heaven.

25 So mortals ate the bread of angels; ♦
he sent them food in plenty.

26 He caused the east wind to blow in the heavens ♦
and led out the south wind by his might.

27 He rained flesh upon them as thick as dust ♦
and winged fowl like the sand of the sea.

28 He let it fall in the midst of their camp ♦
and round about their tents.

29 So they ate and were well filled, ♦
for he gave them what they desired.

30 But they did not stop their craving; ♦
their food was still in their mouths,

31 When the anger of God rose against them, ♦
and slew their strongest men
and felled the flower of Israel.

32 But for all this, they sinned yet more ♦
and put no faith in his wonderful works.

33 So he brought their days to an end like a breath ♦
and their years in sudden terror.

34 Whenever he slew them, they would seek him; ♦
they would repent and earnestly search for God.

35 They remembered that God was their rock ♦
and the Most High God their redeemer.

36 Yet they did but flatter him with their mouth ♦
and dissembled with their tongue.

37 Their heart was not steadfast towards him, ♦
neither were they faithful to his covenant.

38   But he was so merciful that he forgave their misdeeds
        and did not destroy them; ♦
    many a time he turned back his wrath
        and did not suffer his whole displeasure to be roused.

39   For he remembered that they were but flesh, ♦
    a wind that passes by and does not return.

40   How often they rebelled against him in the wilderness ♦
    and grieved him in the desert!

41   Again and again they tempted God ♦
    and provoked the Holy One of Israel.

42   They did not remember his power ♦
    in the day when he redeemed them from the enemy;

43   How he had wrought his signs in Egypt ♦
    and his wonders in the field of Zoan.

44   He turned their rivers into blood, ♦
    so that they could not drink of their streams.

45   He sent swarms of flies among them, which devoured them, ♦
    and frogs which brought them ruin.

46   He gave their produce to the caterpillar, ♦
    the fruit of their toil to the locust.

47   He destroyed their vines with hailstones ♦
    and their sycamore trees with the frost.

48   He delivered their cattle to hailstones ♦
    and their flocks to thunderbolts.

49   He set loose on them his blazing anger: ♦
    fury, displeasure and trouble,
        a troop of destroying angels.

50   He made a way for his anger
        and spared not their souls from death, ♦
    but gave their life over to the pestilence.

51   He smote the firstborn of Egypt, ♦
    the first fruits of their strength in the tents of Ham.

52   But he led out his people like sheep ♦
    and guided them in the wilderness like a flock.

53   He led them to safety and they were not afraid, ♦
        but the sea overwhelmed their enemies.

54   He brought them to his holy place, ♦
        the mountain which his right hand took in possession.

55   He drove out the nations before them
          and shared out to them their inheritance; ♦
        he settled the tribes of Israel in their tents.

56   Yet still they tested God Most High
          and rebelled against him, ♦
        and would not keep his commandments.

57   They turned back and fell away like their forebears, ♦
        starting aside like an unstrung bow.

58   They grieved him with their hill altars ♦
        and provoked him to displeasure with their idols.

59   God heard and was greatly angered, ♦
        and utterly rejected Israel.

60   He forsook the tabernacle at Shiloh, ♦
        the tent of his presence on earth.

61   He gave the ark of his strength into captivity, ♦
        his splendour into the adversary's hand.

62   He delivered his people to the sword ♦
        and raged against his inheritance.

63   The fire consumed their young men; ♦
        there was no one to lament their maidens.

64   Their priests fell by the sword, ♦
        and their widows made no lamentation.

65   Then the Lord woke as out of sleep, ♦
        like a warrior who had been overcome with wine.

66   He struck his enemies from behind ♦
        and put them to perpetual shame.

67   He rejected the tent of Joseph ♦
        and chose not the tribe of Ephraim,

68   But he chose the tribe of Judah ♦
        and the hill of Zion, which he loved.

69   And there he built his sanctuary like the heights of heaven, ♦
       like the earth which he founded for ever.

70   He chose David also, his servant, ♦
       and took him away from the sheepfolds.

71   From following the ewes with their lambs he took him, ♦
       that he might shepherd Jacob his people
           and Israel his inheritance.

72   So he shepherded them with a devoted heart ♦
       and with skilful hands he guided them.

Psalm 79

1   O God, the heathen have come into your heritage; ♦
       your holy temple have they defiled
           and made Jerusalem a heap of stones.

2   The dead bodies of your servants they have given
           to be food for the birds of the air, ♦
       and the flesh of your faithful to the beasts of the field.

3   Their blood have they shed like water
           on every side of Jerusalem, ♦
       and there was no one to bury them.

4   We have become the taunt of our neighbours, ♦
       the scorn and derision of those that are round about us.

5   Lord, how long will you be angry, for ever? ♦
       How long will your jealous fury blaze like fire?

6   Pour out your wrath upon the nations that have not known you, ♦
       and upon the kingdoms that have not called upon your name.

7   For they have devoured Jacob ♦
       and laid waste his dwelling place.

8   Remember not against us our former sins; ♦
       let your compassion make haste to meet us,
           for we are brought very low.

9   Help us, O God of our salvation, for the glory of your name; ♦
       deliver us, and wipe away our sins for your name's sake.

10   Why should the heathen say, ♦
       'Where is now their God?'

11   Let vengeance for your servants' blood that is shed ♦
        be known among the nations in our sight.

12   Let the sorrowful sighing of the prisoners come before you, ♦
        and by your mighty arm
            preserve those who are condemned to die.

13   May the taunts with which our neighbours taunted you, Lord, ♦
        return sevenfold into their bosom.

14   But we that are your people and the sheep of your pasture
            will give you thanks for ever, ♦
        and tell of your praise from generation to generation.

Psalm 80

1   Hear, O Shepherd of Israel, ♦
        you that led Joseph like a flock;

2   Shine forth, you that are enthroned upon the cherubim, ♦
        before Ephraim, Benjamin and Manasseh.

3   Stir up your mighty strength ♦
        and come to our salvation.

4   *Turn us again, O God; ♦*
        show the light of your countenance, and we shall be saved.

5   O Lord God of hosts, ♦
        how long will you be angry at your people's prayer?

6   You feed them with the bread of tears; ♦
        you give them abundance of tears to drink.

7   You have made us the derision of our neighbours, ♦
        and our enemies laugh us to scorn.

8   *Turn us again, O God of hosts; ♦*
        show the light of your countenance, and we shall be saved.

9   You brought a vine out of Egypt; ♦
        you drove out the nations and planted it.

10   You made room around it, ♦
        and when it had taken root, it filled the land.

11   The hills were covered with its shadow ♦
      and the cedars of God by its boughs.

12   It stretched out its branches to the Sea ♦
      and its tendrils to the River.

13   Why then have you broken down its wall, ♦
      so that all who pass by pluck off its grapes?

14   The wild boar out of the wood tears it off, ♦
      and all the insects of the field devour it.

15   Turn again, O God of hosts, ♦
      look down from heaven and behold;

16   Cherish this vine which your right hand has planted, ♦
      and the branch that you made so strong for yourself.

17   Let those who burnt it with fire, who cut it down, ♦
      perish at the rebuke of your countenance.

18   Let your hand be upon the man at your right hand, ♦
      the son of man you made so strong for yourself.

19   And so will we not go back from you; ♦
      give us life, and we shall call upon your name.

20   *Turn us again, O Lord God of hosts; ♦*
      show the light of your countenance, and we shall be saved.

Psalm 81

1   Sing merrily to God our strength, ♦
      shout for joy to the God of Jacob.

2   Take up the song and sound the timbrel, ♦
      the tuneful lyre with the harp.

3   Blow the trumpet at the new moon, ♦
      as at the full moon, upon our solemn feast day.

4   For this is a statute for Israel, ♦
      a law of the God of Jacob,

5   The charge he laid on the people of Joseph, ♦
      when they came out of the land of Egypt.

6   I heard a voice I did not know, that said: ♦
    'I eased their shoulder from the burden;
        their hands were set free from bearing the load.

7   'You called upon me in trouble and I delivered you; ♦
    I answered you from the secret place of thunder
        and proved you at the waters of Meribah.

8   'Hear, O my people, and I will admonish you: ♦
    O Israel, if you would but listen to me!

9   'There shall be no strange god among you; ♦
    you shall not worship a foreign god.

10 'I am the Lord your God,
        who brought you up from the land of Egypt; ♦
    open your mouth wide and I shall fill it.'

11 But my people would not hear my voice ♦
    and Israel would not obey me.

12 So I sent them away in the stubbornness of their hearts, ♦
    and let them walk after their own counsels.

13 O that my people would listen to me, ♦
    that Israel would walk in my ways!

14 Then I should soon put down their enemies ♦
    and turn my hand against their adversaries.

15 Those who hate the Lord would be humbled before him, ♦
    and their punishment would last for ever.

16 But Israel would I feed with the finest wheat ♦
    and with honey from the rock would I satisfy them.

Psalm 82

1   God has taken his stand in the council of heaven; ♦
    in the midst of the gods he gives judgement:

2   'How long will you judge unjustly ♦
    and show such favour to the wicked?

3   'You were to judge the weak and the orphan; ♦
    defend the right of the humble and needy;

4 'Rescue the weak and the poor; ♦
   deliver them from the hand of the wicked.

5 'They have no knowledge or wisdom;
       they walk on still in darkness: ♦
   all the foundations of the earth are shaken.

6 'Therefore I say that though you are gods ♦
   and all of you children of the Most High,

7 'Nevertheless, you shall die like mortals ♦
   and fall like one of their princes.'

8 Arise, O God and judge the earth, ♦
   for it is you that shall take all nations for your possession.

Psalm 83

1 Hold not your peace, O God, do not keep silent; ♦
   be not unmoved, O God;

2 For your enemies are in tumult ♦
   and those who hate you lift up their heads.

3 They take secret counsel against your people ♦
   and plot against those whom you treasure.

4 They say, 'Come, let us destroy them as a nation, ♦
   that the name of Israel be remembered no more.'

5 They have conspired together with one mind; ♦
   they are in league against you:

6 The tents of Edom and the Ishmaelites, ♦
   Moab and the Hagarenes,

7 Gebal and Ammon and Amalek, ♦
   the Philistines and those who dwell in Tyre.

8 Ashur also has joined them ♦
   and has lent a strong arm to the children of Lot.

9 Do to them as you did to Midian, ♦
   to Sisera and to Jabin at the river of Kishon,

10 Who perished at Endor ♦
   and became as dung for the earth.

11 Make their commanders like Oreb and Zeëb, ♦
   and all their princes like Zebah and Zalmunna,

12   Who said, 'Let us take for ourselves ♦
      the pastures of God as our possession.'

13   O my God, make them like thistledown, ♦
      like chaff before the wind.

14   Like fire that consumes a forest, ♦
      like the flame that sets mountains ablaze,

15   So drive them with your tempest ♦
      and dismay them with your storm.

16   Cover their faces with shame, O Lord, ♦
      that they may seek your name.

17   Let them be disgraced and dismayed for ever; ♦
      let them be put to confusion and perish;

18   And they shall know that you, whose name is the Lord, ♦
      are alone the Most High over all the earth.

Psalm 84

1   How lovely is your dwelling place, O Lord of hosts! ♦
      My soul has a desire and longing to enter the courts of the Lord;
         my heart and my flesh rejoice in the living God.

2   The sparrow has found her a house
         and the swallow a nest where she may lay her young: ♦
      at your altars, O Lord of hosts, my King and my God.

3   Blessed are they who dwell in your house: ♦
      they will always be praising you.

4   Blessed are those whose strength is in you, ♦
      in whose heart are the highways to Zion,

5   Who going through the barren valley find there a spring, ♦
      and the early rains will clothe it with blessing.

6   They will go from strength to strength ♦
      and appear before God in Zion.

7   O Lord God of hosts, hear my prayer; ♦
      listen, O God of Jacob.

8   Behold our defender, O God, ♦
      and look upon the face of your anointed.

9   For one day in your courts ♦
    is better than a thousand.

10 I would rather be a doorkeeper in the house of my God ♦
    than dwell in the tents of ungodliness.

11 For the Lord God is both sun and shield;
        he will give grace and glory; ♦
    no good thing shall the Lord withhold
        from those who walk with integrity.

12 O Lord God of hosts, ♦
    blessed are those who put their trust in you.

Psalm 85

1   Lord, you were gracious to your land; ♦
    you restored the fortunes of Jacob.

2   You forgave the offence of your people ♦
    and covered all their sins.

3   You laid aside all your fury ♦
    and turned from your wrathful indignation.

4   Restore us again, O God our Saviour, ♦
    and let your anger cease from us.

5   Will you be displeased with us for ever? ♦
    Will you stretch out your wrath from one generation to another?

6   Will you not give us life again, ♦
    that your people may rejoice in you?

7   Show us your mercy, O Lord, ♦
    and grant us your salvation.

8   I will listen to what the Lord God will say, ♦
    for he shall speak peace to his people and to the faithful,
        that they turn not again to folly.

9   Truly, his salvation is near to those who fear him, ♦
    that his glory may dwell in our land.

10 Mercy and truth are met together, ♦
    righteousness and peace have kissed each other;

11   Truth shall spring up from the earth ♦
        and righteousness look down from heaven.

12   The Lord will indeed give all that is good, ♦
        and our land will yield its increase.

13   Righteousness shall go before him ♦
        and direct his steps in the way.

Psalm 86

1   Incline your ear, O Lord, and answer me, ♦
        for I am poor and in misery.

2   Preserve my soul, for I am faithful; ♦
        save your servant, for I put my trust in you.

3   Be merciful to me, O Lord, for you are my God; ♦
        I call upon you all the day long.

4   Gladden the soul of your servant, ♦
        for to you, O Lord, I lift up my soul.

5   For you, Lord, are good and forgiving, ♦
        abounding in steadfast love to all who call upon you.

6   Give ear, O Lord, to my prayer ♦
        and listen to the voice of my supplication.

7   In the day of my distress I will call upon you, ♦
        for you will answer me.

8   Among the gods there is none like you, O Lord, ♦
        nor any works like yours.

9   All nations you have made shall come and worship you, O Lord, ♦
        and shall glorify your name.

10   For you are great and do wonderful things; ♦
        you alone are God.

11   Teach me your way, O Lord, and I will walk in your truth; ♦
        knit my heart to you, that I may fear your name.

12   I will thank you, O Lord my God, with all my heart, ♦
        and glorify your name for evermore;

13   For great is your steadfast love towards me, ♦
        for you have delivered my soul from the depths of the grave.

14 O God, the proud rise up against me
　　and a ruthless horde seek after my life; ◆
they have not set you before their eyes.

15 But you, Lord, are gracious and full of compassion, ◆
slow to anger and full of kindness and truth.

16 Turn to me and have mercy upon me; ◆
give your strength to your servant
　　and save the child of your handmaid.

17 Show me a token of your favour,
　　that those who hate me may see it and be ashamed; ◆
because you, O Lord, have helped and comforted me.

Psalm 87

1 His foundation is on the holy mountains. ◆
The Lord loves the gates of Zion
　　more than all the dwellings of Jacob.

2 Glorious things are spoken of you, ◆
Zion, city of our God.

3 I record Egypt and Babylon as those who know me; ◆
behold Philistia, Tyre and Ethiopia:
　　in Zion were they born.

4 And of Zion it shall be said, 'Each one was born in her, ◆
and the Most High himself has established her.'

5 The Lord will record as he writes up the peoples, ◆
'This one also was born there.'

6 And as they dance they shall sing, ◆
'All my fresh springs are in you.'

1   O Lord, God of my salvation, ♦
    I have cried day and night before you.

2   Let my prayer come into your presence; ♦
    incline your ear to my cry.

3   For my soul is full of troubles; ♦
    my life draws near to the land of death.

4   I am counted as one gone down to the Pit; ♦
    I am like one that has no strength,

5   Lost among the dead, ♦
    like the slain who lie in the grave,

6   Whom you remember no more, ♦
    for they are cut off from your hand.

7   You have laid me in the lowest pit, ♦
    in a place of darkness in the abyss.

8   Your anger lies heavy upon me, ♦
    and you have afflicted me with all your waves.

9   You have put my friends far from me ♦
    and made me to be abhorred by them.

10   I am so fast in prison that I cannot get free; ♦
    my eyes fail from all my trouble.

11   Lord, I have called daily upon you; ♦
    I have stretched out my hands to you.

12   Do you work wonders for the dead? ♦
    Will the shades stand up and praise you?

13   Shall your loving-kindness be declared in the grave, ♦
    your faithfulness in the land of destruction?

14   Shall your wonders be known in the dark ♦
    or your righteous deeds in the land where all is forgotten?

15   But as for me, O Lord, I will cry to you; ♦
    early in the morning my prayer shall come before you.

16   Lord, why have you rejected my soul? ♦
    Why have you hidden your face from me?

17   I have been wretched and at the point of death from my youth; ♦
     I suffer your terrors and am no more seen.

18   Your wrath sweeps over me; ♦
     your horrors are come to destroy me;

19   All day long they come about me like water; ♦
     they close me in on every side.

20   Lover and friend have you put far from me ♦
     and hid my companions out of my sight.

Psalm 89

1   My song shall be always of the loving-kindness of the Lord: ♦
     with my mouth will I proclaim your faithfulness
          throughout all generations.

2   I will declare that your love is established for ever; ♦
     you have set your faithfulness as firm as the heavens.

3   For you said: 'I have made a covenant with my chosen one; ♦
     I have sworn an oath to David my servant:

4   ' "Your seed will I establish for ever ♦
     and build up your throne for all generations." '

5   The heavens praise your wonders, O Lord, ♦
     and your faithfulness in the assembly of the holy ones;

6   For who among the clouds can be compared to the Lord? ♦
     Who is like the Lord among the host of heaven?

7   A God feared in the council of the holy ones, ♦
     great and terrible above all those round about him.

8   Who is like you, Lord God of hosts? ♦
     Mighty Lord, your faithfulness is all around you.

9   You rule the raging of the sea; ♦
     you still its waves when they arise.

10   You crushed Rahab with a deadly wound ♦
     and scattered your enemies with your mighty arm.

11   Yours are the heavens; the earth also is yours; ♦
     you established the world and all that fills it.

12   You created the north and the south; ♦
       Tabor and Hermon rejoice in your name.

13   You have a mighty arm; ♦
       strong is your hand and high is your right hand.

14   Righteousness and justice are the foundation of your throne; ♦
       steadfast love and faithfulness go before your face.

15   Happy are the people who know the shout of triumph: ♦
       they walk, O Lord, in the light of your countenance.

16   In your name they rejoice all the day long ♦
       and are exalted in your righteousness.

17   For you are the glory of their strength, ♦
       and in your favour you lift up our heads.

18   Truly the Lord is our shield; ♦
       the Holy One of Israel is our king.

19   You spoke once in a vision and said to your faithful people: ♦
       'I have set a youth above the mighty;
          I have raised a young man over the people.

20   'I have found David my servant; ♦
       with my holy oil have I anointed him.

21   'My hand shall hold him fast ♦
       and my arm shall strengthen him.

22   'No enemy shall deceive him, ♦
       nor any wicked person afflict him.

23   'I will strike down his foes before his face ♦
       and beat down those that hate him.

24   'My truth also and my steadfast love shall be with him, ♦
       and in my name shall his head be exalted.

25   'I will set his dominion upon the sea ♦
       and his right hand upon the rivers.

26   'He shall call to me, "You are my Father, ♦
       my God, and the rock of my salvation;"

27   'And I will make him my firstborn, ♦
       the most high above the kings of the earth.

28   'The love I have pledged to him will I keep for ever, ♦
       and my covenant will stand fast with him.

29 'His seed also will I make to endure for ever ♦
   and his throne as the days of heaven.

30 'But if his children forsake my law ♦
   and cease to walk in my judgements,

31 'If they break my statutes ♦
   and do not keep my commandments,

32 'I will punish their offences with a rod ♦
   and their sin with scourges.

33 'But I will not take from him my steadfast love ♦
   nor suffer my truth to fail.

34 'My covenant will I not break ♦
   nor alter what has gone out of my lips.

35 'Once for all have I sworn by my holiness ♦
   that I will not prove false to David.

36 'His seed shall endure for ever ♦
   and his throne as the sun before me;

37 'It shall stand fast for ever as the moon, ♦
   the enduring witness in the heavens.'

38 But you have cast off and rejected your anointed; ♦
   you have shown fierce anger against him.

39 You have broken the covenant with your servant, ♦
   and have cast his crown to the dust.

40 You have broken down all his walls ♦
   and laid his strongholds in ruins.

41 All who pass by despoil him, ♦
   and he has become the scorn of his neighbours.

42 You have exalted the right hand of his foes ♦
   and made all his enemies rejoice.

43 You have turned back the edge of his sword ♦
   and have not upheld him in battle.

44 You have made an end of his radiance ♦
   and cast his throne to the ground.

45 You have cut short the days of his youth ♦
   and have covered him with shame.

46　How long will you hide yourself so utterly, O Lord? ◆
　　How long shall your anger burn like fire?

47　Remember how short my time is, ◆
　　how frail you have made all mortal flesh.

48　Which of the living shall not see death, ◆
　　and shall deliver their soul from the power of darkness?

49　Where, O Lord, is your steadfast love of old, ◆
　　which you swore to David in your faithfulness?

50　Remember, O Lord, how your servant is scorned, ◆
　　how I bear in my bosom the taunts of many peoples,

51　While your enemies mock, O Lord, ◆
　　while they mock the footsteps of your anointed.

52　Blessed be the Lord for evermore. ◆
　　Amen and Amen.

Psalm 90

1　Lord, you have been our refuge ◆
　　from one generation to another.

2　Before the mountains were brought forth,
　　　　or the earth and the world were formed, ◆
　　from everlasting to everlasting you are God.

3　You turn us back to dust and say: ◆
　　'Turn back, O children of earth.'

4　For a thousand years in your sight are but as yesterday, ◆
　　which passes like a watch in the night.

5　You sweep them away like a dream; ◆
　　they fade away suddenly like the grass.

6　In the morning it is green and flourishes; ◆
　　in the evening it is dried up and withered.

7　For we consume away in your displeasure; ◆
　　we are afraid at your wrathful indignation.

8　You have set our misdeeds before you ◆
　　and our secret sins in the light of your countenance.

9   When you are angry, all our days are gone; ♦
       our years come to an end like a sigh.

10   The days of our life are three score years and ten,
          or if our strength endures, even four score; ♦
       yet the sum of them is but labour and sorrow,
          for they soon pass away and we are gone.

11   Who regards the power of your wrath ♦
       and your indignation like those who fear you?

12   So teach us to number our days ♦
       that we may apply our hearts to wisdom.

13   Turn again, O Lord; how long will you delay? ♦
       Have compassion on your servants.

14   Satisfy us with your loving-kindness in the morning, ♦
       that we may rejoice and be glad all our days.

15   Give us gladness for the days you have afflicted us, ♦
       and for the years in which we have seen adversity.

16   Show your servants your works, ♦
       and let your glory be over their children.

17   May the gracious favour of the Lord our God be upon us; ♦
       prosper our handiwork; O prosper the work of our hands.

Psalm 91

1   Whoever dwells in the shelter of the Most High ♦
       and abides under the shadow of the Almighty,

2   Shall say to the Lord, 'My refuge and my stronghold, ♦
       my God, in whom I put my trust.'

3   For he shall deliver you from the snare of the fowler ♦
       and from the deadly pestilence.

4   He shall cover you with his wings
          and you shall be safe under his feathers; ♦
       his faithfulness shall be your shield and buckler.

5   You shall not be afraid of any terror by night, ♦
       nor of the arrow that flies by day;

6   Of the pestilence that stalks in darkness, ♦
       nor of the sickness that destroys at noonday.

7   Though a thousand fall at your side
         and ten thousand at your right hand, ♦
     yet it shall not come near you.

8   Your eyes have only to behold ♦
     to see the reward of the wicked.

9   Because you have made the Lord your refuge ♦
     and the Most High your stronghold,

10   There shall no evil happen to you, ♦
     neither shall any plague come near your tent.

11   For he shall give his angels charge over you, ♦
     to keep you in all your ways.

12   They shall bear you in their hands, ♦
     lest you dash your foot against a stone.

13   You shall tread upon the lion and adder; ♦
     the young lion and the serpent you shall trample underfoot.

14   Because they have set their love upon me,
         therefore will I deliver them; ♦
     I will lift them up, because they know my name.

15   They will call upon me and I will answer them; ♦
     I am with them in trouble,
         I will deliver them and bring them to honour.

16   With long life will I satisfy them ♦
     and show them my salvation.

Psalm 92

1   It is a good thing to give thanks to the Lord ♦
     and to sing praises to your name, O Most High;

2   To tell of your love early in the morning ♦
     and of your faithfulness in the night-time,

3   Upon the ten-stringed instrument, upon the harp, ♦
     and to the melody of the lyre.

4   For you, Lord, have made me glad by your acts, ♦
     and I sing aloud at the works of your hands.

5   O Lord, how glorious are your works! ♦
     Your thoughts are very deep.

6   The senseless do not know, ♦
nor do fools understand,

7   That though the wicked sprout like grass ♦
and all the workers of iniquity flourish,

8   It is only to be destroyed for ever; ♦
but you, O Lord, shall be exalted for evermore.

9   For lo, your enemies, O Lord,
lo, your enemies shall perish, ♦
and all the workers of iniquity shall be scattered.

10   But my horn you have exalted
like the horns of wild oxen; ♦
I am anointed with fresh oil.

11   My eyes will look down on my foes; ♦
my ears shall hear the ruin of the evildoers
who rise up against me.

12   The righteous shall flourish like a palm tree, ♦
and shall spread abroad like a cedar of Lebanon.

13   Such as are planted in the house of the Lord ♦
shall flourish in the courts of our God.

14   They shall still bear fruit in old age; ♦
they shall be vigorous and in full leaf;

15   That they may show that the Lord is true; ♦
he is my rock,
and there is no unrighteousness in him.

1   The Lord is king and has put on glorious apparel; ♦
the Lord has put on his glory
    and girded himself with strength.

2   He has made the whole world so sure ♦
that it cannot be moved.

3   Your throne has been established from of old; ♦
you are from everlasting.

4   The floods have lifted up, O Lord,
    the floods have lifted up their voice; ♦
the floods lift up their pounding waves.

5   Mightier than the thunder of many waters,
    mightier than the breakers of the sea, ♦
the Lord on high is mightier.

6   Your testimonies are very sure; ♦
holiness adorns your house, O Lord, for ever.

Psalm 94

1   Lord God to whom vengeance belongs, ♦
O God to whom vengeance belongs, shine out in majesty.

2   Rise up, O Judge of the earth; ♦
give the arrogant their just deserts.

3   Lord, how long shall the wicked, ♦
how long shall the wicked triumph?

4   How long shall the evildoers boast ♦
and pour out such impudent words?

5   They crush your people, O Lord, ♦
and afflict your heritage.

6   They murder the widow and the stranger; ♦
the orphans they put to death.

7   And yet they say, 'The Lord will not see, ♦
neither shall the God of Jacob regard it.'

8   Consider, most stupid of people; ♦
you fools, when will you understand?

9   He that planted the ear, shall he not hear? ♦
     He that formed the eye, shall he not see?

10   He who corrects the nations, shall he not punish? ♦
     He who teaches the peoples, does he lack knowledge?

11   The Lord knows every human thought, ♦
     that they are but a breath.

12   Blessed are those whom you chasten, O Lord, ♦
     whom you instruct from your law;

13   That you may give them rest in days of adversity, ♦
     until a pit is dug for the wicked.

14   For the Lord will not fail his people, ♦
     neither will he forsake his inheritance.

15   For justice shall return to the righteous, ♦
     and all that are true of heart shall follow it.

16   Who will rise up for me against the wicked? ♦
     Who will take my part against the evildoers?

17   If the Lord had not helped me, ♦
     my soul would soon have been put to silence.

18   And when I said, 'My foot has slipped', ♦
     your loving mercy, O Lord, upheld me.

19   In the multitude of cares that troubled my heart, ♦
     your comforts have refreshed my soul.

20   Will you have anything to do with the throne of wickedness, ♦
     which fashions evil through its law?

21   They gather together against the life of the righteous ♦
     and condemn the innocent to death.

22   But the Lord has become my stronghold ♦
     and my God the rock of my trust.

23   He will turn against them their own wickedness
        and silence them through their own malice; ♦
     the Lord our God will put them to silence.

1   O come, let us sing to the Lord; ♦
       let us heartily rejoice in the rock of our salvation.

2   Let us come into his presence with thanksgiving ♦
       and be glad in him with psalms.

3   For the Lord is a great God ♦
       and a great king above all gods.

4   In his hand are the depths of the earth ♦
       and the heights of the mountains are his also.

5   The sea is his, for he made it, ♦
       and his hands have moulded the dry land.

6   Come, let us worship and bow down ♦
       and kneel before the Lord our Maker.

7   For he is our God; ♦
       we are the people of his pasture and the sheep of his hand.

8   O that today you would listen to his voice: ♦
       'Harden not your hearts as at Meribah,
          on that day at Massah in the wilderness,

9   'When your forebears tested me, and put me to the proof, ♦
       though they had seen my works.

10   'Forty years long I detested that generation and said, ♦
       "This people are wayward in their hearts;
          they do not know my ways."

11   'So I swore in my wrath, ♦
       "They shall not enter into my rest." '

1   Sing to the Lord a new song; ♦
    sing to the Lord, all the earth.

2   Sing to the Lord and bless his name; ♦
    tell out his salvation from day to day.

3   Declare his glory among the nations ♦
    and his wonders among all peoples.

4   For great is the Lord and greatly to be praised; ♦
    he is more to be feared than all gods.

5   For all the gods of the nations are but idols; ♦
    it is the Lord who made the heavens.

6   Honour and majesty are before him; ♦
    power and splendour are in his sanctuary.

7   Ascribe to the Lord, you families of the peoples; ♦
    ascribe to the Lord honour and strength.

8   Ascribe to the Lord the honour due to his name; ♦
    bring offerings and come into his courts.

9   O worship the Lord in the beauty of holiness; ♦
    let the whole earth tremble before him.

10 Tell it out among the nations that the Lord is king. ♦
    He has made the world so firm that it cannot be moved;
        he will judge the peoples with equity.

11 Let the heavens rejoice and let the earth be glad; ♦
    let the sea thunder and all that is in it;

12 Let the fields be joyful and all that is in them; ♦
    let all the trees of the wood shout for joy before the Lord.

13 For he comes, he comes to judge the earth; ♦
    with righteousness he will judge the world
        and the peoples with his truth.

Psalm 97

1 The Lord is king: let the earth rejoice; ♦
let the multitude of the isles be glad.

2 Clouds and darkness are round about him; ♦
righteousness and justice are the foundation of his throne.

3 Fire goes before him ♦
and burns up his enemies on every side.

4 His lightnings lit up the world; ♦
the earth saw it and trembled.

5 The mountains melted like wax at the presence of the Lord, ♦
at the presence of the Lord of the whole earth.

6 The heavens declared his righteousness, ♦
and all the peoples have seen his glory.

7 Confounded be all who worship carved images
and delight in mere idols. ♦
Bow down before him, all you gods.

8 Zion heard and was glad, and the daughters of Judah rejoiced, ♦
because of your judgements, O Lord.

9 For you, Lord, are most high over all the earth; ♦
you are exalted far above all gods.

10 The Lord loves those who hate evil; ♦
he preserves the lives of his faithful
and delivers them from the hand of the wicked.

11 Light has sprung up for the righteous ♦
and joy for the true of heart.

12 Rejoice in the Lord, you righteous, ♦
and give thanks to his holy name.

1   Sing to the Lord a new song, ♦
       for he has done marvellous things.

2   His own right hand and his holy arm ♦
       have won for him the victory.

3   The Lord has made known his salvation; ♦
       his deliverance has he openly shown in the sight of the nations.

4   He has remembered his mercy and faithfulness
          towards the house of Israel, ♦
       and all the ends of the earth have seen the salvation of our God.

5   Sound praises to the Lord, all the earth; ♦
       break into singing and make music.

6   Make music to the Lord with the lyre, ♦
       with the lyre and the voice of melody.

7   With trumpets and the sound of the horn ♦
       sound praises before the Lord, the King.

8   Let the sea thunder and all that fills it, ♦
       the world and all that dwell upon it.

9   Let the rivers clap their hands ♦
       and let the hills ring out together before the Lord,
          for he comes to judge the earth.

10   In righteousness shall he judge the world ♦
       and the peoples with equity.

1 The Lord is king: let the peoples tremble; ♦
he is enthroned above the cherubim: let the earth shake.

2 The Lord is great in Zion ♦
and high above all peoples.

3 Let them praise your name, which is great and awesome; ♦
the Lord our God is holy.

4 Mighty king, who loves justice,
you have established equity; ♦
you have executed justice and righteousness in Jacob.

5 *Exalt the Lord our God;* ♦
bow down before his footstool, for he is holy.

6 Moses and Aaron among his priests
and Samuel among those who call upon his name; ♦
they called upon the Lord and he answered them.

7 He spoke to them out of the pillar of cloud; ♦
they kept his testimonies and the law that he gave them.

8 You answered them, O Lord our God; ♦
you were a God who forgave them
and pardoned them for their offences.

9 *Exalt the Lord our God*
and worship him upon his holy hill, ♦
for the Lord our God is holy.

1 O be joyful in the Lord, all the earth; ♦
serve the Lord with gladness
and come before his presence with a song.

2 Know that the Lord is God; ♦
it is he that has made us and we are his;
we are his people and the sheep of his pasture.

3 Enter his gates with thanksgiving
and his courts with praise; ♦
give thanks to him and bless his name.

4 For the Lord is gracious; his steadfast love is everlasting, ♦
and his faithfulness endures from generation to generation.

1   I will sing of faithfulness and justice; ♦
to you, O Lord, will I sing.

2   Let me be wise in the way that is perfect: ♦
when will you come to me?

3   I will walk with purity of heart ♦
within the walls of my house.

4   I will not set before my eyes ♦
a counsel that is evil.

5   I abhor the deeds of unfaithfulness; ♦
they shall not cling to me.

6   A crooked heart shall depart from me; ♦
I will not know a wicked person.

7   One who slanders a neighbour in secret ♦
I will quickly put to silence.

8   Haughty eyes and an arrogant heart ♦
I will not endure.

9   My eyes are upon the faithful in the land, ♦
that they may dwell with me.

10   One who walks in the way that is pure ♦
shall be my servant.

11   There shall not dwell in my house ♦
one that practises deceit.

12   One who utters falsehood ♦
shall not continue in my sight.

13   Morning by morning will I put to silence ♦
all the wicked in the land,

14   To cut off from the city of the Lord ♦
all those who practise evil.

1   O Lord, hear my prayer ♦
   and let my crying come before you.

2   Hide not your face from me ♦
   in the day of my distress.

3   Incline your ear to me; ♦
   when I call, make haste to answer me,

4   For my days are consumed in smoke ♦
   and my bones burn away as in a furnace.

5   My heart is smitten down and withered like grass, ♦
   so that I forget to eat my bread.

6   From the sound of my groaning ♦
   my bones cleave fast to my skin.

7   I am become like a vulture in the wilderness, ♦
   like an owl that haunts the ruins.

8   I keep watch and am become like a sparrow ♦
   solitary upon the housetop.

9   My enemies revile me all the day long, ♦
   and those who rage at me have sworn together against me.

10   I have eaten ashes for bread ♦
   and mingled my drink with weeping,

11   Because of your indignation and wrath, ♦
   for you have taken me up and cast me down.

12   My days fade away like a shadow, ♦
   and I am withered like grass.

13   But you, O Lord, shall endure for ever ♦
   and your name through all generations.

14   You will arise and have pity on Zion; ♦
   it is time to have mercy upon her;
      surely the time has come.

15   For your servants love her very stones ♦
   and feel compassion for her dust.

16   Then shall the nations fear your name, O Lord, ♦
       and all the kings of the earth your glory,

17   When the Lord has built up Zion ♦
       and shown himself in glory;

18   When he has turned to the prayer of the destitute ♦
       and has not despised their plea.

19   This shall be written for those that come after, ♦
       and a people yet unborn shall praise the Lord.

20   For he has looked down from his holy height; ♦
       from the heavens he beheld the earth,

21   That he might hear the sighings of the prisoner ♦
       and set free those condemned to die;

22   That the name of the Lord may be proclaimed in Zion ♦
       and his praises in Jerusalem,

23   When peoples are gathered together ♦
       and kingdoms also, to serve the Lord.

24   He has brought down my strength in my journey ♦
       and has shortened my days.

25   I pray, 'O my God, do not take me in the midst of my days; ♦
       your years endure throughout all generations.

26   'In the beginning you laid the foundations of the earth, ♦
       and the heavens are the work of your hands;

27   'They shall perish, but you will endure; ♦
       they all shall wear out like a garment.

28   'You change them like clothing, and they shall be changed; ♦
       but you are the same, and your years will not fail.

29   'The children of your servants shall continue, ♦
       and their descendants shall be established in your sight.'

1   Bless the Lord, O my soul, ♦
     and all that is within me bless his holy name.

2   Bless the Lord, O my soul, ♦
     and forget not all his benefits;

3   Who forgives all your sins ♦
     and heals all your infirmities;

4   Who redeems your life from the Pit ♦
     and crowns you with faithful love and compassion;

5   Who satisfies you with good things, ♦
     so that your youth is renewed like an eagle's.

6   The Lord executes righteousness ♦
     and judgement for all who are oppressed.

7   He made his ways known to Moses ♦
     and his works to the children of Israel.

8   The Lord is full of compassion and mercy, ♦
     slow to anger and of great kindness.

9   He will not always accuse us, ♦
     neither will he keep his anger for ever.

10   He has not dealt with us according to our sins, ♦
     nor rewarded us according to our wickedness.

11   For as the heavens are high above the earth, ♦
     so great is his mercy upon those who fear him.

12   As far as the east is from the west, ♦
     so far has he set our sins from us.

13   As a father has compassion on his children, ♦
     so is the Lord merciful towards those who fear him.

14   For he knows of what we are made; ♦
     he remembers that we are but dust.

15   Our days are but as grass; ♦
     we flourish as a flower of the field;

16   For as soon as the wind goes over it, it is gone, ♦
     and its place shall know it no more.

17   But the merciful goodness of the Lord is from of old
        and endures for ever on those who fear him, ♦
    and his righteousness on children's children;

18   On those who keep his covenant ♦
    and remember his commandments to do them.

19   The Lord has established his throne in heaven, ♦
    and his kingdom has dominion over all.

20   Bless the Lord, you angels of his, ♦
    you mighty ones who do his bidding
        and hearken to the voice of his word.

21   Bless the Lord, all you his hosts, ♦
    you ministers of his who do his will.

22   Bless the Lord, all you works of his,
        in all places of his dominion; ♦
    bless the Lord, O my soul.

Psalm 104

1   Bless the Lord, O my soul. ♦
    O Lord my God, how excellent is your greatness!

2   You are clothed with majesty and honour, ♦
    wrapped in light as in a garment.

3   You spread out the heavens like a curtain ♦
    and lay the beams of your dwelling place in the waters above.

4   You make the clouds your chariot ♦
    and ride on the wings of the wind.

5   You make the winds your messengers ♦
    and flames of fire your servants.

6   You laid the foundations of the earth, ♦
    that it never should move at any time.

7   You covered it with the deep like a garment; ♦
    the waters stood high above the hills.

8   At your rebuke they fled; ♦
    at the voice of your thunder they hastened away.

9   They rose up to the hills and flowed down to the valleys beneath, ♦
to the place which you had appointed for them.

10   You have set them their bounds that they should not pass, ♦
nor turn again to cover the earth.

11   You send the springs into the brooks, ♦
which run among the hills.

12   They give drink to every beast of the field, ♦
and the wild asses quench their thirst.

13   Beside them the birds of the air make their nests ♦
and sing among the branches.

14   You water the hills from your dwelling on high; ♦
the earth is filled with the fruit of your works.

15   You make grass to grow for the cattle ♦
and plants to meet our needs,

16   Bringing forth food from the earth ♦
and wine to gladden our hearts,

17   Oil to give us a cheerful countenance ♦
and bread to strengthen our hearts.

18   The trees of the Lord are full of sap, ♦
the cedars of Lebanon which he planted,

19   In which the birds build their nests, ♦
while the fir trees are a dwelling for the stork.

20   The mountains are a refuge for the wild goats ♦
and the stony cliffs for the conies.

21   You appointed the moon to mark the seasons, ♦
and the sun knows the time for its setting.

22   You make darkness that it may be night, ♦
in which all the beasts of the forest creep forth.

23   The lions roar for their prey ♦
and seek their food from God.

24   The sun rises and they are gone ♦
to lay themselves down in their dens.

25   People go forth to their work ♦
and to their labour until the evening.

26   O Lord, how manifold are your works! ♦
      In wisdom you have made them all;
         the earth is full of your creatures.

27   There is the sea, spread far and wide, ♦
      and there move creatures beyond number, both small and great.

28   There go the ships, and there is that Leviathan ♦
      which you have made to play in the deep.

29   All of these look to you ♦
      to give them their food in due season.

30   When you give it them, they gather it; ♦
      you open your hand and they are filled with good.

31   When you hide your face they are troubled; ♦
      when you take away their breath,
         they die and return again to the dust.

32   When you send forth your spirit, they are created, ♦
      and you renew the face of the earth.

33   May the glory of the Lord endure for ever; ♦
      may the Lord rejoice in his works;

34   He looks on the earth and it trembles; ♦
      he touches the mountains and they smoke.

35   I will sing to the Lord as long as I live; ♦
      I will make music to my God while I have my being.

36   So shall my song please him ♦
      while I rejoice in the Lord.

37   Let sinners be consumed out of the earth
         and the wicked be no more. ♦
      Bless the Lord, O my soul.
         Alleluia.

1   O give thanks to the Lord and call upon his name; ◆
make known his deeds among the peoples.

2   Sing to him, sing praises, ◆
and tell of all his marvellous works.

3   Rejoice in the praise of his holy name; ◆
let the hearts of them rejoice who seek the Lord.

4   Seek the Lord and his strength; ◆
seek his face continually.

5   Remember the marvels he has done, ◆
his wonders and the judgements of his mouth,

6   O seed of Abraham his servant, ◆
O children of Jacob his chosen.

7   He is the Lord our God; ◆
his judgements are in all the earth.

8   He has always been mindful of his covenant, ◆
the promise that he made for a thousand generations:

9   The covenant he made with Abraham, ◆
the oath that he swore to Isaac,

10   Which he established as a statute for Jacob, ◆
an everlasting covenant for Israel,

11   Saying, 'To you will I give the land of Canaan ◆
to be the portion of your inheritance.'

12   When they were but few in number, ◆
of little account, and sojourners in the land,

13   Wandering from nation to nation, ◆
from one kingdom to another people,

14   He suffered no one to do them wrong ◆
and rebuked even kings for their sake,

15   Saying, 'Touch not my anointed ◆
and do my prophets no harm.'

16   Then he called down famine over the land ◆
and broke every staff of bread.

17 But he had sent a man before them, ♦
   Joseph, who was sold as a slave.

18 They shackled his feet with fetters; ♦
   his neck was ringed with iron.

19 Until all he foretold came to pass, ♦
   the word of the Lord tested him.

20 The king sent and released him; ♦
   the ruler of peoples set him free.

21 He appointed him lord of his household ♦
   and ruler of all he possessed,

22 To instruct his princes as he willed ♦
   and to teach his counsellors wisdom.

23 Then Israel came into Egypt; ♦
   Jacob sojourned in the land of Ham.

24 And the Lord made his people exceedingly fruitful; ♦
   he made them too many for their adversaries,

25 Whose heart he turned, so that they hated his people ♦
   and dealt craftily with his servants.

26 Then sent he Moses his servant ♦
   and Aaron whom he had chosen.

27 He showed his signs through their word ♦
   and his wonders in the land of Ham.

28 He sent darkness and it grew dark; ♦
   yet they did not heed his words.

29 He turned their waters into blood ♦
   and slew all their fish.

30 Their land swarmed with frogs, ♦
   even in their kings' chambers.

31 He spoke the word, and there came clouds of flies, ♦
   swarms of gnats within all their borders.

32 He gave them hailstones for rain ♦
   and flames of lightning in their land.

33 He blasted their vines and their fig trees ♦
   and shattered trees across their country.

34   He spoke the word, and the grasshoppers came ♦
       and young locusts without number;

35   They ate every plant in their land ♦
       and devoured the fruit of their soil.

36   He smote all the firstborn in their land, ♦
       the first fruits of all their strength.

37   Then he brought them out with silver and gold; ♦
       there was not one among their tribes that stumbled.

38   Egypt was glad at their departing, ♦
       for a dread of them had fallen upon them.

39   He spread out a cloud for a covering ♦
       and a fire to light up the night.

40   They asked and he brought them quails; ♦
       he satisfied them with the bread of heaven.

41   He opened the rock, and the waters gushed out ♦
       and ran in the dry places like a river.

42   For he remembered his holy word ♦
       and Abraham, his servant.

43   So he brought forth his people with joy, ♦
       his chosen ones with singing.

44   He gave them the lands of the nations ♦
       and they took possession of the fruit of their toil,

45   That they might keep his statutes ♦
       and faithfully observe his laws.
           Alleluia.

Psalm 106

1   Alleluia.
       Give thanks to the Lord, for he is gracious, ♦
       for his faithfulness endures for ever.

2   Who can express the mighty acts of the Lord ♦
       or show forth all his praise?

3   Blessed are those who observe what is right ♦
       and always do what is just.

4   Remember me, O Lord, in the favour you bear for your people; ♦
        visit me in the day of your salvation;

5   That I may see the prosperity of your chosen
           and rejoice in the gladness of your people, ♦
        and exult with your inheritance.

6   We have sinned like our forebears; ♦
        we have done wrong and dealt wickedly.

7   In Egypt they did not consider your wonders,
           nor remember the abundance of your faithful love; ♦
        they rebelled against the Most High at the Red Sea.

8   But he saved them for his name's sake, ♦
        that he might make his power to be known.

9   He rebuked the Red Sea and it was dried up; ♦
        so he led them through the deep as through the wilderness.

10   He saved them from the adversary's hand ♦
        and redeemed them from the hand of the enemy.

11   As for those that troubled them, the waters overwhelmed them; ♦
        there was not one of them left.

12   Then they believed his words ♦
        and sang aloud his praise.

13   But soon they forgot his deeds ♦
        and would not wait for his counsel.

14   A craving seized them in the wilderness, ♦
        and they put God to the test in the desert.

15   He gave them their desire, ♦
        but sent a wasting sickness among them.

16   They grew jealous of Moses in the camp ♦
        and of Aaron, the holy one of the Lord.

17   So the earth opened and swallowed up Dathan ♦
        and covered the company of Abiram.

18   A fire was kindled in their company; ♦
        the flame burnt up the wicked.

19   They made a calf at Horeb ♦
        and worshipped the molten image;

20   Thus they exchanged their glory ♦
        for the image of an ox that feeds on hay.

21   They forgot God their saviour, ♦
        who had done such great things in Egypt,

22   Wonderful deeds in the land of Ham ♦
        and fearful things at the Red Sea.

23   So he would have destroyed them,
        had not Moses his chosen stood before him in the breach, ♦
        to turn away his wrath from consuming them.

24   Then they scorned the Promised Land ♦
        and would not believe his word,

25   But murmured in their tents ♦
        and would not heed the voice of the Lord.

26   So he lifted his hand against them ♦
        and swore to overthrow them in the wilderness,

27   To disperse their descendants among the nations, ♦
        and to scatter them throughout the lands.

28   They joined themselves to the Baal of Peor ♦
        and ate sacrifices offered to the dead.

29   They provoked him to anger with their evil deeds ♦
        and a plague broke out among them.

30   Then Phinehas stood up and interceded ♦
        and so the plague was stayed.

31   This was counted to him for righteousness ♦
        throughout all generations for ever.

32   They angered him also at the waters of Meribah, ♦
        so that Moses suffered for their sake;

33   For they so embittered his spirit ♦
        that he spoke rash words with his lips.

34   They did not destroy the peoples ♦
        as the Lord had commanded them.

35   They mingled with the nations ♦
        and learned to follow their ways,

36   So that they worshipped their idols, ♦
        which became to them a snare.

37   Their own sons and daughters ♦
      they sacrificed to evil spirits.

38   They shed innocent blood, ♦
      the blood of their sons and daughters,

39   Which they offered to the idols of Canaan, ♦
      and the land was defiled with blood.

40   Thus were they polluted by their actions, ♦
      and in their wanton deeds went whoring after other gods.

41   Therefore was the wrath of the Lord
            kindled against his people, ♦
      and he abhorred his inheritance.

42   He gave them over to the hand of the nations, ♦
      and those who hated them ruled over them.

43   So their enemies oppressed them ♦
      and put them in subjection under their hand.

44   Many a time did he deliver them,
            but they rebelled through their own devices ♦
      and were brought down through their wickedness.

45   Nevertheless, he saw their adversity, ♦
      when he heard their lamentation.

46   He remembered his covenant with them ♦
      and relented according to the greatness of his faithful love.

47   He made them also to be pitied ♦
      by all who had taken them captive.

48   Save us, O Lord our God,
            and gather us from among the nations, ♦
      that we may give thanks to your holy name
            and glory in your praise.

49   Blessed be the Lord, the God of Israel,
            from everlasting and to everlasting; ♦
      and let all the people say, Amen.
            Alleluia.

1   O give thanks to the Lord, for he is gracious, ♦
    for his steadfast love endures for ever.

2   Let the redeemed of the Lord say this, ♦
    those he redeemed from the hand of the enemy,

3   And gathered out of the lands
      from the east and from the west, ♦
    from the north and from the south.

4   Some went astray in desert wastes ♦
    and found no path to a city to dwell in.

5   Hungry and thirsty, ♦
    their soul was fainting within them.

6   So they cried to the Lord in their trouble ♦
    and he delivered them from their distress.

7   He set their feet on the right way ♦
    till they came to a city to dwell in.

8   *Let them give thanks to the Lord for his goodness* ♦
    and the wonders he does for his children.

9   *For he satisfies the longing soul* ♦
    and fills the hungry soul with good.

10   Some sat in darkness and in the shadow of death, ♦
    bound fast in misery and iron,

11   For they had rebelled against the words of God ♦
    and despised the counsel of the Most High.

12   So he bowed down their heart with heaviness; ♦
    they stumbled and there was none to help them.

13   Then they cried to the Lord in their trouble, ♦
    and he delivered them from their distress.

14   He brought them out of darkness and out of the shadow of death, ♦
    and broke their bonds asunder.

15   *Let them give thanks to the Lord for his goodness* ♦
    and the wonders he does for his children.

16   *For he has broken the doors of bronze* ♦
    and breaks the bars of iron in pieces.

17	Some were foolish and took a rebellious way, ♦
	and were plagued because of their wrongdoing.

18	Their soul abhorred all manner of food ♦
	and drew near to the gates of death.

19	Then they cried to the Lord in their trouble, ♦
	and he delivered them from their distress.

20	He sent forth his word and healed them, ♦
	and saved them from destruction.

21	*Let them give thanks to the Lord for his goodness* ♦
	and the wonders he does for his children.

22	*Let them offer him sacrifices of thanksgiving* ♦
	and tell of his acts with shouts of joy.

23	Those who go down to the sea in ships ♦
	and ply their trade in great waters,

24	These have seen the works of the Lord ♦
	and his wonders in the deep.

25	For at his word the stormy wind arose ♦
	and lifted up the waves of the sea.

26	They were carried up to the heavens
	and down again to the deep; ♦
	their soul melted away in their peril.

27	They reeled and staggered like a drunkard ♦
	and were at their wits' end.

28	Then they cried to the Lord in their trouble, ♦
	and he brought them out of their distress.

29	He made the storm be still ♦
	and the waves of the sea were calmed.

30	Then were they glad because they were at rest, ♦
	and he brought them to the haven they desired.

31	*Let them give thanks to the Lord for his goodness* ♦
	and the wonders he does for his children.

32	*Let them exalt him in the congregation of the people* ♦
	and praise him in the council of the elders.

33 The Lord turns rivers into wilderness ♦
and water springs into thirsty ground;

34 A fruitful land he makes a salty waste, ♦
because of the wickedness of those who dwell there.

35 He makes the wilderness a pool of water ♦
and water springs out of a thirsty land.

36 There he settles the hungry ♦
and they build a city to dwell in.

37 They sow fields and plant vineyards ♦
and bring in a fruitful harvest.

38 He blesses them, so that they multiply greatly; ♦
he does not let their herds of cattle decrease.

39 He pours contempt on princes ♦
and makes them wander in trackless wastes.

40 They are diminished and brought low, ♦
through stress of misfortune and sorrow,

41 But he raises the poor from their misery ♦
and multiplies their families like flocks of sheep.

42 The upright will see this and rejoice, ♦
but all wickedness will shut its mouth.

43 Whoever is wise will ponder these things ♦
and consider the loving-kindness of the Lord.

Psalm 108

1 My heart is ready, O God, my heart is ready; ♦
I will sing and give you praise.

2 Awake, my soul; awake, harp and lyre, ♦
that I may awaken the dawn.

3 I will give you thanks, O Lord, among the peoples; ♦
I will sing praise to you among the nations.

4 For your loving-kindness is as high as the heavens ♦
and your faithfulness reaches to the clouds.

5 Be exalted, O God, above the heavens ♦
and your glory over all the earth.

6   That your beloved may be delivered, ♦
      save us by your right hand and answer me.

7   God has spoken in his holiness: ♦
      'I will triumph and divide Shechem
         and share out the valley of Succoth.

8   'Gilead is mine and Manasseh is mine; ♦
      Ephraim is my helmet and Judah my sceptre.

9   'Moab shall be my washpot,
         over Edom will I cast my sandal, ♦
      across Philistia will I shout in triumph.'

10   Who will lead me into the strong city? ♦
      Who will bring me into Edom?

11   Have you not cast us off, O God? ♦
      Will you no longer go forth with our troops?

12   O grant us your help against the enemy, ♦
      for earthly help is in vain.

13   Through God will we do great acts, ♦
      for it is he that shall tread down our enemies.

Psalm 109

1   Keep silent no longer, O God of my praise, ♦
      for the mouth of wickedness and treachery
         is opened against me.

2   They have spoken against me with a lying tongue; ♦
      they encompassed me with words of hatred
         and fought against me without a cause.

3   In return for my love, they set themselves against me, ♦
      even though I had prayed for them.

4   Thus have they repaid me with evil for good, ♦
      and hatred for my good will.

5   They say, 'Appoint a wicked man over him, ♦
      and let an accuser stand at his right hand.

6   'When he is judged, let him be found guilty, ♦
      and let his prayer be counted as sin.

7   'Let his days be few ♦
and let another take his office.

8   'Let his children be fatherless ♦
and his wife become a widow.

9   'Let his children wander to beg their bread; ♦
let them seek it in desolate places.

10   'Let the creditor seize all that he has; ♦
let strangers plunder the fruit of his toil.

11   'Let there be no one to keep faith with him, ♦
or have compassion on his fatherless children.

12   'Let his line soon come to an end ♦
and his name be blotted out in the next generation.

13   'Let the wickedness of his fathers
        be remembered before the Lord, ♦
and no sin of his mother be blotted out;

14   'Let their sin be always before the Lord, ♦
that he may root out their name from the earth;

15   'Because he was not minded to keep faith, ♦
but persecuted the poor and needy
        and sought to kill the brokenhearted.

16   'He loved cursing and it came to him; ♦
he took no delight in blessing and it was far from him.

17   'He clothed himself with cursing as with a garment: ♦
it seeped into his body like water
        and into his bones like oil;

18   'Let it be to him like the cloak
        which he wraps around him ♦
and like the belt that he wears continually.'

19   Thus may the Lord repay my accusers ♦
and those who speak evil against me.

20   But deal with me, O Lord my God, according to your name; ♦
O deliver me, for sweet is your faithfulness.

21   For I am helpless and poor ♦
and my heart is disquieted within me.

22   I fade like a shadow that lengthens; ♦
         I am shaken off like a locust.

23   My knees are weak through fasting ♦
         and my flesh is dried up and wasted.

24   I have become a reproach to them; ♦
         those who see me shake their heads in scorn.

25   Help me, O Lord my God; ♦
         save me for your loving mercy's sake,

26   And they shall know that this is your hand, ♦
         that you, O Lord, have done it.

27   Though they curse, may you bless; ♦
         let those who rise up against me be confounded,
             but let your servant rejoice.

28   Let my accusers be clothed with disgrace ♦
         and wrap themselves in their shame as in a cloak.

29   I will give great thanks to the Lord with my mouth; ♦
         in the midst of the multitude will I praise him;

30   Because he has stood at the right hand of the needy, ♦
         to save them from those who would condemn them.

Psalm 110

1   The Lord said to my lord, 'Sit at my right hand, ♦
         until I make your enemies your footstool.'

2   May the Lord stretch forth the sceptre of your power; ♦
         rule from Zion in the midst of your enemies.

3   'Noble are you on this day of your birth; ♦
         on the holy mountain, from the womb of the dawn
             the dew of your new birth is upon you.'

4   The Lord has sworn and will not retract: ♦
         'You are a priest for ever after the order of Melchizedek.'

5   The king at your right hand, O Lord, ♦
         shall smite down kings in the day of his wrath.

6   In all his majesty, he shall judge among the nations, ♦
         smiting heads over all the wide earth.

7   He shall drink from the brook beside the way; ♦
         therefore shall he lift high his head.

1 Alleluia.
    I will give thanks to the Lord with my whole heart, ♦
in the company of the faithful and in the congregation.

2 The works of the Lord are great, ♦
sought out by all who delight in them.

3 His work is full of majesty and honour ♦
and his righteousness endures for ever.

4 He appointed a memorial for his marvellous deeds; ♦
the Lord is gracious and full of compassion.

5 He gave food to those who feared him; ♦
he is ever mindful of his covenant.

6 He showed his people the power of his works ♦
in giving them the heritage of the nations.

7 The works of his hands are truth and justice; ♦
all his commandments are sure.

8 They stand fast for ever and ever; ♦
they are done in truth and equity.

9 He sent redemption to his people;
    he commanded his covenant for ever; ♦
holy and awesome is his name.

10 The fear of the Lord is the beginning of wisdom;
    a good understanding have those who live by it; ♦
his praise endures for ever.

Psalm 112

1 Alleluia.
    Blessed are those who fear the Lord ♦
and have great delight in his commandments.

2 Their descendants will be mighty in the land, ♦
a generation of the faithful that will be blest.

3 Wealth and riches will be in their house, ♦
and their righteousness endures for ever.

4 Light shines in the darkness for the upright; ♦
gracious and full of compassion are the righteous.

5   It goes well with those who are generous in lending ♦
      and order their affairs with justice,

6   For they will never be shaken; ♦
      the righteous will be held in everlasting remembrance.

7   They will not be afraid of any evil tidings; ♦
      their heart is steadfast, trusting in the Lord.

8   Their heart is sustained and will not fear, ♦
      until they see the downfall of their foes.

9   They have given freely to the poor;
        their righteousness stands fast for ever; ♦
      their head will be exalted with honour.

10   The wicked shall see it and be angry;
        they shall gnash their teeth in despair; ♦
      the desire of the wicked shall perish.

Psalm 113

1   Alleluia.
        Give praise, you servants of the Lord, ♦
      O praise the name of the Lord.

2   Blessed be the name of the Lord, ♦
      from this time forth and for evermore.

3   From the rising of the sun to its setting ♦
      let the name of the Lord be praised.

4   The Lord is high above all nations ♦
      and his glory above the heavens.

5   Who is like the Lord our God,
        that has his throne so high, ♦
      yet humbles himself to behold
        the things of heaven and earth?

6   He raises the poor from the dust ♦
      and lifts the needy from the ashes,

7   To set them with princes, ♦
      with the princes of his people.

8   He gives the barren woman a place in the house ♦
      and makes her a joyful mother of children.
        Alleluia.

1   When Israel came out of Egypt, ♦
     the house of Jacob from a people of a strange tongue,

2   Judah became his sanctuary, ♦
     Israel his dominion.

3   The sea saw that, and fled; ♦
     Jordan was driven back.

4   The mountains skipped like rams, ♦
     the little hills like young sheep.

5   What ailed you, O sea, that you fled? ♦
     O Jordan, that you were driven back?

6   You mountains, that you skipped like rams, ♦
     you little hills like young sheep?

7   Tremble, O earth, at the presence of the Lord, ♦
     at the presence of the God of Jacob,

8   Who turns the hard rock into a pool of water, ♦
     the flint-stone into a springing well.

Psalm 115

1   Not to us, Lord, not to us,
          but to your name give the glory, ♦
     for the sake of your loving mercy and truth.

2   Why should the nations say, ♦
     'Where is now their God?'

3   As for our God, he is in heaven; ♦
     he does whatever he pleases.

4   Their idols are silver and gold, ♦
     the work of human hands.

5   They have mouths, but cannot speak; ♦
     eyes have they, but cannot see;

6   They have ears, but cannot hear; ♦
     noses have they, but cannot smell;

7   They have hands, but cannot feel;
          feet have they, but cannot walk; ♦
    not a whisper do they make from their throats.

8   Those who make them shall become like them ♦
    and so will all who put their trust in them.

9   But you, Israel, put your trust in the Lord; ♦
    he is their help and their shield.

10   House of Aaron, trust in the Lord; ♦
    he is their help and their shield.

11   You that fear the Lord, trust in the Lord; ♦
    he is their help and their shield.

12   The Lord has been mindful of us and he will bless us; ♦
    may he bless the house of Israel;
          may he bless the house of Aaron;

13   May he bless those who fear the Lord, ♦
    both small and great together.

14   May the Lord increase you more and more, ♦
    you and your children after you.

15   May you be blest by the Lord, ♦
    the maker of heaven and earth.

16   The heavens are the heavens of the Lord, ♦
    but the earth he has entrusted to his children.

17   The dead do not praise the Lord, ♦
    nor those gone down into silence;

18   But we will bless the Lord, ♦
    from this time forth for evermore.
          Alleluia.

1   I love the Lord,
      for he has heard the voice of my supplication; ♦
   because he inclined his ear to me
      on the day I called to him.

2   The snares of death encompassed me;
      the pains of hell took hold of me; ♦
   by grief and sorrow was I held.

3   Then I called upon the name of the Lord: ♦
   'O Lord, I beg you, deliver my soul.'

4   Gracious is the Lord and righteous; ♦
   our God is full of compassion.

5   The Lord watches over the simple; ♦
   I was brought very low and he saved me.

6   Turn again to your rest, O my soul, ♦
   for the Lord has been gracious to you.

7   For you have delivered my soul from death, ♦
   my eyes from tears and my feet from falling.

8   I will walk before the Lord ♦
   in the land of the living.

9   I believed that I should perish
      for I was sorely troubled; ♦
   and I said in my alarm,
      'Everyone is a liar.'

10 How shall I repay the Lord ♦
   for all the benefits he has given to me?

11 I will lift up the cup of salvation ♦
   and call upon the name of the Lord.

12 I will fulfil my vows to the Lord ♦
   in the presence of all his people.

13 Precious in the sight of the Lord ♦
   is the death of his faithful servants.

14 O Lord, I am your servant, ♦
   your servant, the child of your handmaid;
      you have freed me from my bonds.

15   I will offer to you a sacrifice of thanksgiving ♦
       and call upon the name of the Lord.

16   I will fulfil my vows to the Lord ♦
       in the presence of all his people,

17   In the courts of the house of the Lord, ♦
       in the midst of you, O Jerusalem.
           Alleluia.

Psalm 117

1   O praise the Lord, all you nations; ♦
       praise him, all you peoples.

2   For great is his steadfast love towards us, ♦
       and the faithfulness of the Lord endures for ever.
           Alleluia.

Psalm 118

1   O give thanks to the Lord, for he is good; ♦
       his mercy endures for ever.

2   Let Israel now proclaim, ♦
       'His mercy endures for ever.'

3   Let the house of Aaron now proclaim, ♦
       'His mercy endures for ever.'

4   Let those who fear the Lord proclaim, ♦
       'His mercy endures for ever.'

5   In my constraint I called to the Lord; ♦
       the Lord answered and set me free.

6   The Lord is at my side; I will not fear; ♦
       what can flesh do to me?

7   With the Lord at my side as my saviour, ♦
       I shall see the downfall of my enemies.

8   It is better to take refuge in the Lord ♦
       than to put any confidence in flesh.

9   It is better to take refuge in the Lord ♦
       than to put any confidence in princes.

10   All the nations encompassed me, ♦
       but by the name of the Lord I drove them back.

11   They hemmed me in, they hemmed me in on every side, ♦
       but by the name of the Lord I drove them back.

12   They swarmed about me like bees;
       they blazed like fire among thorns, ♦
       but by the name of the Lord I drove them back.

13   Surely, I was thrust to the brink, ♦
       but the Lord came to my help.

14   The Lord is my strength and my song, ♦
       and he has become my salvation.

15   Joyful shouts of salvation ♦
       sound from the tents of the righteous:

16   'The right hand of the Lord does mighty deeds;
       the right hand of the Lord raises up; ♦
       the right hand of the Lord does mighty deeds.'

17   I shall not die, but live ♦
       and declare the works of the Lord.

18   The Lord has punished me sorely, ♦
       but he has not given me over to death.

19   Open to me the gates of righteousness, ♦
       that I may enter and give thanks to the Lord.

20   This is the gate of the Lord; ♦
       the righteous shall enter through it.

21   I will give thanks to you, for you have answered me ♦
       and have become my salvation.

22   The stone which the builders rejected ♦
       has become the chief cornerstone.

23   This is the Lord's doing, ♦
       and it is marvellous in our eyes.

24   This is the day that the Lord has made; ♦
       we will rejoice and be glad in it.

25 Come, O Lord, and save us we pray. ♦
    Come, Lord, send us now prosperity.

26 Blessed is he who comes in the name of the Lord; ♦
    we bless you from the house of the Lord.

27 The Lord is God; he has given us light; ♦
    link the pilgrims with cords
        right to the horns of the altar.

28 You are my God and I will thank you; ♦
    you are my God and I will exalt you.

29 O give thanks to the Lord, for he is good; ♦
    his mercy endures for ever.

Psalm 119

I א Aleph

1   Blessed are those whose way is pure, ♦
    who walk in the law of the Lord.

2   Blessed are those who keep his testimonies ♦
    and seek him with their whole heart,

3   Those who do no wickedness, ♦
    but walk in his ways.

4   You, O Lord, have charged ♦
    that we should diligently keep your commandments.

5   O that my ways were made so direct ♦
    that I might keep your statutes.

6   Then should I not be put to shame, ♦
    because I have regard for all your commandments.

7   I will thank you with an unfeigned heart, ♦
    when I have learned your righteous judgements.

8   I will keep your statutes; ♦
    O forsake me not utterly.

9   How shall young people cleanse their way ♦
      to keep themselves according to your word?

10   With my whole heart have I sought you; ♦
      O let me not go astray from your commandments.

11   Your words have I hidden within my heart, ♦
      that I should not sin against you.

12   Blessed are you, O Lord; ♦
      O teach me your statutes.

13   With my lips have I been telling ♦
      of all the judgements of your mouth.

14   I have taken greater delight in the way of your testimonies ♦
      than in all manner of riches.

15   I will meditate on your commandments ♦
      and contemplate your ways.

16   My delight shall be in your statutes ♦
      and I will not forget your word.

3 ג Gimel

17   O do good to your servant that I may live, ♦
      and so shall I keep your word.

18   Open my eyes, that I may see ♦
      the wonders of your law.

19   I am a stranger upon earth; ♦
      hide not your commandments from me.

20   My soul is consumed at all times ♦
      with fervent longing for your judgements.

21   You have rebuked the arrogant; ♦
      cursed are those who stray from your commandments.

22   Turn from me shame and rebuke, ♦
      for I have kept your testimonies.

23   Rulers also sit and speak against me, ♦
      but your servant meditates on your statutes.

24   For your testimonies are my delight; ♦
      they are my faithful counsellors.

4 ד *Daleth*

25 My soul cleaves to the dust; ♦
O give me life according to your word.

26 I have acknowledged my ways and you have answered me; ♦
O teach me your statutes.

27 Make me understand the way of your commandments, ♦
and so shall I meditate on your wondrous works.

28 My soul melts away in tears of sorrow; ♦
raise me up according to your word.

29 Take from me the way of falsehood; ♦
be gracious to me through your law.

30 I have chosen the way of truth ♦
and your judgements have I laid before me.

31 I hold fast to your testimonies; ♦
O Lord, let me not be put to shame.

32 I will run the way of your commandments, ♦
when you have set my heart at liberty.

5 ה *He*

33 Teach me, O Lord, the way of your statutes ♦
and I shall keep it to the end.

34 Give me understanding and I shall keep your law; ♦
I shall keep it with my whole heart.

35 Lead me in the path of your commandments, ♦
for therein is my delight.

36 Incline my heart to your testimonies ♦
and not to unjust gain.

37 Turn away my eyes lest they gaze on vanities; ♦
O give me life in your ways.

38 Confirm to your servant your promise, ♦
which stands for all who fear you.

39 Turn away the reproach which I dread, ♦
because your judgements are good.

40 Behold, I long for your commandments; ♦
in your righteousness give me life.

6 **ו** *Waw*

41   Let your faithful love come unto me, O Lord, ♦
       even your salvation, according to your promise.

42   Then shall I answer those who taunt me, ♦
       for my trust is in your word.

43   O take not the word of truth utterly out of my mouth, ♦
       for my hope is in your judgements.

44   So shall I always keep your law; ♦
       I shall keep it for ever and ever.

45   I will walk at liberty, ♦
       because I study your commandments.

46   I will tell of your testimonies, even before kings, ♦
       and will not be ashamed.

47   My delight shall be in your commandments, ♦
       which I have greatly loved.

48   My hands will I lift up to your commandments,
         which I love, ♦
       and I will meditate on your statutes.

7 **ז** *Zayin*

49   Remember your word to your servant, ♦
       on which you have built my hope.

50   This is my comfort in my trouble, ♦
       that your promise gives me life.

51   The proud have derided me cruelly, ♦
       but I have not turned aside from your law.

52   I have remembered your everlasting judgements, O Lord, ♦
       and have been comforted.

53   I am seized with indignation at the wicked, ♦
       for they have forsaken your law.

54   Your statutes have been like songs to me ♦
       in the house of my pilgrimage.

55   I have thought on your name in the night, O Lord, ♦
       and so have I kept your law.

56   These blessings have been mine, ♦
       for I have kept your commandments.

8 ⎕ *Heth*

57   You only are my portion, O Lord; ♦
        I have promised to keep your words.

58   I entreat you with all my heart, ♦
        be merciful to me according to your promise.

59   I have considered my ways ♦
        and turned my feet back to your testimonies.

60   I made haste and did not delay ♦
        to keep your commandments.

61   Though the cords of the wicked entangle me, ♦
        I do not forget your law.

62   At midnight I will rise to give you thanks, ♦
        because of your righteous judgements.

63   I am a companion of all those who fear you, ♦
        those who keep your commandments.

64   The earth, O Lord, is full of your faithful love; ♦
        instruct me in your statutes.

9 ⎕ *Teth*

65   You have dealt graciously with your servant, ♦
        according to your word, O Lord.

66   O teach me true understanding and knowledge, ♦
        for I have trusted in your commandments.

67   Before I was afflicted I went astray, ♦
        but now I keep your word.

68   You are gracious and do good; ♦
        O Lord, teach me your statutes.

69   The proud have smeared me with lies, ♦
        but I will keep your commandments with my whole heart.

70   Their heart has become gross with fat, ♦
        but my delight is in your law.

71   It is good for me that I have been afflicted, ♦
        that I may learn your statutes.

72   The law of your mouth is dearer to me ♦
        than a hoard of gold and silver.

73   Your hands have made me and fashioned me; ♦
give me understanding, that I may learn your commandments.

74   Those who fear you will be glad when they see me, ♦
because I have hoped in your word.

75   I know, O Lord, that your judgements are right, ♦
and that in very faithfulness you caused me to be troubled.

76   Let your faithful love be my comfort, ♦
according to your promise to your servant.

77   Let your tender mercies come to me, that I may live, ♦
for your law is my delight.

78   Let the proud be put to shame, for they wrong me with lies; ♦
but I will meditate on your commandments.

79   Let those who fear you turn to me, ♦
even those who know your testimonies.

80   Let my heart be sound in your statutes, ♦
that I may not be put to shame.

11 כ Kaph

81   My soul is pining for your salvation; ♦
I have hoped in your word.

82   My eyes fail with watching for your word, ♦
while I say, 'O when will you comfort me?'

83   I have become like a wineskin in the smoke, ♦
yet I do not forget your statutes.

84   How many are the days of your servant? ♦
When will you bring judgement on those who persecute me?

85   The proud have dug pits for me ♦
in defiance of your law.

86   All your commandments are true; ♦
help me, for they persecute me with falsehood.

87   They had almost made an end of me on earth, ♦
but I have not forsaken your commandments.

88   Give me life according to your loving-kindness; ♦
so shall I keep the testimonies of your mouth.

12 ל Lamedh

89 O Lord, your word is everlasting; ♦
   it ever stands firm in the heavens.

90 Your faithfulness also remains from one generation to another; ♦
   you have established the earth and it abides.

91 So also your judgements stand firm this day, ♦
   for all things are your servants.

92 If your law had not been my delight, ♦
   I should have perished in my trouble.

93 I will never forget your commandments, ♦
   for by them you have given me life.

94 I am yours, O save me! ♦
   For I have sought your commandments.

95 The wicked have waited for me to destroy me, ♦
   but I will meditate on your testimonies.

96 I have seen an end of all perfection, ♦
   but your commandment knows no bounds.

13 מ Mem

97 Lord, how I love your law! ♦
   All the day long it is my study.

98 Your commandments have made me wiser than my enemies, ♦
   for they are ever with me.

99 I have more understanding than all my teachers, ♦
   for your testimonies are my meditation.

100 I am wiser than the aged, ♦
    because I keep your commandments.

101 I restrain my feet from every evil way, ♦
    that I may keep your word.

102 I have not turned aside from your judgements, ♦
    for you have been my teacher.

103 How sweet are your words on my tongue! ♦
    They are sweeter than honey to my mouth.

104 Through your commandments I get understanding; ♦
    therefore I hate all lying ways.

14 נ Nun

105 Your word is a lantern to my feet ♦
and a light upon my path.

106 I have sworn and will fulfil it, ♦
to keep your righteous judgements.

107 I am troubled above measure; ♦
give me life, O Lord, according to your word.

108 Accept the freewill offering of my mouth, O Lord, ♦
and teach me your judgements.

109 My soul is ever in my hand, ♦
yet I do not forget your law.

110 The wicked have laid a snare for me, ♦
but I have not strayed from your commandments.

111 Your testimonies have I claimed as my heritage for ever; ♦
for they are the very joy of my heart.

112 I have applied my heart to fulfil your statutes: ♦
always, even to the end.

15 ס Samekh

113 I hate those who are double-minded, ♦
but your law do I love.

114 You are my hiding place and my shield ♦
and my hope is in your word.

115 Away from me, you wicked! ♦
I will keep the commandments of my God.

116 Sustain me according to your promise, that I may live, ♦
and let me not be disappointed in my hope.

117 Hold me up and I shall be saved, ♦
and my delight shall be ever in your statutes.

118 You set at nought those who depart from your statutes, ♦
for their deceiving is in vain.

119 You consider all the wicked as dross; ♦
therefore I love your testimonies.

120 My flesh trembles for fear of you ♦
and I am afraid of your judgements.

16 ע Ayin

121 I have done what is just and right; ♦
O give me not over to my oppressors.

122 Stand surety for your servant's good; ♦
let not the proud oppress me.

123 My eyes fail with watching for your salvation ♦
and for your righteous promise.

124 O deal with your servant according to your faithful love ♦
and teach me your statutes.

125 I am your servant; O grant me understanding, ♦
that I may know your testimonies.

126 It is time for you to act, O Lord, ♦
for they frustrate your law.

127 Therefore I love your commandments ♦
above gold, even much fine gold.

128 Therefore I direct my steps by all your precepts, ♦
and all false ways I utterly abhor.

17 פ Pe

129 Your testimonies are wonderful; ♦
therefore my soul keeps them.

130 The opening of your word gives light; ♦
it gives understanding to the simple.

131 I open my mouth and draw in my breath, ♦
as I long for your commandments.

132 Turn to me and be gracious to me, ♦
as is your way with those who love your name.

133 Order my steps by your word, ♦
and let no wickedness have dominion over me.

134 Redeem me from earthly oppressors ♦
so that I may keep your commandments.

135 Show the light of your countenance upon your servant ♦
and teach me your statutes.

136 My eyes run down with streams of water, ♦
because the wicked do not keep your law.

137   Righteous are you, O Lord, ♦
    and true are your judgements.

138   You have ordered your decrees in righteousness ♦
    and in great faithfulness.

139   My indignation destroys me, ♦
    because my adversaries forget your word.

140   Your word has been tried to the uttermost ♦
    and so your servant loves it.

141   I am small and of no reputation, ♦
    yet do I not forget your commandments.

142   Your righteousness is an everlasting righteousness ♦
    and your law is the truth.

143   Trouble and heaviness have taken hold upon me, ♦
    yet my delight is in your commandments.

144   The righteousness of your testimonies is everlasting; ♦
    O grant me understanding and I shall live.

19 ק Qoph

145   I call with my whole heart; ♦
    answer me, O Lord, that I may keep your statutes.

146   To you I call, O save me! ♦
    And I shall keep your testimonies.

147   Early in the morning I cry to you, ♦
    for in your word is my trust.

148   My eyes are open before the night watches, ♦
    that I may meditate on your word.

149   Hear my voice, O Lord, according to your faithful love; ♦
    according to your judgement, give me life.

150   They draw near that in malice persecute me, ♦
    who are far from your law.

151   You, O Lord, are near at hand, ♦
    and all your commandments are true.

152   Long have I known of your testimonies, ♦
    that you have founded them for ever.

20 ר Resh

153 O consider my affliction and deliver me, ♦
for I do not forget your law.

154 Plead my cause and redeem me; ♦
according to your promise, give me life.

155 Salvation is far from the wicked, ♦
for they do not seek your statutes.

156 Great is your compassion, O Lord; ♦
give me life, according to your judgements.

157 Many there are that persecute and oppress me, ♦
yet do I not swerve from your testimonies.

158 It grieves me when I see the treacherous, ♦
for they do not keep your word.

159 Consider, O Lord, how I love your commandments; ♦
give me life according to your loving-kindness.

160 The sum of your word is truth, ♦
and all your righteous judgements endure for evermore.

21 ש Shin

161 Princes have persecuted me without a cause, ♦
but my heart stands in awe of your word.

162 I am as glad of your word ♦
as one who finds great spoils.

163 As for lies, I hate and abhor them, ♦
but your law do I love.

164 Seven times a day do I praise you, ♦
because of your righteous judgements.

165 Great peace have they who love your law; ♦
nothing shall make them stumble.

166 Lord, I have looked for your salvation ♦
and I have fulfilled your commandments.

167 My soul has kept your testimonies ♦
and greatly have I loved them.

168 I have kept your commandments and testimonies, ♦
for all my ways are before you.

169   Let my cry come before you, O Lord; ♦
       give me understanding, according to your word.

170   Let my supplication come before you; ♦
       deliver me, according to your promise.

171   My lips shall pour forth your praise, ♦
       when you have taught me your statutes.

172   My tongue shall sing of your word, ♦
       for all your commandments are righteous.

173   Let your hand reach out to help me, ♦
       for I have chosen your commandments.

174   I have longed for your salvation, O Lord, ♦
       and your law is my delight.

175   Let my soul live and it shall praise you, ♦
       and let your judgements be my help.

176   I have gone astray like a sheep that is lost; ♦
       O seek your servant, for I do not forget your commandments.

Psalm 120

1   When I was in trouble I called to the Lord; ♦
       I called to the Lord and he answered me.

2   Deliver me, O Lord, from lying lips ♦
       and from a deceitful tongue.

3   What shall be given to you? ♦
       What more shall be done to you, deceitful tongue?

4   The sharp arrows of a warrior, ♦
       tempered in burning coals!

5   Woe is me, that I must lodge in Meshech ♦
       and dwell among the tents of Kedar.

6   My soul has dwelt too long ♦
       with enemies of peace.

7   I am for making peace, ♦
       but when I speak of it, they make ready for war.

1   I lift up my eyes to the hills; ♦
    from where is my help to come?

2   My help comes from the Lord, ♦
    the maker of heaven and earth.

3   He will not suffer your foot to stumble; ♦
    he who watches over you will not sleep.

4   Behold, he who keeps watch over Israel ♦
    shall neither slumber nor sleep.

5   The Lord himself watches over you; ♦
    the Lord is your shade at your right hand,

6   So that the sun shall not strike you by day, ♦
    neither the moon by night.

7   The Lord shall keep you from all evil; ♦
    it is he who shall keep your soul.

8   The Lord shall keep watch over your going out
        and your coming in, ♦
    from this time forth for evermore.

Psalm 122

1   I was glad when they said to me, ♦
    'Let us go to the house of the Lord.'

2   And now our feet are standing ♦
    within your gates, O Jerusalem;

3   Jerusalem, built as a city ♦
    that is at unity in itself.

4   Thither the tribes go up, the tribes of the Lord, ♦
    as is decreed for Israel,
        to give thanks to the name of the Lord.

5   For there are set the thrones of judgement, ♦
    the thrones of the house of David.

6   O pray for the peace of Jerusalem: ♦
       'May they prosper who love you.

7   'Peace be within your walls ♦
       and tranquillity within your palaces.'

8   For my kindred and companions' sake, ♦
       I will pray that peace be with you.

9   For the sake of the house of the Lord our God, ♦
       I will seek to do you good.

Psalm 123

1   To you I lift up my eyes, ♦
       to you that are enthroned in the heavens.

2   As the eyes of servants look to the hand of their master, ♦
       or the eyes of a maid to the hand of her mistress,

3   So our eyes wait upon the Lord our God, ♦
       until he have mercy upon us.

4   Have mercy upon us, O Lord, have mercy upon us, ♦
       for we have had more than enough of contempt.

5   Our soul has had more than enough of the scorn of the arrogant, ♦
       and of the contempt of the proud.

Psalm 124

1   If the Lord himself had not been on our side, ♦
       now may Israel say;

2   If the Lord had not been on our side, ♦
       when enemies rose up against us;

3   Then would they have swallowed us alive ♦
       when their anger burned against us;

4   Then would the waters have overwhelmed us
         and the torrent gone over our soul; ♦
       over our soul would have swept the raging waters.

5   But blessed be the Lord ♦
    who has not given us over to be a prey for their teeth.

6   Our soul has escaped
        as a bird from the snare of the fowler; ♦
    the snare is broken and we are delivered.

7   Our help is in the name of the Lord, ♦
    who has made heaven and earth.

Psalm 125

1   Those who trust in the Lord are like Mount Zion, ♦
    which cannot be moved, but stands fast for ever.

2   As the hills stand about Jerusalem, ♦
    so the Lord stands round about his people,
        from this time forth for evermore.

3   The sceptre of wickedness shall not hold sway
        over the land allotted to the righteous, ♦
    lest the righteous turn their hands to evil.

4   Do good, O Lord, to those who are good, ♦
    and to those who are true of heart.

5   Those who turn aside to crooked ways
        the Lord shall take away with the evildoers; ♦
    but let there be peace upon Israel.

Psalm 126

1   When the Lord restored the fortunes of Zion, ♦
    then were we like those who dream.

2   Then was our mouth filled with laughter ♦
    and our tongue with songs of joy.

3   Then said they among the nations, ♦
    'The Lord has done great things for them.'

4   The Lord has indeed done great things for us, ♦
    and therefore we rejoiced.

5   Restore again our fortunes, O Lord, ♦
     as the river beds of the desert.

6   Those who sow in tears ♦
     shall reap with songs of joy.

7   Those who go out weeping, bearing the seed, ♦
     will come back with shouts of joy,
          bearing their sheaves with them.

Psalm 127

1   Unless the Lord builds the house, ♦
     those who build it labour in vain.

2   Unless the Lord keeps the city, ♦
     the guard keeps watch in vain.

3   It is in vain that you hasten to rise up early
          and go so late to rest, eating the bread of toil, ♦
     for he gives his beloved sleep.

4   Children are a heritage from the Lord ♦
     and the fruit of the womb is his gift.

5   Like arrows in the hand of a warrior, ♦
     so are the children of one's youth.

6   Happy are those who have their quiver full of them: ♦
     they shall not be put to shame
          when they dispute with their enemies in the gate.

Psalm 128

1   Blessed are all those who fear the Lord, ♦
     and walk in his ways.

2   You shall eat the fruit of the toil of your hands; ♦
     it shall go well with you, and happy shall you be.

3   Your wife within your house
          shall be like a fruitful vine; ♦
     your children round your table,
          like fresh olive branches.

4   Thus shall the one be blest ♦
      who fears the Lord.

5   The Lord from out of Zion bless you, ♦
      that you may see Jerusalem in prosperity
         all the days of your life.

6   May you see your children's children, ♦
      and may there be peace upon Israel.

Psalm 129

1   'Many a time have they fought against me from my youth,' ♦
      may Israel now say;

2   'Many a time have they fought against me from my youth, ♦
      but they have not prevailed against me.'

3   The ploughers ploughed upon my back ♦
      and made their furrows long.

4   But the righteous Lord ♦
      has cut the cords of the wicked in pieces.

5   Let them be put to shame and turned backwards, ♦
      as many as are enemies of Zion.

6   Let them be like grass upon the housetops, ♦
      which withers before it can grow,

7   So that no reaper can fill his hand, ♦
      nor a binder of sheaves his bosom;

8   And none who go by may say,
         'The blessing of the Lord be upon you. ♦
      We bless you in the name of the Lord.'

1   Out of the depths have I cried to you, O Lord;
      Lord, hear my voice; ♦
   let your ears consider well the voice of my supplication.

2   If you, Lord, were to mark what is done amiss, ♦
   O Lord, who could stand?

3   But there is forgiveness with you, ♦
   so that you shall be feared.

4   I wait for the Lord; my soul waits for him; ♦
   in his word is my hope.

5   My soul waits for the Lord,
      more than the night watch for the morning, ♦
   more than the night watch for the morning.

6   O Israel, wait for the Lord, ♦
   for with the Lord there is mercy;

7   With him is plenteous redemption ♦
   and he shall redeem Israel from all their sins.

Psalm 131

1   O Lord, my heart is not proud; ♦
   my eyes are not raised in haughty looks.

2   I do not occupy myself with great matters, ♦
   with things that are too high for me.

3   But I have quieted and stilled my soul,
      like a weaned child on its mother's breast; ♦
   so my soul is quieted within me.

4   O Israel, trust in the Lord, ♦
   from this time forth for evermore.

1   Lord, remember for David ♦
     all the hardships he endured;

2   How he swore an oath to the Lord ♦
     and vowed a vow to the Mighty One of Jacob:

3   'I will not come within the shelter of my house, ♦
     nor climb up into my bed;

4   'I will not allow my eyes to sleep, ♦
     nor let my eyelids slumber,

5   'Until I find a place for the Lord, ♦
     a dwelling for the Mighty One of Jacob.'

6   Now, we heard of the ark in Ephrathah ♦
     and found it in the fields of Ja-ar.

7   Let us enter his dwelling place ♦
     and fall low before his footstool.

8   Arise, O Lord, into your resting place, ♦
     you and the ark of your strength.

9   Let your priests be clothed with righteousness ♦
     and your faithful ones sing with joy.

10   For your servant David's sake, ♦
     turn not away the face of your anointed.

11   The Lord has sworn an oath to David, ♦
     a promise from which he will not shrink:

12   'Of the fruit of your body ♦
     shall I set upon your throne.

13   'If your children keep my covenant
          and my testimonies that I shall teach them, ♦
     their children also shall sit upon your throne for evermore.'

14   For the Lord has chosen Zion for himself; ♦
     he has desired her for his habitation:

15   'This shall be my resting place for ever; ♦
     here will I dwell, for I have longed for her.

16   'I will abundantly bless her provision; ♦
      her poor will I satisfy with bread.

17   'I will clothe her priests with salvation, ♦
      and her faithful ones shall rejoice and sing.

18   'There will I make a horn to spring up for David; ♦
      I will keep a lantern burning for my anointed.

19   'As for his enemies, I will clothe them with shame; ♦
      but on him shall his crown be bright.'

Psalm 133

1   Behold how good and pleasant it is ♦
      to dwell together in unity.

2   It is like the precious oil upon the head, ♦
      running down upon the beard,

3   Even on Aaron's beard, ♦
      running down upon the collar of his clothing.

4   It is like the dew of Hermon ♦
      running down upon the hills of Zion.

5   For there the Lord has promised his blessing: ♦
      even life for evermore.

Psalm 134

1   Come, bless the Lord, all you servants of the Lord, ♦
      you that by night stand in the house of the Lord.

2   Lift up your hands towards the sanctuary ♦
      and bless the Lord.

3   The Lord who made heaven and earth ♦
      give you blessing out of Zion.

1 Alleluia.
    Praise the name of the Lord; ♦
give praise, you servants of the Lord,

2 You that stand in the house of the Lord, ♦
in the courts of the house of our God.

3 Praise the Lord, for the Lord is good; ♦
make music to his name, for it is lovely.

4 For the Lord has chosen Jacob for himself ♦
and Israel for his own possession.

5 For I know that the Lord is great ♦
and that our Lord is above all gods.

6 The Lord does whatever he pleases
    in heaven and on earth, ♦
in the seas and in all the deeps.

7 He brings up the clouds from the ends of the earth; ♦
he makes lightning with the rain
    and brings the winds out of his treasuries.

8 He smote the firstborn of Egypt, ♦
the firstborn of man and beast.

9 He sent signs and wonders into your midst, O Egypt, ♦
upon Pharaoh and all his servants.

10 He smote many nations ♦
and slew mighty kings:

11 Sihon, king of the Amorites,
    and Og, the king of Bashan, ♦
and all the kingdoms of Canaan.

12 He gave their land as a heritage, ♦
a heritage for Israel his people.

13 Your name, O Lord, endures for ever ♦
and shall be remembered through all generations.

14 For the Lord will vindicate his people ♦
and have compassion on his servants.

15   The idols of the nations are but silver and gold, ♦
      the work of human hands.

16   They have mouths, but cannot speak; ♦
      eyes have they, but cannot see;

17   They have ears, but cannot hear; ♦
      neither is there any breath in their mouths.

18   Those who make them shall become like them, ♦
      and so will all who put their trust in them.

19   Bless the Lord, O house of Israel; ♦
      O house of Aaron, bless the Lord.

20   Bless the Lord, O house of Levi; ♦
      you who fear the Lord, bless the Lord.

21   Blessed be the Lord from Zion, ♦
      who dwells in Jerusalem.
            Alleluia.

Psalm 136

1   Give thanks to the Lord, for he is gracious, ♦
      for his mercy endures for ever.

2   Give thanks to the God of gods, ♦
      for his mercy endures for ever.

3   Give thanks to the Lord of lords, ♦
      for his mercy endures for ever;

4   Who alone does great wonders, ♦
      for his mercy endures for ever;

5   Who by wisdom made the heavens, ♦
      for his mercy endures for ever;

6   Who laid out the earth upon the waters, ♦
      for his mercy endures for ever;

7   Who made the great lights, ♦
      for his mercy endures for ever;

8   The sun to rule the day, ♦
      for his mercy endures for ever;

9   The moon and the stars to govern t
for his mercy endures for ever;

10   Who smote the firstborn of Egypt, ♦
for his mercy endures for ever;

11   And brought out Israel from among them, ♦
for his mercy endures for ever;

12   With a mighty hand and outstretched arm, ♦
for his mercy endures for ever;

13   Who divided the Red Sea in two, ♦
for his mercy endures for ever;

14   And made Israel to pass through the midst of it, ♦
for his mercy endures for ever;

15   But Pharaoh and his host he overthrew in the Red Sea, ♦
for his mercy endures for ever;

16   Who led his people through the wilderness, ♦
for his mercy endures for ever;

17   Who smote great kings, ♦
for his mercy endures for ever;

18   And slew mighty kings, ♦
for his mercy endures for ever;

19   Sihon, king of the Amorites, ♦
for his mercy endures for ever;

20   And Og, the king of Bashan, ♦
for his mercy endures for ever;

21   And gave away their land for a heritage, ♦
for his mercy endures for ever;

22   A heritage for Israel his servant, ♦
for his mercy endures for ever;

23   Who remembered us when we were in trouble, ♦
for his mercy endures for ever;

24   And delivered us from our enemies, ♦
for his mercy endures for ever;

Psalm 136

od to all creatures, ♦
25　cy endures for ever.

nks to the God of heaven, ♦
26　mercy endures for ever.

Psalm 137

By the waters of Babylon we sat down and wept, ♦
when we remembered Zion.

2　As for our lyres, we hung them up ♦
on the willows that grow in that land.

3　For there our captors asked for a song,
our tormentors called for mirth: ♦
'Sing us one of the songs of Zion.'

4　How shall we sing the Lord's song ♦
in a strange land?

5　If I forget you, O Jerusalem, ♦
let my right hand forget its skill.

6　Let my tongue cleave to the roof of my mouth
if I do not remember you, ♦
if I set not Jerusalem above my highest joy.

7　Remember, O Lord, against the people of Edom
the day of Jerusalem, ♦
how they said, 'Down with it, down with it,
even to the ground.'

8　O daughter of Babylon, doomed to destruction, ♦
happy the one who repays you
for all you have done to us;

9　Who takes your little ones, ♦
and dashes them against the rock.

1   I will give thanks to you, O Lord,
before the gods will I sing praise to 38

2   I will bow down towards your holy te.
       because of your love and faithfulness
for you have glorified your name   name,
       and your word above all things.

3   In the day that I called to you, you answered
you put new strength in my soul.

4   All the kings of the earth shall praise you, O Lo
for they have heard the words of your mouth.

5   They shall sing of the ways of the Lord, ♦
that great is the glory of the Lord.

6   Though the Lord be high, he watches over the lowly,
as for the proud, he regards them from afar.

7   Though I walk in the midst of trouble,
       you will preserve me; ♦
you will stretch forth your hand against the fury of my enemies;
       your right hand will save me.

8   The Lord shall make good his purpose for me; ♦
your loving-kindness, O Lord, endures for ever;
       forsake not the work of your hands.

Psalm 139

1   O Lord, you have searched me out and known me; ♦
you know my sitting down and my rising up;
       you discern my thoughts from afar.

2   You mark out my journeys and my resting place ♦
and are acquainted with all my ways.

3   For there is not a word on my tongue, ♦
but you, O Lord, know it altogether.

4   You encompass me behind and before ♦
and lay your hand upon me.

is too wonderful for me, ♦
  nnot attain it.

o then from your spirit? ♦
  I flee from your presence?

to heaven, you are there; ♦
  grave my bed, you are there also.

If I t wings of the morning ♦
 and in the uttermost parts of the sea,

9 Eve e your hand shall lead me, ♦
  yo t hand hold me fast.

10 If Surely the darkness will cover me ♦
  a e light around me turn to night,'

11 E darkness is no darkness with you; ♦
  he night is as clear as the day; ♦
  d ness and light to you are both alike.

12 For ou yourself created my inmost parts; ♦
  you kni me together in my mother's womb.

13 I thank you, for I am fearfully and wonderfully made; ♦
  marvellous are your works, my soul knows well.

14 My frame was not hidden from you, ♦
  when I was made in secret
    and woven in the depths of the earth.

15 Your eyes beheld my form, as yet unfinished; ♦
  already in your book were all my members written,

16 As day by day they were fashioned ♦
  when as yet there was none of them.

17 How deep are your counsels to me, O God! ♦
  How great is the sum of them!

18 If I count them, they are more in number than the sand, ♦
  and at the end, I am still in your presence.

19 O that you would slay the wicked, O God, ♦
  that the bloodthirsty might depart from me!

20 They speak against you with wicked intent; ♦
  your enemies take up your name for evil.

21   Do I not oppose those, O Lord, who oppose you? ♦
        Do I not abhor those who rise up against you?

22   I hate them with a perfect hatred; ♦
        they have become my own enemies also.

23   Search me out, O God, and know my heart; ♦
        try me and examine my thoughts.

24   See if there is any way of wickedness in me ♦
        and lead me in the way everlasting.

Psalm 140

1   Deliver me, O Lord, from evildoers ♦
        and protect me from the violent,

2   Who devise evil in their hearts ♦
        and stir up strife all the day long.

3   They have sharpened their tongues like a serpent; ♦
        adder's poison is under their lips.

4   Keep me, O Lord, from the hands of the wicked; ♦
        protect me from the violent
           who seek to make me stumble.

5   The proud have laid a snare for me
           and spread out a net of cords; ♦
        they have set traps along my path.

6   I have said to the Lord, 'You are my God; ♦
        listen, O Lord, to the voice of my supplication.

7   'O Lord God, the strength of my salvation, ♦
        you have covered my head in the day of battle.

8   'Do not grant the desires of the wicked, O Lord, ♦
        do not prosper their wicked plans.

9   'Let not those who surround me lift up their heads; ♦
        let the evil of their own lips fall upon them.

10   'Let hot burning coals rain upon them; ♦
        let them be cast into the depths, that they rise not again.'

11   No slanderer shall prosper on the earth, ♦
      and evil shall hunt down the violent to overthrow them.

12   I know that the Lord will bring justice for the oppressed ♦
      and maintain the cause of the needy.

13   Surely, the righteous will give thanks to your name, ♦
      and the upright shall dwell in your presence.

Psalm 141

1   O Lord, I call to you; come to me quickly; ♦
      hear my voice when I cry to you.

2   Let my prayer rise before you as incense, ♦
      the lifting up of my hands as the evening sacrifice.

3   Set a watch before my mouth, O Lord, ♦
      and guard the door of my lips;

4   Let not my heart incline to any evil thing; ♦
      let me not be occupied in wickedness with evildoers,
         nor taste the pleasures of their table.

5   Let the righteous smite me in friendly rebuke;
         but let not the oil of the unrighteous anoint my head; ♦
      for my prayer is continually against their wicked deeds.

6   Let their rulers be overthrown in stony places; ♦
      then they may know that my words are sweet.

7   As when a plough turns over the earth in furrows, ♦
      let their bones be scattered at the mouth of the Pit.

8   But my eyes are turned to you, Lord God; ♦
      in you I take refuge; do not leave me defenceless.

9   Protect me from the snare which they have laid for me ♦
      and from the traps of the evildoers.

10   Let the wicked fall into their own nets, ♦
      while I pass by in safety.

1   I cry aloud to the Lord; ♦
     to the Lord I make my supplication.

2   I pour out my complaint before him ♦
     and tell him of my trouble.

3   When my spirit faints within me, you know my pa͟
     in the way wherein I walk have they laid a snare for ͟

4   I look to my right hand, and find no one who knows me;
     I have no place to flee to, and no one cares for my soul.

5   I cry out to you, O Lord, and say: ♦
     'You are my refuge, my portion in the land of the living.

6   'Listen to my cry, for I am brought very low; ♦
     save me from my persecutors, for they are too strong for me.

7   'Bring my soul out of prison,
       that I may give thanks to your name; ♦
     when you have dealt bountifully with me,
       then shall the righteous gather around me.'

Psalm 143

1   Hear my prayer, O Lord,
       and in your faithfulness give ear to my supplications; ♦
     answer me in your righteousness.

2   Enter not into judgement with your servant, ♦
     for in your sight shall no one living be justified.

3   For the enemy has pursued me,
       crushing my life to the ground, ♦
     making me sit in darkness like those long dead.

4   My spirit faints within me; ♦
     my heart within me is desolate.

5   I remember the time past; I muse upon all your deeds; ♦
     I consider the works of your hands.

6   I stretch out my hands to you; ♦
     my soul gasps for you like a thirsty land.

7   O Lord, make haste to answer me; my spirit fails me; ♦
     hide not your face from me
       lest I be like those who go down to the Pit.

your loving-kindness in the morning,

8   I put my trust; ♦

the way I should walk in,

    ift up my soul to you.

   me, O Lord, from my enemies, ♦

9 flee to you for refuge.

each me to do what pleases you, for you are my God; ♦

let your kindly spirit lead me on a level path.

Revive me, O Lord, for your name's sake; ♦

for your righteousness' sake, bring me out of trouble.

12   In your faithfulness, slay my enemies,

    and destroy all the adversaries of my soul, ♦

for truly I am your servant.

Psalm 144

1   Blessed be the Lord my rock, ♦

who teaches my hands for war and my fingers for battle;

2   My steadfast help and my fortress,

    my stronghold and my deliverer,

    my shield in whom I trust, ♦

who subdues the peoples under me.

3   O Lord, what are mortals that you should consider them; ♦

mere human beings, that you should take thought for them?

4   They are like a breath of wind; ♦

their days pass away like a shadow.

5   Bow your heavens, O Lord, and come down; ♦

touch the mountains and they shall smoke.

6   Cast down your lightnings and scatter them; ♦

shoot out your arrows and let thunder roar.

7   Reach down your hand from on high; ♦

deliver me and take me out of the great waters,

    from the hand of foreign enemies,

8   Whose mouth speaks wickedness ♦

and their right hand is the hand of falsehood.

9   O God, I will sing to you a new so'
       I will play to you on a ten-stringed

10   You that give salvation to kings ♦
       and have delivered David your servant.

11   Save me from the peril of the sword ♦
       and deliver me from the hand of foreign enemies

12   Whose mouth speaks wickedness ♦
       and whose right hand is the hand of falsehood;

13   So that our sons in their youth
          may be like well-nurtured plants, ♦
     and our daughters like pillars
          carved for the corners of the temple;

14   Our barns be filled with all manner of store; ♦
     our flocks bearing thousands,
          and ten thousands in our fields;

15   Our cattle be heavy with young: ♦
     may there be no miscarriage or untimely birth,
          no cry of distress in our streets.

16   Happy are the people whose blessing this is. ♦
     Happy are the people who have the Lord for their God.

Psalm 145

1   I will exalt you, O God my King, ♦
     and bless your name for ever and ever.

2   Every day will I bless you ♦
     and praise your name for ever and ever.

3   Great is the Lord and highly to be praised; ♦
     his greatness is beyond all searching out.

4   One generation shall praise your works to another ♦
     and declare your mighty acts.

5   They shall speak of the majesty of your glory, ♦
     and I will tell of all your wonderful deeds.

6   They shall speak of the might of your marvellous acts, ♦
     and I will also tell of your greatness.

r forth the story of your abundant kindness ♦

7   ing of your righteousness.

is gracious and merciful, ♦

8   ering and of great goodness.

Lord is loving to everyone ♦
    d his mercy is over all his creatures.

All your works praise you, O Lord, ♦
and your faithful servants bless you.

11   They tell of the glory of your kingdom ♦
     and speak of your mighty power,

12   To make known to all peoples your mighty acts ♦
     and the glorious splendour of your kingdom.

13   Your kingdom is an everlasting kingdom; ♦
     your dominion endures throughout all ages.

14   The Lord is sure in all his words ♦
     and faithful in all his deeds.

15   The Lord upholds all those who fall ♦
     and lifts up all those who are bowed down.

16   The eyes of all wait upon you, O Lord, ♦
     and you give them their food in due season.

17   You open wide your hand ♦
     and fill all things living with plenty.

18   The Lord is righteous in all his ways ♦
     and loving in all his works.

19   The Lord is near to those who call upon him, ♦
     to all who call upon him faithfully.

20   He fulfils the desire of those who fear him; ♦
     he hears their cry and saves them.

21   The Lord watches over those who love him, ♦
     but all the wicked shall he destroy.

22   My mouth shall speak the praise of the Lord, ♦
     and let all flesh bless his holy name for ever and ever.

1   Alleluia.
        O praise God in his holiness; ✦
    praise him in the firmament of his power.

2   Praise him for his mighty acts; ✦
    praise him according to his excellent greatness.

3   Praise him with the blast of the trumpet; ✦
    praise him upon the harp and lyre.

4   Praise him with timbrel and dances; ✦
    praise him upon the strings and pipe.

5   Praise him with ringing cymbals; ✦
    praise him upon the clashing cymbals.

6   Let everything that has breath ✦
    praise the Lord.
        Alleluia.

Canticles

Contents

Opening Hymn and Canticles
at Morning and Evening Prayer

Old and New Testament Canticles
at Morning and Evening Prayer

¶ *Opening Hymn and Canticles at Morning and Evening Prayer*

Benedicite – a Song of Creation

1   Bless the Lord all you works of the Lord: ♦
    sing his praise and exalt him for ever.

2   Bless the Lord you heavens: ♦
    sing his praise and exalt him for ever.

3   Bless the Lord you angels of the Lord: ♦
    bless the Lord all you his hosts;

    bless the Lord you waters above the heavens: ♦
    sing his praise and exalt him for ever.

4   Bless the Lord sun and moon: ♦
    bless the Lord you stars of heaven;

    bless the Lord all rain and dew: ♦
    sing his praise and exalt him for ever.

5   Bless the Lord all winds that blow: ♦
    bless the Lord you fire and heat;

    bless the Lord scorching wind and bitter cold: ♦
    sing his praise and exalt him for ever.

6   Bless the Lord dews and falling snows: ♦
    bless the Lord you nights and days;

    bless the Lord light and darkness: ♦
    sing his praise and exalt him for ever.

7   Bless the Lord frost and cold: ♦
    bless the Lord you ice and snow;

    bless the Lord lightnings and clouds: ♦
    sing his praise and exalt him for ever.

8   O let the earth bless the Lord: ♦
    bless the Lord you mountains and hills;

    bless the Lord all that grows in the ground: ♦
    sing his praise and exalt him for ever.

    Bless the Lord you springs: ♦
    bless the Lord you seas and rivers;

bless the Lord you whales and all tha
sing his praise and exalt him for ever.

    waters: ♦

10   Bless the Lord all birds of the air: ♦
bless the Lord you beasts and cattle;

bless the Lord all people on earth: ♦
sing his praise and exalt him for ever.

11   O people of God bless the Lord: ♦
bless the Lord you priests of the Lord;

bless the Lord you servants of the Lord: ♦
sing his praise and exalt him for ever.

12   Bless the Lord all you of upright spirit: ♦
bless the Lord you that are holy and humble in heart;

bless the Father, the Son and the Holy Spirit: ♦
sing his praise and exalt him for ever.

The Song of the Three 35-65

Benedicite – a Song of Creation
(shorter version)

1   Bless the Lord all you works of the Lord: ♦
sing his praise and exalt him for ever.

2   Bless the Lord you heavens: ♦
sing his praise and exalt him for ever.

3   Bless the Lord you angels of the Lord: ♦
sing his praise and exalt him for ever.

4   Bless the Lord all people on earth: ♦
sing his praise and exalt him for ever.

5   O people of God bless the Lord: ♦
sing his praise and exalt him for ever.

6   Bless the Lord you priests of the Lord: ♦
sing his praise and exalt him for ever.

7   Bless the Lord you servants of the Lord: ♦
sing his praise and exalt him for ever.

8   Bless the Lord all you of upright spirit: ♦
bless the Lord you that are holy and humble in heart;

bless the Father, the Son and the Holy Spirit; ♦
sing his praise and exalt him for ever.

Canticle

let us sing to the Lord; ♦
heartily rejoice in the rock of our salvation.

us come into his presence with thanksgiving ♦
d be glad in him with psalms.

For the Lord is a great God ♦
and a great king above all gods.

4   In his hand are the depths of the earth ♦
and the heights of the mountains are his also.

5   The sea is his, for he made it, ♦
and his hands have moulded the dry land.

6   Come, let us worship and bow down ♦
and kneel before the Lord our Maker.

7   For he is our God; ♦
we are the people of his pasture and the sheep of his hand.

The canticle may end here with 'Glory to the Father…'

8   O that today you would listen to his voice: ♦
'Harden not your hearts as at Meribah,
    on that day at Massah in the wilderness,

9   'When your forebears tested me, and put me to the proof, ♦
though they had seen my works.

10   'Forty years long I detested that generation and said, ♦
"This people are wayward in their hearts;
    they do not know my ways."

11   'So I swore in my wrath, ♦
"They shall not enter into my rest." '

Psalm 95

Glory to the Father and to the Son
and to the Holy Spirit;
as it was in the beginning is now
and shall be for ever. Amen.

1   O be joyful in the Lord, all the earth;
     serve the Lord with gladness
          and come before his presence with a s

2   Know that the Lord is God; ♦
     it is he that has made us and we are his;
          we are his people and the sheep of his pasture.

3   Enter his gates with thanksgiving
          and his courts with praise; ♦
     give thanks to him and bless his name.

4   For the Lord is gracious; his steadfast love is everlasting, ♦
     and his faithfulness endures from generation to generation.

Psalm 100

     Glory to the Father and to the Son
     and to the Holy Spirit;
     as it was in the beginning is now
     and shall be for ever. Amen.

...assover has been sacrificed for us: ♦
1 ...celebrate the feast,

...th the old leaven of corruption and wickedness: ♦
2 with the unleavened bread of sincerity and truth.

1 Corinthians 5.7b, 8

Christ once raised from the dead dies no more: ♦
death has no more dominion over him.

4 In dying he died to sin once for all: ♦
in living he lives to God.

5 See yourselves therefore as dead to sin: ♦
and alive to God in Jesus Christ our Lord.

Romans 6.9-11

6 Christ has been raised from the dead: ♦
the first fruits of those who sleep.

7 For as by man came death: ♦
by man has come also the resurrection of the dead;

8 for as in Adam all die: ♦
even so in Christ shall all be made alive.

1 Corinthians 15.20-22

Glory to the Father and to the Son
and to the Holy Spirit;
as it was in the beginning is now
and shall be for ever. Amen.

Evening Prayer

Phos hilaron – a Song of the Light

O joyful light,
from the pure glory of the eternal heavenly Father,
O holy, blessed Jesus Christ.

As we come to the setting of the sun
and see the evening light,
we give thanks and praise to the Father and to the Son
and to the Holy Spirit of God.

Worthy are you at all times
to be sung with holy voices,
O Son of God, O giver of life,
and to be glorified through all creation.

(or)

Hail, gladdening Light, of his pure glory poured,
Who is the immortal Father, heavenly, blest,
Holiest of holies, Jesus Christ our Lord.

Now we are come to the sun's hour of rest,
The lights of evening round us shine,
We hymn the Father, Son and Holy Spirit divine.

Worthy are you at all times to be sung
With undefiled tongue,
Son of our God, giver of life, alone:
Therefore in all the world your glories, Lord, they own.

All   **Let my prayer rise before you as incense,** ♦
      the lifting up of my hands as the evening sacrifice.

O Lord, I call to you; come to me quickly; ♦
hear my voice when I cry to you.

Set a watch before my mouth, O Lord, ♦
and guard the door of my lips;

All   **Let my prayer rise before you as incense,** ♦
      the lifting up of my hands as the evening sacrifice.

Let not my heart incline to any evil thing; ♦
let me not be occupied in wickedness with evildoers.

But my eyes are turned to you, Lord God; ♦
in you I take refuge; do not leave me defenceless.

All   **Let my prayer rise before you as incense,** ♦
      the lifting up of my hands as the evening sacrifice.

All **Bless the Lord, O my soul.** ♦
O Lord my God, how excellent is your greaess!

You are clothed with majesty and honour,
wrapped in light as in a garment.

The sun knows the time for its setting. ♦
You make darkness that it may be night.

All **Bless the Lord, O my soul.** ♦
O Lord my God, how excellent is your greatnes

O Lord, how manifold are your works! ♦
In wisdom you have made them all;
    the earth is full of your creatures.

When you send forth your spirit, they are created, ♦
and you renew the face of the earth.

All **Bless the Lord, O my soul.** ♦
O Lord my God, how excellent is your greatness!

May the glory of the Lord endure for ever; ♦
may the Lord rejoice in his works;

I will sing to the Lord as long as I live; ♦
I will make music to my God while I have my being.

All **Bless the Lord, O my soul.** ♦
O Lord my God, how excellent is your greatness!

Morning Prayer

A Song of the Wilderness (Advent)

1 wilderness and the dry land shall rejoice, ♦
   desert shall blossom and burst into song.

2 ...ey hall see the glory of the Lord, ♦
   he ajesty of our God.

3 St ...gthen the weary hands, ♦
   a make firm the feeble knees.

4 ...r to the anxious, 'Be strong, fear not,
   your God is coming with judgement, ♦
   oming with judgement to save you.'

5 Then shall the eyes of the blind be opened, ♦
   and the ears of the deaf unstopped;

6 Then shall the lame leap like a hart, ♦
   and the tongue of the dumb sing for joy.

7 For waters shall break forth in the wilderness, ♦
   and streams in the desert;

8 The ransomed of the Lord shall return with singing, ♦
   with everlasting joy upon their heads.

9 Joy and gladness shall be theirs, ♦
   and sorrow and sighing shall flee away.   *Isaiah 35.1,2b-4a,4c-6,10*

Glory to the Father and to the Son
and to the Holy Spirit;
as it was in the beginning is now
and shall be for ever. Amen.

A Song of the Messiah (Christmas)

1   The people who walked in darkness have seen a great light; ♦
those who dwelt in a land of deep darkness,
     upon them the light has dawned.

2   You have increased their joy and given them great gladness; ♦
they rejoiced before you as with joy at the harvest.

3   For you have shattered the yoke that burdened them; ♦
the collar that lay heavy on their shoulders.

4   For to us a child is born and to us a son is given, ♦
and the government will be upon his shoulder.

5   And his name will be called: Wonderful Counsellor;
     the Mighty God; ♦
the Everlasting Father; the Prince of Peace.

6   Of the increase of his government and of peace ♦
there will be no end,

7   Upon the throne of David and over his kingdom, ♦
to establish and uphold it with justice and righteousness.

8   From this time forth and for evermore; ♦
the zeal of the Lord of hosts will do this.   *Isaiah 9.2,3b,4a,6,7*

Glory to the Father and to the Son
and to the Holy Spirit;
as it was in the beginning is now
and shall be for ever. Amen.

A Song of the New Jerusalem (Epiphany)

1   Arise, shine out, for your light has come, ♦
    the glory of the Lord is rising upon you.

2   Though night still covers the earth, ♦
    and darkness the peoples;

3   Above you the Holy One arises, ♦
    and above you God's glory appears.

4   The nations will come to your light, ♦
    and kings to your dawning brightness.

5   Your gates will lie open continually, ♦
    shut neither by day nor by night.

6   The sound of violence shall be heard no longer in your land, ♦
    or ruin and devastation within your borders.

7   You will call your walls, Salvation, ♦
    and your gates, Praise.

8   No more will the sun give you daylight, ♦
    nor moonlight shine upon you;

9   But the Lord will be your everlasting light, ♦
    your God will be your splendour.

10   For you shall be called the city of God, ♦
    the dwelling of the Holy One of Israel.   *Isaiah 60.1-3,11a,18,19,14b*

    Glory to the Father and to the Son
    and to the Holy Spirit;
    as it was in the beginning is now
    and shall be for ever. Amen.

A Song of Redemption (Christmas)

1   The Father has delivered us from the dominion of darkness, ♦
      and transferred us to the kingdom of his beloved Son;

2   In whom we have redemption, ♦
      the forgiveness of our sins.

3   He is the image of the invisible God, ♦
      the firstborn of all creation.

4   For in him all things were created, ♦
      in heaven and on earth, visible and invisible.

5   All things were created through him and for him, ♦
      he is before all things and in him all things hold together.

6   He is the head of the body, the Church, ♦
      he is the beginning, the firstborn from the dead.

7   In him all the fullness of God was pleased to dwell; ♦
      and through him God was pleased to reconcile all things.

Colossians 1.13-18a, 19, 20a

Glory to the Father and to the Son
and to the Holy Spirit;
as it was in the beginning is now
and shall be for ever. Amen.

A Song of Praise (Epiphany)

This Canticle is also known as Glory and Honour.

1   You are worthy, our Lord and God, ♦
    to receive glory and honour and power.

2   For you have created all things, ♦
    and by your will they have their being.

3   You are worthy, O Lamb, for you were slain, ♦
    and by your blood you ransomed for God
        saints from every tribe and language and nation.

4   You have made them to be a kingdom and priests
        serving our God, ♦
    and they will reign with you on earth.   *Revelation 4.11; 5.9b, 10*

    To the One who sits on the throne and to the Lamb ♦
    be blessing and honour, glory and might,
        for ever and ever. Amen.

A Song of Christ the Servant (Lent)

1   Christ suffered for you, leaving you an example, ♦
    that you should follow in his steps.

2   He committed no sin, no guile was found on his lips, ♦
    when he was reviled, he did not revile in turn.

3   When he suffered, he did not threaten, ♦
    but he trusted himself to God who judges justly.

4   Christ himself bore our sins in his body on the tree, ♦
    that we might die to sin and live to righteousness.

5   By his wounds, you have been healed,
        for you were straying like sheep, ♦
    but have now returned
        to the shepherd and guardian of your souls.   *1 Peter 2.21b-25*

    Glory to the Father and to the Son
    and to the Holy Spirit;
    as it was in the beginning is now
    and shall be for ever. Amen.

A Song of Faith (Easter)

1   Blessed be the God and Father ✦
    of our Lord Jesus Christ!

2   By his great mercy we have been born anew to a living hope ✦
    through the resurrection of Jesus Christ from the dead,

3   Into an inheritance that is imperishable, undefiled and unfading, ✦
    kept in heaven for you,

4   Who are being protected by the power of God
        through faith for a salvation, ✦
    ready to be revealed in the last time.

5   You were ransomed from the futile ways of your ancestors ✦
    not with perishable things like silver or gold

6   But with the precious blood of Christ ✦
    like that of a lamb without spot or stain.

7   Through him we have confidence in God,
        who raised him from the dead and gave him glory, ✦
    so that your faith and hope are set on God.   *1 Peter 1.3-5,18,19,21*

    Glory to the Father and to the Son
    and to the Holy Spirit;
    as it was in the beginning is now
    and shall be for ever. Amen.

A Song of God's Children (Pentecost)

1 The law of the Spirit of life in Christ Jesus ♦
   has set us free from the law of sin and death.

2 All who are led by the Spirit of God are children of God; ♦
   for we have received the Spirit that enables us to cry, 'Abba, Father'.

3 The Spirit himself bears witness that we are children of God ♦
   and if God's children, then heirs of God;

4 If heirs of God, then fellow-heirs with Christ; ♦
   since we suffer with him now, that we may be glorified with him.

5 These sufferings that we now endure ♦
   are not worth comparing to the glory that shall be revealed.

6 For the creation waits with eager longing ♦
   for the revealing of the children of God.   *Romans 8.2,14,15b-19*

   Glory to the Father and to the Son
   and to the Holy Spirit;
   as it was in the beginning is now
   and shall be for ever. Amen.

A Song of the Lamb (Ordinary Time)

1 Salvation and glory and power belong to our God, ♦
   whose judgements are true and just.

2 Praise our God, all you his servants, ♦
   all who fear him, both small and great.

3 The Lord our God, the Almighty, reigns: ♦
   let us rejoice and exult and give him the glory.

4 For the marriage of the Lamb has come ♦
   and his bride has made herself ready.

5 Blessed are those who are invited ♦
   to the wedding banquet of the Lamb.   *Revelation 19.1b,5b,6b,7,9b*

   To the One who sits on the throne and to the Lamb ♦
   be blessing and honour and glory and might,
       for ever and ever. Amen.

¶ *Gospel Canticles*

Morning Prayer

Benedictus (The Song of Zechariah)

1 Blessed be the Lord the God of Israel, ♦
   who has come to his people and set them free.

2 He has raised up for us a mighty Saviour, ♦
   born of the house of his servant David.

3 Through his holy prophets God promised of old ♦
   to save us from our enemies,
        from the hands of all that hate us,

4 To show mercy to our ancestors, ♦
   and to remember his holy covenant.

5 This was the oath God swore to our father Abraham: ♦
   to set us free from the hands of our enemies,

6 Free to worship him without fear, ♦
   holy and righteous in his sight
        all the days of our life.

7 And you, child, shall be called the prophet of the Most High, ♦
   for you will go before the Lord to prepare his way,

8 To give his people knowledge of salvation ♦
   by the forgiveness of all their sins.

9 In the tender compassion of our God ♦
   the dawn from on high shall break upon us,

10 To shine on those who dwell in darkness and the shadow of death, ♦
   and to guide our feet into the way of peace.   *Luke 1.68-79*

Glory to the Father and to the Son
and to the Holy Spirit;
as it was in the beginning is now
and shall be for ever. Amen.

Evening Prayer

Magnificat (The Song of Mary)

1   My soul proclaims the greatness of the Lord,
        my spirit rejoices in God my Saviour; ♦
    he has looked with favour on his lowly servant.

2   From this day all generations will call me blessed; ♦
    the Almighty has done great things for me
        and holy is his name.

3   He has mercy on those who fear him, ♦
    from generation to generation.

4   He has shown strength with his arm ♦
    and has scattered the proud in their conceit,

5   Casting down the mighty from their thrones ♦
    and lifting up the lowly.

6   He has filled the hungry with good things ♦
    and sent the rich away empty.

7   He has come to the aid of his servant Israel, ♦
    to remember his promise of mercy,

8   The promise made to our ancestors, ♦
    to Abraham and his children for ever.   *Luke 1.46-55*

    Glory to the Father and to the Son
    and to the Holy Spirit;
    as it was in the beginning is now
    and shall be for ever. Amen.

Night Prayer

Nunc dimittis (The Song of Simeon)

1   Now, Lord, you let your servant go in peace: ♦
    your word has been fulfilled.

2   My own eyes have seen the salvation ♦
    which you have prepared in the sight of every people;

3   A light to reveal you to the nations ♦
    and the glory of your people Israel.   *Luke 2.29-32*

    Glory to the Father and to the Son
    and to the Holy Spirit;
    as it was in the beginning is now
    and shall be for ever. Amen.

¶ Other Canticles

The Song of Christ's Glory

1   Christ Jesus was in the form of God, ♦
    but he did not cling to equality with God.

2   He emptied himself, taking the form of a servant, ♦
    and was born in our human likeness.

3   Being found in human form he humbled himself, ♦
    and became obedient unto death, even death on a cross.

4   Therefore God has highly exalted him, ♦
    and bestowed on him the name above every name,

5   That at the name of Jesus, every knee should bow, ♦
    in heaven and on earth and under the earth;

6   And every tongue confess that Jesus Christ is Lord, ♦
    to the glory of God the Father.   *Philippians 2.5-11*

    Glory to the Father and to the Son
    and to the Holy Spirit;
    as it was in the beginning is now
    and shall be for ever. Amen.

Great and Wonderful

1   Great and wonderful are your deeds, ♦
    Lord God the Almighty.

2   Just and true are your ways, ♦
    O ruler of the nations.

3   Who shall not revere and praise your name, O Lord? ♦
    for you alone are holy.

4   All nations shall come and worship in your presence: ♦
    for your just dealings have been revealed.   *Revelation 15.3, 4*

To the One who sits on the throne and to the Lamb ♦
be blessing and honour and glory and might,
    for ever and ever. Amen.

Bless the Lord

1   Blessed are you, the God of our ancestors, ♦
    worthy to be praised and exalted for ever.

2   Blessed is your holy and glorious name, ♦
    worthy to be praised and exalted for ever.

3   Blessed are you, in your holy and glorious temple, ♦
    worthy to be praised and exalted for ever.

4   Blessed are you who look into the depths, ♦
    worthy to be praised and exalted for ever.

5   Blessed are you, enthroned on the cherubim, ♦
    worthy to be praised and exalted for ever.

6   Blessed are you on the throne of your kingdom, ♦
    worthy to be praised and exalted for ever.

7   Blessed are you in the heights of heaven, ♦
    worthy to be praised and exalted for ever.

The Song of the Three 29-34

Bless the Father, the Son and the Holy Spirit,
worthy to be praised and exalted for ever.

Saviour of the World

1   Jesus, Saviour of the world,
        come to us in your mercy: ♦
    we look to you to save and help us.

2   By your cross and your life laid down,
        you set your people free: ♦
    we look to you to save and help us.

3   When they were ready to perish, you saved your disciples: ♦
    we look to you to come to our help.

4   In the greatness of your mercy, loose us from our chains, ♦
    forgive the sins of all your people.

5   Make yourself known as our Saviour and mighty deliverer; ♦
    save and help us that we may praise you.

6   Come now and dwell with us, Lord Christ Jesus: ♦
    hear our prayer and be with us always.

7   And when you come in your glory: ♦
    make us to be one with you
        and to share the life of your kingdom.

¶ *Te Deum Laudamus*

See Note 7, page 58.

We praise you, O God,
we acclaim you as the Lord;
all creation worships you,
the Father everlasting.
To you all angels, all the powers of heaven,
the cherubim and seraphim, sing in endless praise:
Holy, holy, holy Lord, God of power and might,
heaven and earth are full of your glory.
The glorious company of apostles praise you.
The noble fellowship of prophets praise you.
The white-robed army of martyrs praise you.
Throughout the world the holy Church acclaims you:
Father, of majesty unbounded,
your true and only Son, worthy of all praise,
the Holy Spirit, advocate and guide.

You, Christ, are the King of glory,
the eternal Son of the Father.
When you took our flesh to set us free
you humbly chose the Virgin's womb.
You overcame the sting of death
and opened the kingdom of heaven to all believers.
You are seated at God's right hand in glory.
We believe that you will come and be our judge.
Come then, Lord, and help your people,
bought with the price of your own blood,
and bring us with your saints
to glory everlasting.

The canticle may end here.

Save your people, Lord, and bless your inheritance.
Govern and uphold them now and always.

Day by day we bless you.
We praise your name for ever.

Keep us today, Lord, from all sin.
Have mercy on us, Lord, have mercy.

Lord, show us your love and mercy,
for we have put our trust in you.

In you, Lord, is our hope:
let us never be put to shame.

¶ *Canticles from*
# The Book of Common Prayer

Morning Prayer

Venite, exultemus Domino

1   O come, let us sing unto the Lord :
    let us heartily rejoice in the strength of our salvation.

2   Let us come before his presence with thanksgiving :
    and shew ourselves glad in him with psalms.

3   For the Lord is a great God :
    and a great King above all gods.

4   In his hand are all the corners of the earth :
    and the strength of the hills is his also.

5   The sea is his, and he made it :
    and his hands prepared the dry land.

6   O come, let us worship, and fall down :
    and kneel before the Lord our Maker.

7   For he is the Lord our God :
    and we are the people of his pasture, and the sheep of his hand.

[8 Today if ye will hear his voice, harden not your hearts :
    as in the provocation,
        and as in the day of temptation in the wilderness;

9   When your fathers tempted me :
    proved me, and saw my works.

10 Forty years long was I grieved with this generation, and said :
    It is a people that do err in their hearts,
        for they have not known my ways.

11 Unto whom I sware in my wrath :
    that they should not enter into my rest.]   *Psalm 95*

    Glory be to the Father, and to the Son :
    and to the Holy Ghost;
    as it was in the beginning, is now, and ever shall be :
    world without end. Amen.

The Easter Anthems

1   Christ our passover is sacrificed for us :
       therefore let us keep the feast;

2   Not with the old leaven,
          nor with the leaven of malice and wickedness :
       but with the unleavened bread of sincerity and truth.

1 Corinthians 5.7b, 8

3   Christ being raised from the dead dieth no more :
       death hath no more dominion over him.

4   For in that he died, he died unto sin once :
       but in that he liveth, he liveth unto God.

5   Likewise reckon ye also yourselves to be dead indeed unto sin :
       but alive unto God, through Jesus Christ our Lord.   *Romans 6.9-11*

6   Christ is risen from the dead :
       and become the first fruits of them that slept.

7   For since by man came death :
       by man came also the resurrection of the dead.

8   For as in Adam all die :
       even so in Christ shall all be made alive.   *1 Corinthians 15.20-22*

Glory be to the Father, and to the Son :
and to the Holy Ghost;
as it was in the beginning, is now, and ever shall be :
world without end. Amen.

Te Deum Laudamus

We praise thee, O God; we acknowledge thee to be the Lord.
All the earth doth worship thee, the Father everlasting.
To thee all angels cry aloud, the heavens and all the powers therein.
To thee cherubin and seraphin continually do cry,
Holy, Holy, Holy, Lord God of Sabaoth;
Heaven and earth are full of the majesty of thy glory.
The glorious company of the apostles praise thee.
The goodly fellowship of the prophets praise thee.
The noble army of martyrs praise thee.
The holy Church throughout all the world doth acknowledge thee:
the Father of an infinite majesty;
thine honourable, true and only Son;
also the Holy Ghost the Comforter.

Thou art the King of glory, O Christ.
Thou art the everlasting Son of the Father.
When thou tookest upon thee to deliver man,
    thou didst not abhor the Virgin's womb.
When thou hadst overcome the sharpness of death,
    thou didst open the kingdom of heaven to all believers.
Thou sittest at the right hand of God, in the glory of the Father.
We believe that thou shalt come to be our judge.
We therefore pray thee, help thy servants,
    whom thou hast redeemed with thy precious blood.
Make them to be numbered with thy saints in glory everlasting.

O Lord, save thy people and bless thine heritage.
Govern them and lift them up for ever.
Day by day we magnify thee;
and we worship thy name, ever world without end.
Vouchsafe, O Lord, to keep us this day without sin.
O Lord, have mercy upon us, have mercy upon us.
O Lord, let thy mercy lighten upon us, as our trust is in thee.
O Lord, in thee have I trusted; let me never be confounded.

Benedicite, omnia opera

1   O all ye Works of the Lord, bless ye the Lord :
praise him, and magnify him for ever.

2   O ye Angels of the Lord, bless ye the Lord :
praise him, and magnify him for ever.

3   O ye Heavens, bless ye the Lord :
praise him, and magnify him for ever.

4   O ye Waters that be above the Firmament, bless ye the Lord :
praise him, and magnify him for ever.

5   O all ye Powers of the Lord, bless ye the Lord :
praise him, and magnify him for ever.

6   O ye Sun and Moon, bless ye the Lord :
praise him, and magnify him for ever.

7   O ye Stars of Heaven, bless ye the Lord :
praise him, and magnify him for ever.

8   O ye Showers and Dew, bless ye the Lord :
praise him, and magnify him for ever.

9   O ye Winds of God, bless ye the Lord :
praise him, and magnify him for ever.

10   O ye Fire and Heat, bless ye the Lord :
praise him, and magnify him for ever.

11   O ye Winter and Summer, bless ye the Lord :
praise him, and magnify him for ever.

12   O ye Dews and Frosts, bless ye the Lord :
praise him, and magnify him for ever.

13   O ye Frost and Cold, bless ye the Lord :
praise him, and magnify him for ever.

14   O ye Ice and Snow, bless ye the Lord :
praise him, and magnify him for ever.

15   O ye Nights and Days, bless ye the Lord :
praise him, and magnify him for ever.

16   O ye Light and Darkness, bless ye the Lord :
praise him, and magnify him for ever.

17   O ye Lightnings and Clouds, bless ye the Lord :
praise him, and magnify him for ever.

18   O let the Earth bless the Lord :
      yea, let it praise him, and magnify him for ever.

19   O ye Mountains and Hills, bless ye the Lord :
      praise him, and magnify him for ever.

20   O all ye Green Things upon the Earth, bless ye the Lord :
      praise him, and magnify him for ever.

21   O ye Wells, bless ye the Lord :
      praise him, and magnify him for ever.

22   O ye Seas and Floods, bless ye the Lord :
      praise him, and magnify him for ever.

23   O ye Whales, and all that move in the Waters, bless ye the Lord :
      praise him, and magnify him for ever.

24   O all ye Fowls of the Air, bless ye the Lord :
      praise him, and magnify him for ever.

25   O all ye Beasts and Cattle, bless ye the Lord :
      praise him, and magnify him for ever.

26   O ye Children of Men, bless ye the Lord :
      praise him, and magnify him for ever.

27   O let Israel bless the Lord :
      praise him, and magnify him for ever.

28   O ye Priests of the Lord, bless ye the Lord :
      praise him, and magnify him for ever.

29   O ye Servants of the Lord, bless ye the Lord :
      praise him, and magnify him for ever.

30   O ye Spirits and Souls of the Righteous, bless ye the Lord :
      praise him, and magnify him for ever.

31   O ye holy and humble Men of heart, bless ye the Lord :
      praise him, and magnify him for ever.

32   O Ananias, Azarias and Misael, bless ye the Lord :
      praise him, and magnify him for ever.

                          The Song of the Three Holy Children 35-66

      Glory be to the Father, and to the Son :
      and to the Holy Ghost;
      as it was in the beginning, is now, and ever shall be :
      world without end. Amen.

Benedictus

1   Blessed be the Lord God of Israel :
    for he hath visited, and redeemed his people;

2   And hath raised up a mighty salvation for us :
    in the house of his servant David;

3   As he spake by the mouth of his holy Prophets :
    which have been since the world began;

4   That we should be saved from our enemies :
    and from the hands of all that hate us;

5   To perform the mercy promised to our forefathers :
    and to remember his holy covenant;

6   To perform the oath which he sware to our forefather Abraham :
    that he would give us,

7   That we being delivered out of the hands of our enemies :
    might serve him without fear,

8   In holiness and righteousness before him :
    all the days of our life.

9   And thou, child, shalt be called the Prophet of the Highest :
    for thou shalt go before the face of the Lord to prepare his ways;

10   To give knowledge of salvation unto his people :
    for the remission of their sins;

11   Through the tender mercy of our God :
    whereby the dayspring from on high hath visited us;

12   To give light to them that sit in darkness,
      and in the shadow of death :
    and to guide our feet into the way of peace.   *Luke 1.68-79*

Glory be to the Father, and to the Son :
and to the Holy Ghost;
as it was in the beginning, is now, and ever shall be :
world without end. Amen.

1   O be joyful in the Lord, all ye lands :
serve the Lord with gladness,
     and come before his presence with a song.

2   Be ye sure that the Lord he is God :
it is he that hath made us, and not we ourselves;
     we are his people, and the sheep of his pasture.

3   O go your way into his gates with thanksgiving,
     and into his courts with praise :
be thankful unto him, and speak good of his Name.

4   For the Lord is gracious, his mercy is everlasting :
and his truth endureth from generation to generation.   *Psalm 100*

Glory be to the Father, and to the Son :
and to the Holy Ghost;
as it was in the beginning, is now, and ever shall be :
world without end. Amen.

Magnificat

1   My soul doth magnify the Lord :
      and my spirit hath rejoiced in God my Saviour.

2   For he hath regarded :
      the lowliness of his handmaiden.

3   For behold, from henceforth :
      all generations shall call me blessed.

4   For he that is mighty hath magnified me :
      and holy is his Name.

5   And his mercy is on them that fear him :
      throughout all generations.

6   He hath shewed strength with his arm :
      he hath scattered the proud in the imagination of their hearts.

7   He hath put down the mighty from their seat :
      and hath exalted the humble and meek.

8   He hath filled the hungry with good things :
      and the rich he hath sent empty away.

9   He remembering his mercy hath holpen his servant Israel :
      as he promised to our forefathers, Abraham and his seed for ever.

Luke 1.46-55

Glory be to the Father, and to the Son :
and to the Holy Ghost;
as it was in the beginning, is now, and ever shall be :
world without end. Amen.

1   O sing unto the Lord a new song :
      for he hath done marvellous things.

2   With his own right hand, and with his holy arm :
      hath he gotten himself the victory.

3   The Lord declared his salvation :
      his righteousness hath he openly shewed in the sight of the heathen.

4   He hath remembered his mercy and truth
         toward the house of Israel :
      and all the ends of the world have seen the salvation of our God.

5   Shew yourselves joyful unto the Lord, all ye lands :
      sing, rejoice, and give thanks.

6   Praise the Lord upon the harp :
      sing to the harp with a psalm of thanksgiving.

7   With trumpets also and shawms :
      O shew yourselves joyful before the Lord the King.

8   Let the sea make a noise, and all that therein is :
      the round world, and they that dwell therein.

9   Let the floods clap their hands,
         and let the hills be joyful together before the Lord :
      for he cometh to judge the earth.

10   With righteousness shall he judge the world :
      and the people with equity.   *Psalm 98*

      Glory be to the Father, and to the Son :
      and to the Holy Ghost;
      as it was in the beginning, is now, and ever shall be :
      world without end. Amen.

Nunc dimittis

1   Lord, now lettest thou thy servant depart in peace :
    according to thy word.

2   For mine eyes have seen :
    thy salvation;

3   Which thou hast prepared :
    before the face of all people;

4   To be a light to lighten the Gentiles :
    and to be the glory of thy people Israel.   *Luke 2.29-32*

Glory be to the Father, and to the Son :
and to the Holy Ghost;
as it was in the beginning, is now, and ever shall be :
world without end. Amen.

Deus misereatur

1   God be merciful unto us, and bless us :
    and shew us the light of his countenance, and be merciful unto us:

2   That thy way may be known upon earth :
    thy saving health among all nations.

3   Let the people praise thee, O God :
    yea, let all the people praise thee.

4   O let the nations rejoice and be glad :
    for thou shalt judge the folk righteously,
        and govern the nations upon earth.

5   Let the people praise thee, O God :
    yea, let all the people praise thee.

6   Then shall the earth bring forth her increase :
    and God, even our own God, shall give us his blessing.

7   God shall bless us :
    and all the ends of the world shall fear him.   *Psalm 67*

Glory be to the Father, and to the Son :
and to the Holy Ghost;
as it was in the beginning, is now, and ever shall be :
world without end. Amen.

Authorization Details

¶ The following services and other material in *Common Worship: Services and Prayers for the Church of England* are taken from *The Book of Common Prayer:*

¶ Texts in Morning and Evening Prayer from *The Book of Common Prayer* with permitted variations

¶ Prayers from *The Book of Common Prayer* in Prayers for Various Occasions

¶ The Litany from *The Book of Common Prayer*

¶ Canticles from *The Book of Common Prayer*

The Church of England (Worship and Doctrine) Measure 1974 provides that the forms of service contained in *The Book of Common Prayer* shall continue to be available for use in the Church of England.

¶ The following services comply with the Schedule of permitted variations to *The Book of Common Prayer* Orders for Morning and Evening Prayer where these occur in *Common Worship*:

¶ Morning Prayer from *The Book of Common Prayer* with permitted variations

¶ Evening Prayer from *The Book of Common Prayer* with permitted variations

¶ The following services and other material in *Common Worship: Services and Prayers for the Church of England* are authorized pursuant to Canon B 2 of the Canons of the Church of England for use until further resolution of the General Synod:

¶ The Calendar

¶ A Service of the Word

¶ Schedule of permitted variations to *The Book of Common Prayer* Orders for Morning and Evening Prayer where these occur in *Common Worship*

¶ Prayers for Various Occasions (except Prayers from *The Book of Common Prayer*)

¶ The Litany

¶ Authorized Forms of Confession and Absolution

¶ Creeds and Authorized Affirmations of Faith

¶ The Lord's Prayer

¶ The Order for the Celebration of Holy Communion also called The Eucharist and The Lord's Supper

¶ Thanksgiving for the Gift of a Child

¶ Holy Baptism

¶ Collects and Post Communions

¶ Rules for Regulating Authorized Forms of Service

¶ The Lectionary

¶ Opening Canticles at Morning Prayer, Gospel Canticles, Other Canticles, A Song of Praise (Epiphany), Te Deum Laudamus

¶ The following services comply with the provisions of A Service of the Word:

¶ An Order for Morning Prayer on Sunday

¶ An Order for Evening Prayer on Sunday

¶ An Order for Night Prayer (Compline)

¶ An Order for Night Prayer (Compline) in Traditional Language

¶ The following material has been commended by the House of Bishops of the General Synod pursuant to Canon B 2 of the Canons of the Church of England and is published with the agreement of the House:

¶ Phos hilaron – a Song of the Light, Old and New Testament Canticles at Morning and Evening Prayer

¶ Introduction to Morning and Evening Prayer on Sunday

¶ Short Prefaces for the Sundays before Lent and after Trinity

¶ Introduction to Holy Baptism

Under Canon B 4 it is open to each bishop to authorize, if he sees fit, the form of service to be used within his diocese. He may specify that the services shall be those commended by the House, or that a diocesan form of them shall be used. If the bishop gives no directions in this matter the priest remains free, subject to the terms of Canon B 5, to make use of the material as commended by the House.

¶ Use of the following material falls within the discretion canonically allowed to the minister under Canon B 5:

¶ Collects and Post Communions in Traditional Language

Copyright Information

The Archbishops' Council of the Church of England and the other copyright owners and administrators of texts included in *Common Worship: Services and Prayers for the Church of England* have given permission for the use of their material in local reproductions on a non-commercial basis which comply with the conditions for reproductions for local use set out in the Archbishops' Council's booklet, *A Brief Guide to Liturgical Copyright*. This is available from

Church House Bookshop
Great Smith Street
London SW1P 3BN
Telephone: 020 7898 1300/1/2/4/6
Fax: 020 7898 1305
Email: bookshop@c-of-e.org.uk

or from www.cofe.anglican.org/commonworship. A reproduction which meets the conditions stated in that booklet may be made without an application for copyright permission or payment of a fee, but the following copyright acknowledgement must be included:

> *Common Worship: Services and Prayers for the Church of England*, material from which is included in this service, is copyright © The Archbishops' Council 2000.

Permission must be obtained in advance for any reproduction which does not comply with the conditions set out in *A Brief Guide to Liturgical Copyright*. Applications for permission should be addressed to:

The Copyright and Contracts Administrator
The Archbishops' Council
Church House
Great Smith Street
London SW1P 3NZ
Telephone: 020 7898 1557
Fax: 020 7898 1449
Email: copyright@c-of-e.org.uk

Acknowledgements and Sources

The publisher gratefully acknowledges permission to reproduce copyright material in this book. Every effort has been made to trace and contact copyright holders. If there are any inadvertent omissions we apologize to those concerned and undertake to include suitable acknowledgements in all future editions.

An asterisk * indicates that the prayer has been adapted.

Published sources include the following:

The Archbishops' Council of the Church of England: *The Prayer Book as Proposed in 1928; The Alternative Service Book 1980; Common Worship: Initiation Services; The Christian Year: Calendar, Lectionary and Collects*, all of which are copyright © The Archbishops' Council of the Church of England.

Cambridge University Press: Extracts (and adapted extracts) from *The Book of Common Prayer*, the rights in which are vested in the Crown, are reproduced by permission of the Crown's Patentee, Cambridge University Press.

The Division of Christian Education of the National Council of Churches in the USA: Scripture quotations from *The New Revised Standard Version of the Bible* © 1989 The Division of Christian Education of the National Council of Churches in the USA. Used by permission. All rights reserved.

Thanks are also due to the following for permission to reproduce copyright material:

The General Synod of the Anglican Church of Canada: 'We thank you, almighty God, for the gift of water' (Baptism, p. 355); 'Will you continue in the apostles' teaching and fellowship' (Baptism, p. 359); The Affirmation of Commitment (p. 152) and the Post Communions for Christmas Eve (p. 379), Christmas Day (p. 381), Epiphany 3 (p. 385), 5 before Lent (p. 387), Sunday before Lent (p. 391), Easter 3 (p. 401), Easter 6 (p. 403), Easter 7 (p. 404), Pentecost (p. 405), Weekdays after Pentecost (p. 406), Trinity 4 (p. 410), Trinity 6 (p. 411), Trinity 12 (p. 415), Trinity 14 (p. 417), Last Sunday after Trinity (p. 422), the Transfiguration of Our Lord (p. 438), Holy Cross Day (p. 440), Apostles and Evangelists (p. 428). Adapted from (or excerpted from) *The Book of Alternative Services of the Anglican Church of Canada* © The General Synod of the Anglican Church of Canada 1985. Used by permission.

The English Language Liturgical Consultation: English translation of Gloria in excelsis, Kyrie eleison, Sursum corda, Sanctus and Benedictus, the Lord's Prayer, the Nicene Creed, the Apostles' Creed, Te Deum Laudamus, Agnus Dei, Gloria Patri, Benedictus, Magnificat and Nunc dimittis prepared by the English Language Liturgical Consultation, based (or excerpted) from *Praying Together* © ELLC 1988.

The International Commission on English in the Liturgy: the extended Prefaces for the Sundays before Lent and the Sundays after Trinity (p. 294), Christmas Day until the Eve of Epiphany (p. 303), Ash Wednesday until the Saturday after the Fourth Sunday in Lent (p. 309), the Annunciation of Our Lord (p. 311), the Fifth Sunday of Lent until the Wednesday of Holy Week (p. 313), Ascension Day (p. 319), the Day after Ascension Day until the Day of Pentecost (p. 321); the Collect for the Unity of the Church* (p. 105); Post Communions for the Presentation of Christ in the Temple (p. 386), George* (p. 430), Stephen* (p. 444) and John* (p. 444) are based on (or excerpted from) *The Roman Missal* © International Commission on English in the Liturgy 1973. Used by permission.

The Church of Ireland: the Collects for Christmas 2 (p. 382),
and the Transfiguration of Our Lord* (p. 438) from *Collects and Post
Communion Prayers*, 1995; Post Communions for Palm Sunday (p. 397)
and Easter 4* (p. 402) from *The Alternative Prayer Book*, 1984.
Reproduced by permission.

Church of the Province of Southern Africa: the Collects for
Epiphany 2* (p. 384), Epiphany 3* (p. 385), Lent 5* (p. 396), Thomas*
(p. 436), the Blessed Virgin Mary* (p. 438), Rogation Days (1 and 2)
(p. 104), Harvest Thanksgiving (p. 447), and the Post Communion for
3 before Advent (p. 424) from *An Anglican Prayer Book*, 1989 ©
Provincial Trustees of the Church of the Province of Southern
Africa. Used by permission.

Canterbury Press Norwich: the extended Preface for Easter (p. 317)
reproduced from Alan Griffiths, *We Give You Thanks and Praise*, 1999,
by permission of the publisher.

The Continuum International Publishing Group Ltd: the Post
Communions for Ascension Day* (p. 404), Day of Thanksgiving for
the Institution of Holy Communion* (p. 407), Trinity 11* (p. 415),
2 before Advent* (p. 425) from C. L. MacDonnell, *After Communion*,
1985 © Mowbray, an imprint of The Continuum International
Publishing Group Ltd. Used by permission. The Collects for Epiphany
4* (p. 385), Trinity 15* (p. 417), 4 before Advent (p. 423), and the
Blessed Virgin Mary (p. 438), and Post Communions for Advent 2*
(p. 377), 2 before Lent* (p. 390), Trinity 13 (p. 416), Trinity 20 (p. 421)
and Michael and All Angels (p. 441) from David Silk (ed.), *Prayers for
Use at the Alternative Services*, 1980 © Mowbray, an imprint of The
Continuum International Publishing Group Ltd. Used by permission.

Grove Books Ltd, Ridley Hall Road, Cambridge CB3 9HU:
Collects and Other Endings for Intercession Nos 6 and 7 (p. 289)
from *Intercessions in the Eucharist*, Grove Booklet 77, 1982.

Hodder and Stoughton Publishers: the Collect for Social Justice
and Responsibility* (p. 105) and the Post Communion for Advent 4*
(p. 379) from *Parish Prayers* © Frank Colquhoun 1967.

Jubilate Hymns: 'Lord Jesus Christ, we confess we have failed you,
as did your first disciples...' (Authorized Confession – Cross,
Failure in Discipleship, p. 124); 'Jesus Christ, risen Master and
triumphant Lord...' (Authorized Confession – Resurrection,
Heaven, Glory, Transfiguration, Death, Funerals, p. 125);

'O King enthroned on high...' (Authorized Confession – Trinity, Mission, p. 125); 'We confess our sin, and the sins of our society...' (Authorized Confession – Creation, Harvest, p. 126); 'Lord God, our maker and our redeemer, this is your world and we are your people...' (Authorized Confession – City, World and Society, p. 127); 'God our Father, we come to you in sorrow for our sins ...' (Authorized Confession – General, p. 128); 'May the Father of all mercies ...' (Absolution, p. 135); 'Though he was divine...' (Authorized Affirmation of Faith No. 4, p. 147); 'Christ died for our sins ...', (Authorized Affirmation of Faith No. 5, p. 147); and 'Holy, holy, holy is the Lord God almighty...' (Authorized Affirmation of Faith No. 6, p. 148). 'We believe in God the Father, from whom every family...', (Authorized Affirmation of Faith No. 7, p. 148) from *Church Family Worship*, 1986. Words: Michael Perry © Mrs B Perry/ Jubilate Hymns. Used by permission.

The Methodist Publishing House: 'We thank you, Lord, that you have fed us...'* (Holy Communion – Supplementary Texts, No. 1, p. 297) from *The Methodist Worship Book* © 1999 Trustees for Methodist Church Purposes. Used by permission of Methodist Publishing House.

Oxford University Press: the Collects for the Baptism of Christ* (p. 383) and 2 before Lent* (p. 390), and the Post Communion for Trinity Sunday* (p. 407) from *The Book of Common Worship of the Church of South India*. Used by permission.

The Saint Andrew Press, Edinburgh: Prayers After Communion No. 3 (p. 297), from *The Book of Common Order*, 1994 © The Church of Scotland Panel on Worship.

The European Province of the Society of St Francis: Prayers of Intercession 'As a royal priesthood...' (Baptism, p. 360) and the Collect for George (p. 430). From *Celebrating Common Prayer* © The Society of St Francis European Province 1992 & 1996.

SPCK: 'Almighty God, long-suffering, full of grace and truth ...' (Authorized Confession – General, p. 129) from *My God, my Glory* © Eric Milner-White 1967. Used by permission of the publishers. The Post Communion for Trinity 3* (p. 409) from *All Desires Known* © Janet Morley 1992. Used by permission of the publishers. The Collect for Mothering Sunday (p. 396) and the Post Communions for Mothering Sunday (p. 396) and Trinity 8 (p. 413), and the extended

Preface for the day of Pentecost (p. 321) from *Enriching the Christian Year* © Michael Perham 1993. Used by permission of the publishers.

Trustees of Westcott House, Cambridge: the Post Communions for Advent 3* (p. 378), Lent 1* (p. 393) and Dedication Festival (p. 446).

The Rt Revd Timothy Dudley-Smith: Authorized Affirmation of Faith No. 3 (p. 146) © Timothy Dudley-Smith. Where a CCLI licence is held, this item is covered by the licence and its use should be recorded in the usual way on your CCLI return. Used by permission.

The Revd S.A.J. Mitchell ssc for the extended Preface from the Epiphany until the Eve of the Presentation (p. 305).

The Rt Revd Dr David Stancliffe: the Proper Preface for Eucharist at a Baptism (Baptism, p. 362).

The Rt Revd Dr Kenneth Stevenson: the Post Communion for Trinity 10* (p. 414).

Index of Biblical References

General Index

Lent, Sundays before: Collect and Post
Communion: contemporary **387–91**;
traditional **460–63** – extended
Eucharistic Preface **294** – lectionary **541**
note, **550**

Lent, Sundays of Lent: Collect and Post
Communion: contemporary **393–7**;
traditional **465–9**

Leo the Great (10 November) **15**

Leonard (6 November) **15**

Lesser Festivals – calendar **5–16**, rules
governing **530**

Light, Song of the ('Phos hilaron'), use at
Evening Prayer **58** note, **783**

litanies **111–14** – *Book of Common Prayer*
115–21 – Holy Communion,
supplementary texts **284–7** – *see also*
confessions; intercessions; prayers

liturgical colours, use of **532–3**

local celebrations – calendar **5-16**, rules
governing **530**, transferences, table of
534

Lord's Prayer – contemporary **36, 44,
178, 263, 342** – modified traditional
36, 44, 222, 263, 343 – *Book of Common
Prayer* **64, 70, 74, 78, 96, 120, 229, 242**
– alternative text **106** notes: Holy
Communion Order One **333**,
Order Two **335**

Lord's Supper *see* Holy Communion

Lowder, Charles Fuge (9 September) **13**

Lucy (13 December) **16**

Luke (18 October) **14** – Collect and Post
Communion: contemporary **442**;
traditional **515** – lectionary **586** –
observance **528** note

Luther, Martin (31 October) **14**

Luwum, Janani (17 February) **6**

Macrina (19 July) **11**

Magnificat (Song of Mary) **42, 777**
note, **798**
Book of Common Prayer **76, 777**
note, **811**

Margaret, Queen of Scotland
(16 November) **15**

Margaret of Antioch (20 July) **11**

Mark (25 April) **8** – Collect and Post
Communion: contemporary **431**;
traditional **504** – lectionary **580** –
observance **528** note, **529** note –
transference **534** note

Marriages, on Principal Feasts **525** note

Martha (29 July) **11**

Martin, Bishop of Tours (11 November) **15**

Martin of Porres (3 November) **15**

Martyn, Henry (19 October) **14**

Martyrs of Japan, 1597 (6 February) **6**

Martyrs of Papua New Guinea, 1901 and
1942 (2 September) **13**

Martyrs of Uganda, 1886 and 1978
(3 June) **10**

Mary *see* Blessed Virgin Mary

Mary, Companion of Our Lord (29 July) **11**

Mary Magdalene (22 July) **11** – Collect and
Post Communion: contemporary **436–7**;
traditional **509–10** – lectionary **583** –
observance **528** note

Matthew (21 September) **13** – Collect and
Post Communion: contemporary **440**;
traditional **513** – lectionary **585** –
observance **528** note

Matthias (14 May) **9** – Collect and Post
Communion: contemporary **432**;
traditional **505** – lectionary **540** note,
581 – observance **528** note – transfer to
24 February **6, 9**

Maundy Thursday – Collect and Post
Communion: contemporary **398**;
traditional **470–71** – lectionary **555** –
seasonal provisions **314–15**

Maurice, Frederick Denison (1 April) **8**

Mechtild (19 November) **15**

Mellitus (24 April) **8**

Messiah, Song of the, use at Morning
Prayer **57** note, **776** note, **787**

Methodius (14 February) **6**

Michael and All Angels (29 September) **13**
– Collect and Post Communion:
contemporary **441**; traditional **514** –
lectionary **585** – observance **528** note